LACAN IN AMERICA

THE LACANIAN CLINICAL FIELD

A series of books edited by
Judith Feher Gurewich, Ph.D.
in collaboration with Susan Fairfield

LACAN IN AMERICA

EDITED BY
JEAN-MICHEL RABATÉ

OTHER

Other Press
New York

Production Editor: Robert D. Hack

This book was set in 11 pt. Berkeley by Alpha Graphics of Pittsfield, NH.

10 9 8 7 6 5 4 3 2 1

Library of Congress Cataloging-in-Publication Data

Lacan in America / edited by Jean-Michel Rabaté.
    p. cm. — (Lacanian clinical field)
    Includes bibliographical references and index.
    ISBN 1-892746-63-8 (pbk. : alk. paper)
    1. Psychoanalysis. 2. Lacan, Jacques, 1901– I. Rabaté, Jean-Michel,
    1949– II. Series.
BF173.L13   2000
150.19'5'092—dc21
                                       00-035629

Contents

II
Constructing and Deconstructing
Lacanian Theory

The Lacanian Clinical Field: Series Overview

JUDITH FEHER GUREWICH

Lacanian psychoanalysis exists, and the ongoing series, The Lacanian Clinical Field, is here to prove it. The clinical expertise of French practitioners deeply influenced by the thought of Jacques Lacan has finally found a publishing home in the United States. Books that have been acclaimed in France, Italy, Spain, Greece, South America, and Japan for their clarity, didactic power, and clinical relevance will now be at the disposal of the American psychotherapeutic and academic communities. These books cover a range of topics, including theoretical introductions; clinical approaches to neurosis, perversion, and psychosis; child psychoanalysis; conceptualizations of femininity; psychoanalytic readings of American literature; and more. Thus far ten books are in preparation.

Though all these works are clinically relevant, they will also be of great interest to those American scholars who have taught and used Lacan's theories for over a decade. What better opportunity for the academic world of literary criticism, philosophy, human sciences, women's studies, film studies, and multicultural studies finally to have access to the clinical insights of a theorist known primarily for his revolutionary vision of the formation of the human subject. Thus The Lacanian Clinical Field goes beyond introducing the American clinician to a different psychoanalytic outlook. It brings together two communities that have grown progressively estranged from each other. For indeed, the time when the Frankfurt School, Lionel Trilling, Erich Fromm, Herbert Marcuse, Philip Rieff, and others were fostering exchanges between the academic and the psychoanalytic communities is gone, and in the process psychoanalysis has lost some of its vibrancy.

The very limited success of ego psychology in bringing psychoanalysis into the domain of science has left psychoanalysis in need of a metapsychology that is able not only to withstand the pernicious challenges of psychopharmacology and psychiatry but also to accommodate the findings of cognitive and developmental psychology. Infant research has put many of Freud's insights into question, and the attempts to replace a one-body psychology with a more interpersonal or intersubjective approach have led to dissension within the psychoanalytic community. Many theorists are of the opinion that the road toward scientific legitimacy requires a certain allegiance with Freud's detractors, who are convinced that the unconscious and its sexual underpinnings are merely an aberration. Psychoanalysis continues to be practiced, however, and according to both patients and analysts the uncovering of unconscious motivations continues to provide a sense of relief. But while there has been a burgeoning of different psychoanalytic schools of thought since the desacralization of Freud, no theoretical agreement has been reached as to why such relief occurs.

Nowadays it can sometimes seem that Freud is read much more scrupulously by literary critics and social scientists than by psychoanalysts. This is not entirely a coincidence. While the psychoanalytic community is searching for a new metapsychology, the human sciences have acquired a level of theoretical sophistication and complexity that has enabled them to read Freud under a new lens. Structural linguistics and structural anthropology have transformed conventional appraisals of human subjectivity and have given Freud's unconscious a new status. Lacan's teachings, along with the works of Foucault and Derrida, have been largely responsible for the explosion of new ideas that have enhanced the interdisciplinary movement pervasive in academia today.

The downside of this remarkable intellectual revolution, as far as psychoanalysis is concerned, is the fact that Lacan's contribution has been derailed from its original trajectory. No longer perceived as a theory meant to enlighten the practice of psychoanalysis, his brilliant formulations have been both adapted and criticized so as to conform to the needs of purely intellectual endeavors far removed from clinical reality. This state of affairs is certainly in part responsible for Lacan's dismissal by the psychoanalytic community. Moreover, Lacan's "impossible" style has been seen as yet another proof of the culture of obscurantism that French intellectuals seem so fond of.

In this context the works included in The Lacanian Clinical Field should serve as an eye-opener at both ends of the spectrum. The authors in the series are primarily clinicans eager to offer to professionals in psychoanalysis, psychiatry, psychology, and other mental-health disciplines a clear and succinct didactic view of Lacan's work. Their goal is not so much to emphasize the radi-

cally new insights of the Lacanian theory of subjectivity and its place in the history of human sciences as it is to show how this difficult and complex body of ideas can enhance clinical work. Therefore, while the American clinician will be made aware that Lacanian psychoanalysis is not primarily a staple of literary criticism or philosophy but a praxis meant to cure patients of their psychic distress, the academic community will be exposed for the first time to a reading of Lacan that is in sharp contrast with the literature that has thus far informed them about his theory. In that sense Lacan's teachings return to the clinical reality to which they primarily belong.

Moreover, the clinical approach of the books in this series will shed a new light on the critical amendments that literary scholars and feminist theoreticians have brought to Lacan's conceptualization of subjectivity. While Lacan has been applauded for having offered an alternative to Freud's biological determinism, he has also been accused of nevertheless remaining phallocentric in his formulation of sexual difference. Yet this criticism, one that may be valid outside of the clinical reality—psychoanalysis is both an ingredient and an effect of culture—may not have the same relevance in the clinical context. For psychoanalysis as a praxis has a radically different function from the one it currently serves in academic discourse. In the latter, psychoanalysis is perceived both as an ideology fostering patriarchal beliefs and as a theoretical tool for constructing a vision of the subject no longer dependent on a phallocratic system. In the former, however, the issue of phallocracy loses its political impact. Psychoanalytic practice can only retroactively unravel the ways that the patient's psychic life has been constituted, and in that sense it can only reveal the function the phallus plays in the psychic elaboration of sexual difference.

The Lacanian Clinical Field, therefore, aims to undo certain prejudices that have affected Lacan's reputation up to now in both the academic and the psychoanalytic communities. While these prejudices stem from rather different causes— Lacan is perceived as too patriarchal and reactionary in the one and too far removed from clinical reality in the other—they both seem to overlook the fact that the fifty years that cover the period of Lacan's teachings were mainly devoted to working and reworking the meaning and function of psychoanalysis, not necessarily as a science or even as a human science, but as a practice that can nonetheless rely on a solid and coherent metapsychology. This double debunking of received notions may not only enlarge the respective frames of reference of both the therapeutic and the academic communities; it may also allow them to find a common denominator in a metapsychology that has derived its "scientific" status from the unexpected realm of the humanities.

I would like to end this overview to the series as a whole with a word of warning and a word of reassurance. One of the great difficulties for an American analyst trying to figure out the Lacanian "genre" is the way these clinical theorists explain their theoretical point of view as if it were coming straight from Freud. Yet Lacan's Freud and the American Freud are far from being transparent to each other. Lacan dismantled the Freudian corpus and rebuilt it on entirely new foundations, so that the new edifice no longer resembled the old. At the same time he always downplayed, with a certain coquetterie, *his position as a theory builder, because he was intent on proving that he had remained, despite all odds, true to Freud's deepest insights. Since Lacan was very insistent on keeping Freudian concepts as the raw material of his theory, Lacanian analysts of the sec-*

ond generation have followed in their master's footsteps and have continued to read Freud scrupulously in order to expand, with new insights, this large structure that had been laid out. Moreover, complicated historical circumstances have fostered their isolation, so that their acquaintance with recent psychoanalytic developments outside of France has been limited. Lacan's critical views on ego psychology and selected aspects of object relations theory have continued to inform their vision of American psychoanalysis and have left them unaware that certain of their misgivings about these schools of thought are shared by some of their colleagues in the United States. This apparently undying allegiance to Freud, therefore, does not necessarily mean that Lacanians have not moved beyond him, but rather that their approach is different from that of their American counterparts. While the latter often tend to situate their work as a reaction to Freud, the Lacanian strategy always consists in rescuing Freud's insights and resituating them in a context free of biological determinism.

Second, I want to repeat that the expository style of the books of this series bears no resemblance to Lacan's own writings. Lacan felt that Freud's clarity and didactic talent had ultimately led to distortions and oversimplifications, so that his own notoriously "impossible" style was meant to serve as a metaphor for the difficulty of listening to the unconscious. Cracking his difficult writings involves not only the intellectual effort of readers but also their unconscious processes; comprehension will dawn as reader-analysts recognize in their own work what was expressed in sibylline fashion in the text. Some of Lacan's followers continued this tradition, fearing that clear exposition would leave no room for the active participation of the reader. Others felt strongly that although Lacan's point was *well taken it was not necessary to prolong indefinitely an ideology of obscurantism liable to fall into the same traps as the ones Lacan was denouncing in the first place. Such a conviction was precisely what made this series, The Lacanian Clinical Field, possible.*

Construing Lacan

JEAN-MICHEL RABATÉ

> *To construe:*
>   *1a: to analyze the arrangement and connection of words in a sentence or part of a sentence;*
>   *1b: to combine idiomatically;*
>   *2a: to put a construction on;*
>   *2b: to understand, usually in a particular way.*
>   (Webster's Dictionary)

Is Lacan difficult? Yes, according to a remark often heard: Lacan is perversely obscure, impenetrable, all the more so with an English-speaking audience facing translation problems and increased cultural distance. One might object: Didn't Lacan himself mean to be difficult? Difficulty, it seems, would be intrinsic to a radical pedagogical strategy aiming at forming a new kind of psychoanalyst. This is an insight that is confirmed, for instance, at the beginning of his well-known "The Agency of the letter in the unconscious or reason since Freud," a text that marked his entry into the English-speaking world.[1] Lacan writes: "Writing is distinguished by a prevalence of the *text*

---

1. This essay was first translated by Jan Miel and published in 1966 in *Yale French Studies* n° 36/37, under the title of "The insistence of the letter in the unconscious." The translation is different from that of Alan Sheridan who includes "The agency of the letter in the unconscious or reason since Freud" in his translation of *Ecrits—A Selection* (New York: Norton, 1977).

. . . this makes possible the kind of tightening up that, according to my taste, will leave the reader no other way out than the way in, an entrance which I prefer to be difficult."[2] But he immediately adds a disclaimer: "In that sense, then, this will not be writing." Notwithstanding the almost surrealist implications that might call up a Magritte (with the warning: the words you are reading are not writing), such a constant and deliberate paradox can indeed be seen as the site of Lacan's main effect, of his impact through a Word that will always hesitate before being made either flesh or ink. It is my contention, however, and that of all the authors in this collection, that despite the election of such a paradoxical locus Lacan's difficulty is slowly but steadily vanishing as we enter a new century. By which I do not imply that this difficulty disappears as soon as we understand its rationale. It is rather that, as we move on to another era that might well be called "Lacanian" just as the twentieth century could be called "Freudian,"[3] our reality looks more and more like Lacanian fiction—that is, a truth that has found an adequate fictional structure. Having learned to thread our way through the meanders of a living speech still in quest of a writing, we can now better see the immense difficulties of all kinds against which Lacan was struggling, rather than projecting him as a perverse and cunning trickster of the unconscious.

---

2. Original text in J. Lacan, *Ecrits* (Paris: Seuil, 1966) p. 493. I have modified Alan Sheridan's translation of the essay in *Ecrits—A Selection* (New York: Norton, 1977), p. 147.

3. This collection comes from an international conference that took place at the University of Pennsylvania in April 1998. Its title was "Turn of the Century—End of Analysis?" Most of the essays have been rewritten for publication. I have tried to keep some of the liveliness and excitement of the debates in this retranscription.

In the famous broadcast made in 1973 for French television (illuminated in these pages by Catherine Liu's brilliant commentary), Lacan famously and abruptly began by stating: "I always speak the truth. Not the whole truth, because there's no way, to say it all. Saying it all is literally impossible; words fail. Yet it's through this very impossibility that the truth holds onto the real."[4] As if to prove his point, he concluded with a cryptic riddle sounding like post-Joycean tongue-twisters, or like Beckett's late prose in *Worstward Ho*, forcing the translators to feats of creativity: "between that which perdures through pure dross, and the hand that draws only from Dad to worse"[5]—punning as usual on *père* (father) and *pire* (worse) to suggest that if he is taken as a father by his disciples, this will not bring them many rewards. In between, however, we were warned to be patient: "Ten years is enough for everything I write to become clear to everyone."[6] Quite uncharacteristically, Lacan may have been a little too optimistic here, but we can hope that almost thirty years after, his thoughts and concepts will indeed start to appear "clear as day"—but as blinding as the sun gazed at without blinking; to quote a cryptic phrase from Mallarmé's most obscure and radically unfinished *Book*: "It is clear as day."[7]

However, if *Ecrits*—an immediate and atypical bestseller published in 1966—has by now become "literature" (as Lacan himself noted in front of a bewildered audience at Yale Univer-

---

4. J. Lacan, *Television: A Challenge to the Psychoanalytic Establishment*, ed. J. Copjec, tr. D. Hollier, R. Krauss, A. Michelson, (New York: Norton, 1990), p. 3.

5. Ibid., p. 46.

6. Ibid., p. 45.

7 "*C'est clair comme le jour*," in S. Mallarmé, *Oeuvres complètes* I ed. B. Marchal, (Paris: Gallimard, Pléiade, 1999) p. 608.

sity),[8] this "literature" has not yet achieved the same status as Mallarmé's half-indecipherable last jottings. And even if *Ecrits* has now received the literal critical attention it needed,[9] this collection arises from a wish to go beyond the multiple and redundant "introductions" to Lacan that have multiplied in the last ten years. They have fulfilled an important role, and partly thanks to them, partly because of a deeper historical evolution, we are now ready to use Lacan in a more pragmatic sense, by engaging directly with important debates in a cultural context that he himself has modified, which includes an awareness of the dialectical relationship between transmission and resistance. The authors in this book are all aware of the contested nature of Lacan's heritage. The main framework of this collection is the transatlantic reception of Lacan's ideas, with a focus on the strange discrepancy between the strong impact made by Lacanian ideas in the humanities and social sciences and the ignorance or resistance they are subject to in the field of clinical psychoanalysis. Is the huge difference between Lacan's reception in Latin countries (France, Spain, Italy, and South America mainly) and Anglo-Saxon countries due to cultural gap, to a "jet-lag," as Pommier

---

8. Lacan declared to the students: "There is a new inflection of literature. . . . Everything is literature. I too, produce literature, since it sells: take my *Ecrits*, this is literature to which I have imagined I could give a status which was different from what Freud imagined. . . . I don't think I am making science when I am making literature. Nevertheless, this is literature because it has been written and it sells. And this is also literature because it has effects, even effects on literature." J. Lacan, "Conférences et Entretiens dans des Universités nord-américaines," *Scilicet* 6/7:7, 1976.

9. See the very useful annotations of J. P. Muller and W. J. Richardson, *Lacan and Language: A Reader's Guide to* Ecrits (New York: International Universities Press, 1982).

calls it? No single answer can be provided, or at least it could not be given in a single voice; the book gathers diverse perspectives on the issue of Lacanian cultural translation, articulating several of the essays in an explicitly dialogic confrontation with each other. By including non-Lacanian perspectives, or "dissenters," among the more faithful, the collection aims at creating a coherent "polylogue" and generating a productive discussion. The example of practicing psychoanalysts like Blévis, Braunstein, Feher Gurewich, Gherovici, Pommier, and Tort proves that they can still call themselves "Lacanian" while not being averse to a critical reexamination of major concepts, or textual and political issues.

The main contention underlying their approach is that today, at the dawn of a new century, critical discussions of the Lacanian tradition have to replace the usual introductions to the basics of Lacanian doctrine (often reduced to its structuralist moment). Indeed, a first wave of commentators has succeeded in making sense of Lacan's essential ideas. We should now go beyond explicatory exegeses restating the dual nature of the sign and the notion of the subject split by desire, as well as beyond a mere historicizing and recontextualizing approach to the genesis of Lacan's thought. These introductions to a "Lacan made simple" have been indispensable, but they have tried too strenuously to systematize Lacan's "philosophy" or his "anti-philosophy" (which boils down to exactly the same thing), glossing over hesitations, contradictions, or evolutions that appear today as the most exciting part of his legacy. It is with the wish of assessing Lacan's impact today in English-speaking countries that we want to return to his texts in all their layered complexity.

This is also why we wish to dispel some of the obscurity surrounding his theses, because we feel that Lacan may well be difficult but never obfuscating, or that his difficulty should not paralyze but tantalize. Among the many disguises he chose for himself, there never was that of the abstract metaphysician, of the "speculator" anxious to revise psychoanalytic discourse in the name of a more sophisticated philosophical consistency. His consistency is that of science, of a "science of the subject" that he hoped to found—using all the concepts and discourses he could find on his way, while remaining in touch with the central "experience" his work is based upon— the analytical experience associating two persons through silence and speech. The concepts Lacan kept elaborating during a long and productive career have all proved to be redoubtably sharp and original, pushing psychoanalysis effectively from the nineteenth century, from which Freud barely emerges, to a future perfect we attempt to account for in terms of post-something—post-structuralism, post-modernity, or post-feminism.

Now that we have celebrated one century since Freud discovered the unconscious, since it was in 1897 that he started the self-analysis that led him to discover that "nothing human was alien to him," we may wonder whether the survival of Freudian thought in a new millennium will not be intimately linked with the development of Lacanian discourse. With the rapid development of genetics, biology, and chemistry, one often hears that psychoanalysis is obsolete, that it has lost any scientific credibility. Even if its scientific basis has repeatedly been questioned, psychoanalysis (or the myth it has created) keeps provoking thought and questioning basic assumptions about subjectivity and the human psyche.

The current controversy about the commemoration of Freud in the United States that has recently focused on the

Washington exhibition in the fall of 1998,[10] and various head-lines in magazines such as *Time* and the *New York Times* repeatedly heralding the "death of Freud" nevertheless attest to the vitality of psychoanalysis: like the phoenix it seems to be born again from its ashes and thrive on the opposition it generates. This is why numerous new academic journals have been launched in the last years, and more and more conferences devoted to psychoanalytic readings of film, gender, art, politics, and society. The international focus seems to have shifted toward a more political and critical discourse—and one of the aims of this collection is to assess the reasons of this evolution.

The European or South American equivalent of the debate on Freud in the United States has tended to focus on the controversial figure of Lacan, arguably the most important psychoanalyst after Freud, and on the complex legacy of the numerous schools that have been created in his name, and with the battle cry of a "return to Freud"—by which he meant that psychoanalysts had simply to learn to read all the writings of the founder of their discipline, which never was such an easy task as it appears. The authors gathered here reopen the issue of the various channels through which Freudian ideas have permeated our culture both in Europe and in America to the point that we can hardly describe ourselves or others today without using terms such as *neurotic, psychotic,* or *paranoid* (to say nothing of the adjective *hysterical*). Be-

---

10. The Library of Congress exhibition, *Sigmund Freud: Conflict and Culture,* curated by Michael S. Roth, scheduled originally for 1995, was postponed until October 1998. After D.C., it was shown at the Jewish Museum in New York in the spring of 1999 before being shipped to Vienna. See the collection of essays edited by M. S. Roth, *Freud: Conflict and Culture: Essays on His Life, Work and Legacy* (New York: Knopf, 1998).

yond that popular jargon, it seems that the images of Freud
or of psychoanalysis evoked in, say, France, England, Argentina, Brazil, and in the United States conjure up widely diverging pictures, frameworks that have very little in common.
Is this only due to problems of translation, language, or culture, or to broader institutional and political issues? This
collection will address the tension between national and international traditions in the various theories that claim to be
derived from Freud and from Lacan, and question their link,
since very often Lacan invokes Freud's example to radically
contradict him.[11]

Freud himself insisted on the international aspect of the
movement he had founded, whereas Lacan's motto of a "return to Freud" stresses on the other hand the importance of
languages and cultures in which psychoanalysis has to work.
How far are theories that claim to be universal culture- and
language-bound? Moreover, is the clinical dimension that
could be seen as a universal practice linking various groups
in spite of their theoretical divergence a common ground or
an element that has to be forgotten if these theories wish to
retain all their impact? This collection will try to speak directly
to this important issue: in a typically Lacanian manner, a
number of clinical practitioners choose to address fundamental issues rather than make points based on case studies, as is
regularly done in more traditional Freudian literature. The
several Lacanian clinicians who write here deliberately abstain
from systematic discussions of clinical material, in keeping
with Lacan's often-noted reluctance to engage in case discus-

---

11. I have demonstrated this with regard to the interpretation of
Hamlet in *Jacques Lacan: The Last Word* (New York: St. Martin's Press,
2000).

sions. Even if this did not help to make him amenable to discussion with North American clinicians, the absence of clinical material is part of the book's subject matter and of the problem it addresses.

Indeed, one can note that the fortune of Lacanism in film theory, gender studies, and cultural studies is often the result of a systematic omission of the clinical dimension. The international scholars, historians of culture, philosophers, and practicing psychoanalysts from several countries are gathered here in order to examine Lacan's fundamentalism—by which I do not only mean a fundamentalist reading of Freud's text *à la lettre*, but also the decision to treat fundamental concepts before engaging with issues of clinical practice. Lacan implies that psychoanalysts who merely repeat the original scene devised for them by Freud remain blind to what is central in this very practice: language. Thus, the relevance of language will keep ideological repercussions, especially when we see how a Viennese Freud was translated into English by immigrants often aware that they needed to conform to dominant ideologies if they wished to succeed. The concept of the "French Freud" aims at an inverse translation, at a defamiliarization of the text, soon enriched by new dimensions of knowledge such have been opened by mathematics, topology, philosophy, linguistics, and anthropology.

The more clearly we understand the dimensions of this new context, marked as it is today by other developments, in which gender studies, queer studies, film studies, cultural studies, neo-Marxism, feminism, and the political critiques of nationalism and identities play a more and more important role, the easier, that is, the stronger and the more relevant, Lacan's work will be. This relevance does not preclude contradictory assessments. Indeed, Lacan's dissolution of his own school by a famous letter—whose authenticity has been questioned by Roudinesco[12]—shortly before his death in 1981, led to an even more conflicted scene. This is why Gérard Pommier, who was one of Lacan's disciples, and who was very vocal in the controversies surrounding the institutional debates of the '80s, can testify to the political function of resistances met by Lacanian discourse. Another dissenter is Michel Tort, also involved quite early in these various struggles, who examines Lacan's drift to theoretical paternalism from the late '30s to the main seminars. The concept of the Name-of-the-Father, so central in Lacanian theory, exhibits a troubling proximity to Catholic discourse. Tort's compelling and challenging thesis is that this was Lacan's personal "solution" to the convoluted riddles left open by the Freudian Oedipus complex.

Tort's accusation is not far from Roazen's reproach of theoretical grandiosity doubled by insufficient scholarship. He takes one Seminar as a point of departure and examines with a magnifying glass this Lacanian laboratory. It seems useful to provide a brief account of the status of these Seminars, since they are often invoked in conflicting fashions, and since their hidden existence perpetuates the illusion that they are full of clinical remarks or present an easier Lacan. In these Seminars, Lacan often quotes other clinicians (for instance, Michael Balint or Ella Sharpe) or discusses cases brought by his students (like Rosine Lefort in Seminar I, who provides an exemplary analysis of a Lacanian "Wolfman") rather than examine his own cases. From his first public Seminar at Sainte-Anne,[13] which

---

12. See E. Roudinesco, *Jacques Lacan*, tr. B. Bray, (New York: Columbia University Press, 1997).

13. *Seminar I, Freud's Papers on Technique* (1953–1954) (Paris: Seuil, 1975). Translated by J. Forrester (New York: Norton, 1998).

bristles with original insights and is full of dialogues with interlocutors such as Hyppolite, Anzieu, Mannoni, Granoff, Leclaire, Beirnaert, Rosine Lefort, or less visibly Michael Balint, Anna Freud, and Melanie Klein, to one of the last, Seminar XX,[14] one can measure the ground covered in twenty years. At the other end of the spectrum, in the *Encore* Seminar, Lacan takes a position on the crucial issue of gender, responding to growing feminist dissatisfaction with Freud's and his own alleged phallocentrism. With these groundbreaking "formulas of sexuation," the new grid opens up an original view of sexual difference, opposing the male side of sexuation to the female side. The male side is inscribed under the heading of castration, while a barred Woman can choose to be the "not whole" or "not all," escaping from a defining subjective determination through castration. The feminine side points to a barred Other that keeps strong affinities with the mystical view of a *jouissance* of God—however, men can decide to inscribe themselves under the feminine "not all." This seminar, full of wild puns and improvisations, led Lacan to the discovery of the Borromean knot, in which he soon found an endless source of speculative delight.

A rapid recapitulation of the main Seminars published in French will limn the contours of an evolutionary Lacanian "truth," a truth that had to be transmitted through a discourse that was inseparable from a more writerly, allusive and punning style. With Seminar II,[15] Lacan draws all the theoretical consequences of his forceful distinction between the ego and

---

14. *Seminar XX, Encore* (1972–1973) (Seuil, 1975). Translated as *On Feminine Sexuality: The Limits of Love and Knowledge 1972–1973* by B. Fink (New York: Norton, 1998).

15. *Seminar II, The Ego in Freud's Theory and in the Technique of Psychoanalysis* (1954–1955) (Seuil, 1978). Translated by. S. Tomaselli and J. Forrester (New York: Norton, 1998).

the subject. After a series of discussions linking Freud and Hegel, the Seminar climaxes with wonderful readings of Freud's "Dream of Irma" and of Poe's "The Purloined Letter." These two readings provide a first model, the so-called "L scheme," with which he articulates the three registers of the Real, the Imaginary, and the Symbolic. In the following Seminar,[16] Lacan tackles the issue of psychosis. Starting with Freud's version of the Schreber case, Lacan gives paranoia a rigorous treatment, hitting upon a concept he lacked at the time of his doctoral thesis on psychosis in the '30s: that of foreclosure (*Verwerfung*) coupled with the theory of an unconscious writing. The Seminar then discloses a whole rhetoric of the unconscious: what had been foreclosed in Schreber, generating his psychosis, was the paternal metaphor. In 1956, Lacan elaborates at length the concept of castration and the phallus. In one of the most productive seminars for clinical considerations,[17] one can grasp how the phallus and castration can be brought to bear on the imaginary triad composed of the Mother, the Phallus, and the Child. There, Lacan opposes Castration, the lack of an imaginary object, Frustration, the lack of a real object, and Privation, the lack of a symbolic object, devoting illuminating pages to fetishism, phobia, feminine homosexuality, and perverse fantasies. He also reads Freud's classics, like "A Child is Being Beaten," the "Little Hans" case, and Freud's study of Leonardo. One can see how it was that, armed with the concept of the phallus and a revised sense of castration, Lacan would then reread Freud's

---

16. *Seminar III, Psychoses* (1955–1956) (Seuil, 1981). Translated by R. Grigg (New York: Norton, 1993).

17. *Seminar IV, Object Relations and Freudian Structures.* (1956–1957) (Paris: Seuil, 1994).

major works and rephrase them in a more modern and idiosyncratic language. In 1958, Lacan keeps on reading Freud,[18]
he starts from the *Witz* book to sketch the way jokes disclose
a complex scheme of desire and subjectivity that will resur-
face in "Subversion of the Subject and Dialectics of Desire"
(1966). From the installation of the paternal metaphor to the
prohibition of the mother's body, the subject will learn to pass
through the dialectical hurdles created by the negativity of the
phallus, to either "be or not be the phallus," or "have or not
have the phallus." Molière's comedies and Jean Genet's plays,
or Gide's despair when his wife burned all his letters, help
Lacan define the comic appearance of the phallic object. This
new turn launches Lacan in a series of literary developments
in the following Seminars, and one could almost say that literature has replaced for a time psychoanalytic case studies.

Thus in the famous Seminar on Ethics[19] of 1959–1960,
it is the reading of Marquis de Sade and of *Antigone* that provide the starting point for crucial discoveries. Beginning with
the introduction of the concept of the *Thing* after a patient
reading of Freud's early "*Project of a Scientific Psychology*,"
Lacan criticizes the notion of sublimation, and parallels Kant
with Sade to point out the limits of the moral law. He then
gives a compelling commentary of *Antigone*, a play whose
heroine appears characterized by a blinding beauty whose
main function is to arrest desire "between two deaths." The
Seminar concludes with the paradoxes of ethics, condensed
in the pithy formula: "One should never yield on one's de-

---

18. *Seminar V, The Formations of the Unconscious* (1957–1958) (Paris:
Seuil, 1998).

19. *Seminar VII, The Ethics of Psychoanalysis* (1959–1960). (Paris:
Seuil, 1986). Translated by D. Porter (New York: Norton, 1992).

sire." In 1960–1961, two new interlocutors are Plato with his *Symposium* and Claudel with his historical trilogy.[20] Plato's dialogue leads to a redefinition of "transference love" as the main technical tool of psychoanalysis. Socrates' hidden secret, his *agalma,* the forbidden object of desire for Alcibiades, anticipates on the dialectics of *objet petit a* as cause of desire. Love and desire are closely articulated, even opposed, and Claudel's plays on the Coûfontaine family provide another sense of transference, closer to a "transmission" of desire across several generations. Plato leaves for posterity the emblematic figure of a Socrates who never writes but knows that he knows nothing, except love, thus perhaps "inventing" psychoanalysis, while Claudel's religious critique of the history of modernity yields another perspective: it is through the "humiliation" of a perverse and "real" father that one has to take symbolic paternity into consideration. The result may end up in death and contradict a desire—erotic and never fully sublimated—that remains alive on the side of femininity.

Finally, two other important seminars can be mentioned in this rapid survey. In the seminal Seminar XI, "The Four Fundamental Concepts of Psychoanalysis" (1964),[21] Lacan discusses what he sees as psychoanalysis's "main concepts": the Unconscious, Repetition, Transference, and the Drive. In a very philosophical and dense text, best known for its elaborate disquisition on the opposition between the eye and the gaze, Lacan engages with complex notions: the gap opened by the Freudian unconscious for the subject of certainty, the

---

20. *Seminar VIII, On Transference* (1960–1961) (Paris: Seuil, 1991).
21. *Seminar XI, The Four Fundamental Concepts of Psychoanalysis* (1964) (Paris: Seuil, 1973). Translated by A. Sheridan (New York: Norton, 1978).

reason why gods belong to the Real, the identification of the gaze with the object a, the role of anamorphosis to let the unnamable Thing be glimpsed. Here, the subject is radically split, not only between signifier and signified but also between enunciation and statement: this generates serial rewordings of the Cartesian *ego cogito*, finally under the domination of the Freudian drive, a *Trieb* that always misses a vanishing object. Multiplying new concepts and models, Lacan shows an extraordinary theoretical invention—he begins to think in his own idiom.

A few years later, just after the students' revolt of May 1968, it is a more political Lacan who surfaces in Seminar XVII. In "The Reverse of Psychoanalysis" (1969–1970),[22] we see Lacan reacting with aplomb and savage wit to the radical students who tried to put his teaching in question. Outlining a theory of the "four discourses," the discourse of the University, of the Master, of the Hysteric, and of the Analyst, Lacan uses these discursive formations to account for the entire structure of the social link: four fundamental discursive agencies formalize society understood as a network of signifiers and subjective positions. Society is approached from the specific angle of psychoanalytic practice, a practice that functions by a sort of phenomenological reduction of everything to discourse—while highlighting what is most often forgotten, stressing the role of the subject's desire and enjoyment, asking what key signifiers still provide ideals or programs, finally exhibiting the productive power of unconscious knowledge. The investigation aims at dialecticizing the opposition between knowledge (in the sense of unconscious knowl-

---

22. *Seminar XVII, The Reverse of Psychoanalysis* (1969–1970). (Paris: Seuil, 1991).

edge) and enjoyment, understood as a *jouissance* always deferred under the shape of an elusive "surplus enjoyment." Here one can grasp Lacan's ambition: like Freud before him, he does not hesitate to provide huge cultural syntheses whose applications to everyday life, race, gender, and class are innumerable.

The aim of the various critics, clinicians, and theoreticians called upon here is to live up to Lacan's high ambitions and expectations, not by providing a mimetic homage, but through a polyphony of divergent appraisals modeled on the breadth and variety of these seminars. These seminars helped define step by step a "theory" that was not a philosophy nor an "ontology," but fundamentally an ethics, as the crucial Seminar VII on the "Ethics of Psychoanalysis" magnificently states. In a culture determined by an ideology of endless scientific progress, psychoanalysis reminds us of ethical issues centering around the subject's responsibility. This is why Pommier can go back to Althusser's critique of ideological formation, and denounce a "postmodern condition" entailing the loss of ideals except those provided by a regressive science in which "sexual theories" bypass sexual and political difference. Patricia Gherovici turns to Rorty, who depicts Freud's influence on our culture as lasting and iconic, in a way that tends to assimilate and erase the original shock of his impact into American society. Resistances can be positive in so far as they allow for thinkers like Lacan to bring paradox and contradiction to bear on clinical practice. Lacanian thinkers do not monumentalize his doctrine, nor Freud's, as Nestor Braunstein will show in an astute deconstructive reading of Freud's conception of rememoration and "conviction."

Some resistances met by Lacan's theories can already be accounted for when one considers the difficulty of reading rigorously a seminar as if it was an *écrit*—a written text. This is why the caveats of a renowned historian of psychoanalysis such as Paul Roazen can be put to good use. His critical reading of Lacan's first Seminar highlights omissions, flippant asides, or arbitrary judgments. In spite of Lacan's somewhat cavalier approach to scholarship, it nevertheless remains obvious that his steady pedagogical effort and the breadth of his culture not only did put French psychoanalysis back onto the international map but also forced a radical reexamination of its entire theoretical foundations. Ed Robins's spirited reply reopens the fruitful debate about accusations of "catholicity"; he agrees with Roazen that what matters is to be able to read Lacan closely, while describing an ideal of intellectual rigor completely at odds with either pseudo-philosophical scholasticism or a return to religiosity. The strenuous task of such a reading implies a fierce struggle against ideological resistances.

These resistances are here examined in a specifically American context. Whereas the French transmission has kept the stamp of its Hegelian roots, the American reception has been conceptually more timid and marked by the dominance of psychology, neurosciences, and cognitive sciences, as Kareen Malone demonstrates. She suggests that a slow revolution is taking place in American psychoanalysis, with a professional milieu multiplying signs of interest and betraying a growing need for Lacan. Joseph Smith's testimony is therefore crucial, since he directly addresses the main site of resistance, Lacan's attack on an "ego psychology" presented as ideologically regressive. Smith suggests that Lacan's theory of desire, radical as it is, nevertheless leaves room for a redefinition of the ego. In 1955, Lacan could indeed ascribe all resistances to the subject's ego, defined as the site of an imaginary struggle against the Symbolic.[23] As both Michel Tort and Nestor Braunstein also point out, this problematic of a "symbolic" truth that would come to dispel an imaginary illusion cannot suffice. Braunstein shows the limitation of the Freudian model, with its stubborn insistence on *Ueberzeugung* (conviction). Tort goes further, denouncing as we saw a tendency to find in a religious transcendentalism the absolute foundation for an Unconscious truth (or the truth of the Unconscious).

All this explains why Lacan felt the need to revise his own topology, to overcome the limitations of the binary model opposing signifier and signified, metaphor and metonymy, condensation and displacement, Other and other, subject and ego, and so on, with which he had started. In the late '60s and '70s, he expands into a more subtle and architectonic triangulation: there the Borromean knot posits the theoretical equivalence of the three registers of the Symbolic, the Real, and the Imaginary and leaves at the nexus of the knot a site in which the ego can inscribe itself as a symptom. Such is, very broadly of course, the outcome of the very creative seminar devoted to Joyce in 1976. All of which proves all the more urgently the need to reopen a dialogue with Anglo-Saxon tradition of psychoanalysis, as Michel Tort and Judith Feher Gurewich have started to do.[24] This dialogue had begun not among clinicians but in the field of art theory with some privileged mediators. Thus, as Steven Levine's testimony shows when he reminisces about the magazine *October*, whose role has been exemplary, the transmission of Lacanian ideas in

---

23. *Seminar II*, p. 321.
24. See J. Feher Gurewich and M. Tort, ed., *Lacan and the New Wave in American Psychoanalysis* (New York: Other Press, 1999).

American culture was achieved more through the agency of art and film critics and literature specialists than practicing psychoanalysts.

Other essays in this volume make sense of the North American context, in which Lacanian concepts have often been mediated by film and gender studies or cultural critique. The talent and versatility of a Slavoj Žižek has been instrumental in promoting a trendy Lacanianism applied to popular visual culture. Using the insights developed in Seminar XI, Joan Copjec proposes here an original reading of Lacan's theory of an embodied vision in "The Strut of Vision," while Catherine Liu takes up the issue of the media when she examines how *Television* addresses a "popular" audience. She describes how the intermeshing of technological mediatization and revolutionary posturing in post-Lacanian pedagogy creates both seduction and resistance.

In the particular context of the resistance of scientists, it was important to assess the impact of Sokal's and Bricmont's criticism. In their *Fashionable Nonsense: Postmodern Intellectuals' Abuse of Science*[25] they accuse Lacan of having mistakenly identified the "erectile organ" with "the square root of minus one." Both Pommier and Arkady Plotnitsky deal with their wholesale attack on what they take to be an egregious mistakes that would reflect negatively on the scientificity of the "mathemes." As Plotnitsky shows, this contested mathematical analogy does make sense, especially when it comes to defining the idea of the phallus. Indeed, Lacan's lifelong engagement with mathematics, his standing collaborations with scientists, attest less to a serious purpose or to real com-

---

25. A. Sokal and J. Bricmont, *Fashionable Nonsense: Postmodern Intellectuals' Abuse of Science* (New York: Picador, 1998).

petence than to his need to find a new language that would be as performative as descriptive.

When Nestor Braunstein explores the crucial Freudian concept of *construction*, he can show that Lacan consistently refused the Freudian myth of an archeological retrieval of the past. The only way to avoid the dead end of suggestion would thus lie in a deconstructive practice of psychoanalysis. Consequently, as Erich Freiberger thinks, Lacan would align himself with Wittgenstein's critique of Freud while returning in a very systematic fashion to the insights of Plato—who had, after all, to rationalize and systematize the insights of Socrates, who as we saw might appear as the first psychoanalyst. Lacan's key concept of the phallus (not to be confused with the "erectile organ") corresponds to a more modern sense of a floating currency, whereas Freud's insistence on the "bedrock" of castration seems congruent with an earlier time, when all currencies stayed founded on gold. By keeping the association with the organ while depriving it of its essentialist overtones, Lacan manages to remain Freudian while pushing Freud's insights away from an ideology of biological identity. His idea of a fundamentally comic and deflatable phallus had important repercussions for feminist theory and queer studies.

I have talked about the importance of these theories when accounting for the initial impact of Lacan in the States. As an influential theoretician like Judith Butler has shown, Lacan appears as a thinker who can provide a response to Foucault's analysis of power and subjection, especially when Foucault seems to forget the psychic dimension of subjection. Chris Lane reopens the debate by examining Foucault's hesitations facing psychoanalysis in general and Lacan in particular. His essay on "The Experience of the Outside" posits less Lacan against Foucault than it points to their complementarity. In her turn, Judith Feher Gurewich examines the role of queer theory in the context of Lacan's ambiguous praise of perversion. She is not blind to Lacan's hesitations and ambivalence, a point taken up by Marcianne Blévis when she systematically takes stock of what Lacan has brought to our understanding of female homosexuality. Frances Restuccia confronts directly problems left unresolved by Judith Butler in her "The Subject of Homosexuality: Butler's Elision," while Marcianne Blévis forcibly attacks the mirage of unity provided by the Phallus. As Lacan argued in Seminar XX, there is room for an ethic of femininity that rejects the cult of the Phallus and remains open to the Other. Such an ethic would indeed keep a nostalgic vocation not for the Phallus, but for otherness, to vary slightly Butler's formula. An Unconscious that knows only the One would be homosexual by definition, whereas female homosexuality attempts to position itself in the disturbing axis of otherness, an otherness that can be grasped through Lacan's later graphs and concepts.

I have started these introductory remarks on the proximity between "construing" and "constructing" with considerations of publication and translation. A key term such a *Phallus* might provide a good example on the issue of productive misconstruction—as if the True of Truth would always be not just "half-said" but also, quite literally, systematically "misconstrued." Truth, although impossible to say "all," remains a central concern for Lacan (which triggered the most violent critique from the Derridian camp). Truth does not exist independently from the language *it* inhabits and *we* inhabit as speaking subjects: we cohabit with truth, even when we do not want to see it (which is the most common case). Admittedly, the truth Lacan was seeking in his seminars could not

be given immediately—it had to be staged and produced as if
it was some kind of "difficult" writing being read aloud by a
speaker facing an audience—a situation that is not unlike that
of psychoanalysis. At times, the words on the blackboard
appear illegible, they have been covered by new sentences,
and we once again grasp Freud's magical *Wunderblock*, a writing tablet held by someone who writes with one hand while
erasing with the other.

Thus, if we return to the opening of "The Agency of the
Letter in the Unconscious, or Reason since Freud," which I
have already quoted, it is not to stress the fact that Lacan
flaunts or excuses his own difficulty, since the main origin of
the difficulty appears to be a hiatus between speaking and
writing: "Writing is distinguished by a prevalence of the *text*
. . . this makes possible the kind of tightening up that, according to my taste, will leave the reader no other way out than
the way in, an entrance which I prefer to be difficult."[26] The
way out is the way in, in a startling application to textual
hermeneutics of Pascal's phrase Lacan would often cite: "You
wouldn't have searched for me if you hadn't already found
me." The letter had already started its "agency" especially since
most "written" essays were revised versions of earlier discussions found in the Seminars (in which one can read, for instance, the first installments of a confrontation with Poe or
Sade, an discover pages, that although they are more linear,
are not devoid of complexity). And even if these first versions
are easier in a sense—more relaxed and chatty, more repetitive, the way a Montaigne can use repetition with impercep-

---

26. J. Lacan, *Ecrits* (Paris: Seuil, 1966) p. 493. I have modified Alan
Sheridan's translation of the essay in *Ecrits—A Selection* (New York:
Norton, 1977) p. 147.

tible variations so as to change subtly his point of view—the main issue remains the author's hesitation about the status of writing (or of letters) in his text.

A remark made at the outset of Seminar XX about an earlier Seminar helps make sense of what could otherwise be seen as simple equivocations. When the Seuil had started planning the publication of Lacan's Seminars, wishing to begin with Seminar VII on Ethics, Lacan had declined. This is how he narrates the fact in his own Seminar in the fall of 1972: "It so happened that I did not publish *The Ethics of Psychoanalysis*. At the time, it was a form of politeness on my part—after you, be my guest, be my *worst*. . . . With the passage of time, I learned that I could say a little more about it. And then I realized that what constituted my course was a sort of 'I don't want to know anything about it.'"[27] Despite the overall quality of his translation, Bruce Fink has some trouble finding an equivalent to Lacan's pun on *je vous en prie* and *pire*, a pun that derives its justification from the title of the previous seminar (. . . *Ou pire*). Lacan's story is hard to believe, and the mere suggestion of an all-too-polite host begging others to publish before he does contradicts the most obvious biographical evidence. Yet there is some truth in his reluctance to publish, a misconstrued truth no doubt, at least if we go back to Roudinesco's useful biography. She documents how François Wahl, the Seuil's editor, had to work on Lacan for a long time, pleading and coercing, before he could get him to put together the various texts that went into *Ecrits*.[28] Or one could take

---

27. J. Lacan, *Seminar XX, On Feminine Sexuality: The Limits of Love and Knowledge 1972–1973*, tr. B. Fink (New York: Norton, 1998) p. 1.

28. E. Roudinesco: *Jacques Lacan*, tr. B. Bray, (New York: Columbia University Press, 1997), pp. 322–330.

the lecture on Joyce at the Sorbonne as another example. Lacan read in June 1975 a fairly clear paper; when he was later asked to publish it, he revised it so heavily that the final version has almost no resemblance with the original oral presentation—it is a dense, opaque, punning pastiche of Joyce that is very hard to decipher.[29]

Lacan fundamentally believes that any serious "writing" will be, in some sense, unreadable. This is why he will find in Joyce such a momentous alter ego in the years 1975–1977, and also can present *Ecrits* as a book that is "not meant to be read."[30] However, after that remark, he adds that he was happily surprised to realize that the Seminar on Ethics contained theses that were still valid and could thus "hold water."[31] Alluding once more to the issue of publication of Seminar VII, he remarked that it was futile to try to convince hostile critics, promising that he would rework this Seminar so as to transform it into a real writing.[32] The irony of these remarks is that they introduced another kind of rereading, rather negative and critical this time, performed on his texts by Lacoue-Labarthe and Nancy, two philosophers close to Derrida who take a rather harsh view of Lacan's speculations on language.[33] This reversal can allegorize problems posed by the earlier transmission of Lacanian ideas: the best critics were those who read him closely but ferociously with a devotion that turned

---

29. See J. Lacan, "Joyce le Symptôme II" in *Joyce avec Lacan*, ed. J. Aubert (Paris: Navarin, 1987) pp. 31–36.

30. *Seminar XX, On Feminine Sexuality*, pp. 26.

31. Ibid., p. 27.

32. Ibid., pp. 53–57.

33. See P. Lacoue-Labarthe and J.-L. Nancy, *The Title of the Letter: A Reading of Lacan*, tr. F. Raffoul and D. Pettigrew (Albany: State University of New York Press, 1992).

quickly into hatred, while the devoted followers merely mimicked, repeated phrases that would function as tags, signs of mutual recognition in a group whose identity was constituted by the name of Lacan.

There cannot be any peace or harmony in translation either, but since we can now start reading Lacan in English with more precision, thanks to better translations (which include the forthcoming complete and revised English version of *Ecrits*) the added accuracy will magnify or create new terminological problems. Besides, when so many Lacanian terms are difficult to translate (such is the case of *jouissance*, for instance), Lacan did not wish his main concept of *objet petit a* to be translated into English.[34] In order to avoid its oral transmogrification as "owbjay pteetay," one could easily render it as "object small o" so as to call up the opposition between a "Big Other" and a "small other." Bruce Fink is probably right to call it "object a" in his recent translation of Seminar XX, and to translate the letter of the big Other as A. Since Lacan often writes a barred A for his "barred *Autre*," Fink wishes to avoid confusions with the barred O referring to the empty set of logical theory.[35] Thus we read throughout the Seminar passages such as: "the Other as barred: S (Ⱥ)."[36] From one Other to an Ather: quite a new symbolic family in perspective, an original knot in which we may hope to catch authority and the alterations of symbolic transmission! The

---

34. Lacan probably remembered the tradition that derives from *les grands rhétoriqueurs* in which linguistic riddles and rebuses often include a small *a*, to be read as "*a petit*" so as to call up "*appétit*" (appetite). A good way of sending us on the track of an elusive desire!

35. *Seminar XX, On Feminine Sexuality*, p. 28, note 9.

36. Ibid., p. 81 and passim.

"object a" cause of desire evokes the initial of "analyst" and the scene of substitution in which the analyst finishes by being identified with the *objet a*. An "object o" would have rhymed with the Other, or the main agency underpinning the analyst's silence and meaningful punctuation. Can we half-translate, half-transliterate Lacan's games with letters and graphs? How can we construe Lacan without misconstruing him?

Such hesitation between A and O forces any translator—and therefore any reader, since anyone who opens the text will be requested to rewrite, punctuate and ultimately "construe" a discourse floating between speech and writing—to decide between ultimate beginnings and ultimate ends, to choose between Alpha and Omega. This may prove all too Greek, and perhaps all too apocalyptic a transliteration, but it might be the price Lacan had to pay for the ineluctable displacements and approximations that any transmission entails. Let us therefore begin not at the beginning, nor at the end of a century, but where we are, that is here, and right now.

I

The Transmission of the Lacanian Text: Resistance and Reception

1

The Place of Lacanian Psychoanalysis in North American Psychology

Kareen Ror Malone

BUT WE CAN'T START WITHOUT MENTIONING PSYCHOANALYSIS

In spite of Lacan's significance in the humanities, his direct and indirect contributions to Western philosophy, and his obvious influence in European and South American psychoanalysis, there is little place for Lacanian psychoanalysis in North American psychology. This is not to say that there have not been numerous individuals who have worked to disseminate Lacanian ideas—John Muller comes to mind most especially in the field of psychology; this is not to say that Lacanian analysts have not spoken and explained their ideas to American audiences; this is not to say that there are not home-grown North American clinical psychologists who practice Lacanian psychoanalysis; there are. There are, as well, many other clinicians schooling themselves in Lacan, without being trained exclusively under Lacanian auspices. Such clinicians and academics are reading Lacan's seminars and thinking through the implications of Lacan for American psychoanalytic practice.

Moreover, there are high-profile psychoanalytic perspectives that seem interested in inaugurating dialogues with Lacanian thinking. Some proponents of relational psychoanalysis have attempted to consider Lacanian ideas. Often the interest in Lacan is filtered through an acquaintance with Julia Kristeva or even Judith Butler, or deconstruction, or postmodernism. These are not always propitious starting points. Sometimes, in innovative psychoanalytic texts (ones by Barnaby Barratt[1] or Jane Flax[2] could serve as examples), Lacan will appear as an important interlocutor. In this unexpected role, he is frequently characterized as a less than viable perspective from which to explore new ideas in psychoanalysis. In fact, a Lacanian reader would, at times, be astonished at both what is said about Lacan and the way in which the reach of Lacanian influence is cast. It sometimes sounds as if American psychoanalysts, psychiatrists, and psychologists have to be protected against this phallocentric structuralist with his hordes of South American and Parisian analysts who, with the help of influential literary critics, eagerly await an impending colonization of the American clinical scene. The following probably well-known observations of W. W. Meissner reflect this remarkable way of characterizing Lacan: "Rather than from an empirical examination of clinical data, [Lacanian psychoanalysis] arises from a pre-conceived theory of the nature of language. I find it difficult to negotiate my way through the autocratic, authoritarian, dogmatic style. One can live too close to Lacan; too much intimate contact can trans-

---

1. B. Barratt, *Psychoanalysis and the Postmodern Impulse* (Baltimore: Johns Hopkins Press, 1993).

2. J. Flax, *Disputed Subjects: Essays on Psychoanalysis, Politics and Philosophy* (New York: Routledge, 1993).

mit the fatal virus."[3] In the late 1980s, an allusion to a fatal virus transmitted by intimacy is rather evocative. More pointedly, there has been so little contact between American clinicians and Lacanian approaches that any American characterization of Lacanian clinical work is, to speak more charitably than Meissner, premature.

Still, one encounters a sort of obstinate misreading of Lacan that resembles certain prevalent American (mis)interpretations of Freud. To be honest, there is an extraordinary array of ways in which Freud is understood in the United States and Canada. Still, the approach by which North Americans get the least Freud for their money is the one that portrays him as a biological determinist whose quaint yet pernicious ideas have fallen to the advances of neuroscience and social changes in gender relationships, sexuality, and familial structures.

Perhaps Lacan's admonishment to carefully read Freud, even when Lacan's work obviously stands on its own,[4] accounts for the types of apprehensions many psychoanalytic psychologists feel toward him. Freud is a biological determinist. Lacan becomes a linguistic and structural determinist. Both enforce strict "gender roles" and even if Lacan suggests that gender is an epistemological position (not biological and thus constructed), his formulations of gender are still narrowly sexist. Unlike Freud, Lacan is more interested in the mind than the body. Few contemporary American psychologists or psy-

---

3. Cited in D. Moss, "Thoughts on two seminars of Jacques Lacan with a focus on their difficulty," *International Journal of Psycho-Analysis* 71:704, 1990.

4. J. A. Miller, "Concepts and Contexts," in R. Feldtsein, B. Fink, and M. Jaanus, eds., *Reading Seminar XI* (Ithaca, NY: SUNY Press, 1995), pp. 3–18.

choanalysts have any notion of the significance of "*jouissance*" in Lacan. They simply assume that if Lacan is interested in language, his approach must resemble a Whorfian sociological determinism and indicate an intellectualized clinical practice. I cannot count the many times I have heard American clinicians say that only well-read and intellectual people could be Lacanian analysands (a remark that assumes that Lacanian clinical work is ideological or pedantic). Although directed at Lacan, this remark seems to confuse analytic insight with scientific observation and presumes no specificity to the unconscious. The suspicious wariness of Lacan's intellectualism may also reflect the assumption that the unconscious is only affective and thus any position toward the signifier must rely on conscious cognitive processes. Do these folks not read poetry?

Similarly reductionistic interpretations of Lacan come from astute and thoughtful psychoanalysts. Barratt and Flax, for example, do very creative work in North American psychoanalysis, so it is a bit strange that these very smart authors reduce Lacan to the most deterministic structuralism possible. Even the most innovative know Lacan primarily through some early feminist or literary interpretations (e.g., Jane Gallop or Elizabeth Grosz). Seemingly outside the significant work by Americans working with Lacan, many psychologists turn either to the above sources or trust a well-known American analyst who provides a "can you tell me something short and sweet to say about Lacan." The sad summary is this: Lacan's work is seen as a theory—not as the articulation of a clinical praxis.

Since by now there are enough books in English to contradict this understanding of Lacan, one can assume that other factors may be involved in this continuing (albeit more subtle than Meissner's) suspicion of Lacan. In response to these resistances, it is useless to rehearse the usual cultural generalizations that may account for these resistances to Lacanian approaches. The observation that World War II psychoanalytic immigrants to North America opted for adaptation, or that the ego-oriented approach of some Anglophonic schools is consonant with the American way of life, is true enough. But I don't know if these ideas further the sorts of communications that might foreground a significant hearing for Lacanian ideas. I would hazard that future dialogues may require a reframing of Lacan's significant critiques of ego psychology within American practices in order to more clearly address its disguised replication in Kohutian and interpersonal approaches. There is also a need to further articulate the differences and possible similarities between Lacanian approaches and object relations. Finally, as ably noted by Judith Feher Gurewich,[5] it is worth clarifying that Lacanians read a different Freud than the one assimilated by American practitioners. In a certain sense this means introducing the practice of reading per se, since there is, within the American therapeutic tradition, grounded as it is in medicine and psychology, an implicit bias toward looking. Looking at a book and seeing what is in it is a different sort of exercise than reading.

Whatever the reasons, the continuing resistances to Lacan limit North American psychoanalysis in ways that are unfortunate. The multifaceted debate in psychoanalysis over whether one "interprets," the position of so-called more classical approaches, or "relates," as in providing corrective emotional

---

5. J. Feher Gurewich, "The Lacanian Clinical Field: Series Overview," in J. Dor, J. Feher Gurewich, and S. Fairfield , eds. *The Clinical Lacan* (New York: Other Press, 1999).

experiences or other countertranferential explorations, could benefit from Lacanian insights.[6] A portion of this debate turns on the nature of the unconscious and often remains mired in unproductive suppositions. Is the unconscious a collection of intrapsychic contents[7] that one communicates to the analysand through the interpretation of transference and other relevant observations, or is the unconscious somehow in the "relational" itself? It seems to me that the terms are not fully fleshed out. One must address the structure of the relational (as in the position of the analyst) and the intrapsychic (the topography of the subject) by intellectually transcending the field of imaginary effects. If one's thought puts the ego at the center or sees the oedipal in purely normative terms, the questions this debate inaugurates do not go very far. One merely argues over different ways to identify with the analyst.

There are other impasses as well. There is lively discussion about the place of countertransference, the role of narrativity in the clinic, the foundations of diagnosis in psychoanalysis versus psychiatry, the issue of power, social power, and empowerment in the clinic. Numbers of innovative American therapists are considering the ramifications of Foucauldian notions of power for their work within the clinic. One might consult, for example, the very influential work of Michael White,[8] the influx of feminist thinking in therapy,[9] issues

6. S. Friedlander, "The third party in psychoanalysis: Lacan, the signifier and the symbolic order," *Clinical* Studies 1:17–32, 1955.

7. See S. Frosh, *Psychology and Psychoanalysis* (New York: New York University Press, 1989).

8. M. White, "Deconstruction and Therapy," in S. Gilligan and R. Price, eds., *Therapeutic Conversations* (New York: Norton, 1993).

9. R. Hare-Mustin, "Discourse in the mirrored room: a postmodern analysis of therapy," *Family Process* 33:19–35, 1994.

raised by relational psychoanalysis, or social construction in therapy. But one's ideas of power and agency in analysis and within the constitution and transformation of the psychological life require very sophisticated notions of subjection and rather precise formulations of asymmetry. Throwing together patriarchy and the paternal metaphor, defaulting on transference to a democratic win-win of preoedipal reaffirmation, co-creating narratives of choice with a dash of social critique, is simply insufficient to the complexity of psychic formations in the clinic and to its relationships with the broader social arena. The above admittedly polemic summation does not really do justice to the degree of openness and inquiry that mark certain approaches in the current psychoanalytic and psychotherapeutic scene. It perhaps communicates the frustration of those of us familiar with Lacan who see his relevance for questions in psychology and psychoanalysis but feel stymied as to the point of entry.

THERE'S NO PLACE LIKE NO PLACE:
THE ALLURES OF THE VIRTUAL

This essay is not exclusively concerned with Lacan and his relation to North American psychoanalysis but rather wishes to address a Lacanian contribution to psychology in the United States and Canada. Despite the obvious pessimism about any place in academe for Lacan (outside of the humanities), there are a number of more theoretically astute psychologists who are fundamentally aware of Lacan's importance and influence elsewhere. One finds an occasional article on Lacan and you-fill-in-the-blank in more wide-ranging theoretical journals. Psychologists in Britain have been a bit more innovative in entertaining a Lacanian-informed approach to their researches than have their comparably innovative American counter-parts. One might consult the research of Ian Parker,[10] Corinne Squire,[11] or Valerie Walkerdine.[12]

Still, when one looks at academic psychology in the States, the picture is quite grim. There has been a long-term antipathy between psychoanalysis and psychology, so much so that Erica Burmin[13] refers to psychoanalysis as the repressed of psychology. It is sadly obvious from the history of the discipline that psychoanalysis, even its American varieties, was suppressed by traditional psychology, especially as competing paradigms struggled for hegemony before behaviorism took the flag. Even empirical studies supporting psychoanalysis—and there were many in the 1950s—were dismissed.[14] So although psychoanalysis gained wide acceptance in American culture and wide if eclectic application in clinical practice, it became increasingly disreputable in academic circles.[15] This disrepute continues after the so-called "cognitive revolution,"

10. I. Parker, "Reflexive social psychology: discourse analysis and psychoanalysis," *Free Associations* 4:527–548, 1994.

11. C. Squire "Safety, danger and the movies: women's and men's narratives of aggrzession," *Feminism and Psychology* 4:547–570, 1994.

12. V. Walkerdine, "Working class women: psychologiucal and social aspects of survival," in S. Wilkinson, ed. *Feminist Social Psychologies* (Buckingham: Open University Press, 1996) pp. 145–164.

13. E. Burmin, *Deconstructing Developmental Psychology* (New York: Routledge, 1994).

14. G. Hornstein, "The return of the repressed," *American Psychologist* 47:254–263, 1992.

15. J. Pfister, J. and N. Schnog, N., eds., *Inventing the Psychological* (New Haven: Yale University Press, 1997); and D. Westin, "Social cognition and social affect in psychoanalysis and social cognition," in J. Barron, M. Eagle and D. Wolitsky, eds., *Interface of Psychoanalysis and Psychology* (Washington: APA, 1992) pp. 77–98.

during which mental life again became a suitable topic for psychology. Still, the cognitive revolution has meant some interesting and compelling experimental evidence regarding defensive processes and "unconscious cognition." One must understand that these findings are "discovered" through theories that are often either agnostic or antagonistic to psychoanalytic explanations, which may be why, even in light of experimental leads, psychology remains curiously indifferent to psychoanalytic explanations. Referring to a cognitivist book on the unconscious, Westin (1992) notes:

> Given the accessibility of psychoanalytic writing and the substantial basis now even in experimental work for the existence of unconscious motivational and affective processes, the fact that a book on unconscious processes such as this could be crafted without considering or citing what clinicians have been writing about for 100 years is probably as impressive an empirical demonstration of the existence of unconscious motivation as one could desire. . . . [S]o much of the avoidance of psychoanalytic ideas in this literature [cognitive and social psychology] probably reflects a fear of being associated with a tradition that was totally vilified throughout the training of most of these researchers, beginning with condescending and usually grossly inaccurate coverage of psychoanalysis in introductory psychology classes. [16]

With respect to Freud, psychology may place him on par with William James as one of the few in psychology to have constructed a full theory of the mind. In other words, psychol-

---

16. D. Westin, "Social cognition and social affect in psychoanalysis and social cognition," in J. Barron, M. Eagle and D. Wolitsky, eds., *Interface of Psychoanalysis and Psychology* (Washington: A.P.A., 1992) pp. 77–98.

ogy still wants to claim him. But psychology textbooks spend as much time warning you about his "penis envy" and reactionary Victorian views as they spend explicating his uncanny insight into unconscious functioning.

One might hope that even if traditional psychology, with its abundant rationalism and penchant for experimentation, foregoes Freud, psychoanalysis, (and by default) Lacan, alternative paradigms within the discipline might be sympathetic to Lacanian views of subjectivity and psychic life. Challenges to empiricist psychology should be intrinsic to psychoanalysis and they are explicit in Lacan. But the most vocal advocates for alternative psychological paradigms in North America are grounded in humanistic or hermeneutic perspectives. Humanistic psychologies often take their cue from particular readings of phenomenology and lean toward a view of subjectivity that posits it in the terms of consciousness. Eastern philosophy may supplement the phenomenological basis of alternative approaches. Although Eastern thought often poses quite subtle articulations of important ontological impasses, its Western importation within psychology often serves to emphasize the importance of immediate experience and intuition. Consequently, it reinforces the established phenomenological approach. Thus the bias among traditional critics of psychology would not necessarily promote an opening to Lacan. For their part, Lacanian ideas are not particularly compatible with these alternative perspectives:

> There is nothing then, in our expedient for situating Freud that owes anything to the judicial astrology in which the psychologist dabbles. Nothing that proceeds from quality, or even from the intensive, or from any phenomenology from which idealism may draw re-assurance. In the

Freudian field . . . consciousness is a feature as inadequate to ground the unconscious in its negation . . . as affect is unsuited to play the role of the protopathic subject, since it is a service that has no holder.[17]

Recent critics of psychology emerging from feminist and postmodernist camps may share an interest in putatively Lacanian questions of representation, de-centering the subject. Such critics are aware of the pernicious failures of psychology's focus on individual attributes. Still these perspectives often portray psychoanalysis as part and parcel of the same set of patriarchal and individualistic biases with which they charge the field in general. Thus when pursuing contemporary literature in psychology on Lacan, one could come to the conclusion that more lawyers critically consider Lacanian than do psychologists. Admittedly, the word, "law" does appear frequently in Lacan but so does the word psychology.

As a rule, psychologists critical of the mainstream discipline are not aware of Lacan's prescient observations on academic psychology. Although many of Lacan's critiques of psychology date from the 1950s, they are as relevant today as they were then. Lacan noted the failure to understand the signifying dimensions of experimentation (as of course related to the designs of the experimenter).[18] He decried the manner in which promises of mental hygiene implicitly fortify the often trivial findings of experimental psychology.[19] He saw

---

17. J. Lacan, "The subversion of the subject and the dialectic of desire in the Freudian unconscious" in *Ecrits*, tr. A. Sheridan (New York: Norton, 1977), p. 297.

18. J. Lacan, *The Four Fundamental Concepts of Psychoanalysis*, tr. A. Sheridan, (New York: Norton, 1981), p. 228.

19. J. Lacan, *Ecrits*, p. 297.

how the absolute reification of subjectivity follows from a positivistic comprehension of individual attributes.[20] Lacan even sounds a contemporary Foucauldian alarm when he foresees the following future for psychology:

> Thus in any number of forms, ranging from pious sentiment to ideals of crudest efficiency, through the whole gamut of naturalist propaeduetics, they can be seen sheltering under the wing of a psychologism which in its reification of the human being, could lead to errors besides which those of the physicians scientism would be mere trifles.

> For precisely on account of the strength of the forces opened up by analysis, nothing less than a new alienation of man [sic] is coming into being, as much through the efforts of collective belief as through the selective process of techniques with all the formative weight belonging to rituals; in short a Homo Psychologicus, which is a danger I would warn you against.[21]

Lacan was equally perspicacious about the ideological missteps of traditional humanistic challengers to empiricist psychologies, most explicitly in the way that, like most of Western thought, they "cash out the Other"[22] through the reinvention of unifying cosmologies[23] where consciousness remains "top dog."

-----

20. J. Lacan, "Intervention on transference," in *Feminine Sexuality*, tr. J. Mitchell and J. Rose (New York: Norton, 1985), p. 62.

21. Ibid., p. 64.

22. D. Metzger, personal communication, October, 1997.

23. S. Žižek, *Looking Awry* (Cambridge: MIT Press, 1991).

Given what Lacan and Lacanians do say about psychology (never mind what psychologists would say about Lacan), it would seem that chapter should be shorter than it already is. But, alas, this marriage made in hell between psychology and psychoanalysis cannot be severed despite the industrious efforts of academic researchers. Even Lacan, when not addressing academic psychology, will allude to the contribution of the psychoanalytic dimension to a psychological understanding of human being,[24] and will seriously speak to psychology's missteps as intrinsic to its involvement with the question of subjectivity. Unless of course psychology does finally disappear into neuroscience, biology, history, and sociology, it will continue to stumble across that which creates a subject and that which transforms a subject—perhaps incidentally, perhaps defensively, perhaps directly. Within the context of this tentative yet persistent connection between a fully radicalized psychoanalytic project—Lacan's project— and a psychology that appears mainly in its anomalies, the following will examine a most unlikely candidate for a Lacanian infusion—cognitive psychology.

FINDING THE SIGNIFIER WITHIN THE A-SEXUAL: THE CASE OF COGNITIVE PSYCHOLOGY

After the cognitive revolution in psychology, psychoanalysis continued to be seen as, in the main, irrelevant. The psychodynamic unconscious was portrayed as "hot" and "wet," a seething biological cauldron full of aggressive and sexual

---

24. See J. Lacan, *Seminar VII, The Ethics of Psychoanalysis*, tr. D. Porter (New York: Norton, 1992) pp. 57–70.

passions.[25] No laboratory study of cognition could find these unseemly motivations, and so study of the unconscious was relegated to the back burner. However, the unconscious returned as the cognitive unconscious and it would appear that respectable "evidence" for its existence is well accepted even if the empirical study of the unconscious is a rather specialized pursuit. But does this cognitive beast bear any relationship to any psychoanalytic antecedents?

Past cognitive-psychology research has relied on models of psychic life *qua* cognitive activity that were based on information processing that itself was based on advances in computational models of artificial intelligence. Here a Turing type of machine comprised of functionally specifiable relationships simulates a universal system of symbol manipulation that is independent of its material instantiation. It can be presumed that such systems or engines have no central organizer although a given system's programmer could, it seems, stand as a likely candidate. But within the confines of an ideal functionalism, no central coordinator is needed for the interdependent algorithms to operate correctly. The promise that such computational models held for cognitive scientists and like-minded psychologists are captured in phrases such as the following: "The computer is made in the image of man [sic]." "The brain is the hardware and the mind is the software." Within this perspective, the computer is a model of the working mind. I would guess that many of us find our computers most human when they inexplicably erase hours of work or some virus re-distributes our cognition.

---

25. J. Kihlstrom, T. Barnhardt, and D. Tataryn, "The psychological unconscious/Freud, lost, regained." *American Psychologist* 47:788–791, 1992.

Although I am very critical of traditional psychology, it is fairly interesting that one of the results of its infatuation with the natural sciences is a persistent effort to "drop" out consciousness.[26] Most of those who criticize psychology (although in recent years certainly not all) consider this elision of human consciousness equivalent to the elision of human subjectivity. The cognitive approach drops out consciousness as qualia, treating it as, at best, an emergent property or a particular sort of input or output. But cognitive psychology does not "de-center" consciousness in order to draw more a sophisticated picture of subjective functioning. Rather its aim is to eliminate the subjective dimension altogether. Much like Skinner's black box, the goal is predictable outcomes in response to specific inputs. However, we are really talking about networks, more dependent on systematic interdependencies than linear causality. Still, one can wonder if this branch of psychological science will not prove itself as "sterile" as the earlier grandiose future imagined for trainable pigeons; there is an important difference between behaviorism and cognitive science.[27]

Despite the (albeit sometimes disguised) allegiance to neurological explanations, we are now dealing with an approach to psyche that entertains the effects of formal representational systems. In the case of cognitive science, these formal systems are often treated as self-contained. Nonetheless, the question of the psyche has been thrown a bit closer

---

26. S. Frosh, *Psychology and Psychoanalysis.* (New York: New York University Press, 1989).

27. J. Haugland, "The nature and plausibility of cognitivism," in *Mind Design*, J. Haughland, ed. (Montgomery: Bradford Books, 1981), pp. 243–281.

to what Lacan understands as, in part, essential to the Symbolic Order. Further, it is this order that is seen as defining the specificity of the psychical. Jerome Wakefield[28] explicitly draws out this relationship between the representational and the possible linkage of psychoanalysis and cognitive psychology. In keeping with a Lacanian take, Wakefield argues that it is a mistake for psychologists only to acknowledge (begrudgingly) Freud's clinical insights. Rather, in recognizing the essence of psyche as produced through representation, Freud allows a unique approach to how one studies the human subject. It is thus to Freud's metapsychology, where the relevant principles are formulated, that cognitive psychologists should turn:

> By contrast, Freud argued for the thesis that has become routinely accepted in cognitive science, and indeed might be considered the foundation stone on which cognitive psychology rests, that representationality can be realized in non-conscious brain structures and that therefore, there can be mental states that are not conscious. These states are mental in virtue of being genuine representations, and they are representational in virtue of their being structured so as to represent and thus refer to outside objects. Just like sentences in a book on a shelf, or painting stored in a vault, representational states need not be consciously accessed for them to be true representations.[29]

28. J. Wakefield, "Freud and cognitive psychology" in J. Barron, M. Eagle and D. Wolitsky, eds. *Interface of Psychoanalysis and Psychology*, pp. 66–76.

29. Ibid., p. 81.

As the quotation reveals, the author still retains an adaptational model of the psyche but the tie posited about representation is a significant one. It is a tie between psychoanalysis and cognitive psychology that could best be explored through Lacanian thinking where the Symbolic Order is not added on to the body, the prediscursive, the imagination, or embodied action. Of course, both Wakefield and the cognitivists, in recognizing the autonomy of the signifier in the constitution of the subject, have not yet considered the effects of the signifier as it creates a disjunctive knotting divisible into the Symbolic, Imaginary, and Real orders. Nonetheless, we are a bit removed from trainable pigeons. Moreover, the formalist approach stretches its own positivistic presuppositions. The longer such formalist systems lurk about, the more they become full of holes.

In an essay on Daniel Dennett, a cognitive philosopher, Slavoj Žižek—not a cognitive philosopher—notes the manner in which, for Dennett, signifying chains have usurped psychology's (usually) implicit models of self and self-consciousness.[30] There is nothing before representational schemes, themselves disparate and fragmented. The bias toward immediate experience so characteristic of psychology has disappeared. In its place we find the *ex nihilo* effects of the signifier. Žižek writes:

> In a precise sense the subject is his own fiction, the content of his own self-experience is a narrativization in which memory traces already intervene. So when Dennett

---

30. S. Žižek "Cartesian subject versus the cartesian theatre," in S. Žižek, ed. *Cogito and the Unconscious* (Durham: Duke University Press, 1998) pp. 247–274.

makes "writing it down" in memory critical for consciousness, that is what it is for the given to be taken one way
rather than another, and claims that "there is no reality
of conscious experience independent of the effects of
various vehicles of content on subsequent action (and
hence on memory) we should be careful not to miss the
point: what counts for the concerned subject himself is
the way an event is written down, memorized—memory
is constitutive of my direct experience .[31]

Dennett is close to the views of a growing number in
cognitive science who, using a sort of postmodern evolutionary theory, understand human representation as momentary
and contingent encounters in hit-or-miss situations with some
real. This real is known primarily through its failing, or at best
retroactively. Putting it in the congenial terms of the genre,
lines of descent must always be reconstructed. Success inaugurates a series of replications, an adaptive "fit" of sorts, but
in truth it is only temporary and provisional. Such cognitive
systems are being explored in part because the Turing machine progeny simply did not deliver a sufficiently complex
being. As well, new neuroscientific notions, such as parallel
distributed processing and increasing sophisticated evolutionary thinking, provided new conceptual possibilities.

What is of interest to me, as it was to Žižek, is not the
ascent of new, more groovy biological thinking but the ways
in which the representational system itself is now characterized. Language, cognition, and representation are leaving their
rationalist abodes.[32] In keeping with this "downward slide"

---

31. Ibid., p. 250.
32. See J. Haugland, op. cit.

to Lacanian sensibilities, cognitivists are demanding an examination of embodiment and action. They are expanding research into situated cognition and cultural analysis[33] and importing new ideas from biology. In a way, these strategies supplement the loss to which their dependence upon representation has inexorably led. In Seminar XX, Lacan refers to this encounter with loss and limit that is constitutive of subjectivity but a hard swallow for science. "Stated otherwise, it has become clear, thanks to analytic discourse, that language is not simply communication. Misrecognizing that fact, a grimace has emerged in the lowest depths of science that consists in asking how being can know anything whatsoever."[34] Cognitive science is beginning to see the grimace.

The trick of a Lacanian move requires that one begin by approaching this signifying system outside of the comfort zone of rationality. It further requires that one articulate the relationship between a signifying system and "its cause in the real" without resorting to adaptational analogies from evolution. An analysis of embodiment and sociocultural effects are perceived as necessary by many in the field of cognition.[35] For this embodiment not to be yet another rescue operation for rationalism as philosophy, it must refer to founding of the body in language and thus to one's necessary constitution through the desire of the Other. As suggested by philosopher and cognitive researcher Mark Johnson, primordial forms of

---

33. For example, see E. Hutchins, *Cognition in the Wild* (Cambridge, MA: MIT Press, 1996).

34. J. Lacan, *Seminar XX: Encore*, tr. B. Fink (New York: Norton, 1998), p. 139.

35. G. Lakoff and M. Johnson, *Metaphors We Live By* (Chicago: University of Chicago Press, 1980); E. Hutchins, *Cognition in the Wild.*

embodiment inaugurate human thinking. However, they are not anchored in the mobile acting body as he implies but in a body that comes into being correlative to the object a. Andy Clark, who treats language as the ultimate "artifact," by which he means a "tool" for formatting cognition, still wonders if language may not actually be "a dimension of the user."[36] But if so, then how? And what could what Lacan discretely called "analytic experience" tell us about this constitutive dimension?

More inquiries into the place of language in the genesis of the subject, this time within a communicative logic, might give cognitivists a fuller picture of the reach of human thinking. For unless we seriously approach human desire and motivation, I am not sure that we seriously approach what humans think about. If language uses us, as well as being used by us, how is what we call a *subject* the effect of our induction into language? This is most certainly not a call to social construction, but to a deeper research into the "we" that thinks, represents, imagines, and builds models of the world. One could initially understand this subjective dimension as the remainders from effects of the signifier. Despite all of the awareness of representation, these effects can not be addressed through the presumptions that undergird models from computation. No one doubts, Lacan notes, that computers think, but the acquisition of knowledge is another thing altogether. John Haugland remarks on these same issues:

> When the rationalists took cognition as the essence of being human . . . they meant theoretical cognition. . . .

---

36. A. Clark, *Being There: Putting Brain, Body and World Together Again* (Cambridge, MA: MIT Press, 1998).

Cognitivism is heir to this tradition: to be intelligent is to be able to manipulate (according to rational rules) "clear and distinct" quasi-linguistic representations—but now they are sullied by omissions, probabilities, and heuristics. Deported from the immortal soul, however, they forfeit their original epistemic anchorage in the honesty of God and the natural light of Reason. So bereft . . . the distinction of certain procedures floats adrift. . . . Evolution comes vaguely to mind, but much more needs to be said.[37]

The more that needs to be said may seem to call for yet another Lacan and you-fill-in-the-blank. I can offer only this defense against the presumption of academic irrelevance. There are so many contributions to Western thinking by Lacan, not only in the clinical field and in literature but also in the realm of pedagogy and issues of cognition. Lacan's continual subversion of contemporary discourses, from Heidegger to cybernetics to logic, allowed Lacan to revitalize Freudian psychoanalysis. This cross-fertilization in turn allows others another avenue to profitably think Lacan *contre* Lacan. Perhaps a Lacanian nuance could make the discourse of cognitive science more honest; perhaps it can lend more humanity to the projects of cognitive science. When Lacan addresses the same issues brought forward by John Haugland, he indicates that an even more radical break with rationality is needed:

It is indubitable that the symbolic is the basis of what was made into God. It is certain that the imaginary is based on the reflection of one semblance to another. And yet, *a* has lent itself to be confused with the $S(\cancel{A})$ . . . and

---

37. J. Haugland, op. cit., p. 276.

it has done so by means of the function of being. It is here that a scission or detachment remains to be effectuated. It is in this respect that psychoanalysis is something other than a psychology. For psychology is this uneffectuated scission.[38]

But this separation or scission is the precise point where one pushes the possibility of subjectivity and its ethics to its limit. As long as psychology lurks around this question of subjectivity and aspires to more than ideological proclamations, it must, as a theory, encounter the difficulties of human embodiment and the subject's relation to the Other's desire. Thus one might hope that the science of psychology will take its formalist insights to the internal limits that found human knowledge. In so doing, the discipline could revision its algorithms of problem solving and the calculating subject that slyly reintroduces the terms of consciousness. In its place, one could conceive of a subjective position that would emerge from the effects of the signifier. This would be a subject of desire—for is not such a subject the grounds for "justified belief."

---

38. J. Lacan, *Seminar XX: Encore*, p. 83.

2

Lacan in America

JOSEPH H. SMITH

Perhaps rather perversely, I have persisted in seeing myself as an ego psychologist. This, no doubt, partly in defiance of Lacan's derision of American psychoanalysis, partly because David Rapaport is one of my heroes, and partly out of seeing the thought of Hans Loewald and Roy Schafer, two analysts with whom I am much more identified than with Hartmann, Kris, and Loewenstein, as advances in ego psychology. It is my belief, however, that in the years to come Lacanian and American analysts will give a more serious reading to each other's thought, with more attention to elements in each that might be advantageous to the other. With this hope in mind, I shall indicate a few areas where such mutual understanding might be facilitated. The questions I follow are (1) how might an American analyst approach Lacan's concepts of desire and anxiety, and (2) whether the pleasure principle, primal repression, and identification could be clarified to the advantage of both Lacanians and American readers.

DESIRE

In the era of id psychology, a widespread misinterpretation of Freud was the belief that one should not only become aware of unconscious impulses but also act on those impulses. Failure to do so was thought to imply pathological inhibition. In that trivializing frame of reference, the Lacanian maxim of being true to one's desire could be mistaken as meaning one should do whatever one pleases. Lacan's statement on being true to one's desire, however, implies preservation of "the authentic place of *jouissance*, even if it is empty"[1]—preservation, that is, of access to the place of desire, which is also the place of the drives and of *das Ding*.[2] Authentic decisions are made on the basis of such access. The Lacanian idea arose from Freud's statement that automatic flight in the form of repression of dangerous impulses gives way to an act of judgment on the basis of being able to face dangers. This would include facing impulses and deciding when, how, or whether they are to be enacted. The move from being repressed, impulse-ridden, or inhibited to being able to act on the basis of judgment in accord with and while maintaining access to one's desire is one phrasing of what Lacan depicts as the move from demand to desire. It is also a phrasing of the move from the pleasure principle to the reality principle. But each of these compact statements pertaining to judgment, desire, and the reality principle involve major developments from primitive to advanced structure. The reality principle *is* the pleasure prin-

---

1. *The Seminar of Jacques Lacan, Book VII, The Ethics of Psychoanalysis, 1959–1960,* tr. by D. Porter (New York: Norton, 1992) p. 190. Hereafter referred to as EP.
2. EP, p. 110.

ciple under modified structural conditions, modified, for instance, by resolution of the oedipal complex, submission to the Law, accession to the symbolic order. One's desire is modified in accordance with such development. One's desire is in accord with whom one has authentically become. Had Socrates, for example, accepted the offer of his friends to help him escape from prison, he would not have acted in accord with his desire.

For Lacan, "In so far as [man's] needs are subjected to demand, they return to him alienated. . . . That which is thus alienated in needs constitutes an Urverdrängung (primal repression) . . . but it reappears in . . . man as desire."[3] Desire is neither "the appetite for satisfaction, nor the demand for love, but the difference that results from the subtraction of the first from the second, the phenomenon of their splitting" (E, p. 287). But what could that mean other than that desire is hollowed out, the capacity for desire is established, as a consequence of *recognition* of the two-fold dimension of demand—a recognition that demand, beyond the satisfaction of any particular need is a demand for love, a total demand for all? To recognize a wanting that is impossible is a first step toward recognizing lack as constitutive of human being. The recognition itself transmutes the unconditional element of demand into, as Lacan put it, the absolute condition of desire as constitutive (E, pp. 265, 286–287).

What would approach this thinking in the ordinary reading of Strachey's Freud by English-speaking analysts? The unconditional aspect of wish or demand would be understood in terms of primary process thinking, the identity of perception, primal repression, and the undifferentiated phase men-

---

3. J. Lacan, *Écrits,* tr. A. Sheridan (New York: Norton, 1977) p. 286. Hereafter, referered to as E.

tioned in Chapter 7 of the *Interpretation of Dreams*. Recognizing the difference between the appetite for satisfaction of a particular need and the totalizing demand that that satisfaction should be also a proof of love is like recognizing the difference between the identity of thought and the identity of perception. The image of the object represents the need/drive that, as a danger, is first turned away from. The image returns as the identity of perception, the first instance of the return of the repressed, the primally repressed, in the real. The image, that is, of a prior feeding is not merely an image but an hallucination of the reappearance of the feeding. Since this is wish fulfillment, however, and not actual satisfaction, the difference between the two comes to be recognized.

Once the identity of perception and the identity of thought are differentiated, once the two aspects of demand are recognized, an image, no longer an hallucination, can stand forth as a memory and an anticipation. Imagery at such a level is a precursor or maybe even a species of the language to come. As Lacan wrote, images at this level, "the small curds of representation [have] the same structure as the signifier. [They are] already organized according to the possibilities of the signifier as such" (EP, p. 61). The move from merger to an organization of images is the locus of Freud's original lost object and of Lacan's *objet a*.

Whether conceived as remainder of the real that resists symbolization or as an inner real generated by a system of signifiers in accord with the limits of formalization,[4] the *objet*

---

4. J. Derrida, "Structure, sign, and play," in *Writing and Difference*, tr. A. Bass (Chicago: University of Chicago Press, 1978), pp. 278–293 and repeatedly elsewhere; see also C. Shepherson, "The intimate alterity of the real: a response to reader commentary of 'History and the real,'" *Postmodern Culture* 5:2, 1997.

a is lack, the cause of desire. While incest as remerger with the mother is an impossibility hidden behind a prohibition, the idea that the lost object is *only* generated by the system could be an attribution to the system that denies actual loss. Even if the lost object is a myth of origin, would it not be a myth that echoes the actual loss of merger in the prehistory of each individual? Is not this the meaning of *objet a* as remainder of the real?

THE PLEASURE PRINCIPLE

I believe it must be assumed that the pleasure principle, as a broad principle of self-regulation involving a turn from disequilibrium, is operative in all forms of life, including those prior to cognitive or affective functioning.[5] This is, I think, a bit like Freud's assertion that a original reality ego[6] was operative prior to the pleasure ego or the subsequently established reality ego proper. The reality principle is not a modification of the pleasure principle. It is, instead, the same self-regulatory principle operating under different of structural conditions.[7] Similarly, to speak of a "beyond" of the pleasure principle is to speak of a particular set of structural conditions.

---

5. J. H. Smith, "The pleasure principle," *International Journal of Psycho-Analysis* 58:1–10, 1977.

6. S. Freud, "Instincts and their vicissitudes" (1915). *Standard Edition* 14:136.

7. D. Rapaport, "On the psychoanalytic theory of motivation," in *The Collected Papers of David Rapaport*, ed. M. Gill (New York: Basic Books, 1967), pp. 853–915.

At least some aspects of what Lacan calls the *real* as stumbling block that interferes with direct and immediate satisfaction, Rapaport calls *delay*. The stumbling block itself constitutes a point of disequilibrium necessitating a direction of activity away from or around the block so that the object promising resolution of the original disequilibrium can be approached. As this dealing with delay proceeds, we begin to talk about a reality principle and secondary process functioning. Structural development, the structuralization of the subject, arises by virtue of interference with direct and immediate satisfaction. Without delay, there would be no development. This parallels Lacan's statement that the *objet a,* the remainder that is a piece of the real, is the subject's only access to the Other with the big "O."[8]

Drive, regulated by the pleasure principle, moves toward the object of satisfaction. Notwithstanding Freud's inconsistent phrasing, the seeking is object seeking, not pleasure seeking. Rapaport put it that "the defining characteristic *object* is the outstanding conceptual invention in Freud's theory of the instinctual drive."[9]

PRIMAL REPRESSION

Freud assumed that the unconscious was there, already being structured, prior to repression proper. That assumption required a concept of primal repression. Part of the problem in establishing the definition of primal repression is that pro-

---

8. J. Lacan, *The Seminar of Jacques Lacan, Book X, Anxiety, 1962–1963,* translated by C. Gallagher from unedited French typescripts, session 14.
9. D. Rapaport, op. cit., p. 877.

cesses that have been differentiated in development and can be referred to by differentiated concepts are fused at primitive levels. Primal repression, primary process, and primitive levels of the playing out of the pleasure principle are not sharply delineated concepts that refer to sharply delineated processes.

Originally, the drive away from disequilibrium is represented by idea and affect. Lacan refers to imagery at this level as "the first ideal marks in which the drives are constituted as repressed in the substitution of the signifier for needs" (E, p. 256). Is this not to say that primal repression is simply this turning away from disequilibrium, a turning that is also defined by the concepts of primary process functioning and the pleasure principle?

Regarding primal repression, Lacan also wrote, "This signifier [the *Vorstellungsrepräentanz*][10] constitutes the central point of . . . [primal repression]—of what, . . . having passed into the unconscious, will be, as Freud indicates (...)

---

10. Freud's "biological" view of mind saw drive as the representative (*Repräsentant* or *Repräsentanz*) of bodily disequilibrium in the form of psychic disequilibrium—as a force, that is, within and of the mind. Drive as psychic representative can then achieve representation as idea (*Vorstellung*). The idea, then is the representation of the representative. This phrasing is in accord with Loewald (H. Loewald, "On motivation and instinct theory," in *Papers on Psychoanalysis* (New Haven: Yale University Press 1980), p. 117, and also Freud's "Repression" *Standard Edition* 14:146–158, 1915, where "(ideational) representative" is given as the translation of "*(Vorstellung) Repräsentanz*" (*Gesammelte Werke, 10:250*). (*Vorstellung*) *Repräsentanz* would thus refer to only the idea. This would not invalidate Lacan's idea of the subject fading in being represented by a signifier to a second signifier. (*Vorstellung*) *Repräsentanz*, however, would not name the "binary signifier" (Lacan, *The Four Fundamental Concepts of Psycho-Analysis*, ed. J.-A. Miller, tr. A. Sheridan (New York: Norton, 1978) p. 218. Hereafter, FFC.

the point of attraction, through which all the other repressions will be possible."[11] That repression proper is in any way based on content being drawn into or pulled into the unconscious by the attraction of the previously repressed is a metaphor. It is a metaphor at exactly the level of Ross Perot's warning that, were NAFTA enacted, we would hear a loud sucking noise from the south—the sound of jobs being sucked into Mexico. Repression proper is the unconscious turning away from a danger encountered after the dynamically repressed has already been structured. Both the primally repressed and the properly repressed enter the scene as dangers. But even if a new danger is recognized as dangerous because of its similarity to the previously repressed, it is repressed because it is a danger—not because it is similar.

Loewald saw the drives, both libidinal and aggressive, as psychic representatives that arise and are shaped in early interaction with the mother.[12] In this connection, one need not assume that the wish-fulfilling hallucinatory image is the first

---

11. FFC, p. 218.

12. Regarding the formation of drives, Loewald wrote, "Following a formulation of Freud's—to which he himself and other analytic theorists have not consistently adhered—I define instinct (or instinctual drive) . . . as a *psychic representative* of biological stimuli or processes, and not as these biological stimuli themselves. In contradistinction to Freud's thought in "Instincts and Their Vicissitudes," however, I do not speak of biological stimuli impinging on a ready-made 'psychic apparatus' in which their psychic representatives are thus created, but of interactional biological processes that find higher organization on levels which we have come to call psychic life. Understood as psychic phenomena or representatives, instincts come into being in the early organizing mother-infant interactions. They form the most primitive level of human mentation and motivation" (H. Loewald, "On motivation and instinct theory," in *Papers on Psychoanalysis*, pp. 102–137 and also in the same collection, "Instinct theory, object relations, and psychic structure formation," p. 208).

ideational representation. Such a wish-fulfilling image might cover a prior image of danger. This primordial image of danger, perhaps the precursor of images of the fragmented body or of the witch mother, and its associated affect might be expressed in the infant's cry. Although the cry comes to be interpreted as a call for the mother, it could be originally a crying out against danger, an attack on what will come to be established as inner, a primordial self-attack.[13]

The image of danger would be repressed in a turn to the hallucinatory image of wish fulfillment, which would then be repressed by a turn to a nonhallucinatory image of the object. These are instances of primal repression. That the direction is away from primary process toward secondary process approaches De Waelhens's understanding of primal repression as the repression of immediacy.[14] I would prefer to phrase it, however, that primal repression is the kind of repression that occurs in primary process thinking. Structuralization accomplished in primary process thinking then allows for repression proper. To accord with Lacan's definition of pri-

---

13. This attention to the source of the drive may be the *Anlage* of the ego capacity to track unconscious sources of danger in order that they continue to be avoided. But such high-level functioning would evolve from primitive self attack, from primal masochism. It may be, however, that unconscious tracking applies only to dangers turned away from by means of repression proper. Original (primal) repression begins as a turning from the relatively contentless danger that Freud saw as simply an "excessive degree of excitation" (*Inhibitions, Symptoms and Anxiety. Standard Edition* 20:94, 1926). The navel of the dream may be the limit of the properly repressed, the terminus of what can be tracked, the point at which its connections dip into the unknowable of the primally repressed.

14. A. De Waelhens, *Schizophrenia: A Philosophical Reflection On Lacan's Structuralist Interpretation*, tr. W. VerEecke (Pittsburgh: Duquene University Press, 1978) p. 53.

mal repression, the very first images would have to be taken as "already organized," as Lacan put it, "according to the possibilities of the signifier as such" (EP, p. 61). "The Other," Lacan wrote, "is already there in the very opening, however evanescent, of the unconscious."[15]

ANXIETY AND IDENTIFICATION

Lacan's thought on anxiety is both a reformulation of Freud's first theory of anxiety and a more specific elaboration of the danger signaled in Freud's second theory. That the *objet a* can be the cause of either desire *or* anxiety at least relates desire and anxiety, and recalls Freud's original idea that repressed libido caused or was converted into anxiety. In his second theory, anxiety *signals* danger and induces repression, not simply to avoid anxiety but as an effort to avoid the danger signaled by anxiety.[16] Lacan specifies this danger as pertaining to the unconscious subject.

Lacan's definition of the ego is confined to what American analysts would see as defensive ego activities. American analysts see the ego as developing away from defense and toward being able to face dangers and to acknowledge loss and

---

15. This could be taken as quoting Lacan against himself and in favor of me. I assume unconscious processes to be present from the start and take repression (primal repression) as beginning with the very first turn away from danger, danger as too much excitation. For Lacan, the unconscious as the discourse of the Other arrives with speech and "the first symbolization of the oedipal situation" (*Séminaire I,* 100, as cited in S. Felman, *Jacques Lacan and the Adventure of Insight: Psychoanalysis in Contemporary Culture* (Cambridge, MA: Harvard University Press, 1987), pp. 22 and 122.

16. S. Freud, *Inhibitions, Symptoms and Anxiety. Standard Edition* 20:109, 1926.

lack, in addition to its role in defending against danger. On the assumption, however, that the American and French definitions of ego are the same, Lacanians generally hold that adaptation, in the pejorative sense of adjustment, is the proper goal of analysis propounded by Hartmann and accepted by American analysts. A subspecies of that belief is that American analysts, in line with Ferenczi, Strachey, and Balint (E, p. 246), consider the cure to be wrought by identification with the analyst.

Lacan insisted that "the fundamental mainspring of the analytic operation is the maintenance of the distance between . . . identification . . . and the [*objet a*]" (FFC, p. 273). This is to say that the goal of analysis should be the capacity to love and, thereby, the capacity to grieve; it should not aim for the kind of defensive identification described in "Mourning and Melancholia" that bars love *and* grief. Analysis, Lacan wrote, should go "in a direction that is the exact opposite of identification" (FFC, p. 274). But does such defensive identification exhaust the meaning of identification? Lacan points to another kind. The contrast is similar to that between transference as resistance and transference as that which sustains the progress of analysis.

> Identification with the all-powerful signifier of demand, Lacan wrote, . . . must not be confused with identification with the object of the demand for love. This demand for love is also a regression, as Freud insists, when it produces the second mode of identification . . . [as described in] *Group Psychology and the Analysis of the Ego*. But it is another kind of regression. This is the exit that enables one to emerge from [transference as] suggestion. Identification with the object as regression, because it sets out from the demand for love, opens up the sequence of the transference . . . that is to say, the way by which the identifications that, in blocking this regression, can be denounced. [E, p. 270]

I believe I am on Lacan's side here, but the terms of the argument are murky. I would be inclined to believe, for instance, that Ferenczi, Strachey, and Balint, like the rest of us, sometimes achieved a good result with their patients even though they wrongly believed that it was by virtue of identification with the strong ego or superego of the analyst. Is Lacan saying merely that they know not what they do, or is he saying that any analyst who harbors such a belief can never go beyond the pseudo-cure of defensive identification with the analyst? Surely, what an analyst believes to be essential in analysis must have *some* influence on that analyst's work with patients (E, p. 246). How far can we go in delineating the difference between defensive and nondefensive becoming like one's analyst? Is there a difference comparable with acting out that blocks progress of an analysis and enactments that accomplish or signify progress? By pointing to one kind of identification that enables progress, does not Lacan himself modify his statement that the desire of the analyst and thus the analysis should tend "in a direction that is the exact opposite of identification . . . [toward] the mediation of the separateness of the subject" (FFC, p. 274) into something like, "the analysis should tend in a direction that is the exact opposite of defensive identifications that bar mediation of the separation of the subject."

The transmutation of the unconditional element of demand to the absolute condition of desire is not, of course, a once-and-for-all event. If, as Borch-Jacobsen argues, desire is a desire to be desired as a subject,[17] negating, overcoming, and transcending imaginary identifications is a perpetual task. The key issue here is that if the desire of the analyst (or the

---

17. M. Borch-Jacobsen, *Lacan: The Absolute Master,* tr. D. Brick (Stanford, CA: Stanford University Press, 1991) pp. 208 and 220–225.

mother) is for the patient (or the child) to become a carbon copy of herself, the way out of narcissistic identification tends to be barred. But could not the same problem be hidden in a corrupt form of the demand of the analyst that the patient achieve absolute difference? Might not the stringency of such a demand sometimes be a reaction formation against the desire for the patient to be another me—to be me?

Lacan wrote: "The mirror stage [is] *an identification* . . . the transformation that takes place in the [pre]subject when he assumes an image. . . . This jubilant assumption of his specular image . . . exhibit[s] . . . the symbolic matrix in which the I is precipitated in a primordial form, before it is objectified in the dialectic of identification with the other, and before language restores to it, in the universal, its function as subject" (E, p. 2). The mirror stage identification would not be a defense, even though it "situates the . . . ego, before its social determination, in a fictional direction" (E, p. 2), which can only later and only asymptotically "rejoin the coming-into-being of the subject" (E, p. 2). Instead of a defense, the mirror stage is the way development gets going, a first and necessary step whereby a person can, as Lacan stated, "constitute himself in his imaginary reality" (FFC, p. 144). It would no more be considered a defense than the sight of its own kind necessary for maturation of the female pigeon or the migratory locust (E, p. 3). The fundamental question is whether there are instances throughout development of interaction with another that are necessary triggers, what Chomsky calls "experiential releasing factors"[18]

18. J. H. Smith, "Language and the genealogy of the absent object" in *Psychiatry and the Humanities,* vol. 1, ed. J. H. Smith (New Haven, CT: Yale University Press, 1976), p. 152, and N. Chomsky, *Problems of Knowledge and Freedom* (New York: Random House, 1971), pp. 15, 18, 21, 23, and 43.

for establishing innate capacities whose time has arrived. These might involve becoming like the other but not count as identifications, or at least not as defensive identifications. Chomsky believes, for instance, we do not learn to speak; others speaking trigger a natural development.

What appears on the surface to be identification with the analyst may not be that, even if the analyst thinks so. *Good Will Hunting* ends with Sean (Robin Williams) proudly saying, as would a father: "He stole my line." Not only that, the treatment was characterized throughout by the therapist wholeheartedly revealing sometimes trivial, sometimes personal, intimate aspects of himself and his married life. I suggest, however, that it would be a mistake to see such personal revelations as an invitation for the patient to identify with the therapist. It is, more likely, the therapist risking an engagement with the patient in order to effectively, though indirectly, "interpret" the patient's deployment of intelligence and knowledge as massive ego defense.

Similarly, Sean's repeated insistence in the face of Will's growing anxiety, "It is not your fault," rather than being an attempt to reassure, is the mounting of an unrelenting challenge to Will's conscious belief that he harbors neither guilt nor grief. One does not get at such things in such patients by simply, dryly, and directly interpreting the defense. And also, as anyone knows who has worked with such patients, an expression of tenderness is apt to evoke a violent reaction.

"It's not your fault," in addition to being an expression of tenderness, is also to say, implicitly: "It is much worse than that. It is much more serious, that is, than simply the unconscious, irrational reasons for guilt you harbor. Such 'guilt' only bars access to the loss and grief that, in turn, block access to desire and your own subjecthood." One works toward some such "interpretation" throughout an analysis. To be effective, however, such words can *only* be said indirectly, implicitly, usually with silence when close to the truth and in the face of final moments of protest.

3

What Is Wrong with French Psychoanalysis? Observations on Lacan's First Seminar

PAUL ROAZEN

This presentation is my third attempt to come to terms with the historiographically intriguing problem of French psychoanalysis today. I do not want to repeat anything I wrote earlier, either in connection with Lacan's Benedictine monk brother or the problem of ego psychology. Nor do I feel the need to defend these earlier writings, and the body of my work on Freud. Under the circumstances of this collection of essays I must, however, recur to something mentioned at the outset of my initial book first published in 1968.[1] For almost from the outset of my acquaintance with Freud, I was fascinated by the comparative cultural reception of psychoanalysis, and I wrote a graduate seminar paper in the early 1960s about Freud in Britain as opposed to America. By now the range of my knowledge has expanded, so I know at least something about what happened in France, Italy, Argentina, Rus-

---

1. P. Roazen, *Freud: Political and Social Thought* (New York: Knopf, 1968).

sia, Japan, Mexico, and even India. Yet Freud's position in France remains unique. When Rudolf Nureyev was dying of AIDS in Paris, he was reported to have wondered whether he should seek a psychoanalysis. Freud's influence there has reached by now almost unprecedented heights; it should seem, I believe, no disrespect either to Freud or religion to remark that, while once a priest might be summoned before death, now analysts have come to play a comparable role.

When in 1992 I first gave a talk with the provocative title of the first-half of this subject for the International College of Philosophy and the International Society for the History of Psychiatry and Psychoanalysis in Paris, the place was mobbed. It was not so much the title of my lecture that attracted these people, but the distinguished panel of four analysts who were supposed to be discussing my remarks. Unfortunately it proved, from my point of view, impossible to make much of a coherent statement, since the responding analysts necessarily fragmented the discussion with their own individual observations. But I was told at the time that my proposed talk had, unexpectedly for me, touched on a raw nerve. For in the years since Lacan's death a vacuum has left many with an uncertain hold on what direction they should be moving in.

In 1992 I went armed only with a copy of Lacan's First Seminar in my hands, and today I would like largely to confine my remarks to that one text. I picked that book to try and talk about on ordinary grounds of scholarship. Intellectual historians like myself prefer to start at the beginning, and hence that seminar seems a logical place to proceed from. I realize that there exist different and legally unpublishable versions of Lacan's seminars, and in out-of-the-way cities like Rosario and Tucuman I once saw a whole stack of unofficial accounts of Lacan's seminars. The vexing problem of transcription makes me feel like I might be standing on quicksand, and I am aware of the dangers of constructing a straw man.

But that first seminar did appear while Lacan was still alive, and I feel obliged to do the best I can with the material that is now available in print. I would also like to comment on my frustration that Lacan's medical dissertation on paranoid psychosis remains somehow untranslated into English, although it has appeared in Spanish. I would have thought that all students of Lacan's ideas would like to begin there, but perhaps that is too pedantic on my part. In Freud's case there exist between 20,000 and 40,000 of his letters, which will sometime in the future dwarf in size the twenty-four volume *Standard Edition*. So a tentative spirit behooves anyone working in this field.

Perhaps I should make plain what my own objectives amount to: I am primarily concerned with the history of psychoanalysis as part of intellectual life. I will be contending that one learns little about that subject by examining Lacan's first seminar. You may rightly respond that I have missed the boat, and that one should instead study that seminar as part of understanding what is new and interesting in Lacan's approach. I would not dispute that Lacan's body of work represents one of the most interesting legacies from within psychoanalytic thinking. It bears emphasizing that I am approaching with the standards of intellectual history.

Nietzsche once maintained that it would be to repay one's teachers poorly if one did not challenge them. Let me make some general observations on Lacan's first seminar, which was devoted to Freud's papers on technique. These are essays by Freud that everybody interested in analysis knows almost by heart. They are taught to candidates in training all over the world. But I want to make some sweeping criticisms about Lacan's approach, and then back them up with some noteworthy examples. What I have to say can be extended to many other works emanating from within French analysis, and are relevant not just to this seminar of Lacan's. At the same time I am hoping that my respect for the immense vitality of analysis in France does not fail to get communicated.

First of all, there is, I think, the general problem of what might be called psychoanalytic scholasticism, a static, ahistorical way of proceeding. When I met with Lacan's brother we talked about how the great medievalist Gilson had avoided this pitfall. (At the time at which I first got interested in analysis, I would have thought this charge of scholasticism could best be levelled at the works of Heinz Hartmann, who devotedly tried to tidy up Freud without using any case history material. But he is decidely out of fashion today, and not just because of Lacan's contempt for his approach.) In most institutes of analytic training there is little effort to put these papers on technique by Freud into any kind of proper historical context. I first made that point over twenty years ago, and as the time left to me shrinks I naturally feel more in a hurry. Freud was writing after his difficulties with Alfred Adler had come to a head and while he was already aware of the conflicts brewing with Carl G. Jung. In my opinion Freud's central purpose, as reluctant as he was publicly to talk about matters connected to technique, was to formulate the basis for the discipline of analysis in a way that distinguished it from any of his "deviating" disciples. That historical context to what Freud had to say remains almost always neglected in the way these papers of his on technique are understood.

But the issue of scholasticism is compounded by what I regard as the arbitrary secondary literature that comes up in the course of Lacan's seminar. And this touches on a general problem within the historiography of analysis that is perhaps more true in France than elsewhere. For there are continuities in the history of analysis that cannot be legitimately ignored. Freud's writings on technique have had a follow-up within the literature, but it requires a decent amount of attention to track down which papers bear importantly on what he originally wrote. At the same time it is necessary to be aware not only of the historical development of analytic technique, but also of the ruptures that have taken place. Not only the continuities, but also the discontinuities, require attention. Perhaps the best example of the violation of the occurrence of a discontinuity comes up in the course of Peter Gay's 1988 biography of Freud,[2] generally well regarded in Paris; Gay does not once even mention the name of Wilhelm Reich. As we know, Reich was one of the so-called troublemakers in the history of analysis, yet he made in his time crucial contributions to the area of technique: for example, he insisted on the significance of searching for negative transferences, and the meaningfulness of nonverbal communications. It should be unthinkable to leave him out of any historical account. Gay's way of just ignoring Reich, avoiding him altogether, will not do, and yet it is all too characteristic of the way standard accounts of the history of analysis get constructed.

Let me train my guns on Lacan's seminar itself. (I will be referring to the English translation brought out by Norton, but I have also tried to check that edition against the French.)[3] On page 9, Lacan refers to the significance of Freud's article

---

2. P. Gay, *Freud: A Life for Our Time* (New York: Norton, 1988).

3. J. Lacan, *Seminar I, Freud's Papers on Technique, 1953–1954*, tr. J. Forrester (New York: Norton, 1988).

"Analysis Terminable and Interminable," which Lacan tells us "appeared around 1934." I suppose when speaking off the top of his head Lacan could use a date like 1934, instead of the correct one, which is 1937. For those of us who have devoted care and attention to Freud's last period, three years is no minor matter. Could not in the course of either the editing or the translating the exact year be inserted or provided in a footnote? Then on page 11, Lacan refers to Michael Balint having borrowed a term "from the late Rickman, one of the rare souls to have had a modicum of theoretical originality in analytic circles since Freud's death." Now on what grounds can Lacan's reference to Rickman possibly be justified? Rickman was analyzed first by Freud, later by Sandor Ferenczi, and finally by Melanie Klein. I have it on the authority of Donald W. Winnicott that because of a specific early memory of Rickman's, Freud had advised Rickman to get out of being an analyst. When Ernest Jones in 1932 wrote to Freud of Rickman that "the underlying psychosis must be regarded as incurable," I believe that Jones was echoing Freud's own opinion. Of course, Jones and Freud could both have been in error, but Lacan's singling Rickman out for such striking praise does seem to me to demand some justification. Winnicott, for example, remarked on how useless Rickman's "obsessional" collection of unpublished material proved to be when he examined it following Rickman's death.

On page 12, Lacan announces that "History is not the past. History is the past in so far as it is historicized in the present. . . ." Now Lacan's idea is a fine one, and widely influential, yet it needs qualifying. To take an example already discussed: whether or not Rickman was such a rare soul with "a modicum of theoretical originality" needs to be defended with some sort of scholarly inquiry—on our part, of course, not Lacan's. We cannot simply accept what Lacan said as a matter of faith. Victor Tausk, for instance, had been virtually wiped out of the history books when I was writing my *Brother Animal*; the story of Freud and Tausk as I reconstructed it may even have damaged Tausk in history, in that because of the scandal that arose after the 1969 publication of the first edition of my book it is possible that certain orthodox analysts might have been less likely to cite Tausk than would have been the case before. How history gets "historicized in the present" therefore can be appallingly wayward. Gay's leaving out Reich (in a book subtitled "A Life for Our Time") is a form of presentism that is not acceptable; most of my writing career has been devoted to protecting the lost sheep in analysis, which means counteracting how history has so far been "historicized." When Lacan refers to *"re-writing history"* (p. 14), one has to be careful that Orwell's *1984*, in which truth-holes suck up the past does not get fulfilled. Stalin relied on rewriting history for the sake of making the past disappear, and it should be the objective of intellectual historians to avoid the ideological partisanship of propaganda.

On page 29, Lacan refers to the "reproach" leveled at Freud in connection with "his authoritarianism," but then it seems to me that Lacan does not do anything with that concept. He does go on to warn about the need for "a healthy suspicion of a number of translations of Freud." Here I think there has been a mass of confusion. There are over a dozen translations into French of Freud's little 1925 paper "Negation." It seems to me striking that this five-page paper should have attracted so much attention in France, as opposed to anywhere else in the world. But in general we know that all translations are necessarily interpretations; in English I think that the danger exists that the quest for new translations is bound to lead to making Freud's writings seem more sacred than ever, when in many cases human energy would be better spent acknowledging where he went wrong and trying to get on with thinking along new lines.

On page 49, Lacan refers to Richard Sterba's having in 1934 put something "in a most bizarre manner at the end of an atrocious, though entirely honest, article. . . ." Here Lacan sounds to me at his most breathtaking in his love of paradox, which Theodor W. Adorno shared in a different way: in psychoanalysis, Adorno once maintained, nothing is true but the exaggerations. Sterba was himself a well-educated Viennese analyst, possessing a special interest in art and music, but Lacan's judgment about Sterba's piece seems to me striking. Doubtless Lacan was being playfully enigmatic, and I hope my own reaction does not make me sound an unimaginative pedant. I might have thought an "atrocious" article not worth mentioning, especially if a point had been made in "a most bizarre manner." To say that Sterba's piece had been "entirely honest" in this context was to damn it with faint praise, even though I see no reason in terms of intellectual history for singling out that paper. In 1934 Sterba was hardly a senior member of Freud's circle, and I would have thought that many other works would have been historically more central to be interested in.

On page 55, Lacan waxes explicitly about Freud's "Negation" paper: "This paper shows once more the fundamental value of all of Freud's writings. Every word is worthy of being measured for its precise angle, for its accent, its specific turn, is worthy of being subjected to the most rigorous of logical analyses." Lacan's choice of this one paper seems to me idiosyncratic, historically unjustified, but by now a part of French intellectual life. It also made little sense for Lacan to proceed to distinguish Freud in this one essay from his adherents: "It is in that way that it is distinguished from the same terms gathered together more or less hazily by his disciples, for whom the apprehension of the problems was at second hand. . . . " It seems to me gratuitous for Lacan to take such a swipe at Freud's followers, who for all their deficiencies had a more balanced appreciation for the standing of Freud's essay on "Negation" than Lacan himself.

Then, Lacan on page 59 says of the Wolfman: "The subject is not at all psychotic." What could it mean to say of the Wolfman that he was "not at all psychotic"? Lacan goes on to compound the difficulties: "He just has a hallucination. He might be psychotic later on, but he isn't at the moment when he has this absolutely limited, nodal experience, quite foreign to his childhood, completely disintegrated. At this point in his childhood, nothing entitles one to classify him as a schizophrenic, but it really is a psychotic phenomena we are dealing with." Unpacking these sentences would require great patience. I just want to comment that childhood would seem to have acquired a theological status for Lacan. For what it is worth, in his own reminiscences the Wolfman is reported to have complained that Freud had misdiagnosed him, and that he was in reality schizophrenic. (Despite what Freud wrote about psychoanalysis staying away from schizophrenia, at least once in the 1920s Freud personally treated a patient whom he characterized in a letter as schizophrenic, supposedly the same type as Jean-Jacques Rousseau.)

On the same page, Lacan refers to "one" of Ernst Kris's articles. Would it really be too much to expect of the editorial apparatus that it tell us exactly which of Kris's papers is being referred to? Surely the Kris family would help, even if I have been informally told that Lacan was referring to Kris's

1952 contribution to an issue of the *International Journal of Psycho-Analysis*. James Strachey has been taking a beating lately for his splendid edition of Freud's work, but he never would have allowed himself the laziness of Lacan's editors.

Lacan is rough on Anna Freud, and she had not yet as of the date of this seminar helped drive him out of the IPA. Lacan is obviously being ironic when he refers on page 62 to "all the recent discussions which take the ego of the analysand to be the ally of the analyst in the Great Analytic Work. . . ." The capitalization is designed to show how disaffected Lacan was from any approach to the ego "as an autonomous function. . . ." (Actually it was Hartmann, who briefly practiced in Paris, who proposed the theory of ego autonomy, not Anna Freud.) Lacan maintains that Anna Freud's approach "is intellectualist," as if that were at odds with Freud's, for example in *The Future of An Illusion*. Melanie Klein, as opposed to Anna Freud, is characterized as having had the merits of "her animal instinct" (pp. 67 and 69). Those interested in the vagaries of the history of psychoanalysis should note how British analysts today are keen on denying how heretical Freud deemed Klein's work, for that judgment of his might tarnish the legitimacy of their psychoanalytic standing.

Lacan has many interesting things to say about both Anna Freud and Melanie Klein. But then he maintains on page 80: "We must accept Melanie Klein's text for what it is, namely the write-up of an experiment." Now I do not think we "must" do anything of the sort. Melanie Klein may have been Anna Freud's enemy, and the principle of "the enemy of my enemy is my friend" is an old one, but otherwise there it makes little sense in Lacan's approach to Klein's text. (Klein is widely influential in Paris today, although as far as I know there are no Kleinian centers of analytic training there.) Klein did in fact succeed in making important contributions to the history of analysis, but what is gained by saying that we "must" accept her text for being "the write-up of an experiment"? What on earth is going on by proposing that any analyst's work can be treated simply as "an experiment"? Lacan would seem to be forgetting what he had earlier proposed by the concept of "historicizing" things in the present. Klein needs to be challenged at least as much as any other writer in the history of analysis, and calling any of her work "an experiment" only hides the inevitable subjectivity of her proposals. The curiously important standing that Klein's thinking has in France today can be partly explained by Lacan's influence.

On pages 110 through 112, Lacan refers in passing to Otto Fenichel, Hans Sachs, Sandor Rado, and Franz Alexander. But I wonder how many within French psychoanalysis could distinguish between any of these four writers, showing the strengths as well as the weaknesses of their respective approaches; in the absence of decent scholarship, name-dropping can become a source of mystification. (Julia Kristeva has picked up the habit of tossing around the names of different analysts.) Lacan also pops in one paper of James Strachey's, which Lacan calls a "fundamental article." It is indeed a well-known paper, but should it not be subjected to criticism without ex cathedra calling it "fundamental"? Lacan cannot, in my opinion, get out of how he has presented analysis by his assertion: "There are a number of ways of introducing these ideas. Mine has its limits, like any dogmatic account." (Freud in his *Outline of Psychoanalysis* used the analogy of dogma.) The problem is that readers in France, as well as elsewhere, are unlikely to take away from Lacan's seminar enough of a historical perspective on the different authors he chooses to cite.

Carl G. Jung is rarely mentioned in French psychoanalysis, and there is as yet an unwritten account of the reception of Jung in France. (Paul Riceur was unknowingly echoing Jung in his book *Freud and Philosophy*.) Lacan brings in Jung by means of a discussion that can only obscure Jung's role in intellectual history. Lacan mentions "the need to distinguish the psychoses from the neuroses" (p. 115). Now, historically this is something that Jung, like Lacan a trained psychiatrist, was well aware of. Before World War I, Jung was sensitive to this issue, one which Freud at the time was trying to bridge by the term "narcissistic neuroses" instead of the label of psychoses. (Alan Tyson, the official translator into English of Freud's famous essay on narcissism, once challenged me to try and follow the intricacies of how Freud distinguished himself on narcissism from Jung, since Tyson could make little sense of Freud's subtle polemicizing.) When Lacan refers to "the Jungian dissolution" (p. 115) of the distinction between the psychoses and the neuroses, one might never comprehend what had really happened. It is wholly misleading for Lacan to say: "You are beginning to see, I hope, the difference between Freud's and Jung's appreciation of the place of the psychoses. For Jung, the two domains of the symbolic and the imaginary are there completely confused, whereas one of the preliminary articulations that Freud's article allows us to pinpoint is the clear distinction between the two" (p. 117). Anna Freud and Lacan together viewed Jung as a heretic. But in this passage Lacan is trying to foist off on Freud Lacan's own special distinction between the "symbolic" and the "imaginary." In reality it was not until the 1920s that Freud was even distinguishing between neurosis and psychosis. Lacan is, I regret to say, no more reliable here on Jung than about Klein.

On page 127, Lacan refers to a pioneering article of Sandor Ferenczi's as "very poor." In truth it was, I think, one of the great papers in history, but because of Lacan's immovable opposition to ego psychology he devalued Ferenczi's early attempt to deal with it. I try to keep reminding people of a story that Erik H. Erikson, whom Lacan's son-in-law says Lacan thought was the most dangerous because the best of the ego psychologists used to like to tell: the son of an analyst gets asked what he wants to be when he grows up, and the boy replies "a patient."

While Ferenczi gets blasted, Lacan on page 139 refers favorably to "our dear friend Michael Balint," even though Balint was one of Ferenczi's most loyal followers. On the whole Balint's work, thanks partly to Lacan's influence, is better known in France than almost anywhere else. The whole relation of Ferenczi to Balint is one of those issues that it would be hard, if not impossible, for any reader of Lacan's seminar to make sense of. On page 201, Lacan devotes a special section to Ferenczi's disciple, or it was the editors (presumably with Lacan's approval) who came up with the title "Michael Balint's Blind Alleys." Once again Balint gets referred to as "our friend" (p. 203). The reader will not find, I believe, much in Lacan's remarks that points toward what was most distinctive about Balint's contribution to the history of psychoanalytic thinking. But Lacan specifies his unique purpose: he was trying to "render palpable . . . a certain contemporary deviationism in relation to the fundamental analytic experience. . . ." (p. 203) So Lacan, like Freud and the orthodox tradition in analytic thinking, was trying loyalistically to stick to the position that Freud had first staked out. (Great dissenters like Wilhelm Reich, Sandor Rado, as well as others, tried to maintain that they had been more royal than the king.)

Lacan somehow comments that "up to 1930" Ferenczi "was to some extent considered . . . to be the *enfant terrible* of psychoanalysis." The qualification "to some extent" pulls the rug from under Lacan himself. In fact Ferenczi, who died in 1933, was only in the last few years of his life considered by Freud or anybody else of questionable standing. Perhaps Balint retrospectively romanticized Ferenczi's role, given Balint's own difficulties with Ernest Jones as well as Anna Freud. But, even as late as 1930, Ferenczi was considered one of Freud's most authoritative expositors. And since Lacan also refers to Balint as "our good friend," I would be willing to leave it to future intellectual historians to ferret out in Balint's papers what interchanges were taking place between him and Lacan. (The politics of IPA struggles played a role here, since Lacan was getting support from Balint; Balint in turn could see Ferenczi's ultimate fate in Lacan's organizational troubles. Anna Freud had become more bitter about Ferenczi than Freud himself.)

Within the analytic literature Lacan refers in passing to a paper by Alexander (p. 237), one by Herman Nunberg (p. 240), and also one by Rudolph Loewenstein (p. 243). My problem here is that these three writers are in no sense on a historical par. It should be necessary to put in the context of his theoretical development what Alexander wrote. Also, one needs to understand just how morbidly loyalist the misanthropic Nunberg was. (According to legend Nunberg committed one of the great slips of the tongue in the history of analysis, when he maintained that a patient had been "successfully mistreated.") It would be easy, in my view, to establish the contrast between these two thinkers and Loewenstein. Only in France does Loewenstein, Lacan's own analyst, have any status to speak of. Elsewhere he has been consigned to the category of one of the least significant of analytic writers. In his aim to be "strictly orthodox" Lacan cannot duly credit (p. 267) an idea of Jung's, even when Jung (as in his conception of archetypes, whatever one might think of it) has in reality been also invoked by Freud (in *Moses and Monotheism*, for example). Lacan correctly recognized Edward Bibring's stature (p. 284), cited Nunberg (p. 285) again, and then suddenly dropped down to a different level entirely when he mentioned a nonentity like Willi Hoffer (p. 285). Lest it be thought that my judgment about Hoffer is eccentric, I would like to invoke the British Jungian Michael Fordham having agreed with my view of Hoffer.

At one point Lacan does perceptively interpret a dream of Freud's in terms of Freud's relationship with his wife (pp. 269–270). Lacan not only was way ahead of others in perceiving an important aspect of Freud's feelings about his wife, but Lacan also was "aware of the brutality of his (Freud's) responses to those people who came to him with their hearts of gold, the idealists. . . ." (p. 270). Lacan was outspoken, "fifteen years after Freud's death," in asserting that "we really should not fall to the level of hagiography" (p. 270). It might not be amiss to summarize my approach by saying that at least unconsciously Lacan can be considered a Catholic, even if I do not like the idea of invading someone's privacy by invoking such a characterization. My central point is that the failings I have laboriously pointed out in Lacan's first seminar are representative of a general cavalier approach to Freud in France.

Let me cite some other examples, from writers I happen to admire. Jean Laplanche, with the belief in "the genius of the French language," has proposed to produce "a Freud in French that is . . . Freudian." It is awfully late in the game to think in terms of "the text, the whole text, and nothing but the text." I hope it does not sound wildly immodest of me, but I could write a little book about what I think Freud was doing in those papers of his on technique, and come up with something wholly unlike Lacan's approach; yet I would be closer, I believe, to the ideal of the task of being an intellectual historian. Lacan's seminar almost certainly will be remembered long after what I might write would be recalled; I am not claiming originality as a theorist, just trying to stick to my calling of the study of the history of ideas.

I could take another example from the work of someone else I admire, Kristeva. She happens to have written an Introduction to the French translation of Helene Deutsch's autobiography. Since I wrote Helene Deutsch's biography with her cooperation, I naturally followed up on Kristeva's Introduction, if only because she has—along with Lacan and Simone de Beauvoir—helped keep Helene Deutsch's name alive in France. Kristeva, in writing about Helene's life, reports that she was analyzed by Victor Tausk. When I once mentioned this publicly in Paris, the audience broke out in laughter. The tale of *Brother Animal* is so well known in France that Kristeva's error needed no gloss from me. At the time *Brother Animal* first came out in Paris many thought it was about Lacan and a famous suicide in his circle. But that Kristeva could say that Tausk analyzed Helene Deutsch is one of those incomprehensible reversals that point to what I fear is a dubious use of psychoanalysis in French intellectual life. (Kristeva's great intelligence, beauty, and charm only highlight such a blunder.)

Louis Althusser's engrossing memoir *The Future Lasts Forever*[4] is filled with the rarefied air of the Parisian intelli-

---

4. L. Althusser, *The Future Lasts Forever: A Memoir*, edited by O. Corpet and Y. M. Boutang, tr. R. Veasey (New York: Norton, 1993).

gentsia. Although a committed Marxist theoretician, he takes Freud almost woodenly for granted. Althusser's account of his own tragic life is almost impossible to put down, and the root of much of his trouble may have been that, although he was in analysis for decades, he did not seem to realize, even up to the time of his death, that he might have been medically mishandled. Althusser remained incredibly naive about the efficacy of Freud's method. Although Althusser treats psychiatrists like a new priesthood, as a man of the Left it does not dawn on this otherwise sophisticated Parisian to question any of the key postulates to the Freudian framework he chooses to take as an ideological given. In the memoir he appears appallingly uncritical of Freudian terminology and beliefs. Raymond Aron once accused Althusser of "an imaginary version of Marxism," which I think applies also to his Freudianism. Althusser makes one suspect that the more brilliant the French philosopher, the less contact with common-sense existence he shows. Freud once blamed common sense for most of human troubles, but I find it frightening that ideas are capable of being so addictive. (The visits of Foucault to the hospitalized Althusser underline the significance of the extensive French misreadings of Freud.)

My paper on ego psychology and Lacan covers what I consider the French misconceptions on the topic, and in my book on Erikson I criticized his approach to tragedy; Lacan picked up an authentically Freudian theme when it comes to the tragic dimension of human experience, a point that has been hard for North Americans to accept. Although there is much more to be said about how difficult writing the history of psychoanalysis can be, I want just to touch on one French example: Otto Rank, once Freud's personal favorite, practiced analysis in Paris for over ten years, from the mid-1920s until the late 1930s, and he had a circle of writers, artists, and analysands around him. (His first wife helped me follow the story of early analysis in France.) Yet in Elisabeth Roudinesco's *Jacques Lacan & Co.*,[5] the second volume of her compendious history of analysis in France, Otto Rank's presence in Paris is simply ignored. Rank was, like so many of the other early analysts in Paris, not French, but he has evaporated in Roudinesco for different reasons than why Reich gets dropped from Gay's *Freud*.

Let me conclude on a bold note. Sometimes when I have been in France I have thought to myself: the French are, in the course of a few short years, committing all the mistakes in the history of psychoanalysis over the last hundred years. I never hear in France criticisms of the therapeutic use of the couch, or how analyses may be allowed to go on much too long with the same analyst. Someone like Jung, and Rank too, pointed out long ago the possible authoritarianism implicit in Freud's recommended therapeutic procedure, a point that Jean-Paul Sartre intuitively understood; for a variety of reasons, as I have indicated, Jung still has little influence in France. Voltaire's pungency was not Jung's style. Erich Fromm, rather than Erikson's more discursive approach, has appeal in France, even though it was Erikson who long ago pointed out how psychoanalysis can become an "exquisite" sensory deprivation, an insight that relativizes the classical analytic situation.

I should add that when I presented some of my thinking about what is wrong with French psychoanalysis back in 1992, the first time I cited what I considered a "howler" from Lacan

---

5. E. Roudinesco, *Jacques Lacan & Co.: A History of Psychoanalysis in France, 1925–1985*, tr. J. Mehlman (Chicago: University of Chicago Press, 1990).

the analyst nearest to me murmured, "That is just a mistake," while across the face of another analyst on the panel I thought I could see the thought, "How dare you, a nobody from nowhere, come to criticize."

It is a pleasure in looking at Lacan's first seminar to find him conversant with St. Augustine as well as Sartre. (In an index of all Lacan's seminars Aristotle's name is mentioned more than anyone, followed by Descartes, Hegel, and Socrates.) It has long seemed to me that both Sartre and de Beauvoir played a pivotal role in the reception of Freud in France, even if it generally goes unrecognized. When in Lacan's seminar he alludes to Sartre, I doubt he also was recommending that his audience pay as much attention to Sartre's critique of Freud as I think it deserves. I suppose my notion of what is wrong with French psychoanalysis says too much about my own fairly pedestrian approach. But I do think that as intellectuals we ought not to let slide by the kinds of characteristic distortions that I have tried to point out in Lacan's first seminar.

It should go without saying that I would not have undertaken this unless I thought that Lacan were fully worth the effort of the most sustained sorts of inquiry. He made French psychoanalysis, transforming a second rate Society into one of the greatest contemporary sources of psychoanalytic originality. Jones did the same for the British Society, but he accomplished that objective as an organizer and succeeded via supporting Klein; Lacan succeded by the fertility of his ideas, which have affected French intellectual life as a whole. Lacan brought psychoanalysis and philosophy back together, in a way that is reminiscent of the early Freudians. Just because of the beneficial effects of French psychoanalysis today, it behooves us to be aware of some of its possible shortcomings.

Analysis is by no means coming to an end with a new century, but the past gains power by the way in which we manufacture it. Aspects of psychoanalysis, as in Freud's attack on Christianity, were revolutionary. Fragmentation has also occurred, so that bits of psychoanalytic history have broken off and become isolated. At the same time, we need to be aware of the continous stream of psychoanalytic thinking, without any authoritarian appeal to what might seem to be the "mainstream" of that tradition. What I have written may read like a scold, when in reality I am trying to communicate something of the excitement connected to studying the history of psychoanalysis. Future students will find plenty to work on during the coming years. I have never found a letter of Freud's that bored me, and intellectual historians can do worse than labor over the field that he created.

4

Please Read Lacan!

C. EDWARD ROBINS

In "Lacan's First Disciple: An Interview with Marc-François Lacan," Roazen interviewed the then 84-year-old brother of Jacques Lacan in September 1992, and stated that from their meeting "the Catholic roots" of Lacan's theorizing were laid bare.[1] We also know that Jacques Lacan dedicated his dissertation on paranoia to his brother: "To the Reverend Father Marc-François Lacan, Benedictine of the Congregation of France, my brother in religion" (LFD, p. 325). That dedication sends us back to 1932, before Lacan's many public avowals of atheism. Can one therefore insist that Lacan maintained the same religious, Catholic position throughout his life, which, as Roazen and Roudinesco have pointed out, was the position of his intellectual Catholic mother?

---

1. P. Roazen (1996). "Lacan's first disciple: an interview with Marc-François Lacan." *Journal of Religion and* Health, 35:321–336 (cited as LFD).

Roazen decides to "train his guns on" Lacan's first seminar (W, p. 45),[2] and targets what he calls "distortions" that
we should not allow to "slide by." Roazen's first charge against
Lacan and French psychoanalysis is for what he calls "psychoanalytic scholasticism." In this context, "scholasticism"
is clearly a bad word that implies something like distortion.
Why? Because, for the historian Roazen, Lacan—and French
psychoanalysis in general—is "too Catholic": too philosophical, too theological, too different from Freud's "Jewish
church." In the same interview, Marc-François Lacan told
Roazen, "The first thing Jacques wanted to do was to translate Freud's writings correctly into French." That would have
been the "basis" of all of Jacques's work—to "find the real
meaning of Freud's texts." "But," Marc-François added, "what
St. Thomas would have said now would be very different from
the thirteenth century. Lacan undertook an approach to Freud
in that broad spirit" (LFD, p. 326). Mixing St. Thomas, Freud,
and Jacques Lacan, Marc-François's interviewer seems to have
a clear target: he sees Lacan and French psychoanalysis as
importing Catholicism into psychoanalysis.

Roazen cites Freud as enjoying using religious metaphors, joking that there was no more room for "other popes"
like Adler and Jung in his, Freud's church. He adds: "It is one
thing to try to imagine what it might have meant for a Jew
like Freud to have founded a church; it is altogether a different and more complex matter to follow what it might have

---

2. I refer here to the preceding essay in this collection, "What Is
Wrong with French Psychoanalysis?" The references are to this volume,
hereafter W and page number.

meant for a Catholic like Lacan to break with a Jewish church" (LFD, p. 328). But in the same interview with Lacan's brother, we learn that Marc-François "made no mention of the traditional Christian conception of the Talmud as the origin of Jewish erring" (LFD, p. 333), a theory that I have been unable to find in any Catholic or Christian text. However, he is certainly right to point out that the Church traditionally saw Judaism "in error," from which we know the historical consequences: second-rate social and legal status, ghettoes, the Inquisition. (One example survives in contemporary Flamenco music: suffering is sung in the plaintive wail of the quivering and breaking *canto hondo* voice, rage stomps the heels to the floor crying "*¡Basta!*" "No more!" Voice, guitar, and heels remember the Spain of pain and slaughter of Jews, Moors, and Gypsies.)

Roazen concludes his interview with Lacan's brother by comparing the Lacanian schools to religious orders (LFD, p. 335). Lacan would thus be a Catholic whose "ultimate Other had to be God" (LFD, p. 333)—no matter what Lacan clearly taught on this subject—namely, that "there is no Other of the Other," that the underpinning of the symbolic register simply does not exist. I agree that Lacan's invocation of the Other does keep in play an idea of God (a God more like Martin Buber's "Eternal Thou" that "happens between speaking beings"), and that it is here that Lacan differs from Freud: for Lacan the question of God is not so easily shut, the case is not so easily solved (as Freud thought it was), but it "stays to haunt." It stays to haunt because the symbolic register hinges on the Other as source of our words; it also stays to haunt because if the question of God has any validity whatsoever, it addresses the register of the unknowable, the real.

In another paper by Roazen, "A Plea for Toleration,"[3] we read: "Although it is not evident on the surface, and some of Lacan's atheistic followers would deny it, I find in his work an eloquent restatement of some fundamental Catholic teachings. . . . Oskar Pfister was not the only analyst . . . to try to import Christian principles within the practice and thinking of analysts" (PT, p. 7). Erikson is likewise accused of having tried "to bring Christianity into analysis" (PT, p. 7). In his most recent text, Roazen himself uses the vocabulary of religion: "We cannot accept what Lacan said as a matter of faith" (W, p. 47). Here he writes of "devoted disciples," "devotion" to Freud, making "writings more sacred than ever," "strictly orthodox," and "the new priesthood." Further, note his response to Lacan's insistence on the importance of the non-psychotic childhood of the Wolfman in this way: "Childhood would seem to have acquired a theological status for Lacan" (W, p. 49). Why project "theological" onto Lacan? Why term Lacan's statement as made "ex cathedra" (W, p. 51). Can religion be seen here?

Scholasticism, that "intellectual frenzy" of the middle ages in Europe, was characterized by the proliferation of philosophical and theological texts called *summae*—"sums" or "summits" of knowledge like Aquinas' *Summa Theologica*. Scholasticism was ushered in by the three great commentators on Aristotle—Avicenna, Averroes, and Ben Maimon (Maimonides), who all wrote originally in Arabic. On almost every page of the thirteenth-century *summae*, the names of Avicenna, Averroes, and Maimonides are found. The debt of Aquinas—and us—to them is enormous; they made possible a repossession not only

---

3. P. Roazen (1997). "A plea for toleration." *Clinical Studies*, 3:1–9, hereafter PT and page number.

of matter but especially of the body into an over-Platonized Christianity, thereby granting dignity to the natural sciences. Maimonides was a vigorous adherent of the Aristotelian world view and confronted the same task for the Jewish world that preoccupied the great teachers of medieval Christianity; "staying orthodox" to their own religious traditions proved to be an ordeal—within the Christian camp it meant "staying alive." I mention all this to indicate the depth of the collaboration of Muslim, Jewish, and Christian elements in the scholastic endeavor. The university itself was the achievement of scholasticism. ("Uni-versare" implies that all turn towards the *unum*, the one; and theology considered itself that "one." Philosophy never was content to be the "handmaid" of theology! Of course, by the time of Descartes, and in this country at least, science has taken the place of the *unum* towards which the other disciplines are turned.) It was the University of Paris that became the most representative university of the West: no single *summa* of the entire middle ages derived from anywhere but the University of Paris!

"Scholasticism" is a bad word in another sense: it conjures up unending metaphysical speculation, like "How many angels can dance on the head of a pin?"—and is therefore not "experience-based." Herein lies an historical divide, especially for the Reformation: on the one side the authority of a sacred text and tradition, and on the other the individual's "human experience." It was especially Luther and other Renaissance thinkers like Montaigne who were to insist on the primacy of their own experience over traditional authority. This revolt against scholasticism was swift: Luther began teaching that Aristotle was "the Devil himself"; and under the razor of Occam and other skeptics the "ivory towers of certainty" the medieval schoolmen had so assiduously built began to tumble.

(And yet, with Luther "the Reformer," anti-Semitism and anti-feminism burgeoned.)

In his first few pages of the Schreber case, Freud, in explaining where his theory comes from, contrasts two possible sources, "speculation" and "experience." *Spekulation* (philosophical speculation ungrounded in experience) is to be shunned, and *Erfahrung* (direct experience, here the clinical presentation of Schreber) is to be embraced. Roazen writes that it was Heinz Hartman who deserved the bad name "scholastic" because Hartmann "tried to tidy up Freud without using any case history material" (W, p. 44). Indeed, if one is looking for Lacan's own case material in Lacan's first seminar, one will be disappointed. Lacan gives precious little of his own case material—or his own dreams—as compared with Freud. The word "scholasticism" will thus here imply "too philosophical, too detached from reality, too academic." Is it Lacan's "open style" that Roazen finds "distorted"? Is Lacan impossible to read? Or is it the continental (negative) philosophy inherent in Lacan's—French—approach that Roazen does not agree with? Note what he writes about Althusser: "the more brilliant the French philosopher, the less contact with common-sense existence he shows" (W, p. 57). If I were French I would protest! And who is to define "common-sense existence"? British empiricism imported to America? A philosophy-in-disguise that abhors and ridicules other philosophies.

Now, let us return to the textual criticisms of Lacan's first seminar. I agree with Roazen that Lacan's editor should have corrected a few textual errors, but on many substantive issues I disagree with Roazen. First, it looks as if Roazen had misunderstood the Freud–Jung differences. He writes: "When Lacan refers to 'the Jungian dissolution' of the distinction between the psychoses and the neuroses, one might never comprehend what had really happened. It is wholly misleading for Lacan to say: 'You are beginning to see, I hope, the difference between Freud's and Jung's appreciation of the place of the psychoses. For Jung, the two domains of the symbolic and the imaginary are there completely confused, whereas one of the preliminary articulations that Freud's article allows us to pinpoint is the clear distinction between the two' (p. 117). . . . In reality it was not until the 1920s that Freud was even distinguishing between neurosis and psychosis. Lacan is, I regret to say, no more reliable here on Jung than about Klein" (W, p. 52). It is clear here that Lacan is writing about the two domains of symbolic and imaginary, not about neurosis and psychosis. This misreading of Lacan must be interrogated. Why does Roazen resist Lacan's insistence on the division between the symbolic and the imaginary registers? He retorts throughout this paper by reminding us of anecdotes from Freud's life that do not address the question, from which he asserts that "Lacan is unreliable again." Thus he concludes: "The failings I have laboriously found in Lacan's first seminar are representative of a general cavalier approach to Freud in France" (W, p. 55). "Cavalier" in my dictionary means "haughty, disdainful, domineering." To carefully follow Lacan's exegesis of Freud's article "On Narcissism" in this first seminar is to experience, I would argue, the great esteem Lacan had for Freud. In my opinion, this is Lacan at his best, a thoughtful Freud reader, an exact German reader, who brings of his own to Freud's text as a philosopher-theoretician-historian. But even when Lacan disagrees with Freud (as in the case of Schreber), he is never cavalier; if anything, he appears too obsequious, too forgiving of Freud (as in the case of the Wolf Man).

There is also a controversy about ego psychology. Roazen thinks that "Ego psychology itself arose out of the need to try to get some sound horse-sense into the practice of psychoanalysis" (PT, p. 3). I would say on the contrary that ego psychology arose from the European immigrant analyst's need to accommodate to Adolph Meyer's forty-year iron grip on American psychiatry, and from Meyer's philosophy of "adaptation," which ultimately means conformism to society (also Erikson's dead end). Hence, we fall into a discussion of "the Human Condition." Roazen rails against what he calls "Freud's pessimism": ". . . his negativism about therapy, bordering on nihilism, which can be found in some of Freud's writings. . . . In reality Freud set ego psychology going . . . [it] was especially congenial to the needs of America, did much to correct earlier pessimistic imbalances within psychoanalytic thinking. . . . Lacan did have a genuinely tragic view of the human condition, close to Freud's own central standpoint, which can perhaps be considered a secular version of the doctrine of original sin; but such a viewpoint could never be popular in the States." (LFD, p. 330) That America, it seems, does not want to know the depths of its desperation. That America wants to believe that everything can be fixed, that it is never too late. It is a belief in analysis or therapy, that it can fix everything, and that relationships like man–woman or the family are "naturally healthy" and somehow "salvific." That America believes in positive thinking, not in the death drive. But hiding behind the middle school, an 11- and a 13-year-old boy, camouflaged, with high-power rifles outfitted with scopes, train their cross-hairs only on fleeing girls—the real of sexual difference—and one of last week's battles in the war between the sexes. Or haunting rhapsodies of *Titanic*, impetuous young love, the "heart of the ocean" necklace: glossing over the too-soon icy corpses of thousands.

Roazen sees Lacan as close to the "the tragic view." In classical Rome Seneca wrote plays, far bloodier on stage than the Greeks he was copying from, but the Roman audience simply had no taste for tragic theater; they preferred "live sports" with less plot. It would take some fifteen hundred years before someone in England would resurrect and refashion Seneca's plays and thus reintroduce audiences to tragic theater. (That someone was the high school Latin teacher Freud thought could never have possibly written all these stirring plays!) It is this "tragic view" that would make Roazen's nightmare come true: "truth-holes have already sucked up the past"! There is real loss, irretrievable, forever. Here indeed can one find Lacan's "tragic vision," in words—clear for once—from his seminar on *Ethics*: "The human condition is really that which Freud, in speaking of anxiety, has designated as the ground from where anxiety produces its signal, that of *Hilflosigkeit*, helplessness, distress, out of which man in his rapport to his own self—which is his very death—can count on help from no one."[4]

I can do no better by way of conclusion than to cite Roazen's own anticipated criticism: not that he has missed the boat—unless it were the *Titanic*—but that he should "study what is new and interesting in Lacan's approach." I wish Roazen had clarified for himself the text of Lacan's first seminar, especially Lacan's articulation of the imaginary register, emphasizing our own captivation in aggressive competition, the fight for prestige that constantly circulates among

---

4. This is a literal translation of Lacan's original *Le Séminaire, Livre VII, L'Ethique de la Psychanalyse* (Seuil, Paris, 1986) p. 351. See Dennis Porter's translation in *The Ethics of Psychonaalysis 1959–1960* (New York: Norton, 1992), pp. 303–304.

us; namely, that this is what Freud's *Idealich*—ideal ego—
means, and that we live not "conflict-free" but, in Freud's
words, in "unending conflict." It is because Roazen does not
engage Lacan's ideas in this very first seminar that he fails to
understand the significance of Lacan's mirror stage, and gets
stuck in confusion of the symbolic and imaginary registers
(cf. LFD, p. 20). An historian of ideas must engage ideas: for
instance, is Lacan's formulation of Freud's ideal ego as imaginary accurate or not? Is it useful or not? Lacan's fate in
America could be different if he simply had just begun to be
read.

5

New Resistances to Psychoanalysis

GÉRARD POMMIER

I have entitled my paper "New Resistances to Psychoanalysis," but it could have been called "Jet Lag," or more precisely,
"Double Jet Lag," since it looks as if there were indeed two
jet lags at work here (French phrase, "*décalage horaire*," suggests more specifically a time difference), hence two "time differences" I want to explore. The first time difference is between the United States and France. I am sure it comes as no
surprise to you when I say that, from a French point of view,
psychoanalysis as practiced in the United States appears to
work on a very different time, which is due to considerable
cultural differences. There is, however, another time difference, or gap, a transcultural lag concerning the emergence of
new forms of resistance to psychoanalysis in general and they
are shared by French and Americans alike: this is the main
object of my paper.

In the first place, a conventional way of considering resistances to psychoanalysis would be an optimistic approach
asserting that resistances are a sign of good health and that

they have existed since the very discovery of psychoanalysis. They have affected Freud's followers, as well as society as a whole, to the extent that psychoanalytic discourse has spread by causing scandals. However, this has not prevented psychoanalysis from developing, increasing, and flourishing, and from this point of view the resistances are not as positive as structural. We cannot hope that one day we will finally have finished with resistances to psychoanalysis or that, with correct explanations and good arguments, clever people will finally understand: it is not a matter of being more or less clever but a matter of discourse, or to be more precise, of the *jouissance* contained in discourse.

I would like to rule out a preliminary notion, which would consist in establishing an analogy between resistances in a cure and resistances to psychoanalysis in culture and society. In a psychoanalytic cure, resistances come from one's "ego," that is from the imaginary lure to which the symptoms are suspended; the resistances occur between the ego and the subject of the unconscious, between the ego and the subject of desire. The resistance of the ego is what is required in order to be analyzed. The ego has only one source of power, and it is love. No love, no ego! And as the analyst, this prostitute of the unconscious, will always do his or her best to be loved, you can understand how he or she will try to overcome resistance: first, you have first to accept love, transference love, and then refuse love. For example, by being paid, and if possible well paid. And when deprived of love, this poor ego remains without strength, resistance is overcome. But what is the purpose of this double maneuver? Just to allow unconcious knowledge to appear in discourse. The symptom is this unconscious knowledge, which appears in speech when resistance is overcome. And once it has been decoded in equivalent symptomatic formations in language, this allows for a displacement of the symptom, and a different dialectic between desire and *jouissance*. The generalized equivalence of unconscious formations—for example between a Freudian slip, a dream, and a headache—permit the contradictions of desire to be elevated to the status of a paradox that it is possible to enjoy.

For instance, if a woman is anorgasmic because she tends to superimpose the figure of her husband and that of her father, this is an insoluble contradiction. However, with these same two figures, she could also produce the image of a husband plus a lover. This will perhaps generate some shame, but at least she should now be in a position to get some pleasure. At this very moment, the symptomatic contradiction turns into a paradox: the pleasure of shame. Admittedly, this is not very moral, and I would not want to equate this with a recipe that would pave the way to the end of an analysis. There, a further step is necessary in order to make this paradox compatible with love for just one man. Here is the point where the analyst can be helpful, insofar as he falls in the place of the dead father: he is someone who is loved, while refusing the sexual consequences of love. This transformation of contradiction into a paradox can be seen as an acceptable definition of the end of analysis. As we have seen, the reading of the symptom is possible just insofar as the analyst does not respond to the demand for love. All this being quite difficult of course, and that is why, ultimately, resistance ends up being just the resistance of the analyst: indeed, eventually, the poor guy also wants to be loved, as everybody does.

Now, is this resistance we found to be internal to the treatment of the same order as resistances to psychoanalytic discourse in society? If both were of the same order, this would suggest that all society is in analysis. One can then wonder in analysis with whom—psychoanalysts organized in a social group? Should then one analyze society with its symptoms? This is a hypothesis that Freud had envisaged in *Civilization and its Discontents*[1] and he did not stick to it, because he did not see from what privileged external position an analyst could practice such an analysis. He could not see, and with good reason, who could be such an authority in the position to deliver an interpretation. Of course, we will find in any society people who are "experts" and speak in the media of the unconscious, of the symptoms, of our psychic life, and so on. But they are generally not at all psychoanalysts themselves. These are precisely the representatives of resistance to psychoanalysis and they are sure of getting the most success when they speak against psychoanalysis in the name of psychoanalysis, at least in France.

If, therefore, the resistances within society are something different from the resistance that appears during the cure, how do these resistances apear in the social link? Resistances against psychoanalytic discourse, resistances that no one in particular is consciously planning to set up, are nonetheless at work to a tremendous extent and they are not especially new. Every year, for instance, one announces new discoveries that will finally render psychoanalysis useless. Every three months, a researcher thinks that he or she has discovered the "virus" of schizophrenia, or the "specific gene that causes depression," or abnormal chromosomes responsible for sexual disorders. A disproportionate importance is given to neurosciences and behaviorism, to hormones, to physiology—in short, to any-

---

1. S. Freud, *Civilization and Its Discontents*, tr. James Strachey (New York: Norton, 1989).

thing other than a recognition of the place of unconscious desire. There is an important struggle aiming at assuring us that the origin of desire lies not in the unconscious but in physiology, in the organism, in the nerves and so on; thus any theory that affirms the prevalence of the "ego," either in the organism or in psychology, is bound to succeed.

The resistances tend to increase as well in various types of institutions, for example, health care institutions or institutions of higher learning. There is a strong tendency to marginalize psychoanalysis in psychology, and psychoanalysts are often barred from academic careers. In the same way, the teaching of general psychology in universities is ideological, and presupposes an objectification of the subject. All this is reinforced by reduction of Freudian overdetermination to determism whenever psychoanalysis is taught. Freud always insisted on various contradictory determinations between which the subject remains free to choose. If determism is to reign, if family determination is univocal and absolute, then the subject disappears. Thus, even when psychoanalysis happens to be taught, it is often likely in such a way as to stress the objectification of the subject by determinism. This reduces to nothing the main teachings of Lacan, when he would stress the primacy of the question of the subject and the ethics of the psychoanalytic act.

Similarly, in health care institutions, psychoanalysis cannot avoid marginalization, like classic psychiatry in fact, for both have nearly the same nosography. Nowadays, classical psychiatric nosography and psychoanalytic nosographies are replaced by a new bible, D.S.M. IV,[2] a manual that only lists

---

2. *Diagnostic and Statistical Manual of Mental Disorders*, Fourth Edition Revised (Washington: American Psychiatric Association, 1994).

symptoms for which adequate pills will be provided. Symptoms are cut off from any reference to psychic structures or to the unconscious. One witnesses here a fantastic regression in the enthusiastic return to pharmacological straightjackets, to electric shocks, and to the administration of medication, neuroleptics and antidepressants, in huge proportions.

I will now first to define the common *jouissance* in the social link, in order to show how it resists the psychoanalytic discourse. The normal social link is the tie connecting brothers and all fellow creatures. It is the bond that Freud pointed out in *Civilization and its Discontents*,[3] after having examined the aphorism, "love thy neighbor as thyself." Freud showed that the relationship between all "fellow creatures" consists in exploitation, in abusing one another sexually and brutally. It is only in this light that we can grasp something of resistance, because by showing all this violence, psychoanalysis shows exactly the inverse of the ideals that rule the normal course of social links and mystify the violence implied by these links. But why do we always find such violent relationships between "fellow creatures"?

If we return to Freud's simple sexual pattern, we may consider that each human being has been conceived according to the desire of his mother. Why has she got this desire to have a child, which is not at all a natural one? Desire, you know, is always shocking! Freud says: according to the desire of the penis, according to the *penisneid*. Children come in the place of the missing penis. That means that each human being is first required to identify with the phallus. The whole body becomes the phallus, but a special phallus, since the mother has no phallus. The child is thus required to become a nothingness,

---

3. *Civilization and Its Discontents*, pp. 65–74.

and the child's first encounter with the demand of the mother is an encounter with the death drive. For the mother's sake, the child is confronted with death. Here we reach the question of "to be" and "not to be," of "being" and "nothingness," and I would add that only Freud managed to give its structural explanation to this question because it is only the phallus that carries the contrary values of "being" and "nothingness" and thus provides their dialectic tension and resolution.

I am sorry for Hegel, but as he never gives an explanation of the relationship between "being" and "nothingness" as the keystone of his dialectic, we are obliged to recognize that Freud was the first to show that there is only one signifier, the phallus, which can be at the same time a "being" and a "nothingness." And Freud has shown the sexual meaning of this signifier that has often been repressed by philosophy and by thinking. Now we understand why there is this constant violence between fellow creatures. Each human being is at the same time a "being" and a "nothingness," and the struggle for "being" consists in discharging, in rejecting this "nothingness," on the others. This is the usual structural social link, whose specific modern form is commodity fetishism, as Marx has shown: one very simple way to get one better over one's neighbor is actually, in modern times, capitalist exploitation. In this regard, Althusser remarked that there was a collusion between ego psychology, insofar as it resists psychoanalysis, and all the theories that tend to naturalize the law of the market; that is to say, there is a mode of *jouissance* that adheres precisely in capitalist economy and in the commodity fetishism under whose rules we live today. Thus a collusion implies that the more the discourse of the master triumphs in our capitalist society the more psychoanalysis is threatened.

It is useful in this context to take up the term I have just used of *commodity fetishism*, a term that is at the same time Freudian, in the Freudian sense of the perverse fetish, and that also refers to social ties as well. The term suggests the accelerated dominance of the equivalence of the "market laws," intimating that these laws are beyond our subjective understanding or our ability to change or manipulate them. This goes hand in hand with what I was just referring to, namely the collusion between *homo economicus* and *homo psychologicus*.

I have been a little rough with Hegel, but I have to recognize now that he has shown with the dialectic of the Master and the Slave the normal average of social link, and that is why Lacan has used the Hegelian term of Master to define the "discourse of the Master." But who is the Master? Well, love, of course—our good friend we have already met! The discourse of the Master is only a part, the homosexual part (its more presentable part), of the fact that love is the Master. Because it is with love, with the look of the Other, with the mirror stage, that we attempt to put an end to our nothingness. This creates the normal connection between love and death that we appreciate so much.

The relationship between "fellow creatures" is nothing more than a specific instance of the Master's discourse, that is to say, this particular link of *jouissance* that for each human being consists in trying "to be" or "to exist" by rejecting the part of nothingness inhabiting us onto fellow creatures. This factor is easy to specify historically; capitalist discourse is nothing but a particular version of the Master's discourse, and one can refer to Hegel here again for the terms of the master–slave relationship. We can now see why there is a violent structural resistance between the discourse of the Master as the ordinary social link created by love on the one hand, and the analytic discourse on the other hand.

The fact that unconscious knowledge can appear will limit the Master's efforts to retrieve his *jouissance* by exploiting the Slave. It may even reduce this effort to nothing. Of course, it would be going too far to say that the Master's *jouissance* is reduced to nothing when analytic discourse appears. But we can understand that the *jouissance* of the Master is only efficient if he himself ignores the sexual dimension of his act. This is because there is an irreducible opposition between love and unconscious knowledge, similar to the one I have presented earlier. The Master does not want to know, because if he knew, *jouissance* could disappear. For example, if a man can truly see that in a certain woman he loves only his mother, he will surely have some difficulty in making love to her as a consequence. The same applies to all types of exploitation. Therefore, men will prefer to invent all types of ideals such as neuroscience or ego psychology in order to resist the knowledge of unconscious desire.

To justify violence in the social link, men will invent special pseudo-sciences, for example, the so-called laws of the market; they will say that those laws work as "natural laws," just to forget the *jouissance* of the commodity fetishism. Here we see again the collusion between *homo economicus* and *homo psychologicus* of which Althusser spoke so well. If man could recognize unconscious desire, he would be a subject, the subject of his act, an ethical subject. But, as it is only as an object that he can have *jouissance*, he will prefer to ignore the whole problem. Rather, he prefers to think that his act is not an act but that it concerns itself with universal laws of humanity or the universal laws of psychology, or of the market, in brief, whatever it may be that can objectify what he does, and hence

renders him innocent. *Jouissance* needs this delicious objectification. One can only oppose subjective acts to *jouissance*,
insofar as objectivation is just what it requires. But as the
unconscious is necessary for *jouissance*, this is just the point
at which psychoanalytic discourse can intervene. This is why,
it seems, psychoanalytic discourse has been marginalized as
much as possible, as well as deprived of its most essential
demension. This dimension is that of the subject, of the ethical subjective act—or, precisely, of everything that Lacan has
brought to psychoanalysis.

As far as psychoanalysis exposes how *jouissance* functions
in commodity fetishism, this fetishism loses the essential
characteristic that allows this *jouissance* its unconscious objectivation—this is above all what must not be known so that
jouissance may remain. In this sense, the psychoanalyst is a
kind of devil, he is diabolical; the *diabolos* in Greek is the
person who "unties"—the psychoanalyst unties the knots of
a symptomatic *jouissance*. The psychoanalyst is a devil not
because he wants to do evil—psychoanalysts, it is well known,
are more often good guys—but because he takes away from
jouissance the very kernel that allows the Master's discourse
to take shape. It is in this sense that the analyst is diabolical.
You may have read Fernando Pessoa's *The Devil's Hour*,[4] in
which the Devil explains that he would never hurt a fly, and
that moreover, with him, a woman is always in good company. Unfortunately for him, however, human beings think
that he is an evildoer, and then he at once recognizes that he
is the incarnation of evil. What characterizes the Devil is that
he is not innocent: he knows, and knows that in this reflexive

---

4. F. Pessoa, *L'Heure du Diable*, tr. M. Druais and B. Sesé (Paris: Corti, 1989).

game he can effectively become the incarnation of evil, although he is mostly a good guy (just like analysts are).

Since Freud has not so openly insisted on the question of the subject and of ethics, a certain Freudianism is still socially acceptable, whereas Freud as read by Lacan becomes unbearable, since he puts into question the *jouissance* of the social link in its actual functioning. And we must not forget the fact that every subject (including ourselves) has a tendency to resist psychoanalytic discourse and to prefer the Master's discourse, because, of course, we prefer to love and to be loved.

I would like now to propose a little test that will show how odious psychoanalytic experience can be facing our ideals. We all love Antigone, don't we, this magnificent heroine who braves the laws of the city in the name of higher laws that appear to be placed even higher than our modern humanitarian human rights. But we should ask ourselves a question: Would Antigone have reacted so bravely if she had been in analysis? Would she have acted in the same way knowing that her desire to bury her brother with her own hands was the other side of her desire to kill him, or the result of her ambivalent incestuous love for him? You see then how psychoanalytic discourse can be hated and how there are perhaps good reasons to resist it! And if Antigone had said, "I realize that my passion to bury my brother is as great as my passion to kill him with my own hands, but nevertheless I will not give up on my desire and keep obeying the higher laws"— then this would probably not have made a very good drama.

I will not go much further here, and merely note that we have reached one of the most crucial questions posed by the ethics of psychoanalysis: Does the psychoanalytic cure produce cowards, political cowards unable to care for whatever is happening to the city? I would hurry to answer that the psychoanalytic act, however, fights against the discourse of the Master, and in this way against social or sexual exploitation, even if some analysts ignore that their act is a revolutionary one and not the act of cowards.

You see then in which ways resistance in the cure differs from the resistance in the social link. The resistance that concerns the social knot is a resistance *to* acting, to ethics, and to the subject. It is a resistance against the subject. The resistance in the cure, on the other hand, is a resistance to what disobjectifies him, that is to say, it is a resistance to what would release him from the alienation of his ego. It is a resistance *of* the subject. The very term *resistance* is valid in both cases but does not point to the same thing.

Until now, I have only spoken about structural resistance. If there were nothing but this, one could conclude that we are exactly at the same point as when Freudianism was starting. However, we may have not paid enough attention to accelerated changes in the social link especially these last ten years, and to the new *jouissance* that appears to be at stake there. We may have not paid enough attention to this because we have so far believed with some reason that these resistances were inherent to the structure, that we would always encounter them, and that this would not stop us from developing psychoanalytic discourse. We may think that these resistances as they accumulate would similarly increase the expansion of the psychoanalytic discourse, as they were in some way the inverse of the Master's discourse. We may have believed in the past that though we had powerful enemies, we nevertheless had a good friend, the unconscious itself, and consequently the symptom that it generates, since our best ally in a cure is the symptom itself.

It seems that now we face a new factor, which has to do with the emergence of the discourse of science, especially when it touches upon a very precise point that provokes important modifications in the line of resistance. This is specifically when the discourse of science touches upon the question of sexual reproduction in a new and decisive fashion —with new modes of reproduction and cloning. Today, anybody may think that in order to allow a new human being to be born, what is only required is a spermatozoid and an egg, or even just an egg by itself. And then it seems that all those questions concerning desire, the necessity to love in order to desire, symbolic castration that would be necessary in order to for a child to reach desire, the issue of the *penisneid* and so on, all that sounds suddenly like old stuff completely out of the question, as if now and in the future we had done with all those boring problems posed by relationships between men and women (by which I mean the universal male–female model, which exists similarly and as strongly in hetero- and homosexual relationships).

This is not a point that concerns only psychoanalysis. The main point is that this model of scientific reproduction without desire achieves, from the unconscious point of view, exactly the realization of an "infantile sexual theory." In these theories, children dream that they can have children by oral or anal ways, without any sexual relation. This is why Lacan said in a very Freudian way that "there was no sexual relationship." Scientific dreams have always kept in his perspective the wish of reproduction without sex, following the innocent dream of childhood. And here we have the main point of resistance: with the dream of science, it is actually the victory of children's sexual theories, which corresponds to the triumph of perversion, as the infantile polymorphous perversion. The fact that children are beginning to kill is not a coincidence. Postmodernity is now entering into a childhood dream, and nothing is more difficult to analyze than children, especially when they recognize no parents.

It is thus at the very moment when the discourse of science touches on sexual reproduction that the resistance to psychoanalysis completely changes its mode of operation, insofar as perversion now offers a totally new type of resistance to analysis. With the ideology of science, perversion triumphs three times. First, because there the laws of nature seem stronger than the symbolic law. Read again Spinoza, and you will see that for him—*more geometrico*—there is nothing of good and evil, nothing of ethics, but only what is mathematically correct or incorrect. Second, because science impersonalizes the subject. And third, because when science allows a reproduction without desire it paves the way for the triumph of the perverse polymorphism of childhood.

I will now try to be more specific about what I have called a changes in the nature of resistance to the psychoanalytic discourse. Since there is, as we have seen, something new— of course, from the point of view of the fantasy nothing changes —there is in fact no progress. Nevertheless, the fantasy engenders a certain number of realizations that themselves modify the new possibilities of acting the same fantasies. I wonder, for instance, whether we have given enough attention to what Lyotard, in particular, stated very clearly about the post-modern age. Lyotard defines postmodernism as the end of all the great ideals that had previously guided society— whether they be revolutionary ideas, or even liberal ideas of the progress of humanity. I do not share all his points of view, especially when he declares that all these ideals are now over.

I would rather maintain that these ideals have become unconscious, that they are all brought together under one flag—the ideology of science—that now functions as the current unified ideal of our societies, and becomes a new religion, an ideal that contradicts the law of the unconscious ethics. After all, mathematical laws are in no way concerned with good or evil. In contrast, the unconscious is ethical throughout, since we can know good from evil only because we have an unconscious. The unconscious ushers in repression as the law, the law of incest prohibition, and the prohibition of the murder of the father. Here only we will find the measure of good and evil, and not in nature or in science. This is why perversion has become a new ideal for all neurotics—I am not saying that they are becoming perverse, but I maintain nevertheless that it is this ideal of perversion that seems to them the most practical to obtain *jouissance* (switch on your TV, if you still have one; you can check this out).

Postmodernity marks the end of all ideals in so far as they have a subjective efficiency. As long as humanity has conscious ideals, religious or revolutionary, progressivist or even reactionary ideals, those conscious ideals have a subjective effect. Every subject is required to believe, or not to believe, in those ideals; "to believe" is the free act of a subject. But what will happen if there is nothing more in which to believe, insofar as with science there is nothing in which you have to believe or disbelieve? Science does not require an act of the subject. Science imposes itself *without* needing us to believe in it or not, especially because we do not realize that science involves a new idea—and even a new religion.

All this becomes even clearer if we think of the function of the ideals. They have only one function, namely the repression of unconscious desire. Ideals are necessary to assure repression, and that is what one can find written throughout Freud's texts each time he speaks about religion. The ideals show us unconscious desire itself, but hidden in an inverted form. The most famous example is that of Moses, presented as the father of the Jewish law, even if he has been murdered by the Hebrew tribes. Or, to give another example of an ideal inverting desire, one can refer to the mother of Christ as a Virgin; that is to say that she is a Virgin just as the neurotic wants his mother to be. Or when we speak of God as an Eternal Father, whereas he is the dead father. Thus, insofar as men believe in those ideals, they are still able to repress desire, to keep in their desire unconscious, while following the religious way of repression as something that comes from outside or independently of them. The so-called transcendence of religion is only what humanity does not want to know and this is what psychoanalysis is likely to reveal. The function of ideals in society is to repress unconscious desire. Or, more exactly, it is in the name of some great ideal that you can realize desire, and act as if you were innocent. For example, it is in the name of Christ, or in the name of Marx, or in the name of the laws of the market, that you can kill innocently. It is in the name of good health that you can segregate smokers, in a new trend that is so amusing to observe.

One can easily imagine what will occur in postmodernity when all great ideals have collapsed: it will be directly, that is, without repression, that unconscious desire will try to realize itself. When ideals have collapsed, the subject meets insuperable difficulties in achieving repression, and each time has to put at stake the social link itself as such—since social links, like those of any brotherhood, are built upon a common belief in certain ideals. In this regard, I see no other explanation for the violent resurgence of all type of sects, like religious sects, violent religious fundamentalisms, and integrisms: they have no other role than to try to reestablish ideals. But those new ideals will never be the same as what they were before the emergence of the ideology of science. These ideals are destined to maintain repression despite science; this explains the violence of their expression, a violence that cannot but increase.

And since there is a lack of ideals, psychoanalysis itself will be summoned to play the role of a new ideal, of a worldview, that is to say, the very opposite of what it is. Psychoanalysis will be asked to function as an ideology of postmodernism; one demands of psychoanalysis that it plays the role of a news religion—which is precisely in opposition to what psychoanalysts are daily required to do: to discover those desires that are repressed by ideals.

The death of our great ideals in postmodernity has two related consequences. First, perversion will appear as the best way to reach *jouissance*. For example, in this context, homosexuality will appear as revolutionary or "progressivist," and we will see an extreme confusion between political questions and sexual matters. This creates considerable confusion, because it is one thing to fight against the discrimination of sexual minorities, and quite another to present a sexual choice as a political perspective. After all, one can be homosexual and fascist, and it is quite interesting to notice that this confusion is a good sign of idealization of perversion, despite the fact that perversion is no more funny than neurosis or psychosis. The second consequence is that, when the old ideals are failing, what appears beyond them is just sexual trauma. For example, religion presents the father as dead and castrated; if religion collapses, what can appear beyond the dead father, if it is not the raping father? Therefore we will read more and

more in the headlines stories of sexual traumas and rapes—
thus the enormous contemporary publicity surrounding
issues of childhood sexual trauma, rape, incest, and all the
accompanying legal consequences, including legal issues that
will affect psychoanalysts when they work in institutions.
Indeed, I am astonished when I see that, with all the different
questions concerning pedophilia and incest, we have not seen
more complaints about psychoanalysis in the media until now.

I wish to underline on which points resistances to psychoanalysis have changed. It seems to me that the current
struggle focuses on two points: the scientificity of psychoanalysis, and the question of ethics. There is a strong tendency
to accuse psychoanalysis of having little scientific value. Think
for example of Popper's emphatic disqualification of psychoanalysis as a science. Some analysts themselves are not very
clear on this question. I must remind you that, according to
Lacan, for example in his 1966 Seminar, psychoanalysis deals
only with the "subject of science." Lacan repeated that "the
urgent task at present was to define psychoanalysis as a science." And secondly, this attack against analysis is articulated
to the issue of ethics since science cannot in any way sustain
a code of ethics and is not, as we have seen, concerned with
good and evil, but with accuracy and inaccuracy.

It is from this point of view that one can consider certain books recently published, notably the pamphlet written
by Alan Sokal and Jean Bricmont, *Fashionable Nonsense.*[5] This
book was published in France, but translated from American
articles. It attacks French intellectuals in their writings because they use scientific or mathematical ideas just to look

---

5. A. Sokal and J. Bricmont, *Fashionable Nonsense: Postmodern Intellectuals' Abuse of Science* (New York: Picador, 1998).

brilliant, while proving themselves to be stupid. Sokal and Bricmont notably criticize Lacan for his use of mathematical concepts. Sokal and Bricmont do not see the necessity of importing instruments of knowledge from one field of knowledge to another in order to think and solve completely new problems. However, Bachelard, when he invented the concept of *epistemological break*, could show how the field of a new science is often constituted by the importation or recovery of concepts that are exterior to it. For example, the birth of modern chemistry occurred when the science used a number of concepts it borrowed from alchemy as well as from other sciences, up to the point when chemistry was able to constitute itself as an independent science. In fact, Freud did not just borrow a number of thermodynamic theories in order to define the unconscious and its processes, but one could even say that he has stolen or recovered most of the concepts of classical psychiatry. What is moreover quite funny is that Sokal and Bricmont also do not know that, for example, mathematical physics was constituted by a translation of mathematics into physics. This modern importation, which is only a few centuries old, and which consists in applying mathematical models to matter, thus to physics, is an extension that was never made by the Greeks, Arabs, or Hindus, even if they already possessed perfect mathematical instruments. They would not apply these concepts to the physical world for religious reasons.

Therefore, it is not only at this first level that the critique of Sokal and Bricmont misses Lacan, since there is a second level which escapes them. They do not understand why Lacan uses mathematics or topological models and think these are purely analogical metaphors—which they see as an imposture. They cannot understand that Lacan's "conceptual writing" is a modelization or a mathematical analogy for what is still unknown. Lacan's conceptual writing concerns points in a structure that are outside a discourse, even if they appear to be articulated within this discourse. In order to elaborate these points, we cannot use common signifiers, because signifiers are articulated by them. For example, if we take the concept of *castration*, it remains an incomprehensible psychoanalytic concept in terms of ordinary language. Castration means at once and at the same time the interdiction of *jouissance* by cutting off the genitals and also the condition of desire and of sexual potency! To further clarify the notion, it is better to use a matheme such as ϕ (the symbolic phallus) to write "castration" without confusion.

Conceptual writing is not a metaphor because there is nothing to be metaphorized that would exist prior to it. You can usually produce a metaphor for something that exists independently of it, whereas here this is not the case. Conceptual writing aims at making the invisible visible. In other terms, it concerns a procedure that is, properly speaking, scientific. It aims at rendering visible what is invisible in a specific field—that of the unconscious. It attempts to render what is latent manifest. For example, the Freudian term *penisneid* allows us to see "penis envy," it makes it visible across the desired child, for example, and to subsume all a series of terms (such as, for example, the series linking penis = child = excrement = money).

The question of ethics has become a central problem at the moment when the lines of resistance to psychoanalysis have become displaced. This has occurred precisely because of the ideology of science that levels, that destroys all ideals that form the basis of laws. Where will we find the ground of ethics, if not in the unconscious ground? One could maintain that it is not the business of psychoanalysis to give an ethical point of view on what is happening in society, and that psychoanalysts are only citizens like all the others, who have to submit to common laws, to the common way of life. What I have underline is that what we call "the law" is in no way what we find in the city in the form of ideals or legislation. The law that concerns us is the law of the unconscious, a law that gives to the ethics of psychoanalysis a role that it has not held in the recent past. Psychoanalysis plays the role occupied by religion when religion cannot maintain itself any longer. Of course there is an enormous difference between psychoanalysis and religion, insofar as religion sees the laws as coming from a transcendent power or from God, and analysis refers all the tenets of religion back to corresponding psychical terms. For psychoanalysis, God is unconscious, God is the unconscious. This is where we have to maintain a difficult and important place.

We must thus define an entirely new function for psychoanalysis and present it as a crucial last recourse to ethics. This is the real task we are facing now at the beginning of a new millennium. In a society that hurries to meet with universal and accelerated perversion, there is a new resistance with which we are confronted. I am not saying that perversion is the evil that resists to psychoanalytic discourse. Rather, I am sustaining a position of discourse, in which any ideal and its perversion in our postmodern era can be related to a corresponding psychic fact. This sketches an atheistic program that Lacan, more specifically than Freud, has left to us as providing the very last chance for the subject.

6

Psychoanalysis:
Resistible and Irresistible

PATRICIA GHEROVICI

Richard Rorty opens his review of the English translation of Jacques Bouveresse's *Wittgenstein Reads Freud* with these words: "Suppose that Freud's harshest critics are right. The man himself was a duplicitous, egomaniacal fraud. Psychoanalysts can hardly agree even on what counts as a cure, much less effect one. Freudian ideas have encouraged such abominations as the imprisonment of innocent parents on the basis of 'repressed memories' of abuse, solicited from young children by eager therapists. Should we conclude that there is nothing to be learned from Freud—that we ought, as far as possible, to cleanse our minds and our culture of his ideas?"[1] Why has Freud's name come to embody so many cultural diseases?

The importance of Freud to the history of the twentieth century needs no demonstration. Nevertheless, we should

---

1. R. Rorty (1996). "Sigmund on the couch," *New York Times Book Review*, September 22, p. 42.

welcome the assaults of vindictive detractors and their twisted appreciations of the Freudian "inventions." The critique of psychoanalysis is not without foundation. After a hundred years of history, psychoanalysis is still stirring violent passions. Measuring by the proliferation of critical publications it looks as if Freud's influence today is much greater than decades ago. As criticism of Freud has mounted with virulent ferocity, rather than counterattack or hide in the trenches, we may see Freud-bashing as a sign that psychoanalysis is alive and well and eliciting a controversy that, while being at times ruthless, is however, healthy.

The 1993 cover of *Time*[2] asked with a delay of 54 years, "Is Freud Dead?" Calls to "bury Freud" have proceeded resolutely. Freud actually died in 1939, but his fate seems similar to that of the totemic father: he is more powerful—and feared—dead than alive. Is the death of the father the end of the father or the beginning of his law? Freudian analysts may pay respect to the founder, but they do not truly hold themselves to Freud. The "powers" of psychoanalysis often seem more potent for its critics than for its followers. Today, we can find more than 200 types of officially anti-Freudian therapies in the U.S. involving 10 to 15 million Americans in some kind of talking cure. However, those talking cures that criticize Freudian methods are based ultimately on psychoanalytic principles. Freud has revolutionized the century and has created a new way to look at ourselves and address our problems, yet nobody seems very grateful.

I will avoid the psychoanalytic Catch-22 of considering that opposition to the psychoanalytic method gives evidence of its actual correctness. Classically defined as the obstacle

---

2. *Time* (1993). "Is Freud dead?" November 29.

to the progress of the treatment, "resistance in extension," outside the clinical setting, corresponds to the adverse attitude that the revelations of psychoanalysis awake.[3] The fact that Freud's discoveries are being questioned with such fury testifies, a century after, to the currency of the discoveries of psychoanalysis. This positive sign of resistance to psychoanalysis can change the fate of Freudian psychoanalysis in America where it was transformed into a doctrine too close to a religion, unable to challenge itself and innovate. In the wake of Freud's burial, the best is yet to come. And resistance seems to be the key to this evolution.

In 1984, Rorty already noted that in spite of the overabundance of works devoted to psychoanalysis and the everyday use of Freudian terminology, another few centuries will have to pass to see how useful this new vocabulary is. In the future, will we describe friends and criminals as "neurotic" rather than "wicked" or will patients have to choose between "moral counsel" or an injection, Rorty wondered.[4] Without resistance, the turn of the century is indeed announcing the beginning of the end of analysis. Whether or not we question the scientific status of psychoanalysis, Rorty tells us, we need not give up our common-sense Freudianism. Psychoanalysis, Rorty concludes, merits being part of the lasting monuments of our culture. However, Rorty's identification of Freudianism with quasi-scientific common-sense wisdom is a symptom of the crisis psychoanalysis faces in our contemporary culture. Freud elaborates on resistance at two levels. One

---

3. See J. Laplanche and J. B. Pontalis, *The Language of Psycho-Analysis,* tr. D. N. Smith (London: Hogarth Press, 1973).

4. R. Rorty, "Freud, morality, and hermeneutics," *New Literary History* 12:177–185, 1980.

pertains to the analysand's resistance during the cure, which he approaches both technically and theoretically, offering clues to the analyst in the direction of the treatment. The second conception of resistance is mostly an interpretation of the hostilities that the discoveries of psychoanalysis arouse. Freud argues that the revelations of psychoanalysis inflict a narcissistic wound similar to the one that Copernicus or Darwin produced.

Gérard Pommier's essay in this collection contends that social resistances to psychoanalysis in our culture result from the naturalization of the laws of the market and the *jouissance* of capitalism. Culture resists psychoanalysis by repressing the importance of the social link in the constitution of desire as desire of the Other. This raises issues concerning the capitalist morality of commodity fetishism and the global resistance to an ethics of the subject. Richard Rorty, a philosopher who reflects on Freud and morality and who gladly calls himself the "philosopher of bourgeois liberalism," believes that the revolution announced by Freud, rather than coming to its alleged end, has not yet taken place. Freudianism's great popularity in the first fifty years of this century raises questions: Was it psychoanalysis or rather an adapted and hybridized by-product closer to behaviorism?

In his "History of the analytic movement" (1914)[5] Freud alerts us to the dangers that an enormous interest could produce in the U.S., and he indicates that the fight for psychoanalysis will be decided in a country where the biggest resistance has arisen. Freud highlights France as the least welcoming country in Europe, yet one that paradoxically

---

5. See the volume edited by P. Rieff, S. Freud, *The History of the Psychoanalytic Movement* (New York: Macmillan, 1963).

offered easy access to his doctrine. Already in the 1900s James Putnam was enthusiastically recommending psychoanalysis, while transforming it into a form of Protestantism. He was merely following local conditions that since the nineteenth century produced a situation in which science has replaced and reiterated religion (instead of the worship of God we have the secular and fetishistic worship of science). When the U.S. too readily accepted psychoanalysis, this converted it into a dogmatic ethical and philosophical theory. This construction, however appealing, was far from psychoanalysis. France, on the other hand, resisted, taking much longer to accept Freud's ideas (or even to translate his collected works) but eventually produced a Jacques Lacan.

Psychoanalysis seems to grow stronger where it encounters resistance. But when its primary aim was understood as getting rid of the resistances, the result proved mediocre. The so-called psychoanalysis of resistances used resistances in an attempt to define itself. By focusing on the dissolution of resistances, American psychoanalysis created an optimistic adaptive technique, ego psychology (note that the word *psychoanalysis* has already disappeared). Its reading of Freud's second topic produced a misleading interpretation that stresses defenses and transformed psychoanalysis into an analysis of resistances. Trying to understand "What is it that resists?" the American disciples of Freud crystallized psychoanalysis into an analysis of resistances, where the subject is divided between ego and unconscious, where the drive becomes instinct, sexuality becomes genitality, the phallus a penis, desire simple adaptation, the ego a biological construct, the analyst an ideal, repetition and resistance become defenses, and psychoanalysis consequently becomes a technique of suggestion. The attempt at dissolving resistances also dissolves psychoanalysis.

Psychoanalysis has advanced much more where the most adamant resistance has been encountered—and taken into account rather than simply eliminated—by analysts, by patients, and by the culture at large. Resistance has functioned as a structural requisite to psychoanalysis. This obstacle is not only absolutely necessary, it is propitious.

The concept of resistance precedes that of psychoanalysis. Freud used the term *resistance* before even using the word *psychoanalysis*. In May 1895 he co-authored the *Studies on Hysteria* in which for the first time a definition of *resistance* appears.[6] It is not until 1896 that Freud uses the word *psychoanalysis*,[7] This antecedence of resistance to psychoanalysis leads us to propose that psychoanalysis is created by its resistances.

FROM PATIENTS FALLING ASLEEP TO *THE INTERPRETATION OF DREAMS*

To have a beginning, psychoanalysis needed to be already speaking of resistance. Without resistance there is no psychoanalysis. It is resistance that guides Freud to abandon the tyranny of suggestion, to find psychoanalysis by way of the "cathartic cure." Freud's first treatments of hysteria combined talk therapy and hypnosis. Resistance puts Freud back on track opposing psychoanalysis to hypnosis. He encountered the resistance of the patients who could not fall into a state of

---

6. J. Breuer and S. Freud (1895). Studies on hysteria. *Standard Edition* 2:23, 2:154, 2:268–270.

7. See J. Laplanche and J. B. Pontalis, *The Language of Psycho-Analysis*, p. 351.

somnambulism when he tried to hypnotize them. Freud would command "You are going to sleep! . . . sleep!" to which patients would respond, "But doctor, I'm not asleep." His captious response was "I do not mean ordinary sleep; I mean hypnosis. As you see, you are hypnotized, you can't open your eyes, etc., and in any case, there is no need to go to sleep."[8] Resistance awakes psychoanalysis from its somnambulism, opening the way to the creation of a method that bypasses hypnosis, and is conducted in a state that differs little from a normal one.

Freud took as point of departure the idea that the patient knew something that it was difficult to communicate. He therefore established a solemn commitment: the patient was supposed to say whatever came to mind without criticism and was helped by a light pressure of the hand on his or her forehead. This "small technical artifice" helped to establish transference. This suggestive hand on the forehead found an impediment: a contrary force resisted any access to information that would resolve the trauma. The analysand does not want to know anything of the cause of the illness. This certainty, that rather than "not knowing" the patient "does not want to know" about something repressed, functions as an empty frame. This reinforces transference and allows the analyst to go in a direction opposed to the resistance in order to find the repressed ideas.

It is also resistance that dictates the rules of analytic neutrality. Freud had abandoned hypnoses completely by 1896–1897 and by 1903–1904 he recommends avoiding any physical contact with the patients. Attending to resistance demands an impartial attitude that prevents criticism, gives clues to follow the psychological chain in remembering a

---

8. J. Breuer and S. Freud, Studies on hysteria. *Standard Edition* 2:108.

pathological idea, and helps to discover the secret of neurosis. Resistance uses transference but does not constitute it.[9]

When reading Freud carefully, one sees other functions of resistance: it not only misleads or sets obstacles, it also orients. Resistance is therefore a useful obstacle. In an idea of negative dialectics, resistance appears as the force that maintains the pathological condition but that guides the progression of the cure. Freud poses that the analysand suffers out of ignorance and once this ignorance is overcome it has no other choice but getting cured.[10] Well, as we may all know this is not so simple—there is always a beyond. Not only does the analysand resist the most brilliant interpretations, but the analyst also resists when she cannot overcome what her own complexes and resistances determine.[11] This resistance is clearly represented in the excessive ambition of the *furor sanandi*.

THE RESISTANCE OF THE ANALYST

It is precisely in the analysis of resistances that we find the difference between psychoanalysis and suggestion, Freud establishes.[12] The concepts of transference and countertransference have elicited many discussions and polemics in the

---

9. S. Freud, The dynamics of transference. *Standard Edition* 12:97.

10. S. Freud, Observations on 'wild' psycho-analysis. *Standard Edition* 11:219–230. The task of analysis is to attack resistances that prevent an access to an unconscious knowledge. Freud remarks on the futility of communicating the resistances to the patient or of using pedagogical strategies such as recommending books or attending conferences.

11. S. Freud, The future of an illusion. *Standard Edition* 21:3–58.

12. S. Freud, Further recommendations on the technique of psychoanalysis: Recollection, repetition and working through. *Standard Edition* 145–156.

analytic field. Resistance has not caused so much controversy beside Melanie Klein's claim that resistance can be identi- fied with negative transference—a concept closer to Lacan's conception of resistance—and was part of many of Klein's dissensions with Anna Freud, who interpreted resistance as defense.

Lacan's provocative style is a form of resistance of psy- choanalysis. His system of thought, often perceived as for- biddingly intellectual, his complexity, the inaccessibility of his writings—all that infuriates an American audience—cre- ate on the one hand an obstacle to the transmission of psy- choanalysis but, on the other hand, defy the normalization of media discourse, withstand simplification, resist its trans- formation into a medical subspecialty or a watered down form of psychotherapy.

The problem of resistance is not just a matter of getting rid of it but of finding out why there is resistance. No resis- tance of the analysand can maintain itself without the only resistance that, according to Lacan, is the analyst's.[13] Lacan goes as far as to say that there is only one real resistance, the resistance of the analyst.[14] Analysts resist when they do not understand what they are dealing with. As President Clinton (who was, by the way, the foremost Lacanian president ever), said, "There is not a sexual relationship," even when there may have been intimate physical contact. The belief in this nonexistent rapport is the inertia we call resistance. This calls up echoes of Freud's difficulties with Dora. When an analyst supposes an imaginary completion with an object (Freud's

---

13. J. Lacan, *Seminar II*, tr. S. Tomaselli. (New York: Norton, 1991), p. 13.
14. Ibid., p. 324.

stubborn insistence that Dora was in love with Mr. K.) the analyst resists, interrupting the dialectical process of psychoanalysis.

Patients come to see an analyst thinking that the analyst will know something about why they are suffering. However, this does not mean that the analyst in fact knows, but their supposition of the analyst's knowledge produces the transference that allows the analytic work to start. Transference is an expression of unconscious desires of the analysand within the analytic relationship; it is the foundation of the treatment and the territory through which the cure progresses. Since transference "transfers" the reality of the unconscious to the analytic experience, it needs to be both analyzed and resolved in a successful cure. Transference can become a resistance to the progress of the treatment. When the analysand freely associates and opens up the unconscious, something emerges to block the flow of associations: the analysand may be looking for refuge in the fantasy relation with the object a. If the analyst believes that he or she in fact knows, taking as a fact something that is merely a supposition that allows analytic work to operate, the analysis is doomed. Even when the object of imaginary completude may be psychoanalysis itself, when an analyst believes in a correspondence with an object, she or he resists psychoanalysis.

Can the resistances to psychoanalysis be ultimately that same unique resistance of the analyst? The cultural resistances to psychoanalysis traverse the clinical dimension and they appear in those undergoing psychoanalytic treatment. When Freud told his patients that they were in love with one parent and, as a result, involved in a deadly rivalry with the other, this revelation was not only shocking, it had the effect of an interpretation. Today, when patients come to the office complaining about "an unresolved oedipal complex," this "confession" does not present the specific symptom of a particular patient caught in her subjectivity, history, and particularity but is a universal truth or the application of general knowledge. This in turn becomes a resistance to the uncovering of a specific unconscious meaning. Resistance is a key element in the treatment; it arises when something within the transference has not been articulated. If this block persists, it is because the analyst does not want to hear about something. A better response of the analyst should provide a way to overcome resistance. If the analysand stops analyzing, this, rather than sidetrack the analysis, should be an occasion for the analyst to do something to reestablish the dialectical movement. In the same way that the desire of the analyst sustains psychoanalysis, the only resistance to an unconscious that does not exist outside the analytic setting is the analyst's. In order to work, psychoanalysis needs both transference, which the analyst sustains with her or his desire, and resistance as a useful obstacle.

As we have seen, there is a marked difference between social and individual resistances to psychoanalysis. Whereas within the treatment the resistance can be overcome through interpretation, this device is useless at a societal level. However, both resist the subject of the unconscious. At a clinical level, resistance is both the greatest tool and the greatest enemy of psychoanalysis. Cultural resistances to psychoanalysis are useful obstacles. Left without resistance, psychoanalysis would probably die.

Following Lacan's notion that there is only one resistance, can we say that all resistances, are in fact, counter-resistances of the analyst's? Since Freud writes in the last paragraph of *The Interpretation of Dreams* that desire is indestructible, should therefore the analyst's desire be as indestructible? Lacan qualifies this idea by adding that the analyst's desire is only indefinite in the sense of undefined, meaning that the analyst should never be explicit about a desire that nevertheless remains firm. What is then the responsibility of each analyst: Should he or she sustain psychoanalysis with a desire? An answer would be presumptous, and as Derrida states, resistance remains as the navel (*omphalos*) of psychoanalysis.[15]

Psychoanalysis began with resistance, and psychoanalytic knowledge seems to continue without its being able to assess exactly the function of resistance. Psychoanalysis contains its own resistance: a hole, a scar left by the connection with an intermediate space, like the placenta or any object that belongs to neither baby nor mother. Its destiny is that of any object cause of desire: it must be discarded, lost forever. Resistance is important, since it represents a lost object, an object desired but never attained. It indicates the place of the lack, its necessity and its irreducibility. Resistance causes psychoanalysis. It both threatens and keeps psychoanalysis alive, makes it lacking, inconsistent, makes a hole in it, yet allows it to survive and thrive. In the resistance (hindering) of psychoanalysis lies the resistance (resilience) of psychoanalysis. To the question "What is it that resists?", the recurrent answer is the unconscious, which returns with a vengeance. Or, to play on the German suffixes, the *Wider-stand* (the general image of resistance as butting against something hard) organizes a *Wieder-stand* (literally, a repositioning, a new posture, a dynamic return to a position always more "again" than "against").

---

15. J. Derrida, *Résistances—de la psychanalyse* (Paris: Galilée, 1996).

I will conclude with Freud's own words, words I had the pleasure of hearing in English, thanks to an interview done by the BBC on July 12, 1939. Freud was recorded in his London house: "I started my professional activity as a neurologist trying to bring relief to my neurotic patients. . . . I discovered some important facts about the unconscious . . . the role of instinctual urges and so on. Out of these findings grew a new science, psychoanalysis, a part of psychology, and a new method of treatment of the neuroses. I had to pay heavily for this bit of good luck. People did not believe in my facts and thought my ideas unsavory. Resistance was strong and unrelenting. In the end, I succeeded. . . . But the struggle is not yet over."

7

Lacanian Reception

CATHERINE LIU

The reception of the Lacanian transmission has never gone smoothly; one of the difficulties of his teaching has to do with the problem of how to read or receive his seminars. Can transcripts be read as texts? Should they be read as such? What is at stake in the dissemination and publication of the seminars is not reading at all; it is becoming increasingly evident that readers are being asked to tune into a recording apparatus that has preserved a record of monumental pedagogical performance. Lacan's teaching was a spectacle, and it was in his very theatrical use of language that he made his name and created a scandal. Lacan "live" is what the transcripts want to represent and preserve, and hold in reserve. How does one read Lacan, the spectacle? Unpublished seminars circulate like pirated tapes of live concerts; devoted fans try to circumvent the traditional channels of publishing and distribution. Study groups form in which the recorded word (if not voice) of Lacan can be reanimated by discussion.

How does one "read" a transcript of virtuosic, aphoristic turns of phrase, produced in the heat and the urgency of the moment of improvisation, whether before his overcrowded seminars or in front of microphones and camera? Lacan's prodigious talents of improvisation free up a system of pedagogical associations from the demands of simple communication or transparency. Is it possible to read the transcribed seminars as texts at all, and, if not, then how should we receive them? There is something else to be learned from the record of the performances, something that exceeds a reading, no matter how meticulous, and this something else, this excess, can only be understood if we take into account the historical and technological apparatus that surrounded Lacan's lessons. Lacan is constantly at work, teaching us something about media, mediation, and institutions, but the examination of these lessons have yet to take place in a historiographical manner that has as much to do with an analysis of asset management as it does with theoretical debates.[1]

In the case of Jacques-Alain Miller's interview with Lacan for French television, called Psychoanalysis (the transcript was eventually published under the name of Television),[2] we are presented a Lacanian lesson as "media event." The mode of textual explication or theoretical elaboration seems unable to fully account for the force of Lacanian interventions. Lacan is a medium, establishes himself as such as he tries to clear a space of reassessment outside the official channels of the psy-

----

1. Sherry Turkle's Psychoanalytic Politics: Freud's French Revolution (New York: Basic Books, 1978) provides a sociological study of Lacanianism, and offers one account of Lacanian apostasy and the American reception of his teaching.

2. J. Lacan. Télévision (Paris: Editions du Seuil, 1974).

choanalytic establishment in order to allow us a different relationship to Freud. What his work purports to mediate is nothing less than the distance between Freud and the "here and
now." He takes his lessons on the radio and on television because he is able to exploit the technological media in order to
get his message across the airwaves. Even after his death, he is
productive, as the posthumous seminar industry continues to
produce the official transcripts of his work, transmitted to us
from beyond the grave:

> In nouns such as *telepathy, telephone, telescope,* and *tele-*
> *graph,* the notion of "distance" is preserved only as an ob-
> stacle to be surmounted, either by an intangible "sixth
> sense" (telepathy), or, more frequently, by some sort of
> mechanical device or electronic apparatus (telescope,
> telephone, television).[3]

Lacanian psychoanalytic theory always presented itself as
offering better reception of Freud. If Lacan's theories both
amplified and televised Freudian insights by offering to marry
them to the full force of a non-normative, linguistic, and structural understanding of enjoyment as *jouissance,* Lacan's own
mode of pedagogical transmission allowed him to reach a
wider audience, outside of the range of the orthodox analytic
institutes. His teaching became a televisual network of audi-
tory and visual performances, a record of which exists in the
form of the transcript.

Most of the secondary commentary on the transcript of
Télévision, the interview, offers itself as so many helpful "TV
Guides" who would like to remote-control our mode of re-

---

3. S. Weber, *Massmediauras: Form, Technics, Media* (Stanford: Stanford University Press, 1996), p. 114.

ception. Joan Copjec's brief engagement with the transcript of *Television* reminds us that in it Lacan is offering a parody of his teaching. She then proceeds to demonstrate how film theory has missed the "significance" of Lacan's lessons, arguing quite convincingly for a different reading of desire in psychoanalytic theory than the one promulgated by the most prominent film theorists of the past two decades.[4] About the opening lines of *Television* ("I always tell the truth. . . .") Copjec writes:

> Lacan seems to confirm what we may call our "televisual fear"—that we are perfectly, completely visible to a gaze that observes us from afar (tele meaning both "distant" and, from telos, "complete"). That this proffered image is parodic, however, is almost surely to be missed, so strong are our misperceptions of Lacan.[5]

Copjec focuses on the viewer's tendency to "misperceive" Lacan, and therefore to miss something in Lacanian teaching. The parodic aspect aspect of Lacan's performance is what must be made visible so that we can more clearly see that Lacan is attacking the idea of totalization itself. According to Shoshana Felman, Lacan's incarnation of the televisual medium takes place "less as a statement than a speech act, a performance which enacts at once truth's slippage and the failure of the witness to 'say it all' (to say it whole)."[6] "I always tell the

---

4. J. Copjec, "The orthopsychic subject: film theory and the reception of Lacan." *October* 49:53–71, 1989.

5. Ibid., p. 53.

6. S. Felman. "Lacan's psychoanalysis, or the figure in the screen," *Paragraph* 14 (2):133, 1991.

truth," the opening, speaks in the present-tense temporality of television itself. If Lacan, as Felman asserts, is subverting himself as witness to psychoanalysis in this television interview, he defines one limit of intelligibility, by demanding and defying understanding:

> What can an analyst do, psychoanalytically, on a television programme? In its very terms, the question seems an aporia. What, indeed, can be more contrary to the privacy, the intimacy of psychoanalytic work than the publicity, the ostentatiousness of what is called "show business?" How, in spite of this discrepancy of contexts, can an analyst take a psychoanalytic stance on the television screen?[7]

Felman's rhetorical questions point to the contrast beytween the vulgarity of television and the intimacy of psychoanalytic work. The answer to the first question, "What can an analyst say on TV?" lies for Felman in Lacan's "enigmatic and ironical" performance of self-subversion. Copjec and Felman both offer a clearer picture of Lacan, but the refinement of reception does not really address the question of the medium itself.

For Friedrich Kittler, the difference between Lacanian discourse and the technological medium is less easily resolved as an opposition between private and public, analysis and show biz, fuzzy reception and higher resolution. For Kittler, Lacan was always already being taped and broadcast; he was always speaking to a technically equipped studio audience. Lacan's speech was always ready-made for reproduction.

---

7. Ibid., p. 132.

Lacan names a fully technologized body of psychoanalytic theory, always ready for various forms of mechanical reproduction and media dissemination:

> The master was still speaking, yet only a moment more, and only to say that he was just speaking for a moment.
>
> Needless to say, not to the countless people, women and men, who filled the lecture hall of Saint Anne. They were not even listening; they only wanted to understand (as the master once revealed to the radio microphones of Belgium).
>
> Only tape heads are capable of inscribing into the real a speech that passes over understanding heads, and all of Lacan's seminars were spoken via microphone onto tape. Lowlier hands need then only play it back and listen, in order to be able to create a media link between tape recorder, headphones and typewriter, reporting to the master what he already said. His words, barely spoken, lay before him in typescript, punctually before the beginning of the next seminar.[8]

The tape heads are Lacan's best interlocutors; the addition of visual recording enhances the reproductive accuracy of his teaching. Lacan understood that he has always been on TV, that is, his teaching was ready-made for camera; he demonstrates this understanding by effacing the difference between his televsion audience and the public of his seminars. "For there's no difference between television and the public before

---

8. F. Kittler, "Dracula's legacy," in *Essays: Literature, Media, Information Systems* (Amsterdam: Overseas Publishing Agency, G+B Arts, 1997), p. 50.

whom I've spoken for a long time now, in what is known as my seminar."⁹ Just as the studio audience functions as a metonymical substitute for the broadcast audience of a television taping, his seminar audience stands in for the televisual public that Lacan's word will eventually reach.

His institutional exclusion leaves the charismatic master no choice but to take his teaching to the airwaves; this is why the English translation of the transcript of *Télévision* provides the background documentation of his "excommunication" from the official training institutes. Lacan remains an exception, and we may remember that his analyst, Rudolph Loewenstein, purportedly said, "He is unanalysable."¹⁰ Mary Ann Doane writes that television and televisual information "would seem particularly resistant to analysis."¹¹ There is something about Lacan's teaching that puts him on the side of the medium, rather than the institution. In comparing the televisual medium with photography, Doane writes that as opposed to photography, which deals with pointing to and embalming an image from the past, television's temporal dimension is that of an insistent "presentness." It is a celebration of instantaneousness and its relationship to death is mediated by "the potential trauma and explosiveness of the present. And the ultimate drama of the instantaneous—catastrophe—constitutes the very limit of its discourse."¹²

9. J. Lacan, *Television* (New York: Norton, 1990), p. 7.

10. E. Roudinesco, *Jacques Lacan: Esquisse d'une vie, histoire d'une système de pensée.* (Paris: Fayard, 1993), p. 108.

11. M. Doane. "Information, crisis, catastrophe," in *Logics of Television: Essays in Cultural Criticism*, ed. P. Mellencamp (Bloomington and Indianapolis: Indiana University Press, 1990), pp. 223–224.

12. Ibid., p. 222.

Doane emphasizes the temporal structure of television as producing a medium whose management of information and transmission has to do with its relationship to catastrophe.

The explosiveness of Lacan's performance can be seen in the very drama of his aphoristic declarations, "I always speak the truth. Not the whole truth, because there's no way to say it all. Saying it all is literally impossible: words fail. . . ."[13] The failure of words, the partial nature of truth are announced right away, as the bad news of the day. Felman is right that Lacan is acting as a witness to psychoanalysis, but as a very perverse witness, whose turn towards linguistics is a turn away from hermeneutics. Misunderstanding and nonsense are the source of Lacan's enjoyment of the catastrophe of meaning. Lacan's pedagogical performance almost always takes place as aphoristic pronouncements of the failure of the sexual relation, the failure of meaning, the failure of wholeness, the failure of understanding. Where better to announce this than on television?

Television: A Challenge to the Psychoanalytic Establishment as a publication that tries to situate, both as a media phenomenon and as a historical consequence, Lacan and his colleagues' bitter break with the International Psychoanalytic Association (IPA) and in the form of its French arm, the Société Française de la Psychanalyse (SFP). The dossier of materials bring up a number of important issues having to do with the structure of splits, secessions, conflict, and betrayals on both personal and institutional levels. The IPA's exclusion of Lacan appears as a defensive, bureaucratic move,

---

13. J. Lacan, *Television*, p. 3. Subsequent citations of the transcript of *Television* will appear as T followed by the page number.

designed to preserve a homogeneity in its ranks, and what could be called a reign of mediocrity in its operations; it proves itself unable to tolerate innovation on the level of either theory or technique.[14] Lacan's experimentation with the "short session"[15] was the purported cause of the scandal. In his letter to Ralph Loewenstein, he claims that he was willing to give up the short session in order to maintain his membership in the SFP.[16]

On the one hand, this book (*Television*) provides documentation of some of the struggles within French Freudianism, and functions therefore as an historical document. In Lacan's letter of 1953 to his former analyst, Ralph Loewenstein, explaining to him the coup that was pulled off that banished him from the major French psychoanalytic association, the SFP, Lacan reveals himself to be elegantly submissive and dignified in the manner in which he asks for Loewenstein's support and understanding. In her biography of Lacan,[17] Elisabeth Roudinesco describes Lacan's relationship with Loewenstein as one characterized by an incomplete transference, with the older, more experienced Loewenstein trying to keep down the impetuous, aggressive, brilliant, and arro-

---

14. Anna Freud, still a powerful presence at the time, must have remembered the previous "innovators" in psychoanalytic practice, Jung and Reich most significantly, who went on to recant any kind of adherence to Freudian technique, having found, one in mysticism and the other in orgasm, the grounds for absolute apostasy.

15. At the time of the break, Lacan had been experimenting with analytic sessions of variable length, in which the analyst ended the session when he or she felt it appropriate. See Roudinesco, op. cit., p. 271.

16. See J. Lacan, "Letter to Ralph Loewenstein," in *Television*, pp. 52–70.

17. Roudinesco, op. cit., p. 275.

gant young French doctor. This letter, however, is evidence of an affection between the two, as yet uncolored by Lacan's latter bitterness. According to Roudinesco, Lacan thought Loewenstein was not intelligent enough to be his analyst, but then who possibly could have been?

The free association that failed Lacan on the couch with Loewenstein gave him enough improvisational material to take on the road in the form of the seminar. He is not the first showman to take the detritus of analytic discourse and make something else out of it. Other stars of screen and stage have managed to work their on-the-couch, off-the-cuff material into theatrical monologues; no one else called it a return to Freud. Friedrich Kittler tries to deal with Lacan's technologically wired thinking out loud as an aestheticization of stupidity: "For the first time since man has thought, stupidity is allowed to go on indefinitely."[18] Kittler reminds us that it was the listening public as recording apparatus that both made sense of and encouraged his production of nonsense. The recording apparatus alchemically transforms stupidity into brilliance.

By all accounts, it does seem that the rigid adherence to the fifty-minute session, the protocol for analysts to behave in a blank screen-like manner during all interactions with analysands is a practice that crystallized without Freud's personal endorsement, and only after his death. Freud's own couch-side manner, by many accounts, was any but orthodox, if it is to be judged by his successors' measure. Richard Sterba's account is just one of many that describes Freud's behavior as an analyst as one distinguished by a large degree

---

18. Kittler, op. cit., p. 53.

of flexibility with regard to the constraints that prescribe the analyst's behavior.[19] Freud's status as the founder of and exception to the rule of psychoanalysis is what provides the institutional intolerance of deviation with a paternalistic genealogy that Lacan disrupts or interrupts by making an exception of himself. Lacan understood that IPA's ossification of analytic protocol was something that needed to be challenged, both theoretically and practically. In so doing, he makes an exception of himself by putting the IPA's tolerance of deviation to the test. Uniformity of analytic training was more important than the tolerance of clinical and theoretical speculation and experimentation. One group of French analysts remained in the International Association of Psychoanalysts, dominated as it was for many years by the Central European analysts who were trained either in Germany or Vienna, and the other, smaller group of analysts who decided to work with Lacan, Lagache, and Dolto.

"Who doesn't know that it's with analytic discourse that I've made it big. That makes me a *self-made man*."[20] The IPA did not like the fact that Lacan behaved like a self-made analyst and encouraged the propagation of this idea of self-initiation. The only previous self-made analyst before him was

---

19. "Freud did not hesitate to transcend the so-called classical or orthodox behavior of the analyst as it was prescribed by training institutes. He freely deviated from the straight and narrow path of 'impersonality' and indulged in 'parameters' that would have met with an outcry of indignation by the adherents to a strict and 'sterile' attitude of the analyst, which is supposed to present *the* classical model of the analyst's behavior." R. Sterba, *Reminiscences of a Viennese Psychoanalyst* (Detroit: Wayne State University Press, 1982), p. 123.

20. T, p. 27.

Sigmund Freud himself, whose self-analysis has been fully incorporated as a part of psychoanalytic theory and history. Not only was this new self-made analyst going to continue to make himself big, he was also going to make other analysts, that is, train them according to a theory of self-promotion (this is to be taken in a very literal sense here) that would go against all the teaching and regulations around the training institutes.

According to Roudinesco's biography, Lacan was training too many analysts. At first, Lacan rebelled quietly against the IPA's regulations around the training of analysts by simply taking on too many training analyses. When he was "excommunicated," he theorized his technique openly, and opposed it to the training protocol overseen by the SFP. The training of analysts begins to take place in a radically different way under Lacan's guidance; having been banished by the IPA to an outsider's position, but with enough of a following to establish a school of outside of the IPA's regulatory system, Lacan promulgated and defended his method of initiating analysts:

> I declaim, "No one authorizes the analyst but himself." I
> institute "the pass" in my Ecole, namely the examination
> of what decides an analysand to assert himself as analyst—
> forcing no one through it. It hasn't been heard outside yet,
> I admit, but here inside we've been busy with it, and as
> for my Ecole, I haven't had it that long.[21]

This idea of self-authorized initiation is based on what Lacan understood as the sovereignty of decision in analysis; he minimized external constraints on the training of analysts

---

21. T, p. 29.

in order to refine the concept of initiation. Bureaucratic re-
quirements do not suffice as a rite passage for the analyst in
training. For Lacan, the analysts who have stayed in their "institutes," that is, who have played by the rules of institutional
orthodoxies are

> waiting for a "pass," because they don't want to know any-
> thing about it . . . compensate for it with the formalities
> of rank, an elegant way for them to establish themselves—
> those who demonstrate more cunning in their institu-
> tional relations than in their analytic practices.[22]

In short, these analysts have become bureaucrats and are no
longer even capable of analysis. This is the other aspect of
Lacan's catastrophe: Freudianism has been institutionalized.
The institution has made the training of analysts impossible.
On television, Lacan says that he would like to disturb analysts, through his power of suggestion, by taking them on as
the object of his discourse. There is, however, a limit to the
powers of suggestion:

> There is one situation in which suggestion is powerless:
> when the analyst owes his default to the other, to the
> person who has brought him to the "pass," as I put it, of
> asserting himself as analyst.
>   Happy are those cases in which fictive "passes" pass
> for an incomplete training: they leave room for hope.[23]

Those analysts trained according to the protocols of the IPA,
who have abdicated their sovereignty in favor of the proto-

---

22. T, p. 7.
23. T, p. 4.

cols of analytic initiation, are the ones who are immune to the power of Lacanian discourse; of analysts initiated through the Lacanian pass, they are the ones who give us hope.

The sovereignty of analytic decision is a crucial part of Lacanian practice, and one where the deviation from psychoanalytic orthodoxy is most striking and most disturbing. The decision of the analyst is extended so far as to encompass a new idea about the time constraints in the classical analytic session. In *Television*, he describes the IPA in the following way: "I would say that at present it is a professional insurance plan against analytic discourse. The PIPAAD."[24] By describing the IPA as a pseudo-international, pseudo-analytic organization, Lacan is announcing its catastrophic failure. He offers us an invitation to follow him, to work with him to fill in the blanks of the transcription, as it were, and in doing this labor fall into a kind of analytic free association that does his work for him.

I propose in the following part of this paper that we work for Lacan. For, to expand on the Lacanian practice of self-authorization and analysis, one could cite the Carl Schmitt's theories of sovereignty, decision, and the state. Schmitt tries to generate a theory of jurisprudence and the state from the point of the view of the exception. This is why the notion of sovereignty and the tyrant loom large in his political theology. In Schmitt's analysis of decision in relationship to the law, he emphasizes problems of a purely normative understanding of rights and power, "The decision becomes instantly independent of argumentative substantiation and receives an autonomous value. . . . Looked at normatively, the decision

---

24. T, p. 15.

emanates from nothingness."[25] The decisions of the institutions of psychoanalysis that seek to legislate the limits of orthodoxy in the practice of analysis will also take this form. That the decision is concentrated in the hands of organizations whose actions are formed on elections or votes would not make them, for all that, any less autonomous of maxims and principles of psychoanalytic theory or technique. In fact, there is no substantial psychoanalytic principle that would make Lacan's practice of the short session questionable, but there is an organizational one: the IPA wanted to preserve uniformity in the training of analysts. That the IPA never analyzed its own status as an institution, the nature of its own decisions as such, and its own normative drives would certainly make it intolerant of the one who takes exception by making an exception of himself.

One could say, in support of Lacan's condemnation of the institutions of psychoanalysis, that their power comes from its ability to discipline the exception, to contain the charisma of individuals, and to suppress deviation. Most liberal institutions within the democratic republics are organized in this way, as miniature democratic states, with committees, elections, and consensus-driven decision making that is designed to perpetuate stability, unity, and homogeneity. Integration and assimilation are the goals of such formations; the question of assessment is no longer questioned as judgment is fully institutionalized. As Schmitt describes it, the jurist makes value assessments. "He can construct a unity from everything in which he is interested juristically, provided he remains 'pure.' Unity and purity are easily attained when the

---

25. C. Schmitt, *Political Theology: Four Chapters on the Concept of Sovereignty*, tr. G. Schwab (Cambridge, MA: MIT Press, 1983), pp. 32–33.

basic difficult is emphatically ignored and when, for formal reasons, everything that contradicts the system is excluded as impure."[26]

The break with such an institution is structurally necessary for analysis to take place; so far we can see the logic in Lacan's radicalization of analytic technique. We can supplement his densely evocative language with a theory of decision and analysis that offers a critique of decision, law, and exclusion. We can offer our work of association; Schmitt provides a political background to Lacanian analysis and offers us another means of understanding the question of Maoism here. Maoism, in its most pragmatic form during the Cultural Revolution, was a critique of modernization, bureaucracy, and technocracy; it was also a critique of consensus-driven democratic socialism. Both Schmitt and Lacan share a fascination with Maoist formations of power.

That Lacan understood bureaucratization as an American phenomenon is certainly justified by the post-war reorganization of French higher education that occured as what Kristin Ross has called "a kind of Marshall Plan for intellectuals."[27] Ross's hasty dismissal of Lacan as merely another French structuralist who embraced the denial of the historical event for the time of modernization is a bit flat. She does point out that the ascendancy of structuralism was related to a largely American inspired and American funded attempt to consolidate the power of social sciences by consolidating and restructuring various organizations like the

---

26. Ibid., pp. 20–22.
27. K. Ross, *Fast Cars, Clean Bodies: Decolonization and the Reordering of French Culture* (Cambridge, MA: MIT Press, 1995), p. 186.

Centre d'études sociologiques (CES). The founding of the ENA, the Ecole nationale d'administration, in 1947 guaranteed the modernization of France, a "techno-elite of top civil servants and national administrators."[28] Lacan's reaction against the new bureacracy, and the functionalist ideology upon which it was formed, took place as a critique of the IPA. Lacan was nevertheless calling for a less technical and pragmatic understanding of authority, and refusing to be assimilated as a part of the intellectual "Marshall Plan." This refusal of assimilation or adaptation to what was perceived as a largely American form of institutionalization allowed him to be viciously critical of post-war Freudians. There is a darker side to this resistance that we will have to deal with later.

If the liberal, technocratic, and bureaucratic institution is based on consensus, collectivity, calculability, and conformity, the radical critique of such forms is often dependent on a charismatic master to whom the final decision will devolve. The short session here would again be our concrete example of institutionalized protocols and sovereignty. Lacan gave the power to analyst to decide when the session would end; no longer tied to the fifty-minute session, the analyst is no longer held hostage by a time constraint and his or her analysand's ability to fulfill the fifty-minute protocol. The analyst's decision acts as a radicalized intervention, upping the ante of transference while working through the resistance in the analysand's discourse. The psychoanalytic irregularity of such a situation is also based on the assumption of equivalence: all analysts trained in analytic institutes should offer equiva-

---

28. Ibid., p. 185.

lent analyses and, if we cannot fully control their content, we can regulate their form. The sovereignty of the self-authorizing analyst defies this kind of bureaucratic convention, but localizes the decision in a charismatic master rather than an institutional body. This incarnation of authority very easily becomes a cult of personality. Mao understood how powerful this could be and so did Lacan in their face-offs with their respective enemies.

The charismatic master is the one invited to speak on the airwaves with a broader range of broadcast than that of bureaucratic meeting announcements and memos. Lacan's exclusion provided an opportunity to take his word to a greater crowd; the crowds who attended his seminars have become a part of his legend, but both television and radio interviews offered another kind of opportunity by which the Lacanian transmission could take place. First, he could criticize however cryptically the proponents of what is called ego psychology: Heinz Hartmann's and Rudolph Loewenstein's notions of adaptation and the autonomous ego. Lacan used the televisual medium to perform his own brand of pedagogical excess and performative exclusion by announcing that he did not speak to or for everyone. As in the case of Mao Zedong's thought, aphorisms are collected and transcribed. A reader has no idea whether they were written by master or taken down by a faithful secretary.

Transcription comes out of and leads to transmission. Transcriptions are a form of writing, but the author of such a text is difficult to situate. "Whether one understands oneself to be lifted by inspiration or dashed by melancholia, quietly moved, controlled by muses, or possessed by demons, one has responded to remoter regions of being in that circumstance of nearly transcendental passivity that I am calling 'Dictations.'"[29] Ronell's understanding of taking dictation as a kind of spirit possession casts some light on the relationship between Jacques-Alain Miller and Jacques Lacan. About Miller, Lacan is supposed to have said, "He who reads me understands me." It is obviously not enough just to listen in on the seminar, one must become this reader/transcriber, this mystical scribe, who mythologizes his own relationship with the act of reading, editing, and transcribing. Miller describes what happened when he showed Lacan what he had written in the margins of the text of the transcription, notes as it were, to help guide the reader along:

> In providing them, I attested first of all that the text could be followed, indicating as well, most simply how to read Lacan. For you cannot make anything of it if you try to read it quickly, and besides it can't be done for you end up throwing down the book. You should realize that Lacan is to be read sentence by sentence, that every rhetorical flourish is in fact built upon a structure, and that his playing with language corresponds to lines of reasoning. I showed these marginalia to the doctor one evening in his home in the rue de Lille. For two full hours he poured over them, one by one. When he was through . . . I told him it would be good if he put in a word to distance himself from what was, after all, but my reading, leaving the way open to others. Still standing, he took out his pen again, and without saying a

---

29. A. Ronell, *Dictations: On Haunted Writing* (Lincoln, NE: University of Nebraska Press, 1986), p. xiv.

word, wrote this line: 'He who questions me also knows how to read me.'[30]

Lacan writes out the line so that Miller is in fact forced to "read him"—again. The marginalia show us "how to read Lacan." With Lacan's note, passed to Miller, we the captivated interlocutor can only glimpse at the foundations of a quasi-Biblical and mythic authority that will henceforth be Miller's inheritance; he is the one who understands Lacan because he knows how to "read" him. If Felman has described Lacan's incomprehensibility as a psychoanalytic subversion and a calling into question of witnessing, oath-taking, and communication, what would she make of this declaration, "He who reads me understands me"? What does such a statement do or perform, but seal the authority of the transcriber? For who is the first to "read" Lacan but the one who transcribes his speech?

Those who follow Miller's reading will also understand. Miller will show us the way, because it seems, at least from the dialogue, a possibility of understanding can be found in Miller's marginalia. The care that is demanded in reading "Lacan" is based on the fact that "every rhetorical flourish is built on a structure"; a microscopic exegesis is necessary, but it is not what is given.

The introduction promises that every flourish will bear structural fruit, but it does not produce a reading. The role of Miller as editor, transcriber, and reader of Lacan has not been fully examined; it is a complicated one, and the problem of reading Miller is one that can only be addressed briefly here.

---

30. J.-A. Miller, "Microscopia: an introduction to the reading of television," tr. B. Fink, in J. Lacan, *Television*, pp. xvii–xviii.

If, as Ronell has shown in her analysis of Eckermann's *Conversations with Goethe*, conversations with great men are another mode of taking dictation from them, and accepting the generosity of their tyranny, even from beyond the grave, when the survivor and the inheritor must manage the ongoing transmission of the work. "The supplement of tyranny exerted by the notion of dictation suggests that, even where there is generosity, it is somehow compelled; it is the command performance issued by some unknown force that we can only welcome."[31] The Miller–Lacan couple is one that is based on the tyranny of transcription, the tyranny of a legacy for which one is chosen as the privileged witness.

What is called psychoanalytic teaching is at stake here, as well as the writing of the history of the psychoanalytic movement. It is nowhere more evident than in this collection of texts that Lacan was a master at calling up resistance and ambivalence.[32] Lacan insists more and more vehemently that Freud had established what might be called a nonsemantic theory of both communication in anticipation of Saussure's work in linguistics. Lacan's conjugation of Freudian interpre-

---

31. Ronell, op. cit., p. xiv.

32. My own attempts at following Miller's injunction to read the Lacanian transcriptions did not allow me to access "every rhetorical flourish," but it did lead to a precocious attempt to follow the master's transcribed messages because the message was mediated by a promise that patient reading would bear fruit in the privilege of understanding. The precocity of such patience led to a kind of reading for applications; I used Lacan's transmissions to understand technological media, but the resting point of that understanding was an assumption that Lacanian teaching was the final mediator. In the long run, this patience was merely a deferral of a resistance that was overcome finally by reading of Freud, which is not at all the same thing as picking up Lacan. See my "Telacan: Tiananmen," *Lacanian Ink* 3:19-34, 1991.

tation with the Saussurian signifier proves extremely provocative. Lacan's linguistic reevaluation of psychoanalysis provides a powerful tool for theory and practice, pointing towards an anti-hermeneutic approach[33] whose far-reaching consequences are wrapped up in a psychoanalytic method that promises a radical nonnormativity.

The implicit attack or critique of the institutionalization of ego psychology takes place as an attack on the Americans, that is, the American inheritors of Freud whose stupidity Lacan never failed to find bitterly amusing. As an American transmitter of Lacan, then, one would have to identify with his contempt, and therefore take on the burden, or the pleasures, of a productive masochism. The actual conditions of Lacan's conflict with America lies in his disdain for ego psychology as an adaptive strategy for immigrants. This is what is ignored for the most part by both American and French Lacanians. The ego psychologists for whom Lacan has so much contempt are Central European immigrants to the United States of America. Implied in the following statements is the idea that the stupidity of ego psychology is related to the displacement of Europeans to America. For Lacan, a truly radical, nonadaptive psychoanalysis was only possible for those who stayed home:

> The autonomous ego, the conflict-free sphere proposed as a new Gospel by Mr. Heinz Hartmann to the New York circle is no more than an ideology of a class of immigrants preoccupied with the prestigious values prevailing in cen-

---

33. "The side of meaning, the side we would identify as that of analysis, which pours out a flood of meaning to float the sexual boat. It is striking that this meaning reduces to non-sense: the non-sense of the sexual relation. . . ." T, p. 8.

tral European society when with the diaspora of the war they had to settle in a society in which values sediment according to a scale of *income tax*.[34]

It certainly can be argued that Hartmann's mind-numbingly normative versions of ego autonomy and adaptation were developed by the Central European immigrant as a mode of adaptation to a materialistic culture where the once cherished values of one's country of origin are held in indifference or contempt in favor of a bottom line. Lacan's critique of Hartmann's theories as having an adaptative function appears not only brutal but also inaccurate when one considers the historical fact that there is nothing inherently "American" about the much maligned "American" ego psychology; Hartmann had already given his talk on "*Ich-Psychologie und Anpassungsproblem*"[35] to the Vienna Psychoanalytic Society in 1937. This paper seemed to have provoked some criticism, but was later cited and supported by Anna Freud. Hartmann was arguing for an analysis of spheres of the ego that functioned harmoniously in learning to adapt itself to external reality through the exercise of intelligence, through learning, and through deferral. Hartmann's ego psychology was already preparing the way for its eventual victory on the post-war scene when Anna Freud endorsed an emphasis on the ego's successes rather than its failures. The ego becomes the hero

---

34. J. Lacan, "Responses to students of philosophy concerning the object of psychoanalysis," in *Television*, p. 109.

35. This paper was later translated into English by David Rapaport as "Ego psychology and the problem of adaptation" and published first as a part of *Organization and Pathology of Thought* (New York: Columbia University Press, 1951) and then separately as *Ego Psychology and the Problem of Adaptation* (New York: International Universities Press, 1958).

of the day, regulating conflicts, engineering cease-fires between external conditions and instinctual drives in order to
guarantee peaceful "internal development."[36] It is no surprise
that Hartmann would have no understanding or tolerance of
Lacan's radically dissenting point of view on the psychoanalytic technique and psychoanalytic theory. With Heinz
Hartmann as the President of the IPA at the time of Lacan's
"excommunication," there was no chance of Lacan's gaining
any kind of acceptance from that body. Hartmann was ready
to cooperate with sociology and psychology to establish the
normative categories that would govern the administration
of both mental health and education. In Hartmann's own
words:

> We hope that the study of the conflict-free ego sphere and
> of its functions—and the further exploration of the prob-
> lem of adaptation will open up the no-man's land between
> sociology and psychoanalysis and thus extend the con-
> tribution to the social sciences.[37]

Hartmann's eagerness to come to terms with the social sciences
pays off insofar as the Ford Foundation financed the English
translation of *Ego Psychology and the Problem of Adaptation.*
Kristin Ross reminds us that both the Ford and the Rockefeller
Foundations played crucial roles in the reorganization of the
humanities and the social sciences in post-war France. These
social sciences would seem perfectly compatible with Hartmann's ideas of assessing "total personalities" and their talents. Hartmann suggestion that normal psychology be stud-

---

36. H. Hartmann, *Ego Psychology and the Problem of Adaptation,* p. 11.
37. Ibid., p. 21.

ied in order to understand psychopathology undoes the force of the Freudian intervention. Freud makes what has been marginalized as psychopathology yield insight into normal psychic functioning. He never used the ego to support an idea of normative functions, adaptation, or learning, but in works like "Group Psychology and the Analysis of the Ego" he gives the primal identification and fantasies the final word on precarious ego formations. Hartmann's willingness to make a pact with the winners, the Ford Foundation, the social scientists would of course make him averse to accepting Lacanianism into the fold of orthodox psychoanalysis. Hartmann's work in Vienna was already based on poor readings of Freud and an uncritical attitude towards Anna Freud.

The treacherous stupidity of institutions is perhaps an even more difficult thing to address than the stupidity of Hartmann's ideas. Kittler has pointed out that Lacan's own "stupidity" has to do with the rapt passivity of the recording and transmission apparatus: there is no stopping him. The masterful intervention on any bureaucratic scene has to take place as a violent gesture of pure initiation, creation ex nihilo, but if the force of this gesture is met with no resistance at all, if there is no stupidity, opacity, institutional or otherwise, against which it can exert itself, it must exhaust itself through a degeneration into stupidity. This is perhaps the danger of starting one's own schools, where structural limitations on one's teaching are kept to a minimum; the containment of thought is necessary for the exercise of subversive thinking. This was Nietzsche's lesson, and one as hard to keep in mind as Freud's.

Television serves up a challenge to America. This is evident in Miller's introduction to the collection, entitled "Microscopia." This fictitious dialogue sheds some light on the fantasy of the Franco-American encounter. Miller urges us to read Lacan "sentence by sentence" in his preface to the English translation of *Télévision*. Microscopia: An Introduction to Reading Television" takes place as a fictional dialogue between Miller's French first person singular "I" and a puritanical, charmingly impatient woman, "She," who represents the American reader. A feminine and American resistance to Lacan has been scripted for us. The conversation takes place in New York: the American woman has been given a copy of *Télévision*, which she has read and which she finds infuriating. Her nonreading is the set-up for what transpires between them. "I" must convince her that she has to read Lacan (again). Miller is trying to charm his reader, to compel her to overcome, in this dialogue, a resistance to reading Lacan. The only way to do so, "I" suggests, is "sentence by sentence." For if one does not read sentence by sentence then one really does not read at all. Close reading is perhaps what we are being asked to do here, but a close reading of Miller's own is called for as well. That the dialogue alternates between "I" and "She" points to the missing "You."

The conceit of the encounter between the courtly, experienced French "I" and the naïve, temperamental "She" is staged as an allegory of seduction and misunderstanding, but it also describes a game of "reading together." "I" asks "She" to be patient so that he can teach her a lesson about reading Lacan. They will read together. This conceit is about reading Lacan together, but it also allegorizes the way in which Miller would like to teach us all a lesson (or two). This initiation to Lacan takes place as a seduction, a classic Enlightenment strategy, a reference to Sade's *Philosophy in the Boudoir*, but the fiction of the eighteenth-century-style ingenue whose sexual inexperience and philosophical ignorance will be transformed by her libertine master depends on the temperamental inexperience of the student/victim/object of desire. In "Microscopia," "She" has an eighteenth-century innocence; her impatience and anger make her more charming. She suffers as much from Attention Deficit Disorder as youthful impetuosity, a passionate character, not unbecoming in a clever pupil. She throws the book, *Télévision* to the floor and cries out melodramatically, "Here's your book back!"[38] She is "enraged and horrified" while he compares her with the image of the cover of the book, a reproduction of a fresco painting of a young woman of Pompeii:

> She: Well, I let you vaticinate to your heart's delight, but right-mindedness must nonetheless object to your concept of truth. I call "true" a statement which says what is the case, and "false" one which says what it is not. And I'll stick to my guns.

> I: I don't know if that is what right-mindedness involves, but "what is the case" comes right out of Wittgenstein's *Tractatus.*[39]

Miller sets up scenes like this so that "I" can be playful, learned, and corrective at the same time. Just as "I" compelled "She" to really read Lacan slowly in order to appreciate every word-play, "I" is showing us what the correct American attitude toward reading Lacan might be. About analytic method, "She" exclaims, "So, it certainly is simple: one can say whatever one likes!" "I" replies, "Analytic experience has no other

---

38. Miller, p. xi.
39. Miller, p. xxii.

principle—that's what Freud called free association."[40] After a lesson in the Lacanian theories of the analyst, who is neither ego ideal nor idenficatory object in the analysis, "I" provides some more information on the Lacanian version of psychoanalytic history:

> The fact, if you can believe it, is that "Ego-psychology"— stemming from the work of Anna Freud and Heinz Hartmann—still predominates in America: as a Chicago analyst was telling me yesterday, it has become like wallpaper for American analysts: it's so much in evidence that no one pays attention to it anymore. Ego-psychology so thoroughly deflected Freud's work from its authentic perspective that it is currently suffering the return of what it rejected in the guise of "object relations theory," which is no less partial. Crossing one with the other in varying quantities, as is now done in your country, is no substitute for Lacan's "return to Freud."[41]

"I" got what "She" the real thing, wants: access to Freud. The Chicago analyst plays the role of the native informant. "She" is the one who needs to be informed about her own culture; "I" comes from Paris to New York to tell you what is happening in Chicago. "I" has a trustworthy source there and it must become obvious that Freud's "authentic perspective" has been all but lost to Americans; "She" must be convinced of the fact that the radicalization of psychoanalysis in the hands of Lacanians is also its authentication. It is only through the civilized refinement that "I" has mastered that "She" can be restored to authenticity. The myth that is produced here is

---

40. Miller, p. xxiii.
41. Miller, p. xxxi.

another variation on narratives of Enlightenment: the truth comes to us from France. Americans have no knowledge of their own history or themselves.[42]

There is another association that this encounter brings up, this time with Michel de Certeau's discussion of an etching by Jan Van der Straet, *L'Ecriture conquérante*, representing an explorer, Amerigo Vespucci, meeting an Indian named America. This is how de Certeau describes the etching, and sketches out its importance for his historiographical project:

> Amerigo Vespucci the voyager arrives from the sea. A crusader standing erect, his body in armor, he bears the European weapons of meaning. . . . Before him is the Indian "America," a nude woman reclining in her hammock, an unnamed presence of difference, a body which awakens within a space of exotic fauna and flora. . . . An inaugural scene: after a moment of stupor, on this threshold dotted with colonnades of trees, the conqueror will write the body of the other and trace there his own history. From her he will make a historicized body—a blazon—of his labors and phantasms. She will be "Latin" America . . . what is really initiated here is a colonization of the body by the discourse of power. This is the writing that conquers. It will use the New World as if were a blank, "savage" page on which Western desire will be written.[43]

---

42. If we were to follow Ross's critique of post-war French revisionism, French superiority is based on French innocence of colonialism, racism, and exploitation. French resistance to the American error becomes the message of every import: when French modernity is accepted as being free of all complicity (with the social sciences or a materialistic society), then as Americans we can only agree that it is time to change the wallpaper.

43. M. de Certeau, *The Writing of History*, tr. T. Conley (New York: Columbia University Press, 1988), p. xxv.

The New World has a charmingly Old World flavor in "Micro-scopia," but, unfortunately, psychoanalysis had already arrived on these shores, and it took a form that Lacan found distressingly stupid. "She" was perhaps Miller's Latin America after all: Latin American reception of Miller and Lacan is after all more intense and more enthusiastic than the North American one. In any case, the invitation to reread Lacan comes in the form of Miller's pseudo-seduction. "She" seems convinced by the end of the conversation, which ends with her exclamation after "I" explains that there are no subsitutes for the Lacanian return to Freud, "Lacan! Lacan! Lacan! do something for me now!"[44] This is a sign of her capitulation: from now on, Lacan will be the medium through which her demand will be transmitted, punctuation and all. It will be through the Miller–Lacan couple that our American distance from Freud will be overcome.

It is quite amazing that our charming nonreader "She" had no idea what "free association" is; she certainly did need someone to explain that to her. Even more importantly, she must be informed about the sorry state of affairs in American psychoanalytic institutes. She can be saved because, as de Certeau points out, her body is awakening in the midst of exotically opaque flora and fauna to the desire of the European. The weapons that he wields against her are gentle ones: Old World charm, knowledge of the classics, and access not only to Lacan and Freud but to the American scene itself. Chicago becomes the signifier of the mess that American psychoanalysts have made of Freudianism. Our slumbering American must have not strayed very far from her lush gar-

---

44. Miller, op. cit., p. xxxi.

den and hammock to have missed out on the popularized versions of Freudianism that have shaped American culture and psychology since the end of the war. Stupid as the American Freudians might have been, their influence on American culture has been enormous.[45]

Ego psychology turns out to be another European import, and it is based upon the work of exiled Central European analysts, Jewish and non-Jewish alike, like Anna Freud, Rudolph Loewenstein, Ernst Kris, and Heinz Hartmann, whose attempts at adaptation to the New World no doubt produced symptomatic resistances in their theoretical and clinical work. Their exile from their native cities and countries led them to defend a cultural legacy that was in decline in post-war Europe but, at least in the case of Hartmann, his ego psychology was fully developed in Europe long before he reached these shores. Their readings of Freud tend towards orthodoxy and ossification, and merit thorough criticism. The wholesale dismissal of this body of work, however, as one that is merely wrong or "inauthentic" is based on a refusal to address the question of immigration, exile, and adaptation in the history of psychoanalytic practice after the Second World War. That Lacan lacked a historical perspective on this, being locked in a struggle with institutions like the IPA, is understandable; that we, French and American, continue to ignore the historical conditions of the conflicts and evolution of the psychoanalytic movement is less forgivable, given our more distanced perspective on those events, and the historiographical tools that are available to us.

---

45. The success of the 1999 film *Analyze This* is only one example of cinematic interpretations of the psychoanalytic process.

8

October's *Lacan, or*
In the Beginning Was the Void

STEVEN Z. LEVINE

In reviewing the millennial legacy of Jacques Lacan as it has been transmitted in the United States of America, I have chosen to look in on the Lacanian void, to listen to the Lacanian word, the void of the word, the word of the void, as these fragile phonemes made of nothing but the merest exhalation of air will have flown back and forth from the mouths and into the ears of me and my Eastern European Jewish immigrant forbears as we have struggled during this past century to reconcile in a Gentile land the sacred books of Genesis and, where in Greek it is said, "In the beginning was the Word, and the Word was with God, and the Word was God," while in Hebrew it is written, "In the beginning God created the heaven and the earth. And the earth was without form, and void." In Hebrew the word *void* is rendered *tohu vavohu*, quite like the French phrase *tohu-bohu*, which in the fantasy of my trilingual transference has always helped me imagine that I was speaking in God's unpronounceable tongue while only appearing to mouth poorly the symbols of spoken French. I begin in this abjectly personal way from the bottomless void of my empty word in order to suggest the entangled knots that will not be unknotted in this brief and partial account of my vexed and overdetermined reception of the twenty-odd years of transmission of *October*'s Lacan.

A quarterly journal of Art/Theory/Criticism/Politics as emblazoned on its cover, *October* may still be had at the newsstand at $10.00 a copy. Founded in 1976 by art critic and historian Rosalind Krauss and film critic and historian Annette Michelson (as well as artist and art critic Jeremy Gilbert-Rolfe, who left the magazine after only three issues), the journal is named not after the revolutionary month of October in the new Soviet Russia of 1917, but rather after Eisenstein's film *October* of a decade later, which was to become, by way of deferred action, the Symbolic repetition, remembrance, and working through of the unrepresentable Real trauma of the war and its aftermath. In Eisenstein's film the actor portraying Lenin proclaims the success of the Revolution at the Congress of Soviets, and we are free to imagine without disrespect, I think, either Krauss or Michelson mounting the platform at some future revolutionary tribunal in order to proclaim the emancipation of political and artistic expression from the grip of the moral censor and the greed of the global market. In the service in 1976 of this American bicentennial revolutionary project the editors of *October* prominently conscripted, from among other living and dead European artists and authors, the psychoanalytic texts of Jacques Lacan.

Already in the first issue Rosalind Krauss opens a door to the Lacanian "*vide*" (void) in her article on "Video: The Aesthetics of Narcissism." Focusing on an analogy between the narcissistic projections of the analysand and the self-reflective performances of video artists such as Vito Acconci and Bruce Nauman, Krauss quotes Lacan in characterizing the analytic setting as "an extraordinary void created by the silence of the analyst." "Into this void," she writes, "the patient projects the monologue of his own recitation, which Lacan calls 'the monumental construct of his own narcissism.'" At this moment in the transmission of Lacanian theory just prior to the 1977 and 1978 publication in English of *Ecrits: A Selection* and *The Four Fundamental Concepts of Psycho-Analysis*, Krauss relies on a notion of the analytic project as "one in which the patient disengages from the 'statue' of his reflected self, and through a method of reflexiveness, rediscovers the real time of his own history"[1] Unlike the narcissistic self-infatuation with the mirror-reflection that the feedback loop of video holds out to the artist as its arresting, frozen allure, the self-reflexiveness identified by Krauss with both Lacanian analysis and the modernist practices of artists such as Robert Rauschenberg and Jasper Johns represents a conscious and conscientious discovery of what she calls "the objective conditions" of history and medium in which alone the lived expressiveness of the individual's subjectivity may be fully acknowledged and potentially transformed. At this point in Krauss's work, there is not yet an explicit structural contrast between the static, atemporal Imaginary register of the illusory, alienated *moi*, or ego, and the *je*, or I, that is the mobile Symbolic subject of the chain of signifiers in the unconscious; at this still early date, the existential phenomenology of Merleau-Ponty continues to exercise intellectual authority alongside her principal Lacanian source, Anthony Wilden's 1968 translation of Lacan's famous 1956 essay, "The Function and Field of Speech and Language in Psychoanalysis,"

---

1. *October* 1:57–58, 1976.

with its unfortunately misleading, existentialist-sounding English title, *The Language of the Self*. Although Krauss continues to retain the residually humanistic category of the self in her well-known article, "Notes on the Index: Seventies Art in America," in which Roman Jakobson's so-called "empty" category of the linguistic shifter is introduced, in this article she clearly puts in place the Lacanian opposition between the Imaginary realm of fantasy and the preexistent Symbolic framework of history, convention, and language.[2] This opposition between the self-image in the Imaginary and the self-inscription in the Symbolic is illustrated by Man Ray's famous 1920 photograph of Marcel Duchamp in the guise of his feminine alter ego, Rose Selavy, whose mock-signature sounds out in French the subversive refrain, "Eros, c'est la vie"—Eros is life.

In "Vision in Process,"[3] the Brussels-based critic and aesthetician Birgit Pelzer opens up a view of an intrapsychic Lacanian void that is rather different from Krauss's inital representation of the interpersonal void introduced into the analytic setting by the largely silent dialogical abstinence of the analyst. Referring to the effects upon the viewer of Dan Graham's mirrored video installations of the 1970s as well as to the recent translation in *Ecrits* of "The Mirror Stage as Formative of the Function of the I" of 1949, Pelzer situates the void not between persons but within each individual, now seen as constitutionally split from the multiplicity and fragmentation of its physical and affective embodiment by an externally encountered mirror-image in the illusory unity of which the subject finds an alienating yet also indispensable

---

2. *October* 3:69–70, 1977.
3. *October* 10:105–119, 1979.

identity. "Thus that void is opened," she writes, "in which the labyrinth of desire will grow and rest intact—a desire which is aimless, since its object (the real, or even the drives as irreducible causes of structure) exists precisely at the fantasy's origin and can neither be grasped nor controlled, since it is what grasps and controls."[4] The mysterious name for this lost object-cause of an unattainable since irrecuperable desire is *l'objet petit a* and this empty locus now begins to find its uncanny, unspecularizable place in the pages of the journal along the twisting borders of the Lacanian topology of the Imaginary, Symbolic, and Real orders. For quite some time yet, however, the predominant focus within the magazine will remain fixed upon the Imaginary scenario of the mirror stage, though with the arrival of Joan Copjec as editorial associate a broader Lacanian perspective emerges regarding what she calls in her essay on the films of Marguerite Duras, "The Compulsion to Repeat," "the otherness of body and language each to the other."[5] One name for this otherness will be the void.

The constitutional alienation of the subject in the illusory unity of its external mirror-reflection is repeatedly exemplified in the art reproduced and discussed during the course of the 1980s. In a much-anthologized essay, "The Allegorical Impulse: Toward a Theory of Postmodernism,"[6] the late Craig Owens offers but one of the first of many subsequent readings of the photography of Cindy Sherman as an ethical and political allegory of the social psychology of the mirror stage. Her famous self-representational series of *Untitled Film Stills* is presented as a pointed critique of the "false

---

4. *October* 10:116, 1979.
5. *October* 17:51, 1981.
6. *October* 12:67–86 (1980) and *October* 13:59–80 (1980).

mirror" wherein the generic imagery of Hollywood films and the mass media repeatedly entrap women in a sterile series of "alienating identifications."[7] In "Corpus Delicti," Raoul Ubac's photographic *Portrait in a Mirror* published in the surrealist journal *Minotaure* in 1938 is similarly seen by Rosalind Krauss as "a stunning demonstration of the disarticulation of the self by means of its mirrored double."[8] In "Monet's Series: Repetition, Obsession," I also invoked the dialectic of the mirror stage in reference to the hundreds of paintings of watery reflections by Claude Monet, writing rather cumbersomely of "the narcissistically disenabling, Lacanian recognition that the imaginary posssession of one's private vision of the world depends upon the prior existence of a symbolic system whose repetitions and reflections one must be taught to know."[9] At this time I as yet seem to have known little more than nothing of the Real.

It was at this juncture, with the arrival of the fresh Slovenian-Parisian voice of Slavoj Žižek in the pages of *October*, that the predominant focus began to shift more and more away from the Imaginary and Symbolic vicissitudes of the subject's alienations and identifications as exemplified in installations, video, photography, and painting toward a largely new attention to the texts and films of popular culture in their registration of the traumatic irruption into everyday reality of what we stammeringly term the Real. Joined in many respects by Joan Copjec's insistence on the role of Lacanian theory as a powerful tool in political as well as aesthetic analysis (see her introductory remarks in the special

---

7. *October* 13:78–79, 1980.
8. *October* 33:55, 1985.
9. *October* 37:66, 1986.

issue she edited, "Jacques Lacan: Television,"[10] Žižek's first article for *October* inaugurated his self-appointed radical mission of telling us everything we always wanted to know about Lacan by way of the films of Alfred Hitchcock. If in *Vertigo* (1958) we are asked to see the Imaginary recreation of the lost woman in Kim Novak's uncanny transformation from Judy to Madeleine at the hands of the narcissistic hero played by James Stewart; and if in *North by Northwest* (1959) we are asked to hear the Symbolic substitution of the fictitious name of George Kaplan for that of the neurotic Roger Thornhill played by Cary Grant; then in *Psycho* (1960) we are asked to absorb the bludgeoning return of the Real in the form of the psychotically introjected murdered mother of the killer Norman Bates, played by Anthony Perkins. Slaughtered in the shower where she had figured in the murderous Imaginary scenario of Bates, Marion Crane, as played by Janet Leigh, falls out of the Symbolic narrative of her own life into the Real of the slashed body-in-pieces where her open, sightless, lifeless eye comes finally to incarnate the glassy opacity of the inhuman gaze that fails to reciprocate any human look. As Žižek suggests in "Hitchcock," "it is very tempting to regard these three key Hitchcock films as the articulation of three different versions of filling the gap in the Other," the gap that is otherwise known as the void.[11]

The void of the subject is reopened once again in "Recourse to the Letter," Birgit Pelzer's presentation of the work of Marcel Broodthaers, the deceased Belgian artist who quotes from Lacan's *Ecrits* in his notes and whose challenging work of verbal and pictorial negation "marks out the subject's fate

---

10. *October*, 40:51–54, 1987.
11. *October* 38:104, 1986.

to be an exclusion internal to itself, subsisting in the operation of effacement per se."[12] This blot or stain is the void or
nothing that masks the Real, which Lacan exemplifies in Seminar XI of 1964, published as *The Four Fundamental Concepts
of Psycho-Analysis* (1973; trans. 1978), in the frontally uni-
dentifiable anamorphic object at the bottom of Hans Holbein's famous double portrait, *The French Ambassadors* (National Gallery, London 1533). Looking at this part of the
picture from a very sharp angle from the side, or "Looking
Awry," as Žižek entitles the essay on film and pornography in
which he reproduces the painting,[13] we see "a demented blot—
the skull, the fantasmatic, inert object as the 'impossible'
equivalent of the subject."[14] In "Death in America," Hal Fos-
ter quotes the assistant of Andy Warhol to the effect that "to
paint a skull is to do 'the portrait of everybody in the world.'"[15]

Cézanne, who in a youthful poem once rhymed his
name with *crâne,* also thought the skull a fine object to paint.
As for the subject that is the strict correlate of the skull, its
"desire 'takes off,'" Žižek writes, when 'something' (its object-cause) embodies, gives positive existence to its 'nothing,' to its void." And this nothingness or void that is the
subject of the signifier is the counterpart of the nothingness
or void of linguistic reference: "Such is the effect of the symbolic order on the visible. The emergence of language opens
up a hole in reality, and this hole shifts the axis of our look;
language redoubles 'reality' into itself and the void of the
Thing that can be filled out by an anamorphic gaze from

---

12. *October* 42:181, 1987.
13. *October* 50:3–31, 1989.
14. *October* 38:110, 1986.
15. *October* 75:51, 1996.

aside."[16] By contrast with Holbein's discretely skewed staging of the subject's severed skull, *The Scream* by Edvard Munch (National Gallery, Oslo 1893) presents Žižek with a full frontal face-off with the void in his contribution to a crucial special issue of the journal edited by Parveen Adams in 1991 and entitled "Rendering the Real."[17]

Here then is Žižek, valiantly and vainly attempting to make several passes at encircling the void in the hopes of getting close, but not too dangerously close, to the horrible Thing-in-itself, *la chose freudienne, das Kantische Ding*. First Žižek asks us not to mourn what may seem to be the irreducible avatar of our very own death: "For the 'eclipse' of the subject before the Thing," he writes, ". . . is strictly equal to his emergence, since the 'subject' is precisely the void that remains after all substantial content is taken away." "In Kantian terms," he continues, "because of the inaccessibility of the Thing-in-itself, there always remains a gaping hole in constituted phenomenal reality; reality is never 'all,' its circle is never closed, and the void of the inaccessible Thing is filled out with phantasmagorias through which the transphenomenal Thing enters the stage of phenomenal presence." In Žižek's lexicon, the Kantian Thing is always followed more or less closely by its Hegelian counterpart, for "Hegel radicalized Kant by conceiving the void of the Thing (its inaccessibility) as equivalent to the very negativity that defines the subject; the place where phantasmagorical monsters emerge is thus identified with the void of the pure self." And it is from within the void of my own monstrous self that I thus confront, and silently voice, Munch's voiceless *The Scream*, or so Žižek says: "One

---

16. *October* 50:34–35, 1989.
17. *October* 58:44, 1991.

can say," he writes of the painting, "that the standard modernist reading that conceives it as the manifestation of a monadic subject, desperate at his inability to establish contact with the world, condemned to a solipsistic void—all this falls short insofar as it continues to conceive the subject as substance, as a positive entity whose adequate expression is hindered." (This, incidentally, is the modernist-existentialist position from which Krauss fifteen years earlier had first opened the door to the Lacanian void.) From within the horizon of postmodemism, then, Žižek concludes with one of his oft-repeated signature-locutions, namely, that 'in its most radical dimension, the 'subject' is *nothing but* this dreaded 'void'—in *horror vacui*, the subject simply fears himself, his constitutive void."[18] The title of the article from which these quotations have been purloined is "Grimaces of the Real, or When the Phallus Appears," the reason for which appearance is that along with the void, the voice, and the gaze, identified by Lacan in his 1959 discussion of *Hamlet* as the four object-causes of desire, the Imaginary Phallus of fraudulently permanent erection is in fact the spitting image of the smeared and severed anamorphic distention that Munch has embodied for us not only in *The Scream* but also in *Madonna*, his blasphemous, sperm-bespattered, and alien-looking fetus-accompanied hand-colored lithograph of 1895 (pp. 52–53).

From Žižek's discussion of Munch's anxiously inaudible *The Scream* we need read ahead only some forty pages to encounter the scream once again, unhindered and fully voiced this time in Žižek's chance encounter at the home of Parveen Adams with a traumatically phallic and anti-phallic Thing. In the anecdotal narration of Adams's "The Art of Analy-

---

18. *October* 58:64–67, 1991.

sis,"[19] this potently castrated Thing unexpectedly confronts the unwary Žižek in the form of Mary Kelly's menacingly red X-ed laminated photographic print of a crumpled and knotted woman's black leather jacket. An isolated component of *Corpus*, the first of the four sections of Kelly's 1984–1985 installation of the between times of a woman's life called *Interim*, this disjunctive object takes its title of *Menace* from one of Jean-Martin Charcot's notorious nineteenth-century photographs of female hysterics at the Parisian psychiatric hospital, the Salpêtrière. According to Adams, "at the limit of the analyst's speech there is silence, while at the limit of this artist's images there is emptiness" (pp. 93–94), the subjectifying abyss of the Lacanian void. Caravaggio's decapitated *Head of Medusa* of around 1598 (Uffizi Gallery, Florence) gives timeless echo to the silent scream that soundlessly reverberates in the Lacanian void. In "Voice Devoured," the Russian film theorist Mikhail Yampolsky describes this severed and strangled part object as follows: "Object a is something inexpressible, not inscribable into the structure but defining it; it is a part of the body, torn from it and creating a void, a hiatus, around which the unconscious is formed. . . . Lacan describes desire as a kind of arc that goes out into space from the place in the body where the hiatus of the void is located, then circles around object a and returns to the body. The spatial model of Lacan shows that desire is formed precisely along the edges of the cavity that marks the void—the lack—and is directed around object—as something drawn into this void, or hiatus."[20] "This object," Yampolsky quotes from *The Four Fundamental Concepts of Psycho-Analysis*, "is in fact simply the

---

19. *October* 58:81–96, 1991.
20. *October* 64:74–75, 1993.

presence of a hollow, a void, which can be occupied, Freud tells us, by any object, and whose agency we know only in the form of the lost object, the *petit a*." "The sound emerging from the mouth forms a void, a lack," indeed just as my words of void, my voided words are doing now as you voicelessly mouth them after me, and it is this mortifying yet vivifying void of signification "that introduces a split in the subject."[21] This void is both a wounding and a winding, and "when one approaches this central void which is most interior to the subject and which we call *jouissance*," as Lacan writes in Seminar VII, *The Ethics of Psychoanalysis* of 1959, "'the body tears itself to bits." The quotation here is from François Rouan's essay-memoir, "Circling around a Void."[22]

A Parisian painter who frequently met with Lacan and whose art Lacan owned, Rouan quotes Lacan's views on the void and makes his words his own. "Art finds its necessity," he writes, "when it reaches this capacity to construct a central void that, by means of its very invisibility, manages to indicate the blind spot that is at the center of our thirst for beauty." From beauty to *jouissance*, "where the circulation of the soul between life and death leaves its mark" (p. 88); as an example of this evacuated mark of self-abnegation the painter invokes the ocular passage through the peephole of Marcel Duchamp's testamentary work on which the (anti-) artist labored in secret during the two decades before his death from 1946 to 1966. Entitled *Given: 1. The Waterfall. 2. The Illuminatiny Gas* (Philadelphia Museum of Art), this is what you will see if you would dare to look through the

---

21. *October* 64:75, 1993.
22. *October* no. 65:80, 1993.

hole: "A large part of a female figure, a single arm holding the little lamp, the legs cut off at the knees, the opening of the spread pudenda, hair shaved off leaving only traces, and a fall of curls. Silence: here it's a question of small holes" (p. 86). Unlike Rouan, Lacan need not have availed himself of this Duchampian void for he already owned its scandalous prototype by Gustave Courbet, *The Origin of the World* of 1866 (Musée d'Orsay, Paris). Lacan *en face du con*, the cunt from which he came, in which he came, but to which he can't return. Not even Kant can, whether *avec* Sade or not.

When the feminist art historian Linda Nochlin theatrically appropriated this forbidden word in her College Art Association lecture on Courbet's painting published as "The Origin without an Original,"[23] I understood that while she could use the word I perhaps should not, and indeed we are all familiar with the outrage of many feminist academics, analysts, and analysands who have angrily thrown off the allegedly phallocratic tutelage of the Lacanian yoke. With the recent return to prominence of Melanie Klein as a feminist point of psychoanalytic reference a renewed anti-Lacanian backlash has begun to set in, as in the "Feminist Issues" special issue of 1995, in which the artist Carole Schneemann, who came to notoriety with her nude performances in the 1970s, tells how she now must go to what she calls "Vulva's School" where, with the aid of St. Augustine, Marx, Freud, Lacan, and others, she "discovers she is only a sign, a signification of the void, of absence, of what is not male . . . (she is given a pen for taking notes . . .)."[24] I will not taint her anger with further words of my own.

---

23. *October* 37:77, 1986.
24. *October* 71:41, 1995.

But in one of the latest issues of the journal an emancipatory claim for the Lacanian void continues to be voiced. Coming full circle, back to where Rosalind Krauss had inaugurated the critical journey in the journal's first issue, Parveen Adams now returns us to the work of "Bruce Nauman and the Object of Anxiety," in whose evacuated installation spaces, she writes, "he frees me from the prison where there is less space than I need—in order that I can be."[25] "*Wo Es war soll Ich werden*": where It was, the uncanny object a of the subjectifying void, there—as in the empty, as yet unended stream of my phonemes and pixels here—there I must come to be. And so from Now-Man's timeless video alienation in the Imaginary, to New-Man's accession to the plural places of Symbolic encryption, we finally arrive at No-Man's funereal wreath of burning neon words stamping out the inexorable rites and times of *Life, Death, Love, Hate, Pleasure, Pain* (1979), little letters bravely flickering around a black hole in the Real, one of whose myriad names is the Lacanian void.

---

25. *October* 83:113, 1998.

9

Lacan's New Gospel

MICHEL TORT

Will the turn of the century have meant the end of psychoanalysis? Is it true that we associate psychoanalysis with millenial anguish? Is the year 2000 another year 1000? A doomsday, a day of judgment before its time? At last, psychoanalysis will be unmasked! Yes, there is a sense of apocalypse, of finality. But who is dreaming of the end of psychoanalysis, an end that has been announced so regularly for so many years? Perhaps it is psychoanalysts themselves, if they don't pay attention to the seduction of the Last Judgment, from which they hope to extract themselves painlessly, as from the hell Woody Allen depicts in *Deconstructing Harry*. In this context, Lacan's heritage presents itself as a way of circumnavigating the sensitive cape of the twenty-first century. Yet, the question psychoanalysts face is not just a question of survival. It is a question of knowing under what conditions they will exercise their profession, how they will think and transmit their limited experience.

What indeed is it that we have inherited from Lacan? For one it is his particular way of transmitting psychoanalysis, a rather special transmission process that frequently leads to virulent dissent. Secondly, we have inherited the psychoanalytic theory that he attempted to construct. Finally, and perhaps most importantly, we have inherited what we are not aware of, because he was not aware of it either. It is this latter, darker part of his heritage that I want to focus on here. We can have access to a number of excellent introductions presenting Lacan's psychoanalytic doctrine and even his anti-philosophy. Each of us, however, has been confronted with the extreme difficulty of examining Lacan's constructions, of reading him, in the same way as we have had the freedom to read Freud as psychoanalysts, thanks to him and to many others. The question I pose myself here is this: What did Lacan himself inherit and transmit with regard to the complex question of the Father? It is a decisive question indeed, and for several reasons: first, the question of "What is a Father?" is, according to Lacan himself, at the center of his work. Second, this question is also at the core of the divisions that have split the Lacanian movement. Finally, more recently, this question has become the stomping ground of very divergent interpretations by those who claim to be "institutional" Lacanians. Very schematically and almost as a caricature, I would say, this question can be read in two opposite ways: either one believes that it is possible to find a way of confirming the idea that Lacan introduced the Father for "scientific considerations" (this is, for example, the argument put forward by Guy Le Gaufey[1]; or one emphasizes the positive elements that Lacan contributed to psychoanalysis through his flirtations

---

1. G. Le Gaufey, *L'éviction de l'Origine* (Paris: EPEL, 1994). Le Gaufey postulates an epistemological break between Freud and Lacan on the central issue of the Father.

with theology, particularly Christianity. As will become clear, I hope, my own view diverges from both of these perspectives. I claim that the Lacanian Father is not merely a question, but also a *solution*. It is a solution, *the* paternal solution that Western culture invented a long time ago. It is to Freudian psychoanalysis's immense credit to have produced an interpretation of this paternal solution. To this, our Lacanian heritage contributes yet another problem: the transmittance and modification of this paternal solution.

The Lacanian problematic of the father did not arise out of new questions about the psychoanalytic clinic. It already appeared in an article on the family published in 1938. Let me cite a well-known passage: "Our experience leads us to designate the personality of the father as the main source of major contemporary neurosis. It is the father who is always lacking in one form or another, is humiliated, divided or prosthetic. Quite a number of psychological effects seem to us to derive from the social decline of the paternal imago . . . perhaps the emergence of psychoanalysis itself should be attributed to this crisis."[2] In general, one can easily distinguish between a later theorization of the father and subsequent anthropological and historical considerations about the nature of the father. Such a position, however, seems unacceptable to me. It more or less marks the parameters of what needs to be referred to as Lacan's "question of the father," that is, what I like to call his "paternal solution." How can we characterize this perspective? It establishes a historical relationship between the "major contemporary neurosis" and the degra-

---

2. J. Lacan, "La famille," in *Encyclopédie Française* 1938, 8–40:3–16. Republished as *Les Complexes familiaux dans la formation de l'invidu* (Paris: Navarin, 1984).

dation of the personality of the father. In other words, it presents itself as a general *etiology* of neurosis. Seen from this perspective, what we have is in no way a Freudian construction. One would look in vain in *Civilization and Its Discontents* or in *The Future of an Illusion* to find a conceptualization of this form.

Such an etiologic representation was completely banal at the end of the 1930s, but it continues to find favor to this day. To a certain extent, we can see it developed in the work of Pierre Legendre,[3] who provided Lacan with his judicial-historical double. It is also present in a large number of sociological and anthropological writings that reformulated the question of the father. Yet one notes a strange phenomenon. If, from the 1940s to this day, the father and his inadequacies have been considered successively under the rubrics of role, image, and finally—in Lacan's theory—*function*, the basic problem still remains the same. It involves the various psychological or psychoanalytical categories of inadequacy, dysfunctionality, and causality of paternal etiology, and thus, the paternal solution: How would it be possible to repair this damaged relationship with the father?

A second remark is necessary: as Françoise Hurstel, a psychoanalytic historian of psychology, notes: "Those who showed the most interest in the father's "role" were neither psychoanalysts, psychiatrists or psychologists. . . . They were the Catholics, and particularly the Catholic clergy at the most conservative fringes of the Church. . . . The father is the privileged focus of attention of the clergy, due to his authority

---

3. P. Legendre, *L'Amour du Censeur, essai sur l'ordre dogmatique* (Paris: Seuil, 1974) and *Dieu au Miroir: Etude sur l'institution des images* (Paris: Fayard, 1994).

within the family, an authority founded on the control that is God's wish. If the father fails to assume his role, then the wife endures the well-known disempowerment (*"démission"*) of the father. The themes leave no doubt about the nature of the enterprise: love and authority; conjugal submission of the woman, etc."[4] In brief, the ideological slogan is evident and should be kept in mind in the following discussion. This is how a Catholic from Lyon phrased it in 1942: "God is the model to which every father should refer: the name of the Father is no longer for us merely that of a man, it is above all the name by which Jesus taught us to refer to the omnipotence of God."[5] The theme of the decline of the paternal imago and its reestablishment by making use of the call for order is therefore a Catholic one. It is a Christian representation, particularly strongly expressed during the Vichy period and it is at the basis of the psychiatro-psychological etiology of contemporary disorders. Lacan must be read in front of this backdrop.

Clearly, the formula Lacan developed of the paternal function between 1938 and 1957 attempts to define the function of the father in psychoanalytic terms that claim to distinguish it from its ideological context. Yet, as I will attempt to show, it is far from certain that they make a clean break with their origins. In rereading Lacan's text, it is my intention to bring to light the underlying consistencies of this viewpoint, its major articulations and even its signifiers. In general, the intent to present a logic of the development of Lacanian

---

4. F. Hurstel, *La Déchirure Paternelle* (Paris: Presses Universitaires de France, 1996), pp. 22–24.

5. J. Hours, "Du Père, Spiritualité de la famille." In *Rencontres* (Paris: Editions du Cerf, 1942), 8:52–56.

theory consistent with its explicit objective has resulted in eliminating the real terms in which it is formulated.

What remains is a rapprochement of Lacan's anthropological perspective, the consideration of the clinic, and Freudian theory. We find many explicit indicators of this convergence. In a 1949 discussion, Lacan declares: "The maternal imago is more castrating than the paternal imago. At the end of each of my analyses I have found the fantasy of dismembering the myth of Osiris. It is when the father is lacking in one way or another (deceased, absent, even blind) that the most serious neuroses are produced."[6] The Seminar on Transference (VIII) is devoted in part to the Claudelian trilogy that culminates with *The Humiliated Father*, a title already hinted at in 1938. The following year, in the Seminar on Identification (Session 16), this theme reemerges as the evocation of the small boy "who is requested to follow Daddy's principles, and, as we all know, Daddy, for some time, has had no principles. It is with this reality that all misfortune starts." One could continue to add further references along the same lines. But we need to go further. In fact, it is the theoretical reformulation of the Oedipus complex as a whole that originates in religious representations of the paternal solution.

Lacan's reanalysis of the Oedipus complex starts with his 1938 text, where it presents itself in a very "culturalist" mode. In later years, that is, between 1951 and 1953, such references to anthropology are modified, giving way to a "criticism of the whole schema of the Oedipus complex"[7] marking a new stage

---

6. J. Lacan, "Discussion," in *Revue Française de Psychanalyse*, 1949, p. 317.

7. J. Lacan, *Le mythe individuel du névrosé, ou Poésie et Vérité dans la Névrose*, Centre de Documentation Universitaire (CDU) 1953, p. 33.

of creating the Lacanian Father. In the "Individual Myth of the Neurotic," Lacan writes that "all of analytical theory is constrained by the distance that separates the fundamental conflict, which, in turn, through the mediation of the father, ties the subject to an essential symbolic value. . . . The analyst who takes his place, almost secretly, in this symbolic relation with the subject, this person who has been significantly reduced by our historical decline, is in sum the master, the moral master, the master who initiates these dimensions of fundamental human relations; the other who is ignorant, in a process which can be considered, in a certain sense, to be a means of accessing consciousness, even wisdom by taking possession of the human condition as such."[8] John Forrester's comments on this passage are well taken: "This rapprochement occurs with regards to the real degradation of the actual father; the analysis occurs and evolves in the space, the void, the ambiguity that exists between the degraded figure and that other figure of the father."[9] Meanwhile, the distinction between the *symbolic* and the *imaginary* involves the beginnings of a reformulation of the question of the father. It is not enough to propose—as Guy Le Gaufey has argued—this to be a matter of the disappearance of history as major referent.[10] First, it remains to be proven that the Freudian reference to prehistory coincides with what one could expect to call a "real historical perspective." Second, just as Lacan distinguished between the (Freudian) Oedipus and the symbolic function

---

8. Ibid.

9. J. Forrester, "La dette de l'homme aux rats" in *Etudes Freudiennes*, 33:104 1992.

10. G. Le Gaufey, *L'éviction de l'Origine* (Paris: EPEL, 1994), pp. 148–149.

sustained by the father, he explicitly retained an anthropological perspective.

Simultaneously providing a structural rationale for the
distinction between the symbolic father and the real father,
Lacan writes: "It is clear that the overlapping of the symbolic
and the real is completely elusive and that at least in a social
structure such as ours, the father is always, in one way or
another, a father in conflict with his function, an inadequate
father, a humiliated father, to use the words of Paul Claudel.
There is always a clear dissonance between what the subject
perceives at the level of the real and this symbolic function."[11]
What can we conclude from this? Does it suffice to say that
the beginnings of a *constructed* father will take the place of
the Freudian father, which has already been *provided?* Certainly
we bear witness to a closing of the circle of the paternal metaphor. But we still need to demonstrate how this really relates
to Lacan's point of departure. I believe it is this construction
that transposes the anthropological-religious schema into a
relationship between the symbolic father and his associates on
the one hand, and the symbolic operation itself on the other.
Before developing an ad hoc formulation of what I will call the
Lacanian Oedipus Complex (in Seminars IV and V), Lacan first
needed to transpose the schema into the symbolic operation
in a general way—this is the object of Seminar II. Then he had
to reduce the symbolic echoes of the Christian Father ("in
whose name" the Father can be posited). This eventually became one of the goals of Seminar III.

In fact, Seminar II is already characterized by a spectacu-
lar effort to construct the Symbolic as such. As we know, Lacan

---

11. J. Lacan, *Le mythe individuel du névrosé,* as quoted in *Ornicar?*
1979, 17–18:305.

achieved this when he theoretically overcame the various objections from an audience—consisting of psychoanalysts and others—who had challenged his arguments. They had attempted to blunt the cutting edge of the supremacy and the autonomy of the Symbolic as such. This is why Lacan's insistence on the transcendence of the Symbolic is so striking to those readers who actually listened to the Seminars. One of them particularly recalls an indirect exhortation addressed to Claude Lévi-Strauss not to be afraid and not to lose ground or abandon the sharp polarization that he had introduced between nature and symbolic systems. The reasons given for Lévi-Strauss's alleged "retreat" are instructive:

> Lévi-Strauss is in the midst of abandoning the very sharp bi-partition between nature and symbol which he had established. For reasons which may seem surprising to you, but which he has made quite explicit—he wavers. He is afraid that the autonomy of the symbolic register will once again give rise to a masked transcendentalism, for which—given his affinities and personal sensibilities—he feels only fear and aversion. He does not want the symbol, even in the extraordinarily purified form in which we present it, to constitute a re-emergence of God behind the mask.[12]

In several of her writings, Monique Schneider has analyzed the neo-Platonic drift one finds in many parts of Seminar II (as well as in other texts).[13] Her readings open up the

---

12. J. Lacan, *Seminar II, The Ego in Freud's Theory and in the Technique of Psychoanalysis* (1954–1955) tr. S. Tomaselli and J. Forrester (New York: Norton, 1998), p. 35.

13. M. Schneider, "L'ordre symbolique, la dévoration et l'infanticide," in *La Parole et l'Inceste* (Paris: Fayard, 1990), and "Transcendance du symbolique," in *Retour à Lacan?* (Paris: Fayard, 1981), pp. 217–224.

scene of the apotheosis of the symbolic with the sacrificial cut it implies—an operation that is, to a large extent, coextensive with the Greek *logos*. This theme is taken up again by Christianity, which creates the scene of the Father who acts as separator, eliminating the maternal illusions. Psychoanalysis prolongs this historical struggle of the paternal principle "demystifying the fundamental illusion in the life of man, at least of modern man" and struggling against the "resistance of the incarnate beings that we are" whose "imaginary stops the mediation of the symbolic exchange."[14] Between these pages lurks, as we should note, a reference to modern history that cannot be reduced to a question of structure.

We need to examine what is at stake here. Through these abundant metaphors, Lacan mobilizes the Greek and Christian theological enterprises in their entirety. He acknowledges the place the paternal figure occupies within them. Our main task as psychoanalysts is thus to analyze this oedipal foundation of our representation of God, not just Lacan's word—not just to exploit it. Lacan did not hesitate to doubt the love of the Father, the Freudian rescue of the father, and so on. Consequently, how can we advance in this direction using categories like the symbolic if Lacan inscribes psychoanalysis in the repetition of the sacralizing gesture? Lacan's ironical identification with Moses, who denounces the Golden Calf worshipped by students too sensitive to the imaginary (in this case Serge Leclaire), is typical: "Well, then, you little idolater. I come down from Sinai and break the Tables of the Law."[15]

---

14. *Seminar II*, p. 319.
15. Ibid., p.55.

IN THE NAME OF THE FATHER

"The name of the father" appears as early as the private seminar on the Wolfman: "What religious instruction teaches the child is the name of the father and the son."[16] Lacan provides an important qualification in his text on Schreber: "This surely demonstrates that the attribution of procreation to the father can only be the effect of a pure signifier, of a recognition, not of a real father, but of what religion has taught us to refer to as the Name-of-the-Father."[17] Lacan's stakes have remained unchanged. They are identical to the ones he formulated in *The Individual Myth of the Neurotic* where he juxtaposed "the ever-degraded image of the father" to that of the master who instructs another person who is ignorant of the dimension of fundamental human relations.[18] The analyst assumes the role of the Lord, and psychoanalysis becomes a practice in the reconstruction and recall of the Christian lesson "in the Name of the father." Where the Father is not, one must bring him into existence as the "Name of the Father." Yet the *Name of the Father* detached from the "in the name of the Father" leaves no trace in the operation of a very special kind of relationship, as "Father" here also implies a reference to Jesus. If there is a preliminary issue to consider, it should be this: to pose this question again, but analytically, a question that so far has attracted attention only among theologians.

---

16. Lacan's unpublished Seminar on the Wolfman (1951–1952), quoted by Erik Porge in *Les Noms du Père chez Jacques Lacan* (Paris: ERES, 1997), pp. 24–25.

17. J. Lacan, "On the possible treatment of psychosis," in *Ecrits: A Selection*, tr. A. Sheridan (New York: Norton, 1977), p. 199.

18. See footnote 7, p. 4.

Rather than an analysis of the invocation of Christ, what Lacan provides is its transformation into a psychoanalytic concept. Are we going to say judiciously: "Instead of making use of psychoanalysis and of Oedipus to identify the position of God, as did Freud, Lacan introduces into psychoanalysis a religious term to analyze this Oedipus"?[19] But is this reversal as evident as it seems? The discussion of God's paternity opened the way to the doctrine of the Council of Nicea, which affirmed that the Son was "generated" and not "created" by God, so as to prevent Jesus from being seen like Adam, "created from nothing." It is strange that this entire Christian theological construction—whose main object was, after all, to enable the Father to generate divinely the Son, implying a very particular position of the mother—seems to have presented no particular interest to psychoanalysis, which only retained the opportune discovery of "spiritual paternity."

In *Totem and Taboo* Freud struggled with the whole set of relations involving the mother, the father of the horde, and the sons. When Lacan immediately considers the "Name of the father" as a "sublimation,"[20] he never poses the question of the maternal phantasm, which the son could maintain as a divine filiation to the Father and his strange incarnation. It is this claim that is at the origin of his emergence from Judaism.

Beyond this impasse, there exists further confusion between the nomination of the father in this recognition—a recognition of the role of the father as procreator—and the identification of this function as the "Name of the Father," which links it to Christian religion. Recognition of the father

---

19. E. Porge, op. cit., p. 25.
20. J. Lacan, *Seminar VII, The Ethics of Psychonalaysis*, tr. D. Porter (New York: Norton, 1992), p. 181.

did not, of course, emerge with the advent of Christianity that invented nothing in this domain. Quite to the contrary, the way Christianity dealt with the *Name of the Father* contains a phantasmagoric representation of the relationship with the father, which psychoanalysis needs to analyze instead of incorporating it. It is clear that Christian "spiritual" paternity takes precedence (in that it is more sublime than the Freudian sexual father) over a purely carnal, pagan paternity, or conversely over the figure of a Jewish God as Father and Master. Yet, when Lacan goes about reformulating the Freudian Oedipus complex, he is obligated to reintroduce the element of sexuality. One can predict under what conditions he will do this: the Oedipus, that nest of desire and identification, will have to be structured as a function of the fundamental organizational principle, descended from Christian doctrine, namely the procession of the son from the Father.

Through the representation of the "symbolic," the Father is henceforth firmly inscribed in the signifier. Not only is he a key figure, since he controls no less than the relationship between the signifier and the signified, without meeting any resistance; under the very name of the symbolic, of the order of the signifier, it is his transcendence that endures.

"YES, I COME INTO THE TEMPLE TO ADORE THE ETERNAL"[21]

It is also through the mediation of the notion of "the fear of God" (evoked through Racine's famous opening of *Athalie*) that the Freudian father is going to find himself elevated to

---

21. J. Lacan, *Séminaire III* (Paris: Seuil, 1981), p. 297.

the function of a quilting point *(point de capiton)* between the signifier and the signified. Lacan concludes his reading of *Athalie* with the idea that " . . . the notion of the father, very close to that of the fear of God, gives him [Freud] the most sensitive element in the experience of what I have called the 'quilting point' between the signifier and the signified."[22] Yes, here one can see very clearly how it is not the father that explains God, but it is God who accounts for the function of the father in the signifying system.

The entire analysis of the use of the second person singular pronoun *tu* rather than *vous* in personal addresses towards the subject is conducted in the purest style of mediation of the Other "in our Judo-Christian tradition." In the beginning, therefore there was the *tu* addressed by the Other (God), the only *je* properly speaking being that of this absolute Other who says "I am who I am." One has to find a term that guarantees the Other as the place of Truth, in other words, an earthly representative who brings Truth into the world. This is the Father, who was already known to religion. But to psychoanalysis?

Lacan therefore attributes to Freud his own theological, if not psychoanalytic, question: How does truth come into the world? "Freud really only asked one single question—how does the system of the signifier without which there can be neither incarnation, nor truth, nor justice, how can this literal logos affect an animal that has no interest or patience for it?"[23] Of course, it is impossible to find in Freud a trace of such a question or of this very particular relation to truth. But one cannot deny that a model of such a relation to truth is

---

22. Ibid., p. 304.
23. Ibid., p. 275.

familiar; it already exists in theology. Lacan borrows it in its philosophical version from Hegel as well as Heidegger. Why does he twist things around? The general answer is that truth, justice, law, and so on come about through the system of the signifiers. We should not conclude that we can delegate the representation of this truth to a representative of the "Great Other": a simple Other, a Third Party, some third *parties* would suffice. It is just this ascending gradient that leads to proposing a Great Other that defines theology, even when the process of truth and justice is, like that of analysis, committed to defy such a notion of ascension.

A PATERNAL METAPHOR

Lacan presents his *paternal metaphor* in the seminars on *Object Relations* (1956–1957) and *Formations of the Unconscious* (1957–1958) as well as in other texts published around that time. We know how these famous deliberations brilliantly elaborate on the father with the three registers of the Symbolic, the Real, and the Imaginary. Then we are given the formulation of the well-known paternal metaphor and its proud algorithm. Lacan himself states that thanks to his enterprise, the "Name-of-the-Father was entered into scientific consideration for the first time."[24] It is certain that the schema he constructed marks a *turning point* with respect to the anthropological question with while simultaneously providing a psychoanalytic answer to the question. By defining the story of Oedipus as a normalizing test that follows a well-established

---

24. J. Lacan, "La Science et la Vérité," in *Ecrits* (Paris: Seuil, 1966), pp. 874–875.

process, one can formulate the general structural conditions that passing through the Oedipus narrative must satisfy. From this vantage point one can ask how this passage is either socially facilitated or socially compromised. The commentator can also occupy himself serenely by explaining incessantly the marvelous distinctions that offer a way out of the confusions (like the functions or poles occupied by the penis and the phallus, and so on). Along the same lines, one can also show the productive consequences of this advance in the years subsequent to its presentation, as well as the numerous different directions it has taken. This presentation lives up to the rigor of Lacanian constructions. Yet it seems to me that it also contributes to an uncalled-for simplification of Lacan's elaborations.

In reality, we can anticipate that every new formulation of the Oedipus complex as such, or for that matter, any other concept of psychoanalytic theory, will be confronted with the very effects of its object. Psychoanalysis, spearheaded by Lacan, did not hesitate to remark on this aspect of Freudian theory, while Lacan asked serious questions—and I will be returning to this—about the *père-version* of Freudians, that is, the Freudian version of a father worthy to be loved. Despite the illusions certain people might harbor about the formations of the unconscious, no algorithm provides a complete safeguard. More specifically, as I will argue, two stages need to be distinguished within the Lacanian Oedipus. What are the elements that have assured the success of the new Lacanian formulation since 1956—especially for those people who make institutional claims of being Lacanians? If indeed Lacan, since 1938, repeatedly referred the question of the father to the *paternal solution* so clearly inscribed in religious representation, how does this representation relate to the new Oedipus?

The indisputable elements of Lacan's 1957 construction are without doubt the following: first, in his reading of *Little Hans*, Lacan stresses the link between phobia and its determination by the mother's desire, thus giving a crucial and decisive recognition to what was mentioned almost in passing in the section of *Totem and Taboo*. It was in this text that Freud brought forth his theory of incest and the origin of the social bond by pointing out the privileged relationship between the mother and the youngest son. The Oedipus complex is the force field that cannot be reduced to the child's investments in parental objects; it is constituted by the inscription of Desire in the Other. Another important aspect is the way oedipal normalization assumes that the subject abstracts itself from the position of being the object of desire to which it is assigned. Finally, this issue is fundamentally related to the desiring relationship of the parent insofar as it excludes the subject. Lacan's seminal contribution to the Oedipus narrative rests on these three points. Yet his contribution can and must be dissociated from the *version* that he tended to give, a version determined also by what I have called the *paternal solution*. Here is why.

THE LACANIAN MOTHER

Whoever reads the seminars carefully cannot help but be struck by the picture drawn of the Lacanian mother. This mother is really characterized by her "fundamental dissatisfaction."[25] Structurally, she is prey to penis envy,[26] which puts

---

25. *Séminaire IV, La relation d'Objet* (Paris: Seuil, 1994), p. 202.
26. Ibid., p. 224.

her in a state of dependence and frustration. The back cover of Seminar IV offers a strong depiction of the Lacanian mother: "This unfulfilled, unsatisfied mother, around whom is constructed the child's entire progression towards narcissism, is a real person, she is here, and as all unfulfilled people, she is looking for what she is going to devour—*quaerens quem devoret*. What the child found earlier as a way of erasing his symbolic frustration, is now revealed right in front of him as an open mouth. . . . Here is the real danger which his phantasms reveal to us—the danger of being devoured."[27] Strangely enough, the photograph on the front page of the French edition of this same Seminar IV shows a reproduction of a famous painting by Goya, "Saturn Devouring His Son"! In her threat to devour her child through an act of total consumption, the woman has to be exposed as false. We can observe a permanent confusion between the fantasies of *Little Hans* and those elements that are presented as universal in the mother and the woman. In his entire reading of *Little Hans*, Lacan describes the mother's direct access to the object of her need (the penis-child), but fails to introduce this object within the dialectic of the symbol.[28] It is harder for her to insert herself into the family. This analysis can be strictly superimposed onto the thesis we find among Catholic theoreticians of the 1940s. Does this mean psychoanalysis confirms scientific truth or their truth?

Throughout the seminar on *Ethics*, Lacan blames the mother of Oedipus, Jocasta, for her criminal and incestuous desire—Hamlet's mother suffers a similar fate—thus finding

---

27. J. Lacan, *Séminaire IV: La relation d'Objet*, back cover and p. 195.
28. Ibid., pp. 165–246.

the father innocent, while at the same time repressing the incestuous relation between Antigone and her father.[29] Lacan's passionate antimaternalism is of course barely evident in the purified schema of the paternal metaphor, which presents the mother as completely oriented towards the phallic object of her desire; it remains true, however, that she is the foundation of the schema.

How did we arrive at this point? Starting with the Christianic model of *In the Name of the Father*, the schema of the paternal metaphor is constructed explicitly by its presentation of Oedipus as the executive. In other words, it is a matter of the subject coming to occupy his place of calling in the name of the father. The Lacanian operation consists of identifying and fusing those two processes. The first step corresponds to taking up the Freudian schema of the father's uncertainty and the strange assertion of the cultural superiority of paternity over maternity that Lacan deploys in his conception of the supremacy of the symbolic. The challenge is to substitute paternal procreation with female childbirth; as we know, this representation has been so powerful for centuries that it has been necessary for the female role in procreation to be rediscovered. The challenge here is also to find an answer to the male question of attributing paternity to a *particular* man. But in this context, it is clear that paternity comes from the Father as Master in name and only through his own words. This is the model of political and religious paternity that until recently dominated the West. It is this father, who is "firmly installed in the culture," whom Lacan invokes.

---

29. This is the thesis of P. Guyomard in *La jouissance du tragique* (Paris: Aubier, 1992).

The second step is of a very different nature. It involves an explanation of how a man can be the object of the mother's desire, while the same vectorization enables the oedipal child to separate himself from the delusion of being the object of her desire. It is obvious that the favorable resolution of this operation, which determines the way out of the Oedipus complex, is strictly related to what Lacan himself defines as the intervention of the father as someone real and powerful, in other words as a potent man. Moreover, it is here that one finds the explanation of Lacan's later evolution and the role that he will attribute to the real Father.

Under these conditions, the nomination process necessarily changes the meaning of what is named. This has led certain commentators, such as Philippe Jullien, to the conclusion that "originally, for the child, the father is established as a Name *by the mother*. It is the mother who assigns a position in the symbolic order."[30] Thus the metaphor of the temporal sequence of three stages of becomes contradictory. First, there is the father, who is supposed to represent the law, who "makes the law" for the mother, until in a second stage, he presents all the traits of the Master Father. He is said to possess sovereignty (no less) over the object of his desire. This puts him at an advantage that seems to depend little on the mother's desire, all the more so since he—the Father—is presented as the one who deprives the other and relegates the mother to a law which is not of his own making. Along the way, he does not seem to subscribe to his own desire. He rules but does not desire.

---

30. P. Jullien, *Le Manteau de Noé* (Paris: Desclée de Brouwer, 1991), p. 32.

In the end, Lacan amalgamates the figure of the traditional potentate with the figure of the father who underpins
desire. But you can't have your cake and eat it, too. The schema
contains an untenable and unstable compromise, introducing what would really be a law of desire as incompatible with
the "sovereign" position of the Master Father who imposes
his law as the law of desire. The descriptions of "maternal
castration" as they are represented in the imaginary of the
Lacanian mother set up this phantasmagoric enterprise. Thus
we are able to notice the other aspect of this incoherence. We
are aware of the weight given to the determinant element in
the paternal metaphor. It is "the importance attributed to the
father's speech by the mother." Yet the phenomenon Lacan
tries to describe here is that the importance of this speech
depends in a very precise way on who is actually implicated
in the "desire of the father," that is, who is "potent." Again,
Lacan does not opt for a single answer. The importance of the
speech of the father, just like the idea that he is instituted as
Name by the mother seems more a way of formulating her
submission to the "symbolic order" where the Father as Master makes the law.

What follows is a manifest and unexpected consequence
of the Lacanian schema, destabilized by the intrusion of the
figure of the Master Father into the symbolic order. Either
we assume that, with the decline of the subject's Oedipus
complex, the mother enters the scene by being detached, via
her own passage through the Oedipus scenario, from any
temptation to make the child the object of her desire. In this
case it is *of no use* to let the father intervene to separate the
child from her. Or else, if this is not the case, we do not see
how the father could succeed where there has been a failure.
In both cases, however, the Father finds himself implicitly in

the position of regulating the maternal Oedipus. Yet, isn't this the typically paternal solution, that is solving once and for all the female Oedipus complex by making her a child?

Such would be the inconvenience of pouring new wine into old jugs. The so-called symbolic order has always presented itself as a paternal order. The psychoanalytic novelty is to consider as necessary a phantasmagoric articulation of the father's order. This operation is impossible to achieve if one re-installs the old "Symbolic order." This has been the price to pay for the "father's decadence." The outcome can only be a restoration of the father's role and function. What is at stake is not normativity itself, but a coherent place to assign to the father.

The same equivocation appears most blatantly in Lacan's various attempts to meet the Pope in Rome in 1953. Lacan wished to be granted an interview to discuss "the future of psychoanalysis in the Church." As Roudinesco writes, Lacan wanted to show the importance of Rome for his teaching. In the Sacred City, he could pay homage to the "common father"—as a letter of Jacques Lacan to his brother Marc-François in September, 1953, put it.[31]

LORD PHALLUS, OR THE PENIS OF GOD

It may come as a surprise that I have not yet made any mention of one of Lacanian theory's principal actors, Lord Phallus. It is impossible to ignore the hope psychoanalytic feminism, particularly in America, has placed within it, not to

---

31. Letter of September 1953, quoted by E. Roudinesco, *Jacques Lacan* (Paris: Fayard, 1992), p. 274, note 11.

mention the many subtleties it has employed to find a politically correct use of the term. It seems to me that Judith Feher Gurewich posed this question well in a number of her writings.[32] On the one hand, the idea of the symbolic phallus seems to support the critique of the Freudian reduction of sexual difference to the biological. But the problem resurfaces almost immediately where it has been relegated to—in the Symbolic. In her differentiated critique of Lacan's construction of the symbolic phallus, Judith Butler has forged an ingenious new path. First, she describes in minute detail the extreme difficulties that the phallus, apparently completely distinct from the penis, experiences in becoming symbolic, in losing its imaginary function. She then proposes that it is its performative enunciation where its properties can be found. From this perspective, no one can be stopped from seizing the performative enunciation to use it however he or she pleases, and to speculate otherwise about the differences between the sexes.

We can also consider finding a solution by insisting on the fact that Lacan's challenge was to define the conditions under which desire emerges for the subject beyond its identification with the phallus—what he might *be* for his mother (and not which he either does or does not *possess*). We could emphasize also its negativity. But one will not easily escape from this quandary. The difficulty really remains with the identification of *the object of desire as phallus,* and this problem directly relates to the paternal solution—which I examined earlier in this paper.

---

32. J. Feher Gurewich, "Who's afraid of Jacques Lacan?" in J. Feher Gurewich and M. Tort, eds., *Lacan and the New Wave in American Psychoanalysis* (Other Press, 1999).

Thus, there clearly exists a tension for Lacan, a contradiction between the recognition of a "law of desire" and the
orderly transformation, in all its different aspects, of the term
by the Father. Recognizing a law of desire that directs the
subject to the mother's Other does not require the father to
be presented as the sovereign proprietor of an object, the
phallus. One might even go so far to say that it excludes this.
Lacan himself refers to this, when he develops the thesis of
paternal "per-version," in other words the condition that the
cause of his desire is to be a woman."[33] For the time being,
let's leave aside any other problems this new orientation creates. One thing is certain: the law of desire that it inscribes
has nothing to do with the sovereign position of the pre-
analytic father as owner of a penis. It is easy to see how maintaining this sovereign order in the schema of the paternal
metaphor—where desires "substitute" for each other—quite
naturally leads to a fetishization of the object of desire in the
phallus, possessed by the father since birth, taken away from
the mother, and given back to the child.

In other words, the theorization of the symbolic phallus as signifier of desire appears for what it really is: a *phallic theory* whose author is the child in the phallic stage. The
Lacanian operation that consists of inscribing it in the symbolic in no way changes its origin or its nature, and fails to
resolve the Freudian difficulties. There is no doubt that the
phallic theory needs to be described (and analyzed) as such,
in other words as a *formation* of the unconscious. Not only
does it govern the sexuality of the child of both sexes *during the phallic stage*; it also forms a powerful substructure of

---

33. J. Lacan, *Séminaire RSI* (unpublished, 1975).

the organization of social forms and of power up to this day. This can hardly be taken as the royal road to emerging from the Oedipus dilemma.

For Freud, the construction of the theory of the primacy of the phallus is contemporaneous with dead-ends in the analysis (by Freud himself) of his own daughter Anna.[34] His phallic theory is coextensive with what Freud identified at the end of his life as the radical *rejection of the feminine*, a rejection from which psychoanalysis still needs to extricate itself to this day. The real question is not how to democratize the phallus, but how to rethink radically the theory of sexuality that has been constructed for its greater glory, in that it presents a screen for an excessive *jouissance*—for which the feminine has acted as the figurative embodiment for both sexes.

THE MESSIAH

Having been shoved aside by the IPA, Lacan was unable to conduct his seminar at Sainte Anne in 1963. From 1963 onward, Lacan would time and again remind everyone of the fact that he had been unable to hold this seminar on the *names of the father*. In Lacanian hagiography, this endlessly rehashed experience is readily cited to account for the time it took him to find a solution to the problem that derived from his stress on the primacy of the signifier. He only discovered it in 1975. Lacan's own perspective on this obstacle of speaking of the "Name of the father" presents all the characteristics of a symptom—both in terms of content and tone:

---

34. G. Pragier and S. Faure-Pragier, "Une fille est analysée," in *Revue Française de Psychanalyse* 2:443–457.

The names of the father: in other words, what I promised never to talk about again. There you have it. This is because of certain people, who I no longer need to qualify, who, in the name of Freud, made me hold back on what I was planning to present about the names of the father. Yep. Certainly, this was to make sure they would not have the consolation I was going to provide them; in fact, in some cases they were ignorant of these names, due to repression. It would have been useful to them. This was not really my point. In any case, I know they won't find them all by themselves. They won't find them, as long as they are on Freud's track, i.e., in their psychoanalytic societies.[35]

The most striking aspect of this drift is undoubtedly a curious incrimination of Judaism. We are no longer at the time when Lacan explained that "the" sublime chance of genius perhaps could not alone account for the fact that the son of a patriarchal Jew could draw out of his imagination the Oedipus complex.[36] From then on, he argued that it were precisely those to whom the Name of the father could have been useful who had obstructed him. But why would it have been useful to them in particular? "It was precisely these people to whom it could have been useful who stopped me. I would have rendered them a service in their personal intimacy. These are people who are particularly involved with the Name-of-the-Father; there is a very special clique in the world that one can identify with a religious tradition. It is these people to whom I would have brought some fresh air, and I don't see why I

---

35. *Les non dupes errent*, unpublished seminar, session of November 13, 1973.
36. See footnote 2, paragraph 40.16.

should devote myself particularly to them."[37] Here it is a matter of appealing to the tradition at the origin of psychoanalysis in so far as this tradition is Judaic. But the phrase "a very special clique in the world that one can identify with a religious tradition" recalls, in its own way, Christian anti-Semitism at its best.

Why, in his "Proposition of October 9th, 1967," did Lacan feel the need to state precisely that no member of the IPA perished in the concentration camps—due no doubt to the fact that they belonged to an association structured like an army or the Church, and perhaps also in line with the wishes of Freud?[38] If we have to characterize Lacan's opponents as "the group of Jewish analysts of the IPA who have avoided the concentration-camps," what conclusions should an analyst draw of the wishes of Lacan with respect to his adversaries who did survive?

This declaration stands in dramatic contrast to the letter Freud sent to Arnold Zweig in 1934, in which he pointed out why he had suspended the publication of his *Moses and Monotheism*: "For we live here in an atmosphere of Catholic rigor. It is said that the politics of our country are determined by a certain Father Schmidt. . . . In Rome, my dear Edoardo Weiss has founded an analytical group and published several issues of a *Rivista italiana di psycoanalisis*. Publication ceased abruptly, and, although Weiss had good relations with Mussolini, and obtained from him favorable promises, the banning of the

---

37. J. Lacan. *Séminaire "Ou Pire,"* unpublished seminar, session of June 14, 1972.

38. J. Lacan, "Proposition du 9 Octobre 1967," quoted in E. Porge *op. cit.*, p. 29.

journal could not be prevented. It came directly from the Vatican and the responsibility was Father Schmidt's. Of course, one would anticipate that a publication by myself would create a certain sensationalism that would not escape the attention of the hostile Father. In this way we would be risking here in Vienna a ban on psychoanalysis and an end to all our work."[39] Identifying the analysts of the IPA as Jews, Lacan spews forth all kinds of delirious remarks ("the father's baby donkeys, what a herd, if I had given my seminar, how I would have prepared to stuff their brays back into their throats").[40] In this way Lacan gave in to this familiar Catholic, anti-Semitic pamphleteering, aligning himself with the side of the Hostile Father whom Freud referred to as the so-called Holy Father.

AT LAST, A REAL FATHER

From here Lacan made a complex move. This involved putting into question the origin of the Oedipus myth anew—as a Freudian dream described by the hysteric. No longer was it enough to have gravitated around the "true religion." Lacan proposed that the Freudian Oedipus complex was "unusable," a Freudian invention dictated by the position of the idealized father in which the hysteric placed him. And in Seminar XX, Lacan explains that it was Freud who "saves the Father" once again (after Christ) because he was "a good

39. Freud's Letter of September 30, 1934 to Arnold Zweig in *The Letters of Arnold Zweig and Sigmund Freud*, tr. E. and W. Robson-Scott (New York: Harcourt and Brace, 1970).

40. *Seminar RSI*. March 11, 1975, cited in Porge, *op. cit.*, p. 144.

Jew, who was not entirely up-to-date" (*un bon juif pas tout à fait à la page*).[41]

As is so often the case with Lacan, the acerbic account of an analytical challenge is situated in a theoretical operation that is much more disturbing. Clearly our good Jew, ignorant of the *prestige* of logic as well as of topology and those knots that are so Borromean, could only give birth to the seeds of an Oedipus complex that had yet to be elaborated: "There is some indication on the horizon, in the vapors . . . of what rises up as a hysterical sacrifice."[42] Freud appears therefore as the victim of the hysteric, while Lacan, who would have avoided the traps without simultaneously putting himself in the position of the idealized Father, concludes with a new vision of the Name-of-the-Father. But, strangely, it is only to respond that he is there, when the hysteric calls: namely "the Name so that someone speaks."[43] It is a matter of someone speaking.

From that point on, emerging from the Oedipus complex thus means to extricate oneself from the whole apparatus that Lacan himself had created: the apparatus of the *invoked* and *named* Father. The title of his seminar "Les non dupes errent" already identifies the way in which Lacan is moving ahead by making detours, by treating the subject that he had decided to no longer deal with. Lacan proposed the distinction between the named being and the naming function of the father.

---

41. J. Lacan, *Seminar XX, Encore: On Feminine Sexuality: The Limits of Love and Knowledge 1972–1973*, tr. B. Fink (New York: Norton, 1998), p. 109.

42. J. Lacan, "D'un discours," June 19, 1971, cited in Porge, *op. cit.*, p. 138.

43. Ibid.

To be appointed to something, to have been chosen, and I
do mean chosen, that's what the 'Name of the Father' means
for us at this point in time. I really do mean preferred,
passed before the Name-of-the-Father. It is utterly bizarre
that the social dominates over the knot that literally creates the threads of existence: it is this power of assigning a
name with the aim of restoring an order, an order clad in
iron. What does this mean with regard to a return of the
Name-of-the-Father in the real world, where the Name-of-
the-Father is *verworfen*, excluded, rejected, and where, for
this reason, it designates this foreclosure, which I already
identified as the principle of madness itself, *isn't this naming the sign of a catastrophic degeneration?*[44]

As we can see, the historical perspective of the downfall
of the Father remains a vital issue. From now on, it merely
takes on a new disguise. The reformulation of the Oedipus
version between 1953 and 1957 was not powerful enough
to restore the Father to his place. Lacan needed to take another step towards the neuralgic point that he had already
approached many times before, that is, the point where Christianity and Judaism are equally invested: the *Name of God*.

A PERVERSE FATHER TO RESOLVE
THE OEDIPUS COMPLEX

Parallel to this discussion runs another operation that controls the development of the *père-version*, designed to provide
a way of extracting psychoanalysis from the place Freud at-

---

44. J. Lacan, *Les non dupes errent*, unpublished, March 19, 1974 (emphasis added).

tributed to the father.[45] For Freud, the primary incorporation of the father, the game of identification at the end of the Oedipus, and finally the importance of love of the father all constituted an unconscious limitation of his theory, an aspect of the problem that modulated his versions of the Oedipus complex. For many years, a number of non-Lacanian inquiries have concerned themselves with this question. It seems strange that this aspect struck Lacan himself as he undertook his major recasting of the Oedipus complex in the 1950s.

Lacan refrained from this task due to his own incorporation of the father and of Freud, and the substantial reinforcement of the father in religion that he injected into his analytic problematization. We need to remember Lacan's remark in Seminar IV, when he points out that the Judo-Christian tradition is the only "place which provides answers to questions about the father."[46] We should also note that the typical Christian amalgamation of the term "Judo-Christian tradition" traditionally presents Christianity as a development, a more sophisticated elaboration, a progression of Judaism. This operation had become more difficult from 1963 on, when Lacan had been excluded from the IPA; he had to keep his distance from any relation with Judaism. His reference to the "*per-version of the father*" appears in contexts where it is used as a perverse wordplay on the theorization of the father.

Lacan presents this as a way of discarding the Freudian domination of the imaginary father to the advantage of the real father. Yet this formulation necessarily implies that the predominance of the imaginary father in Freud is not without any reference to perversion. An example would be the

---

45. J. Lacan, RSI 1975, unpublished.
46. J. Lacan, *Séminaire IV*, p. 373. See also p. 364.

form of the initial conceptions of the Perverse Father, which Freud later abandoned. At the same time, Lacan proceeds to erase perversion through derision. From this point on, it identifies the state of mind related to the quandary of no longer knowing if we can still refer to this as the Oedipus complex. Lacan says: "A father does not have the right to respect or love unless said love, said respect is—and you won't believe your ears—*père-versement,* directed at a woman-object that causes his desire (and to whom his desire speaks)."[47] One understands how the progression *toward* the father is in some way inverted in a progression toward woman as object a.

   In a way, Lacan rigorously draws on the consequences of one of the lines of contradiction in the real father, which is necessary to construct the paternal metaphor. In giving priority to what he calls the real father, he acknowledges the *reality of relations of sexualized desire* as decisive elements towards the construction of reality (in which sexualization formulas represent a pseudo-mathematical formulation). He therefore seems to reduce the father to appropriate proportions. From another perspective, however, the normalizing condition that he finally constructs for the father is defined as "perverse." By insisting on the symptoms of the father as compatible with his efficacy,[48] one emphasizes the way out of the normalizing aim itself that played a central part in the earlier stages, since it is through his participation in the symbolic order that the father holds what Lacan considers to be his power. And so the solemn progression toward the Symbolic Father shows itself to be a hodgepodge of circumstances of the 1960s with its side-glances at the Vatican. Behind the

---

47. J. Lacan, *Séminaire RSI,* January 21, 1975. *Ornicar,* 3:107.
48. Ibid.

incense curtain, the latest version of the father reveals itself, a free lover of object a.

Beyond this perverse game on "per-version," it may seem that, bringing into play the real father, the question of the father has at last found its place. But this is certainly not the case. The ascending motion that earlier characterized the Name of the father through his invocation as the symbolic father assumes its ultimate form with the theorization of the Name of the Name of the Name.

TO CONCLUDE

The question of the father, so pervasive in Lacan, is a distinct question about the complex Freudian issue of the Father. No reading of *Moses and Monotheism* is going to help. This text needs to be placed in its historical context, the rise of Nazism, and must be understood as an interpretation—its reference to Christianity included. The current tendency to use it in the context of a Freudo-Lacanian return to the religious, of a Freudo-Christianity, is of the same nature as the construction of a Carmel at Auschwitz. But it can be accounted for. Since the 1970s, the disappointed messianic passion in psychoanalysis has intensified. Lacan's thoughts about the Father contain two contradictory elements: one elaborates strongly on the Freudian opening up of the Oedipus complex by making explicit the conflicting nature of the relations of desire between the sexes. At the same time, it represents a major step backwards when confronted with the ultimate Freudian heritage, which consists of the rejection of the feminine. The second step tends to go all the way back to the source of this advance through a vectorization of the Father, which restores to psychoanalysis its ancient historical and religious solution of the Father as the origin and remedy of all ills.

Psychoanalysis confronts head-on the debasement of the feminine, against which it erects the phallic theory of which Lacan has produced a cleaned-up version. The Freudian female or the Lacanian Woman both designate the power of impulse and desire, which have to be mastered. The Lacanian preoccupation with the preservation of desire in the act is closely related to an anguish in the face of detumescence, which permeates the whole seminar on Anxiety and which is intended to provide a model for desire. The *jouissance* of sexual power, so often passed over in silence, has nothing to do with the obsession with a phallic object fetishized by both sexes. It is foreign to the Hegelian-Christian model that assigns an essential nonsatisfaction to desire and orients it towards a *forcibly sublimated* satisfaction.

One of the merits of Lacan's deviation from Freud's dogma is perhaps that it makes us realize the unknown power of this incarnation of the notorious Great Other represented by Christian religion within psychoanalysis. It is self-evident that the function of the father is a complex issue in our society, but one should immediately add that *it is problematic in all societies*. To invent a golden age of Fathers and create a fanciful history of Paternity is a retrospective illusion of the "paternal solution," whether it is a matter of the Freudian version of history or advancing from the Father of the horde via Moses to our own days, or the saintly Lacanian history of the death of God. The first challenge is then to work toward a real history of the paternal function. One should strive to define the function independently of the phantasmagoric schema of origins and a history mystified by religion.

Not only is the stereotype of the decline of the paternal function inconsistent with minimal historical rigor. It is also an imaginary solution because it deflects attention from the real psychoanalytic problem: the problem of *relations* between the sexes and between generations, which Freud named the Oedipus complex. For Freud, the complex originally remained disconnected or disjointed from the doctrine of the father. When establishing the connection in his own particular way, Lacan produced a remarkable version of the Oedipus complex dominated by an unconscious theory of the promotion of the Father. From our own experience we know full well that analysis occurs *without* a construction based on a faith that needs virtue as a totem for its community of believers.

As analysts, we have the duty to end this patent rift between our experience as analysts and nostalgia for the Father in theory. That is what we mean by *the future of an illusion*. It also states clearly that the illusion *has a future*, even for the twenty-first century. It remains to be seen whether we are going to continue to be busy disseminating it. Since the Renaissance, Europe, and later the West as a whole, have paid dearly for their disenchantment with religious enthusiasm. The Rushdie affair reminds us of the price Islam will still have to pay to kill the Father *symbolically*. Does psychoanalysis consist of pursuing the sinister work of religion by other means? Or more prosaically, will it demolish the great illusion that monotheistic religions have created over the past four millennia?

II

Constructing and
Deconstructing
Lacanian Theory

10

Construction, Interpretation, and Deconstruction in Contemporary Psychoanalysis

NÉSTOR A. BRAUNSTEIN

At the end of a psychoanalytic century the psychoanalytic world becomes puzzling and puzzled. Disagreement reigns everywhere. There is nothing but a few Freudian words that can gather the legatees of the founder. And to those few words (the unconscious, transference, repression) every group, when it is not every analyst, gives a different meaning. The only thing—if it is not the vocabulary and the concepts—that remains in common among analysts can nevertheless be found in the Freudian apparatus taken as the basis of our action: it is a device characterized by a double exigence; the analysand has just to say what happens in her mind, and the analyst has to hear with even attention everything that the analysand says. These are paradoxical commands inasmuch as they speak of freedom (but here freedom is forced by the acceptance of a rule) and of neutrality (only to allow the non-neutral to arise and be considered as such).

If we ask the analysts why they recur to the analytic framework, then we will hear a plurality of divergent reasons and justifications. And what is also different is their way of acting inside the analytic situation according to the different goals they set for their action and according to the quite different ideas they have about the few common words: the unconscious, transference, repression, interpretation, construction. But if we disregard these differences, all psychoanalysts today acknowledge a common origin for their practice, an origin to be found in the Freudian text. That is why I propose in this paper that we should go back once more to this text and find out from it what is the basis for the divergence between Freudian and Lacanian goals, and then, between Freudian and Lacanian techniques.

The not so hidden question behind my propositions would thus be: *Analysis, what for?* Freud has no doubts and he uses the kingly plural *we* to settle the analytic procedure. Freud's answer is clearcut: "We all know that the person who is being analysed has to be induced to remember something that has been experienced and repressed and . . . the other portion of the work, the task performed by the analyst, has been pushed into the background."[1] On this second level, looking at the situation from the analyst's side, she has to *construct* (and that term, according to Freud, is to be preferred to that of *interpret*), or rather to *reconstruct*, what has been forgotten or repressed. The patient *has to remember* and to make a transference from the distant past to the actual situation of psychoanalysis; she has to enact what she cannot remember and has to transfer her cathexis, her investments, from the lost objects to the present character of the analyst.

---

1. S. Freud, "Constructions in analysis," *Standard Edition*, 23:258. *Gesammelte Werke* 16:44, 1937. From now on: *SE* and *GW*.

The analyst acts, following a desire of which Freud makes no secret: "It is familiar ground that the work of analysis aims at inducing the patient to give up the repressions belonging to his early development and to replace them by reactions of a sort that would correspond to a psychically mature condition."[2] The subject is pushed into remembering by the desire of the analyst, which aims at some psychic material defined by Freud himself. It is a search of something that can distinctly named: "It is out of such raw material—if we may so describe it—that we have to put togeteher what we are in search of. What we are in search of (*das Gewünschte*) is a picture of the patient's forgotten years that shall be alike trustworthy and in all essential respects complete (*vollständiges Bild*)."[3] So, in Freud's terms, analyst and analysand go after a commonly induced goal. They go *à la recherche du temps perdu*. Both of them run after a trustworthy image. This is *das Gewünschte* (the object of a *Wunsch*). Something *vraisemblable*, verisimilar, that could be shown as complete. The usual Freudian model of the puzzle is called for again at this point.

Freud has no doubts. His *Gewünschte* is apt to be fulfilled (*Wunscherfüllung*, that brings an echo of the *Traumdeutung*, where it was the law of the dream). To quote him again: "It depends only (*nur*) upon analytic technique whether we shall succeed in bringing what is concealed completely to light (*vollständig zum Vorschein*)."[4] However, he acknowledges two obstacles to his optimism. The first is the utmost complexity of the psychic objects, and the other is our insufficient knowledge of their inner and finer structure, which is still myste-

---

2. Ibid., *SE* p. 257, GW p. 43.
3. Ibid., *SE* p. 258, GW p. 44.
4. Ibid., *SE* p. 260, GW p. 47.

rious, about what we have to construct, to build. Freud's explicit wish gives as a model for the analyst the searcher in the subject's history, the archeologist looking after pieces of memory. These will be reconstructed *in speech*, in an uttered *discourse*, in a *proposition* to be heard by the patient, from whom some kind of reaction is expected. It is the model of a talking analyst who "finishes a piece of construction and communicates it (*teilt mit*) to the subject of the analysis so that it may work upon him; he, then, constructs a piece out of the fresh material pouring in upon him, deals with it in the same way and proceeds in this alternating fashion until the end."[5] Psychoanalysts seldom discuss Freud's utterances but often act in a way that belies them. Nowadays Freud's trust in overcoming the repressed and bringing it to light through interpretations, in recovering memories as a way to cure neurosis, in the value of historical reconstructions, and in fulfilling mnemic gaps has almost disappeared.

Today's analytical world is characterized by different *Zielvorstellungen*, different goal-presentations. Currently, other goal-presentations dominate. To name a few: emotional reeducation, production of a verisimile and reliable narrative offering a new meaning to the patient's life, the restoration of the effects of a maternal defficiency, the compensation (even Borromean) of the failures in the paternal metaphor or the well saying (*bien-dire*) making *jouissance* condescend to desire.

Psychoanalysis "cures" through quite different ways and some people find strange or admirable the fact that every analyst always finds clinical material and examples confirming the interpretations he provides according to his own theo-

---

5. Ibid.

retical grounds about the unconscious, notwithstanding how incompatible these grounds may be. For instance, those who are not Kleinian find that Kleinian analysts produce theoretical and therapeutic effects independently of "bizarre" ideas they could not share. Against this background it could seem that theory is a rescindable obstacle and that our field could be one dominated by a staunch or "healthy" (we often find people who qualify it as such) pragmatism without commitment to truth or even to thought. Everyone is able to hold every possible idea according to his or her own views and nobody can prove anything. The universal claim is that one and the same method is always applied and that from it results are produced that always agree with the therapists' preconceptions. Might it be possible to say that here is the ground for a general disillusion and loss of charm experienced in the analytic field? What are thus analytic theory and thinking for? And, even if thinking is still valued, how can one avoid prejudices against thought viewed as something that hinders action?

In the Freudian model, theory guides the construction given to the patient. How could it be otherwise, if that is the rule in every field of knowledge? Nobody can pretend that an analyst who appears as a radical empiricist acts and speaks in the session so as to follow mere facts, with no preconceptions such as biases, contertransferential prejudices, and so on. The example of a construction given by Freud himself in a text he wrote almost in the deaththroes (in 1937) is that of the introduction of the patient into the oedipal myth and in the *père-version* through the speech of his analyst. We can find this idea even more clearly when he presents the case of feminine homosexuality in 1920. There he says that the analysis goes through ". . . two different stages clearly separated. In a

first phase the doctor gets the necessary data about the patient, familiarizes him with the premises and basic grounds
of the analysis and develops before him the construction of
the origin of his suffering. In a second phase it is the patient
himself who takes at his own the material that has been exposed to him, works with it and, with what is supposedly
repressed in him, remembers what can be remembered and
does his best to recover the rest in some kind of reanimation.
When he accomplishes this task, he can confirm the postula-
tions advanced by the doctor, complete them, and, given the
case, correct them. At so doing, he overcome his resistances,
he changes in the aimed sense and becomes independent from
the medical authority."[6] Such a text clearly shows that what
is called *resistances* charged to the patient's account are the
reasons that induce her to be reluctant regarding the admission of the analytical premises and constructions. What is
expected of her—what is called "resistance" when she be-
trays this expectation—is that she would appropriate the
construction as her own and then be convinced. It looks
paradoxical and indeed it is. When she coincides and if she
coincides with the other's (the analyst's) discourse, she becomes independent of its authority! Overcoming the resistances is synonymous with admitting the analyst's speech
as a convincing truth.

Objections are not unexpected and Freud himself took
them into account: "The danger of our leading a patient astray
by suggestion, by persuading him to accept things which we
ourselves believe but which we ought not to, has certainly
been enormously exaggerated. . . . I can assert without boast-

---

6. S. Freud, "On the psychogenesis of a case of feminine homosexuality," *SE* 18:152, *GW* 12:278, 1920.

ing that such an abuse of 'suggestion' has never occured in my practice."[7] There are perhaps too many negations here. It should be possible to ask the question once more after reading the case history of the Wolfman. There, it is Freud himself who pours his doubts and tries to relativize his constructions while the patient blatantly adheres to the words previously heard from the analyst's mouth because these interpretations are *convenient* for him in all the meanings of the term.

Among psychoanalysts, nobody ignores that the main condition for interpretation is the establishment of transference. The problem is that, as soon as transference is at play, we lose any possibility of proving the truth of the proposed interpretation. Such an interpretation can be and often is efficient, there is no doubt about it. We can say it with words proceeding from a witness who cannot be accused of prejudices against Freudian psychoanalysis. John Klauber writes: "The human mind is satisfied and in some sense healed by what it feels as truth. In the case of psychoanalysis truth is expressed in a system of historic explanation. There may be better and worse historians and there may be historical systems which satisfy some patients by their complexity and subtlety, and others by their simplicity or flexibility. But it is true of nearly all patients that some cogent system of historical explanation is necessary for their satisfaction, involvement and cure, and that these are the resources without which the analyst would be lost."[8] And after some paragraphs, he adds: "Analysts live by interpretation. It brings us emotional and

---

7. S. Freud, "Constructions . . ." *SE* 23:261, *GW* 16:48, 1937.

8. J. Klauber, "On the relationship of transference and interpretation in psychoanalytic therapy," *International Journal of Psycho-Analysis* 53:389, 1972.

intellectual resolution. When we feel we understand something we have to see the way to communicating it. If we are deprived of this satisfaction it is not long before we feel a certain degree of restlessness. And I am not speaking here about the particular situation of a disturbed analyst."[9]

In the already quoted case of feminine homosexuality, Freud admits that the construction is a necessary preparation to the journey, like preliminary exertions to be gone through before mounting the train and going from one station to the other. The construction functions as a Baedeker, informing the patient what she will see during the analysis. Without it both partners would be lost, although with construction nothing can be done, as is also the case with the map before starting to travel, that is to say, before starting the analytic device paving the way to any hearing of the patient's associations. Thus, the construction, like the map, is a necessary guide for the steps to be taken. The acknowledged purpose (*Absicht*) is again the reconstruction of the past.

Freud shifts in his 1937 paper from the word *interpretation* to *construction* and then to *reconstruction*; these terms are taken as equivalent. But it is quite evident that the last two words mean quite different things. The construction is the analyst's production, a *poiesis*, a convenient fiction organizing and giving coherence to the data of a life. The reconstruction alludes to some supposed real "psychic object," already there, broken perhaps but ready to be restored, true and not fictitious, waiting for a possible *restitutio ad integrum*. Let us remember that it is possible to build it up again and "depends only upon psychoanalytic technique *to*

---

9. Ibid., p. 390.

succeed in bringing what is concealed completely to light."[10] The reconstruction is archeological, whereas the construction is hermeneutical. Two different ideas of history collide when it comes to choosing between them. They bring to light different ideas about the past, the goal apt to be reached through the psychoanalytic technique.

We have here two successive steps: first, the Baedeker or map, after which comes the journey allowing to find again (remember, the *wiederzufinden* of the Freudian lost object) what was already known to lie there. Always. Always? Alas, no! The Freudian text regarding this question has been the object of many commentaries widely diverging in meaning and scope and it is necessary to quote it again because it is at the core of our subject: "The path that starts from the analyst's construction ought to end in the patient's recollection: but it does not always lead so far. *Quite often we do not succeed (Oft genug gelingt es nicht)* in bringing the patient to recollect what has been repressed. Instead of that, if the analysis is carried out correctly, we produce in him *an assured conviction of the truth of the construction (eine sichere Überzeugung von der Wahrheit der Konstruktion)* which achieves the same therapeutic results as a recaptured memory. The problem of what the circumstances are in which this occurs and how it is possible that what appears to be an incomplete substitute should nevertheless produce a complete result—all of this is matter of a later inquiry."[11]

Freud had no time left for his inquiry and the problem was to remain open. But in the last pages of his 1937 paper Freud arrives at what seems to be an ironic conclusion, even

---

10. S. Freud, "Constructions . . ." *SE* 23:260, *GW* 16:47, emphasis added.

11. Ibid., *SE* p. 267, *GW* pp. 54–55, emphasis added.

an enactment of his own doubts previously projected onto his imaginary interlocutor. Writing about the conviction induced by constructions, he extends his historic point of departure: not only the hysteric suffers from reminiscences; it is also the case of the delusional patient, since he gets his *conviction* (and we emphasize the use of this word, *Überzeugung,* all over the Freudian writings) out of the part of historical truth included in the delusion. There is truth in delusions; that was something well known after the analysis of Schreber's autobiography. Through delusions, the psychotic substitutes one segment of reality and there he places a fragment of his historic past. The hysteric and the delusional both suffer from reminiscences. But the circle is not yet closed.

There is a new guest invited for dinner and it is an old acquaintance of ours: it is religion, not mentioned as such with its own name. "If we take humanity as a whole we can see that, like the individuals, it develops delusional formations inaccessible to logical criticism and falling in contradiction with the actual reality."[12] How could Freud be so sure about the actual reality, about *Wirklichkeit?* The strength of religion can be explained not as an error but as a truth coming from the forgotten primal times, from the *Urzeiten.* And this is the point at which he arrives and on which he closes his reflection about "Constructions in Analysis."

The hysteric symptom shows the return of the repressed. The same happens with delusions. And so it is in the case of with religion. We must pay attention to what Freud states in *Moses and Monotheism:*[13] "We have learnt from the psycho-

---

12. S. Freud, "Constructions . . ." *SE* 23:268, *GW* 16:65–66.
13. S. Freud, "Moses and monotheism," *SE* 23:130, *GW* 16:239, 1939.

analysis of individuals that their earliest impressions, received at a time when the child was scarcely yet capable of speaking, produce at some times or another effects of a compulsive character without being themselves consciously remembered. We believe we have a right to make the same assumption about the earliest experiences of the whole of humanity. One of these effects would be the emergence of the idea of a single great god—an idea which must be recognized as a completely justified memory, though, it is true, one that has been distorted. An idea such as this has a compulsive character: it *must* be believed. To the extent to which it is distorted, it may be described as a delusion; . . . in sofar as it brings a return of the past, it must be called the *truth*. Psychiatric delusions, too, contain a certain small fragment of truth *and the patient's conviction extends over from this truth on its delusional wrappings.*" Before, in the same paper, he wrote: "The compulsive conviction which attaches to the delusion arises from this core of truth and spreads out on to the errors that wrap it."[14]

Well; very well. But why must we remain only with these three terms: hysteria, delusion, religion? Why limit ourselves at this point instead of posing the presence of truth beyond any particular belief and transforming the idea into a universal thesis? If we take this new step, we are not going beyond the text of Freud himself inasmuch as he said in *The Psychopathology of Everyday Life*[15] that "In the same way that in delusions the feeling of conviction can be inherent to our own mistaken judgements that are by no means pathological." And,

---

14. *SE*, 23:85, *GW*, 16:191.
15. S. Freud, "Psychopathology of everyday life," *SE* 6:256, *GW* 4:285, 1901.

in an even clearer formulation in his text on *Gradiva*:[16] "*We all* [emphasis mine] attach our conviction to thought-contents in which truth is combined with error, and let it extend from the former over the latter. It becomes diffused, as it were, from the truth over the error associated with it and protects the latter, though not so unalterable as in the case of a delusion, against deserved criticism."

As we can see, Freud poses this idea as universal and he considers that there is no essential, substantial difference between delusion and normality. The difference is only a question of gradation. Proceeding one step further, we are driven to see that this universality cannot spare psychoanalysis itself and and the analyst's own knowledge in her theory and practice. There is no metalanguage—this is something that we learn from Lacan's teaching—and the analyst should not be someone pretending to say the truth about truth, or the subject of a speech without failure, the speaker of an enounced statement coinciding with the enunciation, in short, the spokes-woman of a *parole pleine* that, as we all know, language belies and rejects.

Therefore, we are pushed to admit that there are in psychoanalysis kernels of truth and halos of error receiving belief and conviction from the former to the latter. There is no heresy here. In his twelfth *Introductory Lecture on Psychoanalysis* Freud stated it clearly. It is even clearer if we keep in mind the previous quotations: "At our first meeting I lamented the difficulty of providing demonstrations and so of carrying conviction in giving instruction in psychoanalysis. And I have no doubt that you have since come to agree with me. But the

---

16. S. Freud, "Delusion and dreams in W. Jensen's 'Gradiva,'" *SE* 9:81, *GW* 7:109, 1907.

different theses of psychoanlysis are so intimately connected that conviction can easily be carried from a single poin to a larger part of the whole. It might be said of psychoanalysis that if anyone holds out a little finger to it it quickly grasps his whole hand. No one, even, who has accepted the explanation of parapraxes can logically withhold his belief in all the rest."[17] The dominating idea throughout Freud's work is that of a possible total recovery of the missing knowledge, that of an eventual postanalytical transparency of the subject to himself. However, Freud was well aware that this enterprise is doomed, that it will fail. His "quite often, *oft genug, assez souvent*" is, indeed, a universal, an *"always."* There is no complete light falling upon the concealed and, if it happens, it is not because of technical problems. It is for a structural reason that Freud himself indicates; it has a proper analytical name: it is original repression or *Urverdrängung.*

The signifiers of the resigned *jouissance* are not at the subject's disposal. It is impossible to decipher those primal writings of *jouissance* that are offered to multiple and contradictory readings; there is a limit to the possible verbalization, there is a signifier that lacks in the Other, words are lacking to truth and, therefore, truth cannot be said in any language or metalanguage.

Freud already knows this but belies it. "I already know, but even so. . . ." From the abyss opened by the original repression arises the idea of an eventual rescue through a solid theory apt to ground constructions equivalent to what has been lost: a discourse uttered by the analyst like the Other's knowledge (*savoir*), fulfilling the gaps in the subject's *savoir.*

---

17. S. Freud, "Introductory lectures in psychoanalysis," Lecture 12. *SE* 15:192–193, *GW* 11:196–197, 1916–1917.

But the analyst would not be able to say the word lacking in the Other without accepting the call to play the imposture of a full Other, without denying the lack in the Other. Pretending to utter the inaccessible truth, he would place himself as the Real, beyond the Symbolic. Then, he cannot be amazed if he finds that, after the communication of such a "complete" analytical construction, what appears is *hallucination* and not *memory*. "I have been struck by the manner in which in certain analyses, the communication of an obviously apt construction has evoked in the patients a surprising and at first incomprehensible phenomenon. They had have lively recollections called up in them—which them themselves have described as 'ultra-clear' (*überdeutlich*)—but what they have recollected has not been the event that was the subject of the construction but details relating to that subject. For instance, they have recollected with abnormal sharpness the faces of the people involved in the construction or the rooms in which something of the sort might have happened or, a step further away, the furniture in such rooms—on the subject of which the construction had naturally no possibility of any knowledge."[18]

Freud comments that such *metonymical recollections* could be described as hallucinations if a belief in their actual presence had been added to their remarkable clarity. It is easily understood: what has been cut out from the symbolic, what cannot be reminded because it has been the object of a *Verwerfung*, appears in the analyst's construction as a real, leaving the subject with no resources, faded. The memory does not come back. It cannot because it never was.

18. S. Freud, "Constructions . . ." *SE* 23:266, *GW* 16:53.

What could come in this empty place? *A belief.* The *Über-zeugung in der Wahrheit der Konstruktion*, the conviction as an *Ersatz* of an impossible memory. How could we know that a given construction is "an obviously apt" one if we cannot confirm it through recollection? Easy answer: through our own *belief*, our own conviction of working in the reconstruction of some stored past, written in the unconscious memory of the subject, even if she has no access to it. The truth she expected from our analytical knowledge would then be found and confirmed in the conditions of transference.

If our intervention comes from the place of a subject who knows what the truth is, instead of coming from the place of the supposed knowledge subject (as I prefer to translate Lacan's *sujet supposé savoir*), if we speak as masters (*maîtres*) of knowledge, we are agents taking the place of S_1 in the master's discourse, and the answer we find is the fading of the subject, not a divided subject anymore but an object, a dejection thrown out from discourse.

This absolute presence of "truth," through the analyst's speech, is answered by the apparition of the object in the real, with no phantasmatic mediation, no semblance, no "as if," no metaphor. Freud's aforementioned (semi-)hallucination is the name for a return from the real of what cannot be integrated by the symbolic. At this point what we see are dangers arising out of our own conviction that we are able to speak the truth, to go beyond the subject's possibility to symbolize, remember, and integrate a lived history.

Let us return to our common clinical experience: what is essential to determine the subject and his/her desire is the desire of the Other. For everybody this Other is incarnated, embodied, inside the family in which he is born and where he lives his years of childhood. What is decisive for him are

not events that might or might not happen. What is decisive
is his place in the Other's desire, especially the place he occupied in his mother's desire. But the desire of the mother is
not an empirical fact, cannot be reached through enquiry, is
not something that happens to the subject, something that he
would be able to remember afterwards. Who would be able
to remember what he or she was in the mother's desire if the
mother herself could not know because this desire belongs
to her unconscious fantasy?

It is not a question of overcoming any repression. The
only thing we could get is an unstable and precarious knowledge about something never known and impossible to be
known. With Nicolas of Cusa we must admit that there is no
real knowledge when somebody believes that he knows what
cannot be known and that in such a case the only true knowledge consists in acknowledging what cannot be known. And
this admission signals the failure and fall of the supposed
knowledge subject.

From this initial fantasmal status in the desire of the
Other, the subject takes her place in her own fantasy. The
fantasy of a fantasy, that is the ground of the subject, and from
there she can come to demand an analysis and to transform
somebody else into the body of the knowledge she lacks.
Could this ground be unearthed, could she be freed from the
ghosts haunting her, could it be possible for her to reconstruct
in the real, beyond any imaginary shadow, what she really was
in the matrix desire of the Other, in that matrix that is the
desire of the Other?

The subject of psychoanalysis comes to us not as a desert
of words and stories. He is rather overloaded by words and
stories. Of course, by now everybody knows that the unconscious is the discourse of the Other. And for how long and

how much the Other has spoken before! When this subject comes to us he is ready to display before us his heavy burden of constructions coming from different ages or agents.

It is common, perhaps a little too much, to compare the analyst's task with that of the archeologist. How to reconstruct objects that could not leave any trace in memory, like the unconscious fantasies of parents, siblings, grandparents? How could anybody know the truth of what was expected from him at the moment of his or her birth if even those involved in the event and surrounding the subject could not know about it? Every material brought to support a construction can be impeached as partially or totally submitted to the work of censorship, distortion, and repression (*Entstellung*). On such an unknowable basis, mainly upon the unknown of maternal desire transformed into maternal discourse, the individual myth of the neurotic is grounded.

From this originary, primary construction, from this original fiction of the origins arises a second layer of variable thickness, loaded with secondary elaboration: it is the discourse of culture, of paternal constructions, of ideals, of novels that try to establish a certain accord between the fate of the subject and the laws that rule him. From this superfetation of constructions, the retroactive snares can even present as a "fate" the road to be covered before death arrives. There we find fragments of broken pottery to be fixed according to the ideals of an acceptable and made-up truth. As the Cuban writer Eliseo de Diego has said: "To remember is not to live again; to remember is to lie again."[19] It is to integrate screen memo-

---

19. E. de Diego, *Informe contra mí mismo.* (México: Cal y Arena, 1997).

ries in a self-supporting narrative, in an epic where *ego* is the main character.

But we have not come to an end yet. The third geological layer of constructions with which we must cope in analysis is even the most deceitful. It comes from the cultural diffusion of psychoanalysis itself. In his 1937 paper, Freud gives an example of the sort of communication he offers the patient of what he cannot remember. The content of his speech is a story including the subject through this narrative into the oedipal myth, even in a Lacanian version, something that can be heard as, "At first you started by considering yourself as your mother's phallus but afterwards you were expelled from that place because of a fraternal rival and then you had to move forward to find your father (*père-version*), etc." This somewhat distorted (not so much, in fact) presentation of the Freudian model of constructions in analysis is compatible with the other models proposed since Freudian times to build a fresh image of the oedipal or preoedipal past, under the different disguises of a Kleinian paradigm, injecting from the here and now of the analytic situation a reconstruction of primal oral fantasies, or a "modern" model of a psychological restoration of the self, when the analyst reconstructs and repairs the nasty effects of deficient maternal care coming from a not-good-enough mother.

Myths, fictions, novels, semblances, lies, merciful lies, perhaps. It is possible—why not?—that the subject could come to us asking for a new construction, different and better than the ones already at hand, to recompose the smashed pieces of the historical presentation of himself. Yes, it is really possible that he comes to us to be confirmed as a partner in the collective myth, psychoanalytical, mostly oedipal, or some other. Yes, it is possible for him to take us as a Levi-

Straussian shaman who operates by offering him a new integration in the myth of his culture and, given the reality of our culture, that this myth should be the Freudian oedipal myth.

But, isn't it precisely at this point that Lacan rebels and says that "the analysis is not the rite of the Oedipus" and speaks about the "strictly unusable character of the Oedipus complex"?[20] We should say that this reintegration to the myth is what the patient often asks from the analyst. But the analyst will act as such if, and only if, she does not accept the demand, and if in its place she opens the space for the manifestation of the patient's unknown desire. Constructions are what we are asked to build as an answer given to a question. The analyst's attitude is well known: we receive the demand and we *do not* satisfy it. Rather we act contrarywise. Why? Because a construction loaded with meaning, organizing a coherent narrative of the past and integrating the subject into a tragic but conventional view of his own life in the collective community (religion) is not something that works against repression but acts totally in the same direction as repression does. It is the knowledge of the Other, a knowledge with the presumption of being complete and gap-fulfilling, a knowledge aiming at the conviction and belief in a fresh truth more than at the recollection of real events (which, nevertheless, could only be screen memories [*Deckerinnerungen*]). This would be the master's discourse repeated by the university, by the analytical institution with its presumed prestige; it would mean an intervention from the transferential authority of a knowledge against which the analytical discourse is supposed to fight. If the recovery of memories were the goal

20. J. Lacan, *Le Séminaire. Livre XVII. L'Envers de la Psychanalyse.* (París: Seuil, 1991), p. 113.

of analytical action, Freud would never have given up hypnosis and abreaction.

Psychoanalytic ethics is not an epic of the subject. Biographer, historian, novelist, fable-maker, storyteller are not
synonyms of the psychoanalyst. Everyone who is not an oli-
gophrenic of imagination can build several possible constructions, gathering any given set of data of associations and of
memories brought by the patient along a series of sessions. It
is sufficient for that to have some reading code: oedipal, transferential, of the succession of libidinal stages, of the absence
or excess of maternal care or of the paternal metaphor, of the
different ways of organizing the fantasy or about the vicissitudes of castration. There are so many possibilities for the
interpretation and the construction of a more or less successful story, such as Quine's *proxy functions*![21] The number of
these possibilities is only exceeded by the impossibility of
proving their truth, their error or their falsehood. The question of their being more or less false or true is irrelevant. If in
all of them there is a degree of verisimilitude and if there are
no criteria to assess levels of verisimilitude, then they are all
equivalent and the only differential criterion is the faith invested by the analyst in her own interpretative model or the
degree of conviction that she can induce in her patient (see
Ricoeur[22]). In his book *Moses and Monotheism* [23] Freud could
write: "Not even the most tempting probability is a protec-

---

21. W. V. Quine, *Theories and things* (Cambridge, MA: Harvard University Press, 1981).

22. P. Ricoeur, "The question of proof in Freud's psychoanalytic
writings," *Journal of the American Psychoanalytic Association* 25:835–869,
1977.

23. S. Freud, "Moses and monotheism," *SE* 23:17, *GW* 16:114, 1939.

tion against error; even if all the parts of a problem seem to fit together like the pieces of a jig-saw puzzle, one must reflect that what is probable is not necessarily the truth and that the truth is not always probable." In the 1922 paper[24] that we shall consider later he expressed the opposite view: once the pieces of the jigsaw puzzle fit together without leaving gaps between them, one knows that the solution of the puzzle has been reached and that there is no alternative solution.

Skepticism is always sane. Elementary wisdom leads us to say with Wittgenstein that "Whereof one cannot speak, thereof one must remain silent."[25] Whereof one cannot speak, whereof one cannot produce or evoke memories, whereof what organizes verisimilarily a human life, that what one has been in the desire of the Other . . . if we were to use Freudian terms, about the *urverdrängt*, the originally repressed, or if we prefer Lacanian terms, about the signifier of a lack in the Other, the signifier of lost *jouissance*; whereof what is the foundation of all discourse that is not able to be included in the discourse itself. About this incompatibility between *jouissance* and language, why should we speak once we have admitted that any proposition referring to it would be semblance, fiction, construction? *Analysis, what for?* Has it any sense once we have renounced to the goals of the emotional reeducation or the impossible construction of a lost past? And if we are not to dedicate ourselves to this narrative work and to the rhetorical task of constructions that supposedly portray our patients in our discourse, then what will we do instead?

---

24. S. Freud, "Remarks on the theory and practice of dream interpretation," *SE* 19:116, *GW* 13:309, 1923.

25. L. Wittgenstein, *Tractatus Logico-Philosophicus*. (London: Routledge and Kegan, 1990), section 7.0.

It is a pressing question for the theory and practice of psychoanalysis. The practitioner faces two options and must indeed choose. Either he produces meaning through interpretations and constructions, looking for the assent and confirmation signaled by the patient, or he goes against meaning, reduces it and smashes to pieces the imaginary reinforcements that meaning usually produces. Will he *construct* fantasies and historical narratives, or will he *deconstruct* them, thus revealing the fictitious underground of the already existing construction? And, if he chooses deconstruction, he must also answer the question: What for? Why destroy the imaginary basis of an existence? What is he ready to offer as a substitute (if any)?

The family romance and the individual myth both accomplish a function. The imaginary consistence they provide supplies symbolic inconsistence. The strong ego, even reinforced by certain analytic practices, allows one to go on living. Why attack its blessed strength? If the previous constructions show their frailty, why not reinforce or replace them with new fictions guaranteed by a supposed Freudian scientificity or by the institutions Freud founded? There are legions of psychoanalysts who take this path. They admit with us that historical truth cannot be reached and that, should it be reached, it could not be proved either within the analytic situation or elsewhere. However, they acknowledge the necessity of meaningful fictions offering coherence to somebody's life. At last, they coincide with Freud's final ideas considering that what is decisive for the cure is the patient's conviction, even if they cannot say with the same certainty as Freud's that such conviction equates truth. With a *si non é vero é ben trovato* they are satisfied and well served.

Their goal is not that historical truth that would be able to ground a strong scientificity for psychoanalysis but to make audible the "rhetorical voice of psychoanalysis,"[26] understanding "rhetoric" as the use of language for persuasion through speech or writing. As Paul Ricoeur has said, "We must maintain the critical dimension of narrativity, which is just that of self-recognition, of recognition of the other, and of recognition of the fantasy. We may even say, then, that the patient is both the actor and the critic of a history which he is at first unable to recount. The problem of recognizing oneself is the problem of recovering the ability to recount one's own history, to endlessly continue to give the form of a history to reflections on oneself. And working-through is nothing other than this continuous narration."[27] We are tempted to add, as before, in the French phrase, "*cause, cause toujours.*"

The authors who engage themselves in such a way are not interested in the recollection of past experiences and its possible explanatory virtues for the present. They only look after the coherent comprehension of that past. For them, the analytic function is that of producing a continuous and efficient narrative. They don't seem to worry about problems posed by the amount of secondary elaboration necessary to make the construction credible, or about the relation between the acceptance of the narrative and the transferential situation in which it is produced and submitted to the approval of the patient.

This issue has a peculiar importance. The memory, the appearance of recollections, and the way in which they conform and lead to the constitution of a narrative depend on the context of remembering. And that context is, in the analytic

---

26. D. P. Spence, "The rhetorical voice voice of Psychoanalysis." *Journal of the American Psychoanalytic Association* 38:579, 1990.

27. P. Ricoeur, op. cit.

situation, that of a specific transferential relation. It is not seldom that memories come to the analysand. If somebody remembers, she will remember for somebody, for the Other of transference. To remember, always but especially in psychoanalysis, is to remember for (the desire of) the Other. The same thing happens with dreams. The one who hears is a participant in a dream that is being told. The scene, the *Schauplatz* of the dream, calls the adressee to a stage. In every psychoanalysis, to remember, to dream, to communicate (or not) the free associations ordered by the fundamental rule, to produce precisely those associations and not any other, are all effects of transference.

In his paper "Remarks on the Theory and the Practice of Dream Interpretation,"[28] Freud said that "if anyone wishes to maintain that most of the dreams can be made use of (*verwertwaren*, valuable, worthwhile) in analysis are obliging dreams (*Gefälligkeitsträume*, dreams of compliance, dreamt for pleasing the analyst), and owe their origin to suggestion, nothing can be said against that opinion from the point of view of analytic theory."[29] Let us call them *compleasant* dreams, more akin to *gefallen*, instead of *obliging*. What happens in these cases? It happens that the analyst does not preserve the X of his desire and lets the patient know what he expects from him. And the analysand, after receiving the message, returns to the sender his own message in an inverted form. He places himself in the position of offering presents to the analyst, of dreaming to please him (*zu ihn gefallen, Gefälligkeit*). Freud was aware that the attitude leading to the production of pleasing or complacent dreams came from the paternal complex

28. S. Freud, "Remarks . . . ," *SE* 19:116, *GW* 13:309, 1923.

29. Ibid., *SE* 19:117, *GW* 13:310, 1923.

(*Elternkomplex*), that is, from positive transference. It is to please the analyst that dreams end by becoming a motor yielding benefits that support the goals of analysis. We should be more precise: the goals of the analyst. Because "it is the deferential—compleasing (*entgegenkommende*)—work of the cure that loosens repression."[30] In the Standard Edition, we read "the work of treatment has gone half-way to meet it [!] and has loosened the repression."[31]

Freud's trust is not undermined by the acknowledged fact that the patient dreams and—we add—remembers and associates to satisfy what he imagines the analyst expects from him. This is why we are able to explain how is it that every analyst, whatever the technique used, always find the confirmatory material for her theories and can boast of her clinical findings without lying before an audience who is also pleased and waits for new confirmations from her. What Lacan called "the forced card of the clinic" (the English translation states mistakenly "the forced *map* of the clinic")[32] is being played with no respite. And that forced card is nothing less than the use of transference to get compleasant formations of the unconscious. Between the most common of such productions appear what has been called also by Freud "feelings of memory" and "confirmatory dreams."[33] Let us sum up. For Freud constructions are not the consequence of the associative labor of a patient and of her recollections. Rather, they are a preliminary product of the analyst's work. He produces them and

---

30. Ibid., *GW* 13:311.
31. Ibid., *SE* 19:118.
32. J. Lacan, *Écrits*, (Paris: Seuil, 1966), p. 800. *Écrits: A Selection*. (New York: Norton, 1977), p. 299 (mistranslates *carte forcée* as *forced map*).
33. Ibid., *SE* 19:117.

offers them to her and afterwards he receives as an answer the confirmatory material taking the form of memories and complacent dreams.

In some passages of his 1922 paper he speaks about "some" (how many?, we wonder, specially when "some" in the English translation comes from the German "*manchen*," meaning "many") patients who only produce corroborative dreams for the constructions uttered by the analyst. Then he writes that "doubt says"—yes; it is *doubt* speaking by itself, "*der Zweifel sagt*" transformed in the English version into "the doubt arises"—"that these corroborative dreams may be entirely without evidential value, since they may have been imagined (*phantasiert*), in compliance with the physician's words instead of having been brought to light from the dreamer's unconscious. This ambiguous position cannot be escaped in the analysis, *since with these patients unless one interprets, constructs, and propounds, one never obtains access to what is repressed* in them" [emphasis added].[34]

We could reassure ourselves by thinking that this activity of ours loosens repression. But is it so certain? Why should it not be, rather, given the vast variety of results produced by the variety of analysts, a consequence of love, of transferential love? We can also argue in a syllogistic way. Let us admit Freud's initial formula: the dream is a wish-fulfillment. Then we can take another consecrated formula correlated to the former: the desire is the desire of the Other. With these two premises we can ask: What is the wish involved in the transferential situation? Now, let us agree with Freud when he says that the "worthwhile (*verwertwaren*)" dreams in psychoanalysis are dreams of compliance. After placing together this argu-

---

34. Ibid.

ments, we must arrive to an inescapable conclusion: *the dream is a wish-fulfillment . . . of the analyst*. This was Freud's own case as an analyst of his own dreams when he wrote *Die Traumdeutung*. And Lacan didn't miss the point when he clearly stated: "We know that he laid it down as a rule that the expression of a desire must always be sought in the dream. But let us be sure what he meant by this. If Freud admits, as the motive of a dream apparently contrary to his thesis (*Gegenwunschträume* in the *Traumdeutung*), the very desire to contradict him on the part of the subject whom he had tried to convince of his theory, how could he fail to admit the same motive for himself from the moment that, having arrived at this point, it was from another that his own law came back to him?"[35]

And what about the patient? Most of the time he tries to comply and to please in order to be loved and accepted by the interpreter, who, according to Freud's desire, started by expressing his wish for the admission of a construction coherent with his way of thinking and understanding psychoanalysis. Freudian technique, as it comes from Freudian recommendations, is unequivocal. The construction does not proceed from the material brought by the patient but from the analytical theory itself, mainly the oedipal theory. The repeated accusation against psychoanalysis that is was oedipizing can be well founded and just, even if we can support the adverse idea that it ought not be so. When the analyst provides some construction it is necessarily based on a certain theoretical preconception coming from what was learnt through previous analysis, through Freud's or some other's texts or through the analyst's own analysis carried out, most probably, according to the same oedipizing criteria.

---

35. *Écrits*; in French, p. 268; in English, p. 58.

There is the manifestation of some knowledge involving a desire: it is the desire of the Other disguised as an analyst. We can follow Freud when he poses that in such a way ("look at the Montgolfier") we place a magnet that can attract and bring to consciousness what has been repressed. In such a case, can we be sure that we are not inducing a new alienation into our own desire and knowledge, instead of overcoming the repressive process? It is a transcendental question. Perhaps it is the most important reason for understanding the ethical foundation of the analytical silence and for justifying Lacanian skepticism regarding interpretation as well as Lacan's mistrust of constructions.

If those are manifestations of a supposed knowledge subject, they could not be instruments of liberation with regard to the oppresive repression. Interpretations and constructions would rather be the reinforcements of repression through the work and combined action of the Master's and the University's discourses. That is why the essence of the analytic discourse is a wordless discourse, without propositions meant to transmit knowledge, with no ratification of familiar novels and individual myths, without pretending the replacement of a childish and naive knowledge for a sophisticated and presumably psychoanalytic new one.

Let us compare Freudian and Lacanian techniques. In the latter we find cuts, punctuations, plays with equivocations in grammar, homophony, and logics. Every analytic intervention seems to be guided by a single goal: that of debasing meaning—meaning feeding the symptom, as Lacan used to say in his last years. The discourse of the analyst is raised beyond and against those three layers of constructions that we already mentioned: maternal, cultural, and psychoanalytical. It has to be a meaningless and wordless discourse.

In Lacan we find a clear denunciation of that "we all know what is what has to be induced in the analysed" (already quoted) told by Freud. From the very beginning the question is settled: every memory involves a falsification, every official history is the result of an activity of the ego as it happens also with every supposed reconstruction of the forgotten past. Neither the analysand nor the analyst stand for supporting those semblances of truth. The issue is not, however, to ignore memory. Absolutely not. Memories and the whole set of (re)constructions working through the past are a fact and nobody can shy away from it. It is nothing less than the raw material for analytic work. The analyst hears it and allows the possibility through the transference of his being taken as an object inside that very history. We must not ignore that every analytical session is a punctual and a decisive event in the course of that history. Thousands of mirages have to appear, fantasy must bloom, narcissistic endearments of the subject himself or projected upon others ought to be set into motion, many novels must be told. This is the marrow and the bone of the cure—the combined action of all modalities of alienation—reanimated in order for its *non*confirmation through the use of the analyst's deterrent weapons of equivocation and through the dissolving power of silence and scansion.

There is an antinomy between meaning and truth, inasmuch as meaning excludes the real, and the real, reluctant to any wording, only allows the half-saying, the *mi-dire* of truth. Truth means and only means that a signifier is lacking in the Other. It has no objective content expressed through propositions filled with meaning.

This radical skepticism towards truth, towards a full speech, towards all promises of fulfillment, takes us out from the mirage of construction to the opposite place: deconstruction, destruction, and, in the very first place, destitution of that subject incarnating the supposed knowledge, now debased. Implicitly what is denounced is the analytic swindle (*l'escroquerie analytique*). After that debasement there is no more somebody to receive the complaints because there is no Other to keep the balance of the given and taken or to offer compensations for the lack. The subject has to live beyond meaning and sense, beyond the eternal or the natural father who could guarantee or authorize him.

The thesis that I sustain here is that the construction is not the reconstruction of a forgotten past. It is nothing but the proposition of a fantasy, supported by the transferential authority that comes to reinforce and not to face and dissolve the power of the Other. The goal of analysis cannot be the same as the goal of religion, as happens when the place of the supposed knowledge subject is preserved.

If we accept what I have said until now, we will be aware of ethical differences—appearing as technical ones—that separate Lacan from Freud. To complete our task we must hear a new character, a character created by Freud himself. This character is named *"der Skeptiker,"* not to be confounded with *"der Zweifler,"* the dubious, that appear in the same 1922 paper. For *der Skeptiker* there is nothing like recovered memories in analysis. For him these are mnemic hallucinations, illusions (*Erinnerungtäuschungen*), semblances.[36] Freud makes his skeptics say that they could hardly be a retrieval of recollections when so often there is no question of forgotten events but of unconscious fantasies that the analytical communication of a construction has moved to the front of the stage, and that they do not end in a memory but in the feeling of a sub-

---

36. S. Freud, "Remarks . . . ," *SE* 19:115, *GW* 13:308, 1923.

jective conviction (*ein Gefühl subjektiver Überzeugung*). *Über-zeugung*, conviction, in the truth of the construction, as we have already seen by reading first the 1937 paper.

For the skeptic, this road leading to conviction is blocked forever. If the analyst's word telling a construction is just a fantasy, a rational fantasy, the only thing that can be expected is a *feeling of recollection* (an *Erinnerungsgefühl*), a mirage of memory. Perhaps this is the closing point for my paper on constructions: I wish to offer a proper name to represent the Freudian *Skeptiker*, and that name would be one of the most prominent names in the philosophy of our century, that of Ludwig Wittgenstein. And my closing point should become a new starting point, a new task: to discuss the complex relation linking Freud to Wittgenstein. We can just offer the thesis that the Lacanian subversion of psychoanalysis, acting well beyond the "return to Freud," would take into account Wittgenstein's critique of the Freudian thesis about the unconscious. A Lacanian critique may be elaborated quite independently of the possible knowledge that Lacan could have or not about Wittgenstein's objections to the Freudian unconscious.

11

"Heads I Win, Tails You Lose": Wittgenstein, Plato, and the Role of Construction and Deconstruction in Psychoanalysis and Ethics

ERICH D. FREIBERGER

The question of the validity of psychoanalytic constructions raises a disconcerting problem for both psychoanalytic theory and the philosophical tradition alike. Freud's insistence that the analyst's task is to reconstruct the analysand's forgotten memories is problematic for psychoanalysis because it has frequently been used by critics of psychoanalysis to call into question the validity of psychoanalytic knowledge. The problem is equally disturbing for philosophy because of its very centrality, inasmuch as the epistemological question it raises is essentially the same problem raised by the debate between traditional dogmatic metaphysics and the various critical methodologies that oppose it, from Kant's critical philosophy to Wittgenstein's ordinary language analysis and Derridean deconstruction. The problem posed by psychoanalytic constructions is essentially the following: What is the status of our hypotheses of the real? Do they represent adequate knowledge that somehow accurately describes it? Or are they simply fantasies?

In "Constructions in Psychoanalysis," Freud tells us that the analyst's task is "to construct" what "has been forgotten out of the traces of what it has left behind." This analytic

> work of construction, or if it is preferred, reconstruction, resembles to a great extent an archaeologist's excavation and reconstruction of some dwelling-place that has been destroyed or buried in some ancient edifice. The two processes are in fact identical, except that the analyst works under better conditions and has more material at his command to assist him, since what he is dealing with is not something destroyed but something that is still alive— and perhaps for another reason as well. Just as the archaeologist builds up the walls of the building from the foundations that have remained standing, determines the number and position of the columns from the depressions in the floor and reconstructs the mural decorations and paintings from remains found in the débris, so does the analyst proceed when he draws his inferences from the fragments of memories, from the associations and from the behavior of the subject of the analysis.[1]

The problem raised by this approach is how such constructions might ever be vouchsafed or verified, and this is the obstacle on which Freud's account founders, for the notion that the pathogenic memory can be reconstructed raises the epistemological question of the analyst's access to the truth of his constructions. What are the grounds of his certainty?

---

1. S. Freud, "Constructions in psycho-analysis," *Standard Edition* 23:259, 1937.

How can he know the truth of his construction? This question is essentially the same question Freud raises about the status of the primal scene in the case of the Wolfman: Is the primal scene a real experience or is it a fantasy retroactively transformed into the primal scene by deferred action? In what follows I will appeal to Wittgenstein's ordinary language analysis to illustrate how a linguistically oriented approach to the question of construction shows Freud's treatment of the issue to be laden with metaphysical presuppositions that decisively mislead his understanding of both analytic theory and technique. What I propose is that there is a similarity between Wittgenstein's critique of the traditional philosophical "problems" and Lacan's critique of the imaginary, which can explain how Lacan's rejection of interpretation and construction successfully avoids the epistemological difficulties encountered by Freud's approach.

From a Lacanian perspective, the question of whether the primal scene is real or imagined is, strictly speaking, irrelevant, because Freud conceives the analyst's task as producing a conviction in the truth of his construction, whether it is confirmed by the patient's recollection or not. On this view the analyst's task is not to reconstruct the pathogenic origin, in a way that represents a completely self-transparent revelation of the patient's repressed wishes, but to subvert the various imaginary constructions that the subject brings into analysis. The reason for this difference is that Freud's idealized understanding of the repressed content (indeed to think of it as a content already reifies it) simultaneously universalizes and reifies the psychic object, transforming it into an hypostatized essence. It is this imaginary hypostatization of the repressed— and not the actual dynamic of the transference—that leads Freud to insist that the analyst must induce the analysand to accept the truth of his construction, whether it is confirmed by free association or not. Thus, a Lacanian approach would appear to accept the criticism that analytic interpretation adheres to the principle of "heads I win, tails you lose," to which Freud's essay responds. From a Lacanian perspective such a dogmatic approach violates the ethical character of psychoanalytic practice by transforming the discourse of the analyst into the discourse of the master. It also raises the question of whether Freud properly characterized the dynamics of the transference at work in his own practice.

Freud's dogmatic conception of the repressed content leads him to overlook the extent to which primary repression necessarily limits the subject's access to his repressed desire. As what inaugurates the subject's passage into discourse, primary repression cannot itself be included in the discourse it founds. This suggests that there is a crucial difference in technique between Freudian and Lacanian psychoanalysis. Recently Néstor Braunstein has argued that psychoanalysis and the transference upon which its curative effect depends is not to be construed as operating through a process of construction, but rather as operating through the deconstruction of the various constructions that the subject brings to the analysis: the constructions of the maternal discourse, those of the discourse of the dominant culture, and even those of psychoanalytic theory itself. Although this claim is developed in terms of Freud and Lacan, a passing reference to Wittgenstein suggests that this deconstruction is conceived not so much in Derridean but in Wittgensteinian terms. In what follows I will briefly indicate what a Wittgensteinian approach to the question of construction has to offer psychoanalysis.

Wittgenstein's conception that a word's meaning is its use offers an approach to the problem of psychoanalytic constructions that paradoxically condemns such constructions to the status of illusions, or semblances, while simultaneously offering a way to save the phenomena of psychoanalytic practice by showing that this so-called problem is only an apparent one.[2] For if meaning is merely ascribable to the use of a word, then the status of an analytic construction is, strictly speaking, irrelevant provided it has its effect in the language game of analysis. To put the point differently, we might say that Wittgensteinian analysis provides a way to analyze analysis itself by permitting us to describe what analysts actually do, rather than forcing us to rely on their sometimes unreliable reports of what they think they do. Thus, Wittgenstein provides a way to deconstruct Freud's notion of construction that takes account of its curative effect in the transference, without committing psychoanalysis to any idealized conception of meaning that would transform psychoanalysis into either a metaphysics or the rite of Oedipus. This suggests that Lacan's emphasis on the importance of language in psychoanalysis turns the apparent failure of Freud's account of construction into an advantage. Where the repressed is conceived as a function of a linguistic process it can no longer be reified as a determinate content that the analyst reconstructs. On this view, Lacan's lack of trust in interpretation and his rejection

---

2. When Wittgenstein says that a word's meaning is simply its use (cf. *Philosophical Investigations*, tr. G. E. M. Anscombe [Englewood Cliffs, NJ: Prentice Hall, 1953] §30, §41, §43, §138, §197, §532, §556), this amounts to a refusal of depth that offers a way to account for the uncertain status of Freud's constructions. At the same time, however, this refusal is paradoxically what motivates Wittgenstein's various criticisms of unconscious motivation. Thus, Wittgenstein's limitation of meaning to use is at once his philosophy's greatest strength and its greatest weakness when it is applied to psychoanalysis.

of the procedure of construction and reconstruction might be seen as a response to Wittgenstein that overcomes his objections to psychoanalysis by incorporating a Wittgensteinian deconstruction of meaning (or something very much like it) into his revision of Freudian theory.

To see how Wittgenstein's thought can be construed as simultaneously hostile and friendly to psychoanalysis, let us examine his critique of the construction of meaning. In a discussion of games in the *Philosophical Investigations*, Wittgenstein remarks how similarities between games "crop up and disappear" such that our examination produces "a complicated network of similarities overlapping and crisscrossing: sometimes overall similarities and sometimes similarities of detail."[3] How are we to make sense of these shifting similarities? Do they have a single essence? What ties them into a unity? Wittgenstein calls their similarity a "family resemblance," and then in a direct attack on the traditional concept of meaning that is suggestive of the tenor of his entire approach he turns to the analysis of number:

> And for instance the kinds of number form a family in the same way. Why do we call something "a number"? Well, perhaps because it has a—direct—relationship with several things that have hitherto been called number; and this can be said to give it an indirect relationship to other things we call by the same name. And we extend our concept of number as in spinning a thread we twist fibre on fibre. And the strength of the thread does not reside in the fact that some one fibre runs through its whole length, but in the overlapping of many fibres.

---

3. L. Wittgenstein, *Philosophical Investigations*, 32e.

> But if someone wished to say: "There is something in common to all these constructions—namely the disjunction of all their common properties"—I should then reply: Now you are only playing with words. One might as well say: "Something runs through the whole thread—namely the continuous overlapping of those fibers."[4]

The point of this passage is that there is no essential meaning to any concept at all. For Wittgenstein meaning is, rather, merely constructed out of its use, as fibres are woven together to form a thread. Thus, the meaning of what we call "number" is nothing more than a direct relationship to its use, that is, it is a direct relationship to "other things that have been hitherto called number." As a result there is no common essence to these constructions. Instead, the family resemblance "number" is merely constructed in each case out of its immediate usage, which constitutes a direct or indirect link to other usages.

Let us consider what happens if we compare this account of the construction of meaning (which is in fact a deconstruction of the traditional notion) with Freud's account of analytic construction. First of all, the notion that meaning is constructed as nothing but a use that establishes a direct or indirect relationship to other uses in the same family recalls the way dream construction occurs by displacement and condensation. Second, we find that each such relationship, or meaning, is grasped as a construction, in a way that parallels Freud's description of the analyst's act of construction (just as it also parallels the process of the "construction" of the dream described in *The Interpretation of Dreams*). The ana-

---

4. Ibid., 32e.

lyst gathers associative material, dreams, and repetitive actions that are used to develop constructions, just as the construction of meaning is based on direct and indirect relationships of association. But the most important point is that there is no hypostatized essence of any particular construction, just a series of acts that are woven together into a thread, or "family," of resemblances. This suggests that the construction is a never-ending task, which, of course, implies that the task of analytic reconstruction would be equally unending and hence impossible.[5] What is important here, then, is not the idea of some essential meaning, but rather the notion that meaning is only grasped or constructed through its use. This use may be determined by a particular context (and thus, the various parental constructions that patients bring with them to analysis are remarkably similar to the family resemblances that Wittgenstein mentions here), but the important thing is that this approach to the construction of meaning implies that meaning is never fixed, but is only constituted through its use.

If we apply this notion that meaning is constituted by its use to analytic constructions, it appears to suggest that analytic construction has little hope of arriving at its goal, because its goal is an illusion. Thus, in some of Wittgenstein's discussions of Freud he occasionally appears to be harshly critical of any notion of unconscious motivation.[6] The result of this comparison then, is that on Wittgenstein's terms analytic construction must be something other than the discovery of a single enduring essence (or an actual primal scene or

---

5. Compare *Philosophical Investigations*, §87, 41e.

6. L. Wittgenstein, *Lectures and Conversations on Aesthetics, Psychology and Religious Belief*, ed. C. Barrett (Oxford: Basil Blackwell, 1966) pp. 22–27, 42–52.

repressed traumatic event) which constitutes "the ground" of the subject's associations. On the other hand, however, Wittgenstein would be the first to point out that this does not necessarily mean that psychoanalytic constructions are false. To pose the problem this way merely indicates a muddle. There is no deep object of our analysis, no "essential" or "primal" scene to be discovered. Rather, we know what a word's meaning is through its use, and this use is simply what occurs in the language game in which it is employed. In this view, analysis might be regarded as a language game, like any other in which the meaning of the analytic constructions are nothing but the use in which they are employed as they gain a functional meaning in the transference. This Wittgensteinian approach to the problem of construction suggests an alternative that Freud did not consider because he was misled by the metaphysical presuppositions of his epistemology into reifying the repressed content and construing it as an idealized essence. But notice as well that, on this view, the problem of the truthfulness of the analyst's constructions (e.g., whether the primal scene is a real event or a fantasy) drops entirely out of account, because the very notion that there is a repressed "content" is itself revealed to be a semblance, or a false construction of meaning into which grammar has seduced us. One might, of course, object that analysis cannot be properly called a language game, because there is no such thing as an "ordinary use" of language in psychoanalysis, but this would fly in the face of Wittgenstein's text.[7] Analysis is a game (although a highly complex one) with a definite use as much as any other.[8]

---

7. *Philosophical Investigations*, p. 215e.

8. Take for example something that occurred on the flight to this conference: Flight attendant: ". . .if there is anything we can do to make

But what does saying analysis is a language game tell us about what actually happens in analysis? Certainly there are words in analysis. And, notwithstanding Lacan's call for a posture of analytic silence that is more deconstructive than constructive of any grand narrative of the patient's history, there frequently are constructions of meaning and the construction of interpretations in analysis. But what do these words do? Is it so easy to say? In Wittgenstein's terms the best we seem to be able to say is that this meaning is nothing more than the use to which these constructions are put in the trans-

---

your flight more comfortable please do not call." How would Wittgenstein address this slip, this failure to say "please do not hesitate to call"? Not as if she meant to say one thing, but actually said another, which reveals her unconscious will, or another that thinks in her place; rather, he would simply treat it as if this is what she intended. She "meant" to say "do not call." One could of course "try psychoanalytically to discover the causes" of this intention by examining her past, behaviour, but her meaning is never to be distinguished from its use (cf. *Philosophical Investigations*, p. 215e). Psychoanalytic explanation merely looks at another use: the use in the transference. In other words, Freud is telling us to extend the domain of what we consider to be a term's use beyond the domain of the ordinary, just as Freud says in the quote from Schiller at the beginning of Chapter II in *The Interpretation of Dreams*, where dreams are looked at as if they revealed another use when regarded in the context of other apparently absurd thoughts: "Looked at in isolation, a thought may seem very trivial or very fantastic; but it may be made important by another thought that comes after it, and in conjunction with other thoughts that may seem equally absurd, it may turn out to form a most effective link." In psychoanalysis, use is simply extended beyond the range of ordinary language, just as it is in philosophical, and particularly ethical, discourse. In this sense both forms of discourse go beyond the existing world, as Wittgenstein himself remarks of ethical discourse in "A Lecture on Ethics" in *Philosophical Occasions 1912–1951*, ed. J. Klagee and A. Nordmann (Indianapolis: Hackett Publishing Company, 1993) p. 44. Regarded this way, perhaps psychoanalysis, like philosophy, is simply a more complex language game that shows itself to have "a use" beyond that of ordinary language.

ference. But perhaps this is something after all. What Wittgenstein offers is a way to think about psychoanalysis and psychoanalytic construction that has nothing to do with either meaning or the apparent referents of speech. If we thus consider neurotic illness as a language game that has gone awry (or perhaps as a variant game in which use is short-circuited and words are used to produce symptoms rather than more standard uses in the game), then what does it matter if in curing this symptom analysts play another language game, which turns around the transference, and requires one's complicity in the necessary fiction or semblance of the construction that the subject expects from the analyst?[9] This fiction would be analysand's supposition that the analyst is a subject who knows, which inaugurates the transference. Analysis could then be construed as proceeding through the destruction of this supposition, so that this transferential supposition might be replaced by the understanding that the Other is lacking. Given the almost infinite variety of possible analytic interpretations, what is surprising here is that analysis works at all. Thus we should not find it strange that we can form an interpretation of a repressed content, but rather we

---

9. Compare Wittgenstein's claim: "The sign-post is in order—if, under normal circumstances, it fulfills its purpose" (*Philosophical Investigation*, §87, p. 41e). We could say that analysis helps return the use of signs to their "normal circumstances" in the game of everyday speech, and if this reduces analysis to a normative role of the forms of life in which it is embedded then so be it. Either words have a use or they don't, and if we use them in the context of a game then there is no way to prevent this game from constituting a norm. This is similar to what Lacan says about the phallic order in *Encore*. There is no way to avoid the fact that language is at least minimally normative in the sense that it inaugurates a rule of substitution that always leaves something out of account; not everything can be said.

should find it remarkable that so many different interpretations appear to attain their effect.[10] For in the end there can be no guarantee of the validity of an interpretation, and not just because it cannot be verified, but rather because primal repression excludes the possibility that the subject might find the words in which everything can be said. Thus, instead of citing the close of the *Tractatus*, "whereof one cannot speak, thereof one must remain silent," we can cite an alternate passage from the *Philosophical Investigations* that is more appropriate to our present theme:

> I use the name "N" without a *fixed* meaning. (But that detracts as little from its usefulness, as it detracts from that of a table that it stands on four legs instead of three and sometimes wobbles). Should it be said that I am using a word whose meaning I don't know and am talking nonsense?—Say what you choose, as long as it does not prevent you from seeing the facts, and when you see them, there is a good deal that you will not say.[11]

Clearly this characterization of "seeing the facts" could be applied to both ordinary usage and to the analyst's interpretation and handling of the transference. What I am suggesting is that this quotation can be applied to the way the analyst manages the relationship between the patient's constructions and the deconstruction of those constructions in the transference.

---

10. Compare §524 *Philosophical Investigations*, p. 142e, "Don't take it as a matter of course, but as a remarkable fact that pictures and fictitious narratives give us pleasure, occupy our minds. ('Don't take it as a matter of course' means: find it surprising, as you do some things that disturb you. Then the puzzling aspect of the latter will disappear, by your accepting this fact as you do the other.")

11. Ibid., p. 37e.

Thus, the subject's speech appears in a way that has no fixed meaning accessible to analytic construction, but this does not in the least detract from its usefulness in the formation of neurotic symptoms. What does it matter what the subject says so long as it does not prevent the analyst from seeing "the facts," which are not any idealized entities but simply how this speech is used? When the analyst sees these facts there is a great deal he will not say, just as there is a great deal the subject will not say when he receives his own message back in inverted form in the transference. What he will not say is a necessary consequence of his insight into the function of primal repression.

This notion that not everything can be said and that there can be no fixed meaning to our words is put even more starkly in a later passage that decisively indicates the limits of analytic construction: "if God looked into our minds he would not be able to see whom we were speaking of."[12] What this inability to say everything means is that, from a Wittgensteinian perspective, we might say that it makes no difference whether the analyst's constructions name real experience or fantasies. It makes no difference whether they hit the mark, because they never can anyway, given the fact that words and things—desires and demands—are never interchangeable. On Wittgensteinian grounds it makes little difference whether the analyst's constructions are correct, provided one not insist upon saying everything and soliciting the patient's conviction.

Another way to see how Wittgenstein and Lacan appear to be engaged in parallel tasks is to consider his frequent denunciation of the pretensions and the delusions of the philosophical tradition. Thus, Wittgenstein writes:

---

12. Ibid., p. 217e.

> We feel as if we had to penetrate phenomena: our inves-
> tigation, however, is not directed towards phenomena,
> but as one might say, towards the *"possibilities"* of phe-
> nomena . . . our investigation is therefore a grammatical
> one.[13]

Traditionally, the goal of philosophy has been to banish misunderstandings but, in a way that is reminiscent of Lacan's
critique of the philosophical tradition in *Encore*, Wittgenstein
denounces philosophy for falling prey to the greatest misunderstanding of all, namely that there is a "final analysis of
our forms of language and so a *single* completely resolved form
of every expression"[14] that grants God the possibility of a
perfect analysis of the whole. We might think of this as the
illusion that Lacan denounces when he suggests that man has
confused woman with God, by mistaking the *Grand A* of the
symbolic order for his *petit a*, of an intuition of the whole that
he imagines is enjoyed by God.[15] Wittgenstein makes a similar point in different terms when he says:

> We eliminate misunderstandings by making our expres-
> sions more exact; but now it may look as if we were mov-
> ing towards a particular state, a state of complete exactness;
> and as if this were the real goal of our investigation. . . .
> This finds expression in questions as to the *essence* of
> language, of propositions, of thought.—For if we too in
> these investigations are trying to understand the essence
> of language—its function, its structure—yet *this* is not

---

13. *Philosophical Investigations*, §90, p. 43e.
14. Ibid.
15. *Le séminaire de Jacques Lacan: Livre XX, Encore* (Paris: Seuil, 1975) p. 77.

what those questions have in view. For they see the essence, not in something that already lies open to view and
that becomes surveyable by a rearrangement, but something that lies *beneath* the surface. Something that lies
within, which we see when we look *into* the thing, and
which analysis digs out.[16]

Wittgenstein is telling us that the lure of an ultimate ground,
of depth, is itself an illusion. There is no essence, anymore than
there is a final analysis. There is only the possibility of inquir-
ing into structure and function, which already appear on the
surface. Thus, meaning is nothing more than use; it is only
grammar that seduces us into thinking it is something more.

This shows that Wittgenstein is engaged in a "deconstruction" of the traditional notion of meaning. We can get a clear
idea of how this Wittgensteinian deconstruction would treat
Freud's image of reconstruction as archaeology if we consider
the following paragraph from the *Philosophical Investigations*:

Where does our investigation seem to get its importance
from, since it seems only to destroy everything that is interesting, that is, all that is great and important? (As it
were all the buildings, leaving behind only stone and
rubble). What we are destroying is nothing but houses of
cards and we are clearing up the ground of language on
which they stand.[17]

Where Freud proposes that the analyst's task involves the
reconstruction of a repressed complex that is conceived as a
determinate entity, a Lacanian approach to the repressed com-

---

16. Ibid.
17. Ibid., §118, p. 48e.

plex is far more Wittgensteinian in that it commends a deconstruction of the various constructions with which the
analysand arrives at analysis. Rather than reinforce the analysand's constructions of meaning, Lacanian analysis conceives
its task as the deconstruction of these constructions to reveal
the particular way in which the analysand has been subjected
to the symbolic register.

Having established that Lacanian analysis involves a kind
of deconstruction, I would now like to discuss how the psychoanalytic conception of this "deconstruction" or subversion
of the analysand's address as an ethical task might help us to
reconsider the relation between psychoanalysis and traditional
metaphysics.

If, as has already been suggested, there is a parallel between psychoanalysis and metaphysics with respect to their
approach to the question of meaning, this raises a problem
for the relation between "construction" and "deconstruction"
in both fields, for psychoanalysts are not the first to have
traced the subject's itinerary through three levels of construction, followed by a fourth that destroys them.[18] Indeed, in
what can only be called a remarkable act of *anamnesis*, it appears that the Lacanian account of analytic deconstruction has

---

18. I am proposing his levels of construction and deconstruction are
strikingly similar to the four levels of the divided line (510a–511e) that
Socrates proposes as one of three images of the Good "beyond being" (509c)
at the end of book VI of Plato's *Republic*. When Socrates is asked "What is
the good?" at 506b–d, he responds by saying that he is not at all sure he
can say, nor that his interlocutor can understand, but he can provide a
"child," or the interest on the Good, which will substitute for the absent
father or principal, of which he does not give an account. He then proceeds to lay out three images (the sun, the divided line, and the cave) and
tells us that each can be used to interpret the other. The key point is that
as the Good is "beyond being," no image can represent it.

rediscovered the four levels of Plato's divided line with an almost uncanny precision. Thus, we find that the constructions stemming from the maternal discourse correspond to fantasy at the first level; the constructions of the discourse of culture correspond to what Plato calls *pistis* or faith in conventional opinion; the constructions of psychoanalytic theory correspond to the level of *dianoia*, or the type of thinking one uses in the sciences or in theory generally.[19] According to Socrates's image, each level corresponds to a type of thinking. The first of these three kinds of thinking depend on images; the fourth level, dialectical thinking, is said to rest "on the hypothesis" of the first three, and seeks to destroy them. Although I do not have time to do more than to provide the briefest sketch, let me suggest what I make of this surprising correspondence.

In the *Philosophical Investigations*, Wittgenstein frequently suggests that many of the "problems" that Socrates raises in the dialogues by piling analogy on analogy are in fact only pseudo-problems or conflicts between language games, which he "clears away" with his analytic method of reducing meaning to its use. But what if Plato were involved in a similar enterprise? What if he too were, in fact, merely doing the reverse, that is, propounding or inducing such conflicts in order to show how Socrates suggests the necessity that his interlocutors engage in just such a "deconstruction" of these problems? In this view, Socrates' true goal would be to illustrate

---

19. Thus Plato's image of the Good might be seen as involving what Wittgenstein calls "a method of projection according to which the image of the sign was the sign itself" (*Philosophical Investigations*, §366). It is a projection of the impossibility of grasping the nature of the sign through images; a projection that presupposes its own destruction in order for it to be understood.

something about the nature of his interlocutors' ethical position with respect to the alienating function of language, rather
than to propound a theory of forms. This would mean that
the three images of the Good in the *Republic* (the sun, the cave,
and the divided line) might be seen as Plato's way of describing something analogous to primal repression inasmuch as
they show how the foundation of all discourse always stands
outside the discourse that it founds. Or, to put it more con-
ventionally, these images would be Plato's insight into the fact
that the ethical Good always stands beyond the system of language from which the search for its description is inaugurated.
Now, what is this insight, if not an understanding of the fact
that the Good in philosophical explanation and its description in ordinary language constitute incompatible language
games?[20] What is this Good beyond being, in other words, if
not a Wittgensteinian insight into the fact that language tends
to reify the object of its search? Could it be that like Lacanian
psychoanalysis and the Wittgensteinian deconstruction it calls
to its aid, Plato's dialogues are an attempt to orchestrate this
conflict, which spurs us into perplexity, and confusion, so that
we might be prompted to "deconstruct" these illusions for

20. Compare *Philosophical Investigations* §496, p. 138e. Because the
word "good" is *pros hen* equivocal, or homonymous, to talk about the Good
in general as an *explanation* and to *describe* particular good things is to play
two incompatible language games. The Good in general cannot be discussed
without granting it a sense that is inapplicable to particular things, and
vice versa. I am proposing that Plato is intentionally involving us in just
such a conflict of language games, to engage our interest and to lead us to
an understanding that the forms do not exist; an understanding that, like
Wittgenstein, reduces problems "to the ground of language on which they
stand." It is always from this "ground" that Socrates inaugurates his search
for an ethical standard that might regulate our conduct. The fact that this
search is only undertaken in private dialogue is also significant here.

ourselves? What I am proposing is that this insight into the equivocal nature of the word "Good" is used to formulate a philosophical "problem" that Socrates then uses to sting others into philosophical perplexity. Thus, contrary to the entire Platonizing tradition in Western Metaphysics, I am proposing that neither Plato or Socrates necessarily believes that these "problems" actually have a metaphysical solution as Wittgenstein occasionally appears to hold.[21] In this account, the traditional Platonist interpretation of the forms as metaphysical entities is "cleared up" by being sublated into an ethical practice closely resembling Lacan's account of psychoanalytic practice, rather than a platonist metaphysics. It is, I propose, just such an approach to the question of the real that Lacan is trying to suggest in his remarks about the Good in the metaphysical tradition in *Encore*, where in a now infamous passage on sexual difference Lacan rewrites the formulae of the predicate calculus to develop a proposition that links the modality of the necessary to the impossible.[22] Like the treatment of the Good beyond being in the *Republic*, what Lacan is suggesting is that the real exerts a necessary influence on the subject, and yet its very necessity is at the same time impossible to convey within the symbolic order of language. Thus, analysis is, in Lacan's view, an ethical task to the extent it is involved not with articulating universally applicable theories of moral conduct but with tracing (in Socratic fash-

---

21. Indeed, what could such a solution be? To ask what would it look like is already to fall prey to an imaginary lure that this solution might present itself in the form of a picture.

22. Compare *Encore*, p. 59, together with Lacan's introduction of his alteration of the predicate calculus to suggest this equation of the necessary and the impossible on p. 78.

ion) the particular effects of this incapacity to name the real for a particular subject.

What reading Plato in conjunction with Lacan and Wittgenstein suggests is the possibility that Plato is not just a naive metaphysician whose dependence on myth suggests, as Hegel has it, that his thinking "belongs to the pedagogic stage of the human race."[23] What if he is up to something else than propounding an idealist or even a rationalist metaphysics? Perhaps Plato's use of myth and image is an attempt to state something about the limits of reason, together with an insight into the consequences of this limit for ethical conduct. What if he is simply propounding what appears to be a metaphysics for the sole purpose of having it subverted in the destructive/interpretive act that transforms it into an ethical practice? Plato is well aware of what he is doing. He is engaged in something very like a Wittgensteinian "destruction," which recognizes the necessity of appealing beyond the system of the cultural constructions of ordinary language in order to discover not a real entity, but the possibility—already implicit in the language of the crowd, just as it is implicit in Wittgenstein's notion of meaning as use[24]—of articulating *another standard* for our conduct than the parental, conventional, and theoretical constructs that hold us in the sway of their imaginary power.

The fact that Plato and psychoanalysis both commend the necessity of a destruction of prior constructions raises a

---

23. G. Hegel, *Lectures on the History of Philosophy*, vol. II (London: Routledge and Kegan Paul, Ltd., 1894) p. 20.

24. Indeed, note how the close relationship between theory and opinion is already suggested by the fact that the second and third part of the line are of a similar length.

question about the Lacanian understanding of this process, for to elucidate this destruction by an appeal to Wittgenstein fails to emphasize the implicit construction that precedes it. One might well ask if Lacanian analysts see any value or truth in the these constructions that are destroyed. In other words, if they are going to assert that analysis is an ethical practice, it would appear they might also have to acknowledge that there is some positive value in the constructs with which the subject arrives at analysis, if only for the fact that they are necessary hypotheses of this process of "destruction" with which the analysis will end. There is an implicit relationship between the fiction of these constructions and the ethical truth of which they are said to be semblances, but it is never positively named as such. The closest Lacan comes is to raise the question of "the analyst's desire,"[25] but what the object of that desire would be is never named.[26] Indeed, it remains quite mystical and esoteric, inasmuch as its origin in the inversion of traditional metaphysics implies that it lacks any unifying principle that might guarantee its communicability.

In any event, if there is no value to these prior constructions, then I am not sure it is intelligible to speak as Lacanians do of an "ethics" of psychoanalysis. On the other hand, if they

---

25. J. Lacan, *The Four Fundamental Concepts of Psychoanalysis* (New York: Norton, 1977), pp. 9–13.

26. Perhaps the analyst's desire is simply a desire to sustain an insight into the nature of *paideia*, which can never be positively named without destroying its essential character. Thus, the analyst would be like the unrecognized great men Kierkegaard describes in *The Two Ages*, who hold open the possibility of meaning through their "negative support" of their generation. S. Kierkegaard, *The Present Age* (New York: Harper and Row, 1962), p. 81.

grant that they do have a value, then it would seem that they have an obligation to articulate in more universal terms how this contributes to their ethical practice. They must acknowledge the ethical value and the positive necessity of these prior constructs as a prior basis for the deconstructive practice they promote. It is at this juncture that most Lacanians insist that they are only interested in psychoanalysis, and not in philosophy or ethical theory. Nevertheless, the claim that analysis is an ethical practice would seem to require a more complete justification.

What I have in mind is that these "semblances" of familial, social, and scientific constructions must function as necessary lures if the transference is to end in the subject's destruction of these semblances. Any theory that, like Wittgenstein's, only goes about "clearing the ground of language" cannot take account of the value and necessity of these antecedent stages, and thus stands, by its own admission, outside the domain of ethics.[27] Thus, using Wittgenstein to get at the ethical char-

---

27. Compare L. Wittgenstein, "A Lecture on Ethics," in *Philosophical Occasions 1912–1951* (Indianapolis: Hackett, 1993), p. 42. "Now I want to impress on you that a certain characteristic misuse of our language runs through *all* ethical and religions expressions. All these expressions *seem*, prima facie, to be just *similes*. . . . As soon as we try to drop the simile and state the facts which stand behind it, we see that there are no such facts." Compare also p. 44, "I see now that these non-sensical [ethical] expressions were not non-sensical because I had not yet found the correct expressions, but that their non-sensicality was their very essence. For all I wanted to do with them was *go beyond the world* and that is to say beyond significant language. My whole tendency, and I believe the tendency of all men who ever tried to write or talk Ethics or Religion was to run against the boundaries of language. This running against the walls of our cage is perfectly absolutely hopeless."

acter of psychoanalysis would appear to be doomed from the outset.

For Wittgenstein, philosophical analysis is only a destruction of problems to the ground of language on which they stand, and this yields neither an ethics nor an aesthetics, inasmuch as it only refers to the existing state of the world.[28] You cannot proceed from this analysis to talk about the ethical value of any of the constructions that he destroys; all you can say is that meaning is use in ordinary descriptive language. But clearly these constructions do have a value from a psychoanalytic perspective, for they contain the particularity of the desire that emerges from them. And although these constructs are not themselves the ethical truth to be discovered, what Plato's divided line shows us is that they can become the foundations for the possible realization of such a truth. Indeed, the very notion of semblance demands that there must be an original look given by the ground of language (upon which our concepts stand), and this implies that a construction is already at work within this ground in a way that such negative approaches fail to elucidate.

If the metaphysical tradition has always looked at ethics as articulating a universal or categorical truth, then Lacan is proposing we substitute this for a particular truth: the truth of the subject's desire. This emphasis on particularity would imply that the truth of the subject's desire (or the function of the particularity of how the subject is marked by the trauma of its accession to language) is somehow implicit in the constructs that have determined it. This alone would give these

---

28. *Philosophical Investigations*, §77, p. 36e; compare also "A Lecture on Ethics," p. 38.

constructs an ethical value, for in a very definite sense, if we take Freud's notion of psychic determinism seriously, these constructs can never be completely destroyed. At best one can come to accept their determining effect, and thus use this acceptance as the ground from which to articulate another possible standard for our conduct.

12

On Lacan and Mathematics

ARKADY PLOTNITSKY

Imaginary roots are a subtle and wonderful resort of the divine spirit, a kind of hermaphrodite between existence and non-existence (inter Ens and non Ens Amphibio).

—Leibniz

As I was, in October of 1997, contemplating the idea of this essay, an e-mail arrived from a physicist friend of mine. The message concerned Lacan and reflected the recent events sometimes referred to as the "Science Wars," in the wake of Paul Gross and Norman Levitt's book *Higher Superstition: The Academic Left and Its Quarrel with Science*[1] and physicist Alan Sokal's hoax article published in the journal *Social Text*.[2] Sokal and his co-author, Belgian physicist Jean Bricmont, had then just published their book, *Impostures intellectuelles*,[3] devoted to the misuse or even abuse (alleged by the authors) of mathe-

---

1. I refer here and, unless indicated otherwise, throughout this essay, to the English edition, J. Lacan, *Écrits: A Selection*, tr. A. Sheridan (New York: Norton, 1977).

2. A. Sokal, "Transgressing the boundaries—towards a transformative hermeneutics of quantum gravity," *Social Text* (Spring/Summer, 1996), pp. 217–252.

3. A. Sokal and J. Bricmont, *Impostures intellectuelles* (Paris: Odile Jacob, 1997).

matics and science by some leading French intellectuals. Lacan's work appears to be seen by the authors as arguably the most notorious case of this alleged abuse, and some of Lacan's statements they cite were bound to attract a special attention, which prompted my friend's e-mail. It said:

> Does Lacan really talk about the penis and the square root of minus 1 with a straight face, as reported in Saturday's *NY Times* article on the Sokal and Bricmont book? And if so, is there any way to view this as anything but complete nonsense? I am testing the limits of my open-mindedness. These seem to go beyond them.

I shall, by way of replying to these questions here, sketch an argument applicable to Lacan's usage of mathematical ideas other than imaginary numbers (such as the square root of -1), for example, those borrowed from topology and mathematical logic, two other prominent areas of mathematics ventured into by Lacan. I shall deal directly, however, only with imaginary numbers and Lacan's argument, leading to the statement in question, in "The Subversion of the Subject and the Dialectic of Desire in the Freudian Unconscious."[4] It is worth noting at the outset that, as a psychoanalytically informed reader would be aware (my physicist friend wasn't), the erectile organ of Lacan's statement is not the same as the penis. It may not even quite be seen as the phallus, defined by Lacan in the same essay as "the image of the penis," but instead as in turn the *image* of the phallus—the image of the image of the penis.[5]

---

4. J. Lacan, *Écrits*, pp. 318–320.

5. Indeed, as will be seen, if considered as the square root of -1 of Lacan's "algebra" (which, I shall argue here, is not mathematics), "the erectile organ" in Lacan is a formalization of the image of the image of the penis.

I shall more or less bypass the "Science Wars" debates here.[6] Regardless of potential problems with the work of Lacan and other authors under criticism, arguments against them by Gross and Levitt, Sokal and Bricmont, and other recent critics in the scientific community can hardly be seen as ethically, scholarly, and intellectually appropriate, or indeed as in accord with the spirit of scientific inquiry itself. Let me hasten to add that I here refer specifically to the "Science Wars" criticism, such as that by the authors just mentioned, and not to the views or opinions concerning these subjects of the scientific community in general. Indeed, it is my view that such critics as Gross and Levitt or Sokal and Bricmont do not represent, and should not be seen as representing, science and scientists. The criticism of these particular authors is disabled by: a) their lack of necessary familiarity with specific subject matter, arguments, idiom, and context of many works they criticize; b) their inattentiveness to the historical circumstances of using mathematical and scientific ideas in these works; c) their lack of the general philosophical acumen that is necessary for understanding most of the works in question; and d) their insufficient expertise in the history and philosophy of mathematics and science. These factors, which are, as will be seen, manifest in Sokal and Bricmont's "treatment" of Lacan, make any constructive criticism virtually impossible. Lacan's statement in question is a part of a complex psychoanalytical and philosophical conceptual assemblage, and of an equally complex textual network. It makes little, if any,

---

6. A. Plotnitsky, "'But it is above all not true': Derrida, relativity and the 'Science Wars,'" *Postmodern Culture*, 7.2 (Winter 1997); and "On Derrida and relativity: a reply to Richard Crew," *Postmodern Culture* 8.2 (Winter 1998).

sense without taking both and their context into account, or without translating Lacan's ideas into a more accessible idiom. Even such translations are bound to retain considerable complexity for the general audience. The psychoanalytical or even philosophical substance of Lacan's argument requires no mathematics as such, which one can "decouple" from this argument by "translating" Lacan's statements containing mathematical references into statements free from them. The reverse, however, cannot be done: one cannot decouple "Lacan" from the "mathematics" he uses. One cannot meaningfully read Lacan's mathematical or quasi-mathematical statements by extracting them from their psychoanalytical and philosophical content and context.

Admittedly, the task of reading Lacan is not easy, in view of his idiosyncracies, convolutions, fragmented or even spasmodic textual economy, and other complications, in part resulting from the fact that one usually deals with transcripts of oral presentations. Luckily, I need not deal with these problems here, since I need not fully spell out Lacan's psychoanalytical argument for my purposes. My argument and claims are of a different nature. They concern, first, the *way* mathematics is used in Lacan, not the mathematical accuracy of his mathematical references (although, as will be seen, Lacan is far from being as bad on this score as some of his critics claim), and second, *philosophical* rather than psychoanalytical dimensions of Lacan's work. More generally, I am interested in the interconnections between, on the one hand, philosophical and, on the other, mathematical ideas. I am also interested in the structure of *philosophical concepts* as such, and Lacan's concepts will be here considered as philosophical concepts. Such concepts often entail an engagement of different disciplines and fields of inquiry. The term "concept" itself is used here in the sense Deleuze and Guattari give it in *What Is Philosophy?*,[7] rather than in any common sense of it, such as an entity established by a generalization from particulars, or indeed "any general or abstract idea," as Deleuze and Guattari argue, via Hegel. A philosophical concept is an irreducibly complex, multilayered structure—a multi-component conglomerate of concepts (in their conventional sense), figures, metaphors, particular (ungeneralized) elements, and so forth. This complexity is, I argue, manifest in Lacan's concepts. Psychoanalytical dimensions of Lacan's conceptual economy are a separate matter, which I will not be able properly to consider here, although they are of course crucial to Lacan's work.[8] This essay, thus, concerns primarily the philosophical component of Lacan's discourse, and the role of mathematics there will be considered accordingly. I shall return to the question of the relationships between mathematics and philosophy at the end of this essay. It may be recalled here, by way of justifying this approach, that Lacan's essay "The subversion of the subject . . ." was originally a contribution to a philosophical conference entitled "*La Dialectique*."[9] Its first reference is Hegel and *The Phenomenology of the Spirit*. Hegel is one of the key, even if mostly implicit, subjects of the essay, indelibly inscribed in the phrase "the dialectic of desire" of its title. The structure of philosophical concepts is, in my view, where Lacan's usage of mathematics most fundamen-

7. G. Deleuze and F. Guattari, *What is Philosophy?*, tr. H. Tomlinson and G. Burchell. (New York: Columbia University Press, 1994).

8. See in particular G. Le Gaufey, *L'éviction de l'origine* (Paris: E.P.E.L., 1994) and G. Le Gaufey, *L'incomplétude du Symbolique* (Paris: E.P.E.L., 1996).

9. See *Ecrits, A Selection* (New York: Norton, 1977), p. 292.

tally belongs and the best perspective from which this usage can be meaningfully considered.

From this perspective, there is a way, at least one way, to argue that the statement in question and the *connections* (rather than an identification or even a metaphor) between the erectile organ and the square root of −1 make sense. Ironically, in order to pursue this argument one has indeed to know something not only about Lacan but also about imaginary and complex numbers, and their history. On that score, Sokal and Bricmont appear to be rather less informed than they could have been and, even more ironically, in some respects perhaps less informed than Lacan was. They appear to be taking complex numbers for granted as a self-evident mathematical object. The situation, however, is more complicated, both mathematically and, especially, philosophically.

Accordingly, it may be useful to review basic facts concerning imaginary and complex numbers, and numbers in general.[10] Given their crucial role in defining first irrational and then complex numbers, square roots will be my primary focus. Let us recall, first, that the square root is the mathematical operation reversing the square of a number. The square of 2 is 4, the square root of 4 is 2 or, of course, −2, which is of some significance here. I hope I will be forgiven for being so

---

10. The discussion to follow is indebted to a number of technical and semitechnical accounts, in particular, E. Cartan, "Nombres complexes. Exposé, d'après l'article allemand de E. Study (Bonn)" (which, along with Study's article itself appears to shape most accounts of the subject by mathematicians), Reinhold Remmert's chapter, "Complex Numbers" in Heinz-Dieter Ebbinghaus et al., *Numbers* (which, too, follows Cartan rather closely), and David Reed, *The Figures of Thought*. I am grateful to David Reed for especially helpful discussions of several key mathematical and philosophical questions to be addressed here. I am also grateful to Barry Mazur, Michael Harris, and David Mermin for productive exchanges on these subjects.

elementary, but I want even those who know nothing, or forgot everything, about mathematics—unlike Plato we do admit them into the Academy these days—to understand my argument. Besides, things get more complicated rather quickly. Thus, the square root of 2 is already a far more complex matter, both mathematically and philosophically, although it is of a rather straightforward mathematical genealogy. One needs it if one wants to know the length of the diagonal of the square. This is how the Greeks discovered it. If the length of the side is 1 the length of the diagonal is the square root of 2. I would not be able to say—nobody would—what its exact numerical value is. It does not have an *exact* numerical value: it cannot be represented (only approximated) by a finite, or an infinite periodical, decimal fraction, and accordingly, by a regular fraction—by a ratio of two whole numbers. It is what is called an *irrational* number, and it was the first or one of the first such numbers—or (they would not see it as a number) mathematical object—discovered by the Greeks, specifically by the Pythagoreans. The discovery is sometimes attributed to Plato's friend and pupil Theaetetus, although earlier figures are mentioned. It was an extraordinary and, at the time, shocking discovery—both a great glory and a great problem, almost a scandal, of Greek mathematics. The diagonal and the side of a square were *mathematically proven* to be incommensurable, their "ratio" irrational. The very term "irrational"— both *alogon* (outside logos) and *arreton* (incomprehensible) were used—was at the time of its discovery also used in its direct sense. The discovery, made by the Pythagoreans against themselves, may be seen as the "Gödel theorem" of antiquity.[11]

---

11. It is worth noting here that the method used in the proof—an argument based on the so-called excluded middle (still the most common

It undermined the Pythagorean belief that, as everything rational, the harmony of the cosmos was expressible in terms of (whole) numbers and their commensurable ratios (proportions). This discovery was also in part responsible for a crucial shift from arithmetical to geometrical thinking in mathematics and philosophy. For, while the diagonal of the square was well within the limits of geometrical representation, it was outside those of arithmetical representation, as the Greeks conceived of it.

We now call fractions and whole numbers *rational* numbers. Rational numbers together with irrational numbers (such as roots of all powers and still other irrational numbers, such as *pi*, which cannot be represented as roots or even as solutions of polynomial equations) are called *real* numbers. Real numbers can be either positive or negative, or zero (the latter, incidentally, unknown to the Greeks).[12] The main reason for using this term is that real numbers are suitable for measurements, in particular of the length of line segments, straight or curved, in the material world around us, the world of things that are, or appear to be, real. We can also represent and visualize them as points on the continuum of the straight line. We can do all standard arithmetic with real numbers and generate new real numbers in the process—add them, subtract them, multiply them, divide them, and so forth. (The same is true for rational numbers, but, because of division, not for whole numbers.)

---

and effective form of mathematical proof)—was originally used by Parmenides and Zeno, and formed one of the foundations of dialectic, the invention of which is credited to them.

12. It is worth observing here that the mathematical legitimacy of negative numbers, too, was a matter of a long debate, extending to the eighteenth century.

Now "there's the rub"—the square root. If a number is positive, there is no problem. We can always mathematically define its square root and calculate it to any degree of approximation. However (this is the rub), in the domain of real numbers the square root can be defined, can be given mathematical sense, only for positive numbers. This is so for a very simple reason (recall that the square root is the reversal of the square): whether you square a positive or a negative number—that is, multiply any number by itself—the result is always positive. Thus, 2 times 2 is 4, and −2 times −2 is also 4, and the same is true for 1 and −1—the square of both is 1. In a sense, square roots of negative numbers, such as −4 or −1, do not exist, at least in the way real numbers exist, or appear to exist. This is why, when introduced, they were called *imaginary*, and sometimes even *impossible*, numbers.

Why bother, then? First, from early on it appeared (correctly) that one could operate with square roots of negative numbers as with any other numbers—add them, subtract them, multiply them, divide them, and so forth. Moreover, the impossible square root of −1 appears most naturally in the simplest algebraic equations, such as $X^2 + 1 = 0$. This is how the square root of −1 and other "imaginary quantities," as they were called, made their first appearance during the Renaissance. Indeed, roots of negative numbers naturally emerge throughout mathematics. In short, on the one hand, mathematics at a certain point appeared to need to be able to deal with square roots of negative numbers, beginning with −1. On the other hand, it was clear that such "numbers" could not be any numbers already available.

It took the mathematical community a while (nearly two centuries) to accept the mathematical legitimacy, let alone reality, of these new numbers, and rigorously to define them.

Their status as mathematical objects has remained in question for much longer, especially in philosophical terms of their mathematical reality, or as concerns their possible role in describing material reality, as in physics (which remains a complex question to this day). The resolution required a very great and protracted effort and the best mathematical minds available. It was achieved by a seemingly simple, especially from our vantage point, but in truth, at least at the time, highly nontrivial stratagem—by formally adjoining the square root of −1 to real numbers. This "simple" resolution amounted to the introduction of new numbers and of a new kind of number, which could be manipulated in the manner of all other numbers. This is why they were first called first imaginary (and sometimes impossible) numbers, and then complex numbers, which are entities a little more complicated than square roots, although they have been known for just as long. The square root of −1, also called i, is the simplest such number. Other complex numbers are written in the form A + Bi, where A and B are real numbers (in the case of imaginary numbers A = 0). The square root of −1 may be seen as the fundamental element, by adjoining which to the old domain of real numbers the new domain is generated. Just as real (or rational) numbers do, complex numbers form what is in mathematics called a *field*—a multiplicity with whose elements one can perform standard arithmetical operations, with the outcome being again an element of the same multiplicity.

With the introduction of *complex* numbers it also became possible to represent the whole system on the regular real (in mathematical sense) two-dimensional plane, with the line representing real numbers serving, symbolically, as the horizontal axis and the line representing imaginary numbers (strictly, square roots of negative numbers) as the vertical axis in the Cartesian-like mapping of the plane. The square root of −1 or i would be plotted at the length equal to 1 above zero on the vertical axis. In this representation the domain of complex numbers is two-dimensional, in contrast to the one-dimensional domain of real numbers as represented by the line. This representation is sometimes called the Argand plane, although it was the great, one of the greatest ever, mathematician Karl Friedrich Gauss who legitimized it as part of giving legitimacy and perhaps reality to complex numbers.[13] "You made possible the impossible" was a phrase (which also refers to complex numbers) used in a congratulatory address on the on the 50-year jubilee of his doctorate. In 1977 the German Post Office issued a stamp illustrating the Gauss-Argand plane to celebrate the bicentenary of his birth in 1777 (obviously a very lucky sequence of numbers).

The picture, however, is not without complications, although I can only indicate some among the complexities involved, not offer a full argument here. In particular, the real two-dimensional plane is—this is a mathematical fact—mathematically *not* the same object as complex numbers. Complex numbers, such as the square root of −1, and their operations, may be "represented" and "visualized" geometrically, via the two-dimensional real plane, only as a kind of *diagram* (the Gauss-Argand "plane")—a schematic illustration, comprehensive (point by point) as it is—but *not* in themselves, not as mathematical objects with their actual (indi-

---

13. Gauss was also one of the discoverers of the non-Euclidean geometry, which discovery he, however, suppressed for twenty years for fear of being laughed at by philistines, or perhaps for the reason the Pythagoreans thought it wise to conceal the existence of the irrationals. Gauss did not think, as it happened rightly, that the world was quite ready for this.

vidual and collective) mathematical properties.[14] The main
reason for this is that a real (in mathematical sense) point on
the two dimensional plane, for example, with Cartesian (now
indeed Cartesian rather than Cartesian-like) coordinates, is
not a "number." In contrast to real numbers and their geometrical representation as the (real) line, there is no "natural"
way to conceive of all necessary arithmetical operations, in
particular multiplication or division (addition and subtraction are not a problem)—that is, in the way the real line is
"naturally" converted into arithmetics in the case of real number. As a result, complex numbers as such cannot in all rigor
be seen as *represented* as points on the two-dimensional real
plane and indeed are epistemologically unavailable as a visualizable or, more generally, geometrical object. Their properties
can, of course, be spelled out and rigorously comprehended
algebraically. In the sense of algebraic representation, there
is no epistemological difference between real and complex
numbers (although there are fundamental differences in algebraic properties of two domains). Ultimately, complex numbers may remain not only imaginary, but, at least geometrically, strictly unimaginable. They (in the ultimate structure
of their properties and attributes) are certainly nonvisualizable
as such, at least not in the way real numbers are. Epistemologically, at least in terms of its geometrical representability,
the square root of −1 or, more accurately, the signifier "the
square root of −1" signals—"represents"—the ultimate lack
of geometrical representation. It is something that in itself is
geometrically unvisualizable or unrepresentable, or, one might

---

14. In the language of mathematics, these two objects are not iso-
morphic, insofar as one can assign (as will be seen, one can) to the real
plane an algebraic structure at all.

say, geometrically unepistemologizable. This radical epistemological complexity of mathematical complex numbers explains the ambivalent attitude toward them on the part of the
key figures involved in their discovery or creation.[15]

It could appear "wondrous strange" indeed, and to some
outright bizarre, that the theory of complex numbers has

---

15. Thus, Augustin-Louis Cauchy (1789–1857), a contemporary of
Gauss and a great mathematician in his own right, had reservations concerning the geometrical representation of complex numbers throughout
his life. He considered them purely symbolic (algebraic) entities and at one
point even attempted a general mathematical definition of "symbolic
expression" in explaining his attitude—to some discontent among his colleagues. (See Remmert's commentary in Ebbinghaus et al., *Numbers*, 62–63).
This situation and a more general problem of geometrical representation
of post-eighteenth century mathematics that it reflects has far-reaching
implications for modern mathematics, such as topology, of some of which
Lacan appears to be aware. It is also worth noting here that certain, indeed
quite radical, epistemological complexities are involved in the case of real
numbers as well, or indeed of all numbers. I cannot consider these subjects here. Lacan aside, however, the question may well be: Do we know
what is the number like the square root of –1, or indeed –1 (which, as I
said, gave mathematicians some pause even as late as the eighteenth century), or for that matter 1? It may be recalled that Frege once said that it is
scandalous that we do not know what numbers really are. Lacan was aware
of some of these complexities, as is clear from his comments on foundations of mathematics, including some of those cited by Sokal and Bricmont
in *Imposture intellectuelles* (pp. 32–38). These passages cause Sokal and
Bricmont much aggravation. In truth, however, they are at worst harm-
less, and often there is nothing especially wrong with them—if, again, one
tries to understand Lacan's actual argument where these passages are used.
In general, Lacan and other radical thinkers in question in recent debates
appear to be more aware of and attentive both to the philosophical dimension of the mathematical concept in question and their history themselves,
and to the philosophical thought (often in turn quite radical) of the key
mathematical and scientific figures involved than their recent critics in the
scientific community. This difference, too, is far from irrelevant to the
nature of the debates in question.

anything to do with the erectile organ. Given, however, the preceding discussion and some knowledge of Lacan, it is not so difficult to see that Lacan's "formula" is in fact not so strange. The epistemological point just made concerning complex numbers—their ultimately unavailability to visualization and perhaps any geometrical conceptualization, while they seem to be represented as points on the two-dimensional real plane —gives one a hint here. The erectile organ may be seen as theorized by Lacan as a symbolic object (also in Lacan's sense of the symbolic), specifically a *signifier* (in Lacan's sense), that is epistemologically *analogous* to the signifiers one encounters in the case of complex numbers, specifically the square root of –1. Within the Lacanian psychoanalytic configuration, any image, in particular a visual image, of the erectile organ, including that of an "erectile organ," can only be an *image* of the *signifier*—the signif*ier*, not the signif*ied*. (I shall further comment on this point presently.) This signifier itself is fundamentally, irreducibly nonvisualizable. At the limit, this signifier—that is, its ultimate structure of, once again, the signif*ier* designated as the erectile organ—may be inconceivable by any means, which epistemology or de-epistemization, and specifically de-visualization, are crucial to most of Lacan's key concepts. Indeed, this signifier is in fact or in effect unnameable, for example, again, as the erectile organ, or the phallus, which, as I said, may not be the same as the erectile organ within the Lacanian economy of subjectivity and desire. That is, we can formally, "algebraically" manipulate its image or images, or names, or further formal symbols associated with it, just as we can formally manipulate complex numbers within their mathematical system, which Lacan's "algebra" in part mimics but to which it is not identical. At the same time, however, we do not really know and perhaps cannot in principle conceive, at least from within the Lacanian psycho-analytical situation (defined by this economy of inaccessible signifiers), what the erectile organ really is as a *signifier* and what its properties are, if we can speak in terms of properties here. The *image* of this signifier, and in particular its visual image, would, then, be analogous to the geometrical, hence visualizable, representation of complex numbers, and in particular of the square root of –1, of which the erectile organ becomes an *analogon* within the Lacanian psychoanalytic "system," rather than being a *mathematical* imaginary number.[16] The situation may even be more subtle, insofar as one may need to deal with further levels of formalization—that is, within still other "formal" symbols and structures associated with signifiers, such as the erectile organ—at which the analogy in question actually emerges. Let me stress that (whether one is within Saussure's or Lacan's scheme of signification) in question here is the irreducible inconceivability of the erectile organ as the *signifier*, not the *signified*. Its signified (such as, in Saussure, the concept behind it) and its referent, whatever they may be, may be in a certain sense even more "remote" and "inaccessible" or inconceivable. One would still need, however, to think in terms of the ultimate inaccessibility (which is not to say identity in terms of their functioning) of all three—the signifier, the signified, and the referent, which should be considered in the register of the Lacanian Real.[17]

---

16. Here and below the term *analogon* may also be understood in its Greek sense, as connoting a parallel or "proportionate" relation, rather than identity, of one *logos* (here as "discourse") to another.

17. See Note 28 below. It can be argued (although I cannot pursue this argument here) that the *epistemologically* analogous triple inconceivability is also encountered in modern, and perhaps all, mathematics, in particular in the mathematics of complex numbers.

My main argument here may be summarized as follows. Both the signifier of the erectile organ in the Lacanian psychoanalytic field and the square root of -1, (i) in mathematics, may be seen as fundamental formal, *symbolic*, entities that enable an introduction of, and may be seen as structurally generating, two new symbolic systems—that of the Lacanian psychoanalysis (his [re]interpretation of Freud's oedipal economy) and the field of complex numbers in mathematics. In each case, the introduction of these new symbols allows one to deal with problems that arise within previously established situations but that cannot be solved by their means: a pre-analytic situation, or a more naively (for example, by way of misreading Freud, conceivably, to a degree, even by Freud himself) constructed analytic situation in psychoanalysis (where one needed to, and in the previous regime could not, approach certain particular forms of anxiety), and the system of real numbers in mathematics (where one needed to but could not rigorously define complex numbers in order, for example, to solve certain polynomial equations). In both cases, the philosophical-epistemological status of these new symbolic systems is complex. In particular, in question are: a) the extent to which such systems represent or otherwise relate to, respectively, psychological/psychoanalytic and mathematical reality (with the question of material reality in the background in both cases—the question of the Real in Lacan's case); and b) the extent to which the properties of such symbolic systems and of their elements, such as what is designated as the square root of -1, (i) in mathematics, or the erectile organ in the Lacanian analysis, can themselves be accessed and specifically visualized by means of images, such as the geometrical representation of complex numbers or the image we form perceptibly or configure theoretically (and these are subtly linked in turn) of the erectile organ in the Lacanian psychoanalytic situation.[18]

In mathematics, these complexities, historically reflected in the term *imaginary numbers*, are, I would argue, not altogether resolved even now, although since and following Gauss most mathematicians stopped worrying philosophically. Leibniz may well have given the problem its most glamorous expression: "Imaginary roots are a subtle and wonderful resort of the divine spirit, a kind of hermaphrodite between existence and non-existence (*inter Ens and non Ens Amphibio*)."[19] Perhaps Descartes, who was one of the first to give serious consideration to imaginary roots and their nature, and indeed was first to use the very term *imaginary*,[20] and who was the inventor of analytic geometry (which fundamentally relates

---

18. One must keep in mind here the difference between complex numbers, or indeed any mathematical object, and the Lacanian system in question as concerns their respective relationships with materiality (whether one sees the latter in terms of material reality in the classical sense or not). In the case of the Lacanian system, the relationships between the symbolic and the material are more immediately germane, somewhat similarly (although not identically) to the way mathematical models function in physics. In the case of mathematics, its symbolic systems may be seen as more or less independent of material objects—that is, such as those considered in physics, since other forms of materiality are irreducible in mathematics as well, and of course there is still the question of nonmaterial mathematical (or for that matter Lacanian) reality. I have considered the question of mathematical reality and its relations to physics in "Complementarity, Idealization, and Limits of the Classical Conceptions of Reality," in *Mathematics, Science and Postclassical Theory*, eds. B. H. Smith and A. Plotnitsky (Durham, NC.: Duke University Press, 1997).

19. Cited by Remmert (Ebbinghaus et al., *Numbers*, p. 58).

20. E. Cartan, "Nombres complexes. Exposé, d'après l'article allemand de E. Study (Bonn)." In E. Cartan, *Oeuvres Complètes*. (Paris: Editions du centre national de la recherche scientifique, 1984) Vol. II, 1, pp. 107–247.

geometrical and algebraic mathematical objects), should be given the last word here: "One is quite unable," he said, "to visualize imaginary quantities."[21] Unless the last word is Lacan's, who in "*Desire and the Interpretation of Desire in* Hamlet," says: "the square root of −1 does not correspond to anything that is subject to our intuition, anything real—in the mathematical sense of the term—and yet it must be conserved, along with its full functioning."[22] This may need to be more precisely stated, but is in essence right, and this statement grounds and guides my analysis here. It may be seen as an updated rendition of Leibniz's early assessment: "From the irrationals are born the impossible or imaginary quantities whose nature is very strange but whose usefulness is not to be despised,"[23] although numerous subsequent statements by leading mathematicians can be cited.

In the same passage Lacan also speaks of imaginary numbers as "irrational." The passage is cited both in Sokal's hoax article and *Impostures intellectuelles* as an example of Lacan's confusion of irrational and imaginary numbers. Lacan's usage, however, does not appear to me due to the lack of understanding of the difference between real irrational numbers and imaginary numbers imputed to him by Sokal and Bricmont. Instead it may be seen as a reflection of his sense of imaginary numbers as an extension of the idea of irrational numbers—both in the general conceptual sense, extending to its ancient mathematical and philosophical origins, as considered

---

21. The statement occurs in "La géométrie," published in 1637; it is cited by Remmert (Ebbinghaus et al., *Numbers*, p. 58).

22. J. Lacan, "Desire and the interpretation of desire in *Hamlet*," tr. James Hulbert, *Yale French Studies* 55/56:11–52.

23. Cited by Remmert (Ebbinghaus et al., *Numbers*, p. 55).

earlier, and in the sense of modern algebra—that is correct
and displays, conceptually, a better sense of the situation on
Lacan's part than that of Sokal and Bricmont. The description
of irrational and imaginary numbers in their book is hardly
edifying as concerns the substance and the beauty of the subject. It is also imprecise and misleading insofar as it suggests
that there is no connection between irrational and imaginary
numbers. Indeed, they claim even more strongly that they
have nothing to do with each other.[24] This is simply wrong.
The profound connections between them define modern algebra. Certainly, complex numbers, beginning with i, are
irrational numbers as the latter are defined by Sokal and
Bricmont (as unrepresentable by a ratio of two whole numbers): no real fraction can be found to represent them, since
no real number of any kind can represent them. The latter is
not a minor or trivial point, and one can hardly think that
Sokal and Bricmont could be unaware of it. In general, I am
not here holding Sokal and Bricmont responsible for their
treatment of numbers as such, inadequate and imprecise as it
is. They are physicists, not mathematicians or historians or
philosophers of mathematics, and it is, in general, not their
responsibility to know (or be precise about) mathematics and
the philosophy and history of mathematics. It is, however,
their responsibility to know those aspects of all three that they
consider in Lacan, and, assuming that they do, it is their responsibility to carefully consider and appropriately explain
these issues, if they want to criticize Lacan.

The erectile organ of the Lacanian or, as Lacan argues
(in part "against" Freud himself), already Freudian system is,
then, analogous to the mathematical square root of -1—*analo-*

---

24. Sokal and Bricmont, *op. cit.*, p. 31.

gous, but *not identical*. Indeed, the proper way of conceiving of the situation is to see the erectile organ, or, again, a certain formalization of it, *as* (as defined by and as defining) "the square root of –1" of the Lacanian system itself—that is, as an *analogon* of the mathematical concept of the mathematical square root of –1 within this system—rather than anything identical, directly linked, of even metaphorized via the mathematical square root of –1.[25] In a word, the erectile organ *is* the square root of –1 of Lacan's system; the mathematical square root of –1 is *not* the erectile organ. There is no mathematics in the disciplinary sense in Lacan's analysis, only certain structural and epistemological analogies or homologies with the mathematics of complex numbers, most particularly the following. *First*—the structural analogy—the erectile organ, as a signifier, or indeed *the* signifier (in Lacan's sense), belongs to and gives rise to a psychoanalytical system different from the standard one or ones (based on misreadings of Freud, conceivably to a degree by Freud himself), and to a different formalization—"algebra"— of psychoanalysis, a formalization that is more effective both conceptually and in terms of the ensuing practice. *Second*—the epistemological analogy—the erectile organ, as a signifier, or again *the* (Lacanian) signifier of this system, while and in a sense

---

25. To the extent that one can speak of the metaphorical parallel, it operates at the level of two systems themselves. This, let me note in passing, is a classical Lacanian move, and it is often found elsewhere as well. For example, Poe's *The Purloined Letter* (in *Écrits*, the French edition) is read by Lacan as textualizing the scene and indeed the field of psychoanalysis, and is reread by Derrida as the scene of writing in Derrida's sense in "Le facteur de la vérité" (*The Post Card*), as part of his deconstruction of Lacan. In the sense just explained, however, one can also speak of a certain "repetition" of Lacan on Derrida's part, albeit a repetition in the sense of Derrida's *différance* as the interplay of differences and similarities, distances and proximities, and so forth.

because it governs the economy of the system, can only be approached by means of tentative, oblique, and ultimately inadequate metaphors. It is ultimately inaccessible, along with its signified and its referent, at the limits inaccessible even as that which is absolutely inaccessible but definable in terms of independent properties and attributes.

In order to explain the reasons for my argument, I shall sketch here some of Lacan's logic and "algebra," *mimicking* complex numbers, without fully spelling out the structure of Lacan's key concepts—such as the subject, the signifier, desire, or indeed the erectile organ—which would require a perusal of a much larger textual field. Lacan defines a signifier, in general, as "that which represents the subject for another signifier," rather than for another subject.[26] The signifier "S" is introduced—first as the "signifier of a lack in the Other [*Autre*], inherent in its very function as the treasure of the signifier." Ultimately, however, "S" is "the signifier for which all the other signifiers represent the subject: that is to say, in the absence of this signifier, all the other signifiers represent nothing, since nothing is represented only *for* something else." This signifier is argued to be "be symbolized by the inherence of (−1) in the whole set of signifier." This signifier is (symbolized as) the −1 of the psychoanalytical system in question in its "algebraic" representation ("algebra" is, again, that of Lacan). "As such, S is inexpressible, but its operation is not inexpressible, for it is that which is produced whenever a proper noun is spoken." In other words, "S" is operationally formalizable and this formalization is expressible.

---

26. J. Lacan, *Ecrits*, p. 316. See also the discussion in "Of structure as an inmixing" in *The Languages of Criticism and the Science of Man*, ed. R. Macksey and E. Donato (Baltimore and London: Johns Hopkins University Press, 1970), pp. 193–194.

The radical epistemology delineated earlier emerges already at this point, insofar as "S" is inexpressible as such. However, the *formal* object corresponding to "S" in Lacan's "algebra"——1—is analogous to the epistemology of the mathematical -1, rather than of the square root of -1, which is radically inaccessible (at least to a geometrical representation) even as a formal object.[27] Then, however, another signifier, "s"—the symbolic square root of -1—is derived, and is defined as that which is radically inaccessible, *unthinkable*, for the subject—both as such, similarly to "S," and, I would argue, more radically, at the level of the corresponding element of the formal "algebra" built by Lacan. More generally, there are two interactive but distinct levels of the economy and epistemology of the signifier in Lacan—the more general conceptual level (subject, the phallus, lack, and so forth), which is not quasi-mathematical, and the level of a certain "algebra," which is quasi-mathematical and at which the analogy between this "algebra" and mathematics must be considered. The signifier "s" is not yet equated with the erectile organ at this point. However, a certain radically inaccessible signifier is argued to be inherent in the dialectic in the subject, indeed as *the* signifier ultimately generating this system or, again, yet another formalization of it, as the square root of -1 of this formalization, rather than the 1 or -1 ("S") of the system. According to Lacan, "This [i.e., that which is designated or, again, formalized as the square root of -1] is what the subject lacks in order to think himself exhausted by his *cogito*, namely that which is unthinkable for him" (although, we

27. See, however, Note 15 above. The question, crucial here, of "negativity," in psychoanalytical or (via Hegel) philosophical terms, in Lacan would require a separate discussion.

might add, appears as representable to him). "But," Lacan asks next, "where does this being, who appears in some way defective in the sea of proper names originates?"

In order to answer this question, Lacan maps the passage from the imaginary to the symbolic order, especially as regards the phallic imagery. First, thanks to Freud's "audacious step," the phallus is argued to acquire the privileged role in the overall economy of signification in question, via the castration complex. Here one must keep in mind the difference between Freud and Lacan insofar as the Lacanian economy of the signifier (replacing Freud's "signified") is concerned, in particular as it relates to the phallus and the difference between the phallus (as a Freudian signified) and what Lacan here designates as the erectile organ as a signifier. The latter, moreover, may need to be seen as formalized yet further as "the square root of −1," thus adding yet another "more distant" level of signification.[28] Then, moving beyond, if not against, Freud, Lacan argues as follows:

> The jouissance [associated with the infinitude involved
> in the castration complex in Freud] . . . brings with it the
> mark of prohibition, and, in order to constitute that mark,

---

28. One can speak of "distancing" here only with considerable caution. For, although a certain efficacious materiality of the Lacanian Real can be seen as, in a certain sense, more "remote," it cannot be postulated as existing by itself and in itself, as absolutely anterior, prior to, or otherwise independent of signification. Hence, it cannot be seen as something from which the distance of signifiers can be unequivocally "measured." One can speak in these terms only provisionally. Nor can the overall efficacity of the Lacanian signification be contained by this materiality: this efficacity, along with its effects, such as signifiers, is fundamentally reciprocal in nature, including as concerns the relationships between materiality and phenomenality.

involves a sacrifice: that which is made in one and the same act with the choice of its symbol, the phallus.

This choice is allowed because the phallus, that is, the image of the penis, is negativity in its place in the specular image. This is what predestines the phallus to embody the *jouissance* in the dialectic of desire.

We must distinguish therefore between the principle of sacrifice, which is symbolic, and the imaginary function that is devoted to that principle of sacrifice, but which, at the same time, masks the fact that it gives it its instrument.[29]

It follows, according to Lacan, that it is the erectile organ—the image or, better, the signifier as an un-image of the phallus, and thus un-image of the image of the penis (in the Lacanian symbolic order)—that is subject to the equation of signification at issue.[30] It is, then, as such and only as such that the erectile organ is the square root of −1—that is, as "the square root" within, and of, the Lacanian system itself in the symbolic order of its operation, or, again, more accurately, of a certain formalization of that system. "Thus the erectile organ comes to symbolize [again, also in Lacan's sense of the symbolic] the place of *jouissance*, not in itself, or even in the form of an image, but as part lacking in desired image: that is why it is equivalent to the square root of −1 of the signification produced above, of the *jouissance* that it restores by the co-efficient of its statement to the function of the lack of signi-

---

29. *Écrits*, p. 319. Here one would need, of course, to consider the question of sacrifice in Lacan, via Hegel, in particular in the *Phenomenology*, and, then, Alexandre Kojève and George Bataille, both of whom are clearly on Lacan's mind here as well.

30. The difference between the erectile organ and the phallus would be inscribed accordingly, as indicated earlier.

fier −1."[31] Accordingly, "the signification of the phallus" so conceived conforms to the economy of the inaccessible signifier. It can be shown that neither the signified nor the referent are simply suspended here, and are in fact conceived of as ultimately inaccessible as well, via the Lacanian Real. For as Lacan says, "if [the erectile organ's role], therefore, is to bind the prohibition of jouissance, it is nevertheless not [only] for these formal reasons."[32] Instead it is due primarily to a complex materiality, ultimately related to the Real and its epistemology. Indeed, the Real in Lacan's sense may be seen as this materiality (rather than reality). It may be best conceived as a certain radical (but not absolute) alterity inaccessible to a metaphysical configuring, oppositional or other, in particular as anything that can be seen as possessing any attributes (perhaps even the attribute of existence in any way that is or will ever be available to us) independently of our engagement with it.

To summarize, within the Lacanian psychoanalytical situation, the *image* or the *signifier* of the erectile organ is a scandal—in either sense, but most crucially in terms of its psychoanalytic management, or the difficulty or even impossibility thereof. In this latter sense it is not unlike what the square root of −1 in mathematics was epistemologically at some point. Lacan's approach is to refigure it as a symbolic object—specifically in Lacan's sense of the juxtaposition between the symbolic and the imaginary. In the register of the

---

31. *Écrits*, p. 320. It is significant that Lacan says, "equivalent" and not "identical," which, again, suggest the difference between Lacan's "algebra" and that of the actual mathematical complex numbers, rather than a claim of their identity on Lacan's part.

32. Ibid.

imaginary "the signification of the phallus," while conceivably involving to *inaccessible* signifieds and referents, may be seen as defined by *accessible signifiers*, but (in part as a consequence) is psychoanalytically useless. In the new system (in the symbolic register) the Lacanian signifiers themselves, in particular the erectile organ, are ultimately inaccessible. By the same token, a symbolic system (in Lacan's sense of the symbolic) is introduced as the dialectic of desire and castration, which enables the subject defined by this system and/as the Lacanian analytical situation to function. The symbolic object itself in question is given a specific formal structure, just as the square root of –1 is in mathematics. From this perspective, the erectile organ is not a real unity or oneness, positive or negative, neither 1 nor –1, or even anything merely fragmented, analogous to either mathematical real rational or real irrational. Instead it is a "solution" of the psychoanalytic equation that contains oneness—1—and the negative of oneness— –1—as terms, but that makes the "solution" itself, while in a certain sense formalizable, inaccessible even at the level of the signifier, which, to the degree they offer us any image of it, all our imaginaries and visualizations ineluctably "miss," along with the signified and the referent—the Real, keeping in mind the qualifications made earlier.[33]

    I am not certain to what degree Lacan's epistemological ideas were derived from the epistemology of mathematical complex numbers. It is not inconceivable, especially given his statements cited here. He also knew enough mathematics and mathematicians to draw this parallel and to use it. I suspect that he was at least aware of these epistemological connec-

---

33. See Note 28.

tions, as some of the statements cited above would indicate, even if he did not actually derive his scheme from the epistemology of complex numbers. There are, however, other candidates for the sources of this epistemology of the inaccessible at all levels of signification—the signifier, the signified, the referent—in more immediate semiotic terms, in the work of Saussure and Hjelmslev, on the one hand, and C. S. Peirce, on the other, or in more philosophical terms in the radical philosophy in the wake of Kant and Hegel, certainly in Nietzsche, although one can trace some of these ideas to Plato and the pre-Socratics.

It is, then, only in the sense of the square root of −1 of Lacan's system, as just delineated, and not of the mathematical system of complex numbers, that the erectile organ is the square root of −1. This argument would clearly invalidate a kind of critique that Sokal and Bricmont level at Lacan, were their critique to survive far lesser levels of scrutiny. Unwittingly, Sokal and Bricmont's own comment in fact says as much: "Even if [Lacan's] 'algebra' made sense, the 'signifier,' and 'signified' and the 'statement' contained in it are not numbers."[34] Of course not; this is the whole point.[35] It is clear even from the most cursory reading that Lacan never says they are. Indeed in a sentence introducing the formula in question, the sentence *cited* by Sokal and Bricmont, Lacan says: "Thus by calculating that signification *according to the algebraic method used here*"[36]—that is, according to Lacan's "algebra," not the

---

34. Sokal and Bricmont, *op. cit.*, p. 32.
35. The reader may be spared the rest of Sokal and Bricmont's sentence, equally ironic in its confirmation of my point here and equally remarkable in its naivete and blindness.
36. J. Lacan, *Ecrits*, p. 317, emphasis added.

actual mathematics of complex numbers, which is my point here.

Lacan's constructions here considered may have been designed primarily for psychoanalytical purposes, although such purposes in Lacan are a complex matter. Either way, this construction is accomplished by way of an invention and construction of philosophical concepts in the Deleuze and Guattari sense, which activity defines philosophy itself, according to their *What is Philosophy?* It is, in my view, this construction that gives us the best sense of Lacan's usages of mathematics. This point also allows me to close here by giving a reasonably definite, although not definitive, answer to the question of what is the place of mathematics in Lacan. Mathematics sometimes functions in Lacan's texts in a more direct and less complicated fashion of metaphor, illustration, and the like. For example, on some occasions certain constructions of modern topology, such as the Möbius strip and the Klein bottle, serve Lacan to find that which "we [can] propose to intuition in order to show" certain complex configurations entailed, Lacan argues, by neurosis, or psychosis,[37] although the overall situation is ultimately more complex on these occasions as well. I do think, however, the primary and most significant usage of mathematical concepts in Lacan is as components of his own multilayered—irreducibly nonsimple—concepts, conforming to Deleuze and Guattari's definition (or concept) of the philosophical concept. The pres-

37. J. Lacan, "Of structure as an inmixing of an otherness prerequisite to any subject whatever," in *The Languages of Criticism and the Sciences of Man: The Structuralist Controversy*, pp. 186–200.

ence and role of such concepts in Lacan is, in my view, unquestionable. Virtually any given sample of Lacan's text manifests such concepts. In "The Subversion of the Subject,"[38] imaginary numbers are only a portion of a conceptual and metaphorical conglomerate, many components of which are borrowed from various domains—literature, religion, philosophy, or whatever—and many of them would require the kind of analysis just given.

This view shifts Lacan's usage of mathematics into the philosophical from the psychoanalytic register, in accord with Deleuze and Guattari's ideas in *What is Philosophy?* It is of some interest that the book, while examining the difference between philosophy (defined by deployment of concepts) and other fields, in particular mathematics, science, and art, Deleuze and Guattari omit psychoanalysis from this argument altogether. The relationships between psychoanalysis and philosophy have of course been the subject of important recent investigations, such as Derrida's, especially in *The Post Card*[39] (where Lacan is the main subject, along with Freud, and Heidegger), or elsewhere in Deleuze and Guattari, especially in *Anti-Oedipus*,[40] and indeed in Lacan's essay in question, the essay also on Hegel. We know from these investigations that philosophy and psychoanalysis are multiplied and perhaps irreducibly entangled, both historically and conceptually. This entanglement, however, is not symmetrical, and

38. J. Lacan, *Ecrits*, p. 320.
39. J. Derrida, *The Post Card*, tr. A. Bass (Chicago: University of Chicago Press, 1987).
40. G. Deleuze and F. Guattari, *Anti-Oedipus: Capitalism and Schizophrenia*, tr. Robert Hurley, Mark Seem, and Helen R. Lane (Minneapolis: University of Minnesota Press, 1983).

this asymmetry may entail a different (and more fundamental) role mathematical concepts and mathematics play in the philosophical *vs.* psychoanalytic thought and discourse. Indeed, one may see Lacan's usage of mathematics as an attempt to change this asymmetry, at least at a certain point, as part of his attempt to make psychoanalysis more scientific or, with Freud, to affirm its scientific character. In the process, Lacan did, I think, manage to enrich our understanding of the nature and complexity of the project of mathematics and science. The success of his deployment of mathematics and science in psychoanalysis *qua* psychoanalysis is a different question, given the very nature of his thought, work, and text. This argument may make mathematics primarily a part of Lacan's work as an inventor of concepts and, hence, as a philosopher, rather than a psychoanalyst (to the degree that these can be distinguished in Lacan's case). At the very least, the role of mathematics in Lacan is fundamentally philosophically mediated, in Hegel's sense of mediation [*Vermittlung*]. That, however, may well be how mathematics has always functioned outside its own sphere, and indeed often within it.

13

The Body as Viewing Intrument, or the Strut of Vision

JOAN COPJEC

If anything has stirred American academics in the last several years, it's the much-trumpeted observation that bodies matter. This observation has produced a veritable cornucopia of corporeal kinds. Volumes have been written and compiled on bodies, all carefully zoned, peeled open layer by layer, categorized by function (as in: the embodied observer, the embodied speaker, the embodied judge—you get the picture), differentiated by class, racialized, genitalized (notice I didn't say *sexualized*), and just basically scrutinized in all the nooks and crannies of their differences from some abstract, idealized form. This *unairbrushing* and proliferation of bodily forms harbors the belief that it was a misguided focus on the signifier that led us down the ideologically retrograde, if illusorily rosy, path of decorporealization. Analysis of our world as a system of signifying relations yielded, we are told, merely ideal subjects: projected points of comprehension or enunciation, absolutely abstract, detached from bodies and all their powers, limitations, and demands.

The current revenge of the body, or of interest in the body, is, then, a revenge against the soma-denying power of the signifier. But while in outline this interest portends a project of enormous merit, in practice it has proved disappointing. For the recent barrage of books on embodiment has evidenced almost total ignorance of the body as such, the body as component of our human existence. The reason for this is that the agitating observation—bodies matter—is trivial. *Of course*, I do not mean that it is insignificant, only that it says too little. Or, put more fully, to state—as though one need only revenge or answer their neglect—that "bodies matter" is to bury the crucial *questions*: 1) What's the matter of bodies? where to ask of what they are made is to acknowledge that they are not simply found, but constitute themselves; and 2) What's the matter with bodies? Why do they suppurate (for that's the word for it) so much trouble for themselves? Why does human embodiment manifest itself as a pitched battle between our bodies and our biology (or, as we will see, our physiology), such that it would be a mistake to take them as synonymous? To be embodied means, of course, that we are not just anybody, but *this* body *here*. But why does our corporeal particularity manifest itself in cravings such that we are constantly overeating or starving ourselves, cutting up other bodies into little pieces, or prostrating ourselves at another's feet? In other words, why, even in their "basic" pursuits of nourishment and sex, are human bodies given to compulsion, inhibition, sadism, idealization? Animals, we may say, have bodies, too, but not such exotic pleasures, such perverse tastes. Their instincts, like our drives, are a kind of nonconscious knowledge of what they must do. The difference is that instinct, which suits animals for survival, is determined by nature, while drives, which are determined neither by nature nor the society in which we live but by each individual embodied subject, often jeopardize survival. It would be a mistake, then, to confuse drive with will or whim, since it is not easily nor consciously altered; on the contrary, it exerts an unrelenting, internal pressure on the body, which the body is unable to escape and will is unable to oppose.

Though the concept of drive pays heed to what is often called the human body's *perversion* or deviance from the natural order, only bad faith would prevent us from admitting that the notion of a nonnatural body is a contradiction in terms and therefore untenable. A body is clearly a part of nature. If one wants to hold onto the notion of drive (and psychoanalysis has given us many reasons why we should), the only way to avoid contradiction is to assume that the notion implies not an overriding so much as a redefinition of nature. Which is precisely why, of all Freud's notions, that of the drive has had the least success in attracting supporters; it obliges a kind of rethinking that only the boldest of thinkers would dare to undertake. The question one must ask is: How does drive determine human embodiment as both a freedom from nature and a part of it? In sum, the conviction that bodies matter does not exonerate us from having to ask this fundamental question, "What is a body?"

However much we have learned about the body in recent years, we've learned next to nothing that would lead us to pose, let alone answer, such a question, nothing that would cast light on the "perversions" of human embodiment.[1] Ei-

---

1. The essays on the Freudian/Lacanian notion of the drive in *Reading Seminar XI: Lacan's Four Fundamental Concepts of Psychoanalysis*, ed. R. Feldstein, B. Fink, and M. Jaanus (Albany, NY: SUNY Press, 1995); the special issue of *Umbr(a)* 1 (1997), ed. D. Collins and *Umbr(a)* Collective

ther it is assumed that we already know what a body is, in which case we are condemned to operate with some empiricist notion gleaned from a vague knowledge of science, or we are treated to the description of some historical construction of the body, in which case we are obliged to consider ourselves simple creatures of clay. Let us settle on one example of this sort of side-stepping, that provided by the notion of the embodied *observer*. In the late 1970s, it is true, the theoretical attempt in film to analyze vision as a signifying practice did produce a subject that no body could be: a monocular subject of pure, abstract seeing, who occupied no space, was subject to no temporal fluxuations, and laid claim to no sexual identity, except—notoriously—by default. In *Techniques of the Observer*, Jonathan Crary[2] challenges this description of the film spectator by mounting a historically informed argument against it. At the end of the nineteenth century, he tells us, the observer suddenly acquired a body, one that took up space, changed over time, and could be examined in all its contingency by empirical science. Unlike the earlier, abstract observer—which was configured by the camera obscura and the geometry that informed it—this corporealized observer was both the subject of autonomous perception and the object of administrative scrutiny. The aberrant perceptions of its all too human eyes—retinal afterimages, light distortions, blurring, and the like—that is, perceptions constituted *by the body it-*

(Center for the Study of Psychoanalysis and Culture, University at Buffalo); and Charles Shepherdson's new book from Routledge, *Vital Signs: Nature, Culture, Psychoanalysis*, go a long way toward correcting this situation.

    2. J. Crary, *Techniques of the Observer: On Vision and Modernity in the Nineteenth Century*, (London and Cambridge, MA: MIT Press, 1990).

self, were no longer dismissed as carnal errors requiring rational correction, but were instead taken seriously as positive phenomena in their own right—the better to be put to use by a developing capitalism.

While the argument for such a shift from an antioptical or geometrical model of vision to an optical or physiological one is amply documented and inventively argued, we have reason to doubt its soundness on a number of points. The first of these is the most general one, that the transition from a geometrical to a physiological model of vision marks the transition from an abstract to a corporealized observer. The support given for this argument is mainly of the following commonsensical sort: since the camera obscura was constructed around a single point of projection while the stereoscope was constructed around two, the first must have been aimed at the mind's eye and the second at the actual eyes of the embodied subject. Or: since geometry is an abstract science, it supposes an abstract subject, while physiology, which studies the body, supposes a carnal observer. Now, from these sorts of assumptions a guess as to what Crary means by embodiment is a simple affair. In the Cartesian vocabulary that Crary cites, it means that the observer is *res extensa* and not merely *res cogitans*, that is, the observer is extended substance rather than purely thinking/seeing thing, or *cogito*; in nontechnical language, the observer, whatever else it may be, *is* matter, a bounded, finite thing interposed between other things, and as matter it impinges necessarily and meaningfully on vision in ways that can be physiologically studied and manipulated. I do not doubt that physiological science held such a notion of the body; what I doubt is its veracity. Additionally, I would question the broad assumption that this notion represented a more materialist account of vision; in fact, it can be easily shown that it is decidedly more *abstract* than the geometrical account.[3] Anyone who needs convincing should treat himself to reading about the wild shenanigans of these physiologists, who kept coming up—despite themselves, one imagines—with reasons for embracing the blind man as the only proper subject of their experiments, and constantly found themselves in cahoots with spiritualists, vitalists, and other such positivist clowns. In any case, the risibility of these experiments exposes their incapacity, for reasons hinted at above, to account for the facts of human— as opposed to animal—embodiment.

Crary does not blink, one notices, when he cites the passage from the *Meditations* where Descartes, in the process of describing the construction of a camera obscura, asks his readers to imagine an eye—it could be the eye of an ox, he adds parenthetically—at the lenticular entrance to the darkened chamber.[4] To this offhand remark Crary offhandedly responds, "this only indicates that for Descartes the images observed within the camera obscura are formed by means of

---

3. I am thinking here of Althusser's argument that the enslavement of positivism to empirical "fact" is what renders it an *abstract* science. See the essays by T. Gunning, "Phantom Images and Modern Manifestations: Spirit Photography, Magic Theater, Trick Films, and Photography's Uncanny," (in *Fugitive Images: From Photography to Video*, ed. P. Petro, (Bloomington and Indianapolis: Indiana University Press, 1995) and A. Zupancic, "Philosophers' Blind Bluff" (in *Gaze and Voice as Love Objects*, ed. R. Salecl and S. Žižek (Durham, NC, and London: Duke University Press, 1996) for the hilarious details of positivism's self-entanglements.

4. In *The Origin of Perspective* (London and Cambridge, MA: MIT Press, 1995) Hubert Damisch points out that light passed into the perspective apparatus not through a "pinhole" exactly, but through a lentil-shaped opening that could better accommodate the physical shape of the observer's eye.

a cyclopean eye, detached from the observer, possibly not even a human eye."[5] That is, since the eye at issue here is not a physical one—insofar as it is the *cogito*, pure seeing/thinking that counts—the eye's actual characteristics are irrelevant. The problem is, however, that when Crary later examines the physiological model of vision, we cannot help recalling this passage from the *Meditations*, and its Bunuelian sleight of hand. For, in the later optical experiments, all indications are that the human eye that was the object of its study might just as well have been the eye of an ox. Physiological science goes awry, first of all, by equating stimuli that are radically different in origin and nature. Thus, "a dryness of the mucous membrane of the pharynx or an irritation of the mucuous membrane of the stomach," that is, the physical manifestations of thirst and hunger, are treated on the model of "a strong light fall[ing] on the eye,"[6] even though the pangs of human hunger and thirst need have nothing to do with the presence or absence of food in the stomach or moisture in the mouth, and how well one sees may have nothing to do with the intensity of available light. But these two types of stimuli—those with a purely physiological source and those that originate in the drive—cannot be distinguished merely by determining whether they originate externally or internally; what differentiates them are two separate concepts of cause. While physiological stimuli and the responses to them are understood to be governed by simple scientific laws, or regularities, drive stimuli are thought to provoke responses not cal-

5. J. Crary, *Techniques of the Observer*, p. 47.
6. S. Freud, "Instincts and their vicissitudes," *Standard Edition* 24:118, 1915.

culable in advance. This is not to say that the latter do not enter into causal relations, but that these relations are "more complex," as Freud said; or, as Lacan would later argue, in them cause and effect are not welded together to form one principle, as is the case with the fixed and stable relations that bind stimulus to response.[7] While the latter are governed by a scientific law, drive stimuli arise where a gap in such laws occurs. To illustrate, Lacan invokes an image of the crushed body of a suicide lying on the pavement. This image would undoubtedly prompt different causal explanations from a physiologists and a psychoanalyst; that it is only a human body that is ever suicided would not enter into the considerations of the physiologist, whose explanation would most likely give more weight to the force of gravity.

The fundamental error of *Techniques of the Observer* is, I am arguing, its unthinking acceptance of the mind/body dualism of Cartesian philosophy. It is this dualism that grounds the distinction Crary makes between the geometrical model of vision, which supposedly disregards the body entirely in favor of abstract consciousness, and the physiological model, which reduces the body to its empiricist definition. This history presents us with a false choice between no body at all and a kind of "bodiless body," lacking both in generic (that is, human) and in individual specificity. This choice precludes any possibility of his coming to terms with the corporealized vision of a human subject, insofar as this subject constitutes a direct challenge to that dualism. But if his initial error ultimately leads him to misjudge the nature of the corporeal

---

7. J. Lacan, *The Four Fundamental Concepts of Psycho-Analysis*, ed. J.-A. Miller, tr. A. Sheridan (London: Hogarth Press and the Institute of Psycho-analysis, 1977), p. 22.

observer, it also causes other problems along the way, including a throughgoing misrepresention of that geometry that informs Renaissance perspective and its "universalist" claims.

This is not to say that this misrespresentation originates with Crary. Since the point of his argument is not to challenge film theory's analysis of Renaissance perspective as what set in place an abstract observer, but to question the hegemony of this model of vision beyond the late eighteenth century, he accepts without question film theory's analysis—and mistakes. As is known, film theory attempted to prop up its notion of cinematic visuality on the analysis of the gaze that Lacan offers in *Seminar XI*, though the reading of Lacan it produced was so severely flawed that it ended up taking a position completely at odds with his. Where film theory and Lacan diverge, Crary not only follows the former, he often sharpens its argument. This is the case, for example, on the question of the observer/spectator's placement vis-á-vis the visual field. Crary works diligently to secure a rigorous separation of the observer from the observed. Essentially he argues that the geometrization of vision places observation not only *outside* the body, but *outside* the visible world, as well, whereas the physiological model places the body of the observer *within* the world and observation *within* the body. Relying on these "age-old assumptions"[8] regarding the simple exteriority of body and world, Crary interprets ideologically the textbook argument that states that Renaissance painting

---

8. In *The Visible and the Invisible*, ed. C. Lefort, tr. A. Lingis (Evanston: Northwestern University Press, 1968), Merleau-Ponty admonishes, "We have to reject the age-old assumptions that put the body in the world and the seer in the body, or, conversely, the world and the body in the seer as in a box," p. 138.

introduced a visual objectivity that quickly displaced the subjectivity of medieval painting. He and film theory interpret this objectivity as a *mis*recognition fostered by the belief that the observer could indeed transcend his or her body and world and thus truthfully comprehend it.

Lacan does not dispute the textbook argument concerning the Renaissance invention of painterly objectivity, but he interprets it in a radically different way. This difference is plain in statements such as this: "the geometral dimension enables us to glimpse how the subject who concerns us is *caught . . . in the field of vision*."[9] That is to say, Lacan argues that Renaissance painting makes the spectator *enter the image*, not exit from it. He takes literally the name given to this model of vision by underlining the fact that all we see, we see from a certain *perspective*. In fact, the relevance of Lacan's lengthy discussion of anamorphosis is that it focuses attention on the *impurity* of the visual field of the painting insofar as it consists not only of *what the spectator sees*, but something more: the vanishing point, which is nothing other than *what the spectator contributes to what she sees*.[10] This does not mean that quattrocento painting rendered the spectator visible or transparent to herself in the manner in which Descartes's ideal observer became transparent to herself. If the spectator is there in the painting, she is not grasped there as coincident with the thought she has of herself.

---

9. J. Lacan, *op. cit.*, p. 92 (my emphasis).

10. J. Lacan, *Seminar XIII: L'objet de la psychanalyse* (unpublished seminar), May 4, 1966. I would like to thank Cormac Gallagher for allowing me to consult his unpublished English translation of this seminar. Further references to *Seminar XIII* will be to the date of the oral transmission.

That Lacan's extended disavowal of the supposed similarity between Descartes's abstract observer and the observer
of Renaissance painting should have fallen on such deaf ears
among film theorists is no surprise. The missed encounter can
perhaps be chalked up to the fact that film theorists mistook
anamorphosis for an occasional rather than a structurally
necessary phenomenon or, more generally, to the notorious
difficulty of Lacan's paratactical style of argumentation. But
if the particulars of his argument were not immediately clear,
its context is unmistakeable, and this alone should have sent
up warning flares to those intent of nailing down the Cartesian lineage of his observer. For these sessions on the gaze
are no diversionary foray into the territory of "applied psychoanalysis"; they are, rather, an attempt to develop one of
psychoanalysis's fundamental concepts: that of the drive. Renaissance perspective is supposed by Lacan to provide the
exact formula of the *scopic drive*, that is, the formula not of
an abstract vision, but of embodied seeing. As was suggested
above, the concept of the drive is the vehicle by which Freud
collided head-on with Cartesian dualism, the means by which
he strove to account for the facts of an incarnate subjectivity.
Listen once more to the definition he gives of the drive in his
essay, "Instincts and their Vicissitudes": "[drive] appears to
us as a concept on the frontier between the mental and so-
matic . . . as a measure of the demand upon the mind for
work in consequence of its connection with the body."[11] This
demand (which is precisely *demand* in the Lacanian sense)
is that call for a more complex response from the corporeal
subject (which is to say, the subject as such of psychoanaly-

---

11. S. Freud, *Standard Edition* 24:121–122.

sis) than any that could be accommodated within a physiological, stimulus–response model of investigation.

But what is it that *justifies* this argument? What allows
one to state that geometrical perspective gives the exact form
of the relation of the *corporeal* subject of vision to the visual
field? What allows Lacan to claim that it is the headless subject of the drive, rather than the purely cognitive subject of
rationalism, which is (pre)figured by Renaissance painting?
The answer to these questions hinges on a clear understanding of the aims and effect of artificial perspective. To arrive at
such an understanding, it is first necessary to distinguish *artificial perspective*, which emerged in the sixteenth century out
of a revolution in geometry, from its predecessor, *natural
perspective*. Wherever this distinction is overlooked, confusion results, as happens in Crary's and film theory's account
of Renaissance perspective.

> What is that thing which does not give itself, and which if it were
> to give itself would not exist? It is the infinite!
> —Leonardo da Vinci

At the beginning of the sessions of *Seminar XIII* that are
devoted to perspective, Lacan poses the basic question to
which his explanation will be the response: "What precisely
is the subject, this place necessitated by the constitution of
the objective world?"[12] What is it that gives rise to this question? One possible answer is Renaissance painting, for there
we find that the objectivity of the space it brings into being
coheres around—rather than cancels out—the perspective of
the subject. How are we to understand *subject* and how are
we to understand *perspective* such that this is true, that is, such

---

12. J. Lacan, *Seminar XIII*, May 4, 1966.

that the objectivity of the world necessarily implies their constitutive role? What can it mean to say that the objectivity of the world is dependent on the subjectivity of the subject?

If projective geometry and Renaissance painting—into which the figure of the artist himself begins to appear with enough regularity to make it a significant phenomenon—provide the first demonstration of this truth, its philosophical justification will lag centuries behind, receiving its first elaboration only at the end of the eighteenth century, from Kant. For, despite these precocious sixteenth-century demonstrations, objectivity was thought by philosophy generally to be arrived at not via the subject, but via an adequate representation of an independently existing world, through the conformity of thought to things. This view of objectivity placed a lot of faith in thought, which is assumed to be up to the task of representing being; as the scholastic doctrine would have it, objective truth meant *adaequatio intellectus ad rem*. Descartes delivered the first major blow to thought and its representations when he placed them under the parching light of his doubt, though he did stage a last-minute rescue by exempting one thought from the general destitution. This one thought he declared to be adequate to its object; here, at last, thinking was taken to conform to being, for the subject, or the *cogito*, *is* (according to Descartes) the thought it has of itself. Thought had, nevertheless, by this Cartesian gesture, already been stripped of most of its power when Kant arrived on the scene to wrest from its hold the last bit of being. Relativism, historicism, multiculturalism, all the modern and postmodern antifoundationalist or sceptical movements spring directly from Kant's radical dethronement of thought and representation, his divorcement of thought from being, such that the former came to be considered absolutely powerless to guarantee the latter. But Kant differs from his sceptical followers in that he believed—despite his own denigration of thought—that we could still meaningfully speak of objectivity. In other words, the caricature of the Kantian position, wherein he is supposed to have exposed the fact that we have access only to subjective appearances, never things-in-themselves, simplifies his position by skirting the issue of objectivity, which Kant himself confronted.

This is where we rejoin Lacan, who 1) wisely pauses to take the Kantian position seriously and to ask what *subject* means in this case, what a subjective constitution of objectivity means, and 2) promises to answer by formulating the relation of the subject to extension, by which he means its body and its world, or the class of all there is. (Here Lacan claims not to follow, but to supplement Kant.) Now, between Kant's bill of divorcement, which created the modern problem of objectivity, and the psychoanalytic attempt at solution lies a long, troubled history of other philosophical attempts to reattach being, and hence objectivity, to the world as it is represented to us by thoughts. Since Kant had stated that it was "transcendental synthesis" that converted arbitrary or subjective perceptions into an objective or necessary world, philosophy after him set out in two different directions to translate this procedure into its own terms. "Empiricists understood [it, i.e., the transcendental synthesis or imagination, to be a matter of] a psychological rapport between representation and sensation . . . what exists as actual [was taken to be] what is perceivable by our senses."[13] Idealists and phenomenolo-

---

13. A succinct and useful account of this philosophical history is found in R. Kearney, "Surplus Being: The Kantian Legacy" (in *From Phenomenology to Thought, Errancy, and Desire*, ed. B. Babich (Dordrecht,

gists, on the other hand, took perception to mean "appearance to consciousness," where consciousness was understood as productive. Notice the way this potted history seems to parcel itself out in "Crary-like" categories: either consciousness or the body, either idealist synthesis or empirical sense impressions—one has to choose.

Psychoanalysis would come along to offer a different solution and thus demonstrate that these alternatives do not exhaust the field of possibilities. But why should psychoanalysis have a position on this philosophical problem? The answer is that the problem came knocking directly at Freud's door, without philosophical mediation, initially, as the problem of hallucinatory satisfaction. Since the mythical "first" satisfaction of the infant's needs leaves behind a memory trace, or *representation*, of satisfaction, the question arises: Why does the infant not simply recathect this fantasmatic trace of reality, which it harbors internally, instead of seeking some other, "external" reality? What incentive is there for the child to search elsewhere for some other object? Later, the deliria of psychotics would pose this question anew: What is it that distinguishes the "objective" thoughts of most subjects from the "subjective" ones, the deliria of psychotics, who seem to experience a "loss of reality"?

We know that Freud first sought an answer in the agency of the ego, and that this answer was expressed in Kantian terms: it was to the *synthetic* function of the ego that he looked

---

Boston, London: Kluwer Publishers, 1995), p. 76. On the Kantian notion of objectivity, D. Henrich is the best source; see the first chapters of his books *The Unity of Reason* (Cambridge, MA: Harvard University Press, 1994) and *Aesthetic Judgment and the Moral Image of the World* (Stanford, CA: Stanford University Press, 1992).

to restore objectivity to a psychical system potentially over-whelmed by delirious thoughts. But the ego did not turn out to be up to its assigned task, for as Lacan's anti-ego psychol-ogy polemic never let us forget, the ego is mired in the same muddy waters it was meant, originally, to titrate. It attracts and repels thought, takes them into itself or casts them out, according to imaginary criteria, that is, according to whether these thoughts are similar or dissimilar to those that form the ego's core. This criterion is hardly adequate grounds to ren-der a judgment of existence, imaginary agglutination being a far cry from the synthesis of transcendental imagination.

The Schreber case, his most sustained attempt to come to grips with psychosis, forced Freud radically to rethink the "reality-testing" function of the ego; it also unearthed an ex-traordinary psychoanalytic discovery: the psychotic not only suffers from a *loss of reality*, but from a *loss of his body* as well. Schreber tells us this when he exposes the conspiracy against him in these words: *"I should be handed over to a certain per-son in such a manner that my soul should be delivered up to him, but my body . . . should be transformed into a fe-male body, and as such surrendered to the person in question with a view to sexual abuse."*[14] Freud notes that a number of Schreber's delusions are of a hypochondriacal nature and concludes that such ideas are an invariable accompaniment of the disease that afflicts him.[15] The point is not simply that the psychotic's body beomes saturated with libido; this satu-ration seems to eat away, to *decompose*, its corporeal support. This does not mean simply that the psychotic has no *image*

---

14. S. Freud, *Standard Edition* 12:44, Schreber's emphasis.
15. Ibid., p. 56.

of his body, and it certainly does not mean that he has no biological body; it means that the psychotic has no body in the material sense: he has no "weight," no corporeality, and thus remains unanchored to his world. This is why the psychotic's own attempts at recovery so often involve delusional constructions of an ersatz body, such as that of the "influencing machine," which Freud's colleague, Victor Tausk, describes in all its peculiary excrescent detail. This machine, Tausk writes, is "a machine of mystical nature. The patients are able to give only vague hints of its constuction. It consists of boxes, cranks, levers, wheels, buttons, wires, batteries, and the like. Patients endeavor to discover the construction of the apparatus by means of their technical knowledge. . . . All the forces known to technology are utilized to explain . . . the marvelous powers of this machine by which the patients feel themselves persecuted. . . . It makes the patient see pictures. . . . It produces, as well as removes, thoughts and feelings by means of waves or rays . . ."[16]

This "paranoia somatica" is not simply a "projection" of the psychotic's own body, as Tausk suggests, but a makeshift construction that attempts to make up his own body's loss. This cursory corporeal contraption (to paraphrase Schreber) restarts the world, which would otherwise collapse. Through

---

16. V. Tausk, "On the Origin of the 'Influencing Machine' in Schizophrenia," tr. by D. Feigenbaum (1933), in *The Psychoanalytic Reader*, edited by R. Fliess, (New York: International Univesities Press, 1948), p. 54. This paper was first read and discussed at the Vienna Psychoanalytic Society in January 1918 and was published in German the following year. I have argued elsewhere that the image of "Fama," which appears in Book IV of Virgil's *Aeneid*, is a classic example of "paranoia somatica"; all eyes, ears, tongues, and mouths, she gets the narrative going again at the point it threatens to come to an end.

a steady accretion of functions and parts, these machine bodies acquire more and more complexity as the disease wears on; this complexity, Tausk reasons (à la Freud), serves to increase the intellectual interest that one takes in them and thus weakens the power of the libidinal siege that holds the psychotic's body hostage.

I should point out that while the study of psychosis may have forced Freud to change his mind about the function of the ego, it did *not* change his mind about the mechanism necessary for the production of "objectivity," or, as he says, "reality." From the ego to the influencing machine the mechanism at issue is *inhibition*, specifically the inhibition of libido. This means that where the philosophical tradition that followed Kant sought to *add* something to representation to produce objectivity, psychoanalysis from its beginning sought to *subtract* something, namely *jouissance*. This includes Lacan's definition of psychosis as the foreclosure of the Name-of-the-Father, which basically means that the interdiction or inhibition of *jouissance* is inoperative in this psychical structure. From this psychoanalytic history one other crucial point needs to be drawn: the inhibition or subtraction at issue does not lead to *abstraction* in the ordinary sense. That is, the subtraction of *jouissance* does not efface or neglect the body; far from it—subtraction *creates* the body. In short, the psychoanalytic position is this: *no objectivity without incorporation, without the body.*

> The donkey that goes straight to the fodder knows as much about the properties of the straight line as we do.
> —Leibniz

Within the context of this discussion of artificial perspective, Leonardo da Vinci and his scientific and artistic explorations of the human body spring almost automatically to mind. How is it that he succeeded where psychotics fail? What distinguished his creations from their delusional constructions? To say that his creations prove his possession of a body (which frequently figures in his paintings themselves), while theirs reveal a lack is merely to put off answering the real question: How did he acquire his body? How did he beat off the predatory, vulture-like kite whose "violent caresses" not only initiated his obsession with the flight of birds, but threatened to devour his body?

The case of Leonardo, Renaissance man, driven by a prodigious scopophilia as well as a thirst for scientific knowledge, allows us to settle several remaining questions and, at the same time, to clear up some potential misunderstandings. First, though I have been trying to elaborate a distinction between a subjective, even delusional reality and an objective reality, one must not forget that this objectivity is *subjectively* constituted, that is, I am not speaking naively of a reality that stands on its own, independent of a subject's thoughts and representations. Freud says of Leonardo's scientific research not that it uncovers the truth of a prior and free-standing reality, but that it "contained some of the features which distinguish the activity of unconscious instincts—insatiability, unyielding rigidity, and *the lack of an ability to adopt to real circumstances.*"[17] Now, once adaptation to reality is seen as part of the *problem* of ego synthesis or, better, of ego "agglutination," the *failure* to adapt takes on a positive value and, indeed, takes over the role formerly assigned to the ego.

---

17. S. Freud, *Standard Edition* 11:133, my emphasis.

What we see developing here in Freud's study of Leonardo is the notion of what Lacan will later call *fantasy*; not fantasies (plural), or hallucinatory fulfillments of desire, but fantasy (singular) as what *frames* our world and *forms* our desires. Fantasy, in the singular, *is* psychoanalysis's translation of Kant's notion of transcendental synthesis or transcendental imagination. Just as Kant recovered from Hume's sceptical conclusion that the world's coherence is a quality attributable not to the world, but merely to our perceptions as they are bundled by our imagination, so, too, did Freud recover from his first faulty attribution of coherence to the ego. Both thinkers move beyond an immanent to a transcendent notion of unity by asserting—and here I will switch to a third vocabulary, neither Kantian nor Freudian, but that of artificial perspective—by asserting that the point of synthesis or the point of view of the fantasy is not reducible to that of the observer, but is located *farther back*: "at his back—or . . . 'behind his head.'"[18]

But from where does this other, anterior point emanate if not from the subject? To whom does it belong if not the subject who—I have been arguing, after all—constitutes the objectivity of the world? Kant, Freud, and Renaissance perspective, in their different ways, offer the same answer. This anterior point, this *gaze* (to give it a name appropriate to its emergence in the visual field, specifically) belongs to no one, comes from no one; it is radically anonymous. Nor is it an *ideal point* that transcends (in that old, pre-Kantian sense) the ability of any individual to embody it. No, if the strange but important Kantian claim that *objectivity itself is perspectival*

---

18. H. Damisch, *op. cit.*, quoting Pascal, p. 121.

is to make any sense, the gaze can only emerge from a blockage of subjective sight itself. There is simply no other source
for it. My world opens up, becomes bigger than me only at
the point where my failure to "take it all in," to see everything,
is acknowledged. Only as a result of this blockage of perspectival vision do my thoughts and representations make room
for the nonintrusive existence of others. In other words, the
gaze that forms the unconscious fantasy or the point of synthesis that forms the "objective" world is not an object of any
thought or any representation; it is simply *supposed*, or (to
put it differently) it is simply the "embodiment" of the possibilities opened up by noting the obstacles to sight.

The gaze is not only a kind of guarantee that there is *more*
to see than what I am actually seeing—a kind of *behind* not
visible from my perspective, but which is imagined, nevertheless, as a "rounding out" of an object in a way that is con-
sistant with what I can see from its front. In Vermeer's *The
Geographer*, for example, the geographer's body is turned almost completely toward us, the viewers.[19] We do not see his
back, nor do we see the whole of the armoire in front of which
he is standing, partially blocking our view of it. Yet we read
the painting *as if* the geographer had a back and the armoire
a base that is simply, owing to our perspective, obscured from
sight. The gaze also suggests that a view *different* from my own,
one that might undermine my perspective, is also possible. It
is for this reason that one can speak of *the* subject of uncon-

---

19. One could argue that the denigration of representation is directly
thematized in this painting by the way the geographer's drawings have so
carelessly been left lying on the floor. Preliminary sketches, discarded
errors? Certainly the air of dignity representation once had no longer clings
to them.

scious fantasy, even though this subject is not the same from day to day and is always in conflict with itself. This is also why we can speak of *a* social space, though this space may be claimed by warring points of view. The gaze allows a self-differing identity to "hold itself together," without sacrificing this difference. Now let me tell you why this is a salutary idea, rather than a paranoid one, in either the colloquial or clinical sense.

As is known, feminists greeted the notion of the gaze with hostility, as just another male hoax, a way of stripping woman of the power of her look in order to grant ultimate power to the "male gaze." Where this feminist interpretation goes wrong is in its assumption that the gaze originates at a definite point, outside the field of vision. This misinterpretation is supported by an incorrect reading of the "distance point." Besides a vanishing point (which marks the inclusion of the eye of the observer, her point of view, in the visual field), Renaissance paintings also contain a distance point (which indicates that a distance from the visual field must be taken in order to see it). Crary and feminist film theorists err by believing that this distance can be metrically measured, that it yields the exact location of the gaze. (This is, of course, one of the errors that results from not distinguishing the metrically based geometry of Euclid from projective geometry.) This is not the case. The distance point produced by projective geometry indicates only *that* a distance must be taken; it does not tell us where to stand (not even ideally) in order to see everything. It is this distance point that Lacan refers to when he speaks of the point of the gaze, which he locates inside the field of vision. The gaze marks the fact that between the observer's point of view and an objective vision *there is a cleavage*. This can be stated more clearly still: the gaze indicates that there is no place to stand that would offer a complete view; this acknowledgment is as much of objectivity as we ever get—which is not the same as saying that we get none.

The gaze does not embrace the entire visual field, on the contrary, it is what makes it impossible for this field to be grasped from any point of view. Artificial perspective makes this fact visible by embedding the vanishing point, or point of view, within the space of the representation. Yet it is not possible to conclude that this viewpoint thus reveals itself as *relative*, since there is on offer no other point from which such a judgment could be made. Outside the vanishing point where we stand looking, there is only the distance point, the point of the gaze, which marks the limit of our vision. This is hardly a spot we can scale in order to see the view from above.

Earlier I argued that by confusing classical and projective geometry, Crary had misunderstood the nature of infinity in Renaissance painting; he equates it with *infinite extension*, with the receding horizon. We are now in a position to understand the difference between this and the infinity introduced by artifical perspective, which is manifest not in the structure of infinite extension but in *the structure of the envelope*.[20] One must be careful, however, for to argue that Renaissance painting reveals that the corporeal subject is not only inserted into his world, but that it is this very insertion that makes the world possible, is *not* to argue that the subject is *enveloped* by the world. In other words: the *structure of the envelope* is not a *structure of envelopment*, where *envelopment* means *enclosure*. What the first structure avoids precisely is the notion of a subject stuck in a world whose limits are drawn

---

20. J. Lacan, *Seminar XIII*, May 4, 1966.

around it. If the notion of unconscious fantasy differs from that of ego adaptation, it is not only because the former implies a reality that is constructed, while the latter implies one that is found, but also because the coil of fantasy estranges the subject from its surrounding, even as it inserts him or her into it, insofar as these surroundings come into being not simply via the subject's look, but also via the look (harbored within the subject's own) of an outside observer.

But what does this envelope structure have to do with infinity? Whereas potential infinity results from withholding or deferring the limit of the visible world, by placing it on an ever receding horizon, always just out of sight, Renaissance paintings give the limit of the visible by subtracting something from its interior. Actual infinity is both that which is subtracted *and* the envelope structure—or what I've called the coil of fantasy—that results from this subtraction. Actual infinity, as what, in Leonardo's words, does not give itself, gives the limit that allows the world to form without closing itself off or without enclosing the subject within it. Visual space circles around this hole, this limit that marks the withdrawal of infinity. In short, the difference between potential and actual infinity is that the latter posits a point of convergence where all the sightlines meet, while the former only endlessly approaches it.

But what's happened to the body? Have we lost it once again? Let us return one more time to Leonardo, who has something to teach us not only about infinity but about its relation to the body as well. The study of Leonardo undertaken by Freud is curiously entangled with the question of inhibition. Freud keeps returning to the notorious slow pace of the artist's production, his inability to complete his paintings, his withdrawal from the field of amorous relations. These returns spell trouble. It's as if the analyst were dissatisfied with his explanations, as if he thought something was not being properly sorted out. By *Inhibitions, Symptoms, and Anxiety*, things have become clearer; Freud has found the distinction he had need to make earlier: an *inhibition* is not necessarily a *symptom*. Some inhibitions have no pathological origin. If every "inhibition is the expression of a *restriction of the ego-function*,"[21] then some such restrictions are beneficial; the ego must be reigned in to prevent it from becoming eroto-genetically overwhelmed, to prevent paranoia. An excess of erotogeneity, or *jouissance*, has the effect of impairing bodily functioning, as when the erotic significance of the throat or arm produces a cough or a paralysis. Freud offers what he terms a "rather absurd analogy" to illustrate: in such cases of impairment, he says, the body behaves "like a maid-servant who refuses to go on cooking because her master has started a love affair with her."[22]

This analogy is too rich to be sure what point Freud is trying to make with it. He seems to be offering it as illustration of a pathological inability to work, yet the distinction he has just introduced between inhibitions and symptoms makes another reading possible, for the maid-servant's inhibition may also be seen as a *nonpathological defense against against working for her master*. That is, it may be necessary to distinguish between an inhibition that *impairs* and an inhibition that *produces* the body. In *Television*, Lacan defines the drive as the point at which the signifier "gears into the body."[23] The suggestion of a military invasion by foreign forces is entirely

---

21. S. Freud, *Standard Edition* 20:89.
22. Ibid., pp. 89–90.
23. J. Lacan, *Television: A Challenge to the Psychoanalytic Establishment*, ed. J. Copjec, tr. D. Hollier, R. Krauss, A. Michelson (New York: Norton, 1974), p. 37.

apt. We know that the original signifiers with which a mother addresses her child are received as a traumatic, because incomprehensible, *demand* to which the speechless child can respond with nothing but the *jouissance* of that part of its body that has felt the signifier's violent touch. To be rigorous, however, one would have to concede that it is premature to speak of the body at this point. The body proper only comes into existence in answer to a certain braking or inhibition of *jouissance*, which does not repress it, but—what? *sublimates* it. Here, too, the psychoanalytic point is quite different from its vulgarization. Sublimation—again, a kind of abstraction—does not efface, but creates the body.

But how? And what is the difference between those notoriously slippery terms, *sublimation* and *repression*? To Freud's murky distinction, I would hazard the following clarification: sublimation inhibits *jouissance* by converting it into a signifier; the surplus that remains after this operation is, by definition, repressed. One can still turn this clarification into nonsense, however, by imagining that this signifier has any positive content, that *jouissance* can be *signified*. This false step would once again sink the concept of sublimation, which is meant to explain how a subject can produce thoughts that are not symptomatic, that are neither inhibited by sexualization nor burdened by sexual content.

If *jouissance* can become a signifier, the only signifier it can become is a negative one. Sublimation must be, then, the articulation of a limit, an inhibition. As signifier, *jouissance* signifies its own prohibition.

As Freud says, the drive is a demand for work made on the subject as a consequence of its corporeality. But whether this demand strips the subject of its body and indentures the subject to the service of the Other, or produces its body and places him in the service of his own insistence, is determined by whether or not the drive is sublimated. Leonardo's inhibitions, many of which smack of sublimation, not only free him from the deadly grip of his mother's demand, they also demonstrate that self-indentureship is not the same as self-mastery. For, like consciousness, the body comes into being at the point where it splits off from itself.

Though this analysis of perspective wins back the body, it seems to lose the political/historical reference to capitalism, which Crary maintains by linking the phenomenon of commodification to the second, physiological model of vision. I would suggest, however, that this reference ought to be brought in earlier, since the geometrization of vision surely helped lay the groundwork for the emergence of capitalism. I would therefore like to restate my complaint that Crary approaches the issue of abstraction's relation to the body in the wrong way. Asking "What was abstracted?" and answering "The body," he misses the opportunity to pose a more productive question: What effect did abstraction have on the body?

The geometrization of vision was the beginning of a general quantification or mathematicization that prepared the way for a money economy based on exchange value: the chiseling away of the bumps and curls, the relief, of uniqueness that left us with the flat surface of a general equivalency. This operation of quantification totally eliminated particularity or uniqueness in the older, precapitalist sense, which is not to say that "quality" [24] was simply lost. It was, rather, *significantly*

---

24. This part of my discussion makes use of Jean-Claude Milner's extremely interesting arguments in *Le triple du plaisir* (Paris: Verdier, 1997); *quality* is the word Milner uses for what becomes unsituatable within the mathematicized world of capitalism.

lost, that is, its absence was marked. This was enough to make it the object of the most fervent of quests and, potentially, the very undoing of capitalism itself—were it not for the fact that it conveniently resurrects "quality" through the fetishization of commodities. This resurrection of lost uniqueness also takes place on the level of the body, through the fetishization of body *parts* that become backlit with the glow of quality, of that object lost to universal quantification. The body in early capitalism is thus divided between the sensuous body, manipulable by market forces, and the *jouissant* body, gripped by a useless—or intransigent—form of enjoyment.

> Kennedy, dying, expresses himself in his final action: *falling and dying, on the back seat of a black presidential car, in the weak embrace of his American petit-bourgeois wife.*
> —Pier Paolo Pasolini

To Crary I would like to cede one further point: he does convincingly underscore that a transformation has taken place in the field of the visible. He associates this transformation with the introduction of technologies—such as the stereoscope, telescope, cinema, and photography—that construct a *binocular*, rather than a monocular, vision. But if we throw out the argument that this shift can be attributed to the substitution of a corporeal observer for an abstract one, how *can* we explain it? Let me try to answer this question by examining one such instance of this newer mode of vision. For the stereoscope, the technology that epitomizes, for Crary, this second model, I will substitute a pair of binoculars—a specific pair, those used in the penultimate sequence of Pasolini's film *Salò*. This is the scene of the final torture and execution of the sadistic libertines' young victims. The libertines are not content only to participate in the torture; most of their en-

joyment comes from watching the scene—through binoculars. All the scenes of torture are viewed through their binoculars, whose shape frames the image we see on the screen,
masking its edges and central section. What sort of image is
this?

Pasolini himself gives us some clues as he ruminates on
the Zapruder film: "the only possible film of Kennedy's death,
all other points of view are missing: that of Kennedy and
Jacqueline, that of the assassin . . . that of those with a better
vantage point . . . etc."[25] His argument is that this 8 mm long
take of the Kennedy assassination is a *subjective shot*; as such
it exists, unrelievedly, in the *present tense*, "makes no sense,
or if it does, it does so only subjectively, in an incomplete . . .
way," and exludes all other points of view. What is immediately striking about this description is its complete reversal
of the ordinary view that the Zapruder film is our only visual
document of this traumatic historical event. Pasolini, inad-
vertently, makes us see that the traumatic event may not have
been the assassination, but the film—which instantiates a new
mode of vision, the same one, in many important respects,
with which he closes *Salò*.

The first thing to note is that *subjective* here no longer
has the same sense it does in Kant; on the contrary, it represents *a suppression of Kantian subjectivity*, or of what we would
call in cinematic terms *point of view*. It is the point-of-view
shot, filmed over the shoulder of some character, that dominates cinema, allowing that same "objectivity" to emerge that
Kant associated with it. Subjective shots, which are taken from

25. P. P. Pasolini, "Observations on the long take," *October* 13:4,
(Summer 1980).

the exact position of some character and which are usually accompanied by some *visual distortion of the image*, are rare.

Subjective shots are disturbing, I would argue, insofar as they substitute an obvious external frame of the image for the "internal frame," or limit within the image. From this substitution results the complete elimination of distance, which gives the image an overwhelming presence, or places it, in Pasolini's terms, unrelievedly in the present tense. In *Salò*, for example, the scenes of torture have an almost suffocating nearness about them, an inalienable closeness that is almost palpable. Indeed, one of the libertines turns the binoculars around to look through the wrong end, as if the reduction of the image might distance it; it does not, of course, since perspective—with its correlation of size and distance—has been demolished. In these scenes, the depth of field associated with Renaissance space is collapsed largely through the elimination of sound. Watching in total silence, the libertines participate in an "observation" that has been reduced to a single sense. Sound would have helped to define a limit to vision and thus produced some sense of depth; its absence adds to the unbearable closeness of the image.

But the unbearable closeness and inalienable subjectivity of these images do not tell the whole story; what must also be commented upon is the extreme corporeal violence depicted in them: the cutting off of a tongue, the plucking out of an eyeball from its socket, the removal of a victim's scalp. A growing consensus (Crary included) suggests that there is a new aesthetic (or antiaesthetic) of ugliness or of a savage deformation that owes its existence to the modern dimension of *velocity*, which twists and tortures form. A speeded up temporality demolishes the dimension of space and, with it, beautiful form. This explanation strikes me as

superficial, since it does not account for the structural transformation at issue.

What the *Salò* sequence makes clear is that this transformation is a matter of *the drive, not acceleration*. More specifically, there seems to be a *jamming* in the sublimation of
the drive. Where formerly it had entailed the production of
an empty or contentless object (object a, in Lacan's terms),
which could not be represented nor consumed but appeared
rather as the surplus of representation and consumption, sublimation now seems to give rise to a new sort of consum-
able object. In *Salò*, that object is shit—which is served and
eaten at a resplendent banquet. That is, the nothing—the
surplus or indigestible of consumption itself—is eaten as if
it were something, as if it were nourishing and consum-
mable. "I know very well that this is shit, but I'll eat it anyway": *this* is disavowal.

Freud argues that sublimation is connected with the drive
to know. In the newer model of vision—which Crary calls
physiological and I call perverse—this drive, propelled by the
surplus object that escapes it, is stilled by the phenomenal
appearance of the object. Instead of a drive to know and a
research, there is a state of knowing and—display; instead of
the creation of aesthetic and scientific objects, the frozen ar-
chitectures of aestheticism and the empty artifices of science.
This artifice is everywhere on display in *Salò* and in the Nazi
regime; it is precisely what Benjamin was talking about when
he talked about the "aestheticization of politics."

I would like to close with some observations about the
body as it exists in this perverse model of vision. Earlier, I
said, capitalism's project of quantification encountered an
exception that refused to allow the dissolution of every body
into a general equivalency, that is, some body parts came to

incarnate an impossible (because lost) "quality." Thus, somebody could become the object of our sexual longing. It is now
beginning to seem that the body has lost this power of incarnation. This fact creates a problem for sexual pleasure, whose
only site is the body, and only the body of the Other. The
problem is how to "other" the body, how to guarantee its
otherness from my own and thus make it an object of enjoyment. *Salò* presents two solutions. First, as Lacan pointed out
in his work on Sade, the sadist's victims are endowed with an
inviolable beauty, undamaged by what is inflicted on them.
In this case, it is clear that the body does not incarnate but *is*
the object a; the surplus object confronts me as artifice.

The second solution is presented in the final sequences
of the film. The primary victim of the courtyard tortures is
the winner of the "most beautiful ass contest," a difficult contest in which to distinguish oneself, given the problem of resemblance. A winner is neverthless chosen and his reward is
to be subject to a torture that will do what? Further distinguish him, assert his otherness. The body, no longer "backlit" by the object a, no longer the incarnation of what has been
lost to quantification, can now only provide pleasure by proving that it is a different body, and this difference can only be
evidenced by the fact that its suffering is not only not my own,
but is the very source of my enjoyment.[26]

---

26. I again borrow from the thesis of Jean-Claude Milner.

14

The Experience of the Outside: Foucault and Psychoanalysis

CHRISTOPHER LANE

> *Perhaps some day . . . [e]verything we experience today in the mode of a limit, or as foreign, or as intolerable will have returned to the serenity of the positive. And whatever currently designates this exteriority to us may well one day designate us.*
> *Only the enigma of this exteriority will remain.*
> —Michel Foucault,
> "Madness, the Absence of Work" (1964)

> *Already all confusion. Things and imaginings. As of always.*
> —Samuel Beckett, *Ill Seen Ill Said* (1981)

Summing up his objections to psychoanalysis in his classic study *Madness and Civilization*, Michel Foucault declared that psychoanalysis "has not been able, will not be able, to hear the voices of unreason."[1] "Psychoanalysis can unravel some of the forms of madness," he cautioned, but "it remains a stranger to the sovereign enterprise of unreason. It can neither liberate nor transcribe, nor most certainly explain, what is essential in this enterprise." To correct this skewed vision— and show us what is "maddest" about the history of reason —Foucault urged us not to "measure and justify madness

---

1. M. Foucault, *Madness and Civilization: A History of Insanity in the Age of Reason*, tr. R. Howard, 1961 (London: Tavistock, 1967), p. 278; hereafter abbreviated M.

through psychology." He argued instead that the various bodies promoting rationalism must "justify [themselves] before madness."

To many Foucauldians, these words stand as a judgment that psychoanalysis sides with rationalism in attempting to bring patients to reason. Yet Foucault advanced a very different thesis in the sixth chapter of *Madness and Civilization* and in later work, claiming that psychoanalysis *surpasses* conventional psychology in its ability to engage with unreason. Since many critics have accepted only the conclusion of Foucault's study, I want to revisit these nonidentical perspectives on psychoanalysis; they reveal a disagreement about objectivity, judgment, and perceptions of reality that we are far from having resolved.[2] The impasse at which Foucault arrived concerning psychoanalysis and unreason also manifests itself in Foucauldian and new historicist work, despite—and sometimes because of—critics' attempts to represent subjectivity as an effect of external causes.

That Jacques Lacan engaged frequently with this impasse is commonplace among his readers. Lacan's 1955 *écrit*, "The Freudian Thing," is an extensive meditation on the analytic

---

2. When Alan Sokal ridiculed various cultural studies arguments about the construction of reality, for example, his hoax essay in *Social Text* and co-authored study, *Fashionable Nonsense* (1998), partly crystallized one side of this debate. See A. D. Sokal, "Transgressing the boundaries: toward a transformative hermeneutics of quantum gravity," *Social Text* 46–47:217–52, 1996; and with J. Bricmont, *Fashionable Nonsense: Postmodern Intellectuals' Abuse of Science* (New York: Picador, 1998), especially pp. 1–17 and 50–105. A longer version of this essay argues, however, that Sokal and Bricmont, in conflating psychoanalysis with cultural studies, have not only simplified Freud and Lacan, but greatly impoverished recent perspectives on causation.

repercussions of the ego's "incompatibilities with reality [*discordances à la réalité*]",[3] and Lacan drew on this discordance to insist that the subject is split and at variance with reality. The ego is homologous with neither the subject nor the external world, he argued, because the ego is not the "seat" of consciousness. "I am not wherever I am the plaything of my thought," he declared in the late 1950s; "I think of what I am where I do not think to think."[4] In advancing these deliberately paradoxical and counterintuitive claims, Lacan complicated suggestions of a simple rapport between unconscious and external reality—claims to which I'll return. In the interests of representing subjectivity largely as an "effect" of discourse, however, Foucauldians and new historicists either ignore or dismiss these claims; they promote an argument about external causation that eschews any notion of the unconscious. Since this latter approach reinforces the study of ideology at the expense of psychic understanding, rendering subjectivity politically transparent and self-identical, my essay builds on Lacan's remarks to advance the following propositions: first, Foucault's ambivalent relationship to psychoanalysis demonstrates that he tried to modify its premises about the unconscious, psychic failure, and "indefinite" causality;[5] second, many Foucauldians have misread this ambivalence, turning it erroneously into an all-out critique of Freud and

---

3. J. Lacan, "The Freudian thing, or the meaning of the return to Freud in psychoanalysis" (1955), *Écrits: A Selection*, ed. J.-A. Miller, tr. A. Sheridan (1966; New York: Norton, 1977), p. 135.

4. J. Lacan, "The agency of the letter in the unconscious or reason since Freud" (1957), *Écrits: A Selection*, p. 166.

5. J. Lacan, *The Four Fundamental Concepts of Psycho-Analysis*, ed. J.-A. Miller, tr. A. Sheridan (1973; New York: Norton, 1978), p. 22; hereafter abbreviated *FFC*.

Lacan; and third, while Lacan's and Foucault's arguments are often similar, it is Lacan's, I suggest, that gives us the more sophisticated and politically useful account of the subject's conflict with reality.[6]

FOUCAULT AND THE UNCONSCIOUS

If I dispute the note on which Foucault concluded *Madness and Civilization*, it is because his account of psychoanalysis and unreason was neither complete nor entirely accurate. As John Rajchman reminds us, "[i]n his famous *Rome Discourse* (1953), Lacan in fact offers a definition of psychosis as 'language without discourse' which Foucault, ten years later, was to make the central terms of his definition of modernist writing."[7] "[I]n the 1930s," Rajchman continues, "when Heidegger, reading Hölderlin, was lecturing on the essence of art, and Janet was calling his patient Roussel a '*pauvre fou*,' Lacan was arguing that a revolution in psychiatry would follow from a detailed linguistic study of the *écrits*

---

6. I present this claim quite starkly to acknowledge the enormous weight of contrary opinion, which claims repeatedly that psychoanalysis has little or nothing—or *nothing precise*—to say about the social. For just four examples of recent work refuting these claims, see S. Žižek, *The Sublime Object of Ideology* (New York: Verso, 1989); S. Žižek, *For They Know Not What They Do: Enjoyment as a Political Factor* (New York: Verso, 1991); R. Salecl, *The Spoils of Freedom: Psychoanalysis and Feminism after the Fall of Socialism* (New York: Routledge, 1994); and J. Copjec, *Read My Desire: Lacan against the Historicists* (Cambridge, MA: MIT Press, 1994); hereafter abbreviated *RM*.

7. J. Rajchman, *Michel Foucault: The Freedom of Philosophy* (New York: Columbia University Press, 1985), p. 20.

of the mad."[8] Such chastening reminders not only undermine the perceived originality of Foucault's study of madness, but remind us why Foucault did not—and could not—represent Freudian and Lacanian psychoanalysis as perpetrators of noxious power/knowledge.[9]

To do justice to Foucault, we should acknowledge that the reception of *Madness and Civilization* differed radically from its conception as a doctoral thesis.[10] According to David Cooper, Foucault later appeared to support one of the prin-

---

8. Ibid., p. 20; see also J. Derrida, "'To do justice to Freud': the history of madness in the age of psychoanalysis," tr. P.-A. Brault and M. Naas, in *Foucault and His Interlocutors,* ed. A. I. Davidson (Chicago: University of Chicago Press, 1997), p. 61; hereafter abbreviated *TJ.* My argument owes much to Derrida's close reading of Foucault's *Madness and Civilization* (1961); *Mental Illness and Psychology* (1954; 1962), tr. A. Sheridan (New York: Harper and Row, 1976); and *The Birth of the Clinic: An Archaeology of Medical Perception,* tr. A. Sheridan (1963; London: Tavistock, 1973).

9. Foucault avowed: "It is very well to look back from our vantage point and remark upon the normalizing impulse in Freud; one can go on to denounce the role played for many years by the psychoanalytic institution; but the fact remains that in the great family of technologies of sex, which goes so far back into the history of the Christian West, of all those institutions that set out in the nineteenth century to medicalize sex, [psychoanalysis] was the one that, up to the decade of the forties, *rigorously opposed* the political and institutional effects of the perversion-hereditary-degenerescence system." M. Foucault, *The History of Sexuality, Vol. 1: An Introduction,* tr. R. Hurley (New York: Pantheon, 1978), pp. 157–158, my emphases; these texts hereafter abbreviated *HS.* I elaborate further on the implications of this passage in *The Burdens of Intimacy: Psychoanalysis and Victorian Masculinity* (Chicago: University of Chicago Press, 1999), pp. 12–26.

10. As David Macey notes, "by 1969, [*Madness and Civilization*] had, to its author's surprise, become part of an anti-psychiatry movement which easily mutated into a positive celebration of madness, and its author could actually be accused of 'psychiatricide' by the very academics and clinicians who had taught him in the 1940s and 1950s." D. Macey, "Michel Foucault: *j'accuse*," *New Formations* 25:8, 1995.

cipal tenets of antipsychiatry—that unreason, in defying civilization, lays down a path to our freedom. Cooper alludes to this claim when writing in his introduction to the English translation of Foucault's book, "[M]adness has in our age become a sort of lost truth" (M, p. vii). Foucault nonetheless cautioned at the start of his book: "we must speak of that initial dispute [between reason and non-reason] without assuming a victory, or the right to a victory" (M, p. xii). And though he later wrote a preface to Gilles Deleuze and Félix Guattari's *Anti-Oedipus* (1972), praising the book's attempt to release unreason from capitalism's "desiring-machines,"[11] Foucault couldn't leave the argument at this point. Nor could he resolve it in *Madness and Civilization*, whose conclusion, as I note above, varies with the final paragraph of its sixth chapter, "Doctors and Patients."[12] Insisting there that "we must do justice to Freud," Foucault argues that "Freud went back to madness at the level of its *language*, reconstituted one of the essential elements of an experience reduced to silence by positivism; he did not make a major addition to the list of psychological treatments for madness; he restored, in medical thought, *the possibility of a dialogue with unreason*" (M, p. 198; final emphasis mine). "It is not psychology that is in-

---

11. M. Foucault, preface to G. Deleuze and F. Guattari, *Anti-Oedipus: Capitalism and Schizophrenia*, tr. R. Hurley, M. Seem, and H. R. Lane, (1972; Minneapolis: University of Minnesota Press, 1983), pp. xi-xiv.

12. Derrida points up this disparity in *TJ*, especially pp. 64–65 and 78, eventually noting that Foucault "firmly places the same Freud (in general) [and] the same psychoanalysis (in general) sometimes on one side and sometimes on the other of the dividing line, *and always on the side of the Evil Genius*—who is found sometimes on the side of madness, sometimes on the side of its exclusion-reappropriation, on the side of its confinement to the outside or the inside, with or without asylum walls" (p. 80; original emphasis).

volved in psychoanalysis," Foucault insists at the end of this chapter, "but precisely an experience of unreason that it has been psychology's meaning, in the modern world, to mask" (*M*, p. 198).

According to *Madness and Civilization*, Chapter 6, we "do justice to Freud" by unmasking the assumed homology between psychoanalysis and psychology. Freud brings the result to our attention in *Group Psychology and the Analysis of the Ego* when announcing his desire to steer between "the Scylla of underestimating the importance of the repressed unconscious, and the Charybdis of judging the normal entirely by the standards of the pathological."[13] And throughout Foucault's career there are clear indications that he wanted this "justice to Freud" to prevail—sometimes in ways *improving* Freud's formulations—precisely to augment psychoanalysis's "experience of unreason" (*M*, p. 168).[14] As Derrida remarks, one way of reading Foucault's statement, "[i]t is not psychology that is involved in psychoanalysis," is to assert unambiguously that "there is, in psychoanalysis, *already no more* psychology" (*TJ*, p. 65; original emphasis). Published five years after *Madness and Civilization*, Foucault's *Order of Things* em-

---

13. S. Freud, "Group psychology and the analysis of the ego," *Standard Edition* 18:138, 1921.

14. One sees hints of this corrective tendency in Foucault's 1954 essay on Ludwig Binswanger and Freud, such as pp. 36–37, where Foucault acknowledges what Melanie Klein and Jacques Lacan add to Freud's conception of dream, reverie, and fantasy. Foucault, "Dream, imagination, and existence" (1954), tr. F. Williams, *Review of Existential Psychology and Psychiatry* 19(1):29–78; 1984–1985; hereafter abbreviated *D*. For an interesting account of Foucault's perspective on Freud, see J. W. Bernauer, *Michel Foucault's Force of Flight: Toward an Ethics for Thought* (Atlantic Highlands, NJ: Humanities Press, 1990), esp. pp. 167–174.

phatically supports this last claim, in the process distancing his work from *Madness and Civilization's* concluding remarks about psychoanalysis and unreason. Foucault asserts at the start of *The Order of Things* that he wants "to reveal a *positive unconscious* of knowledge."[15] And psychoanalysis, he argues throughout this impressive critique of the human sciences, far outweighs ethnology in scope and interpretive value, because it aids Foucault in revealing "the outer confines of representation" (*OT*, p. 378). Additionally, these "outer confines"—"Desire, Law, and Death"—bear intimately on the way we perceive unreason, for as Foucault argues, "[i]n setting itself the task of making the discourse of the unconscious speak through consciousness,"

> psychoanalysis is advancing in the direction of that fundamental region in which the relations of representation and finitude come into play. Whereas all the human sciences advance towards the unconscious only with their back to it, waiting for it to unveil itself as fast as consciousness is analyzed, as it were backwards, psychoanalysis, on the other hand, points directly towards it, with a deliberate purpose—not towards that which must be rendered gradually more explicit by the progressive illumination of the implicit, but towards what is there and yet is hidden, towards what exists with the mute solidity of a thing, of a text closed in upon itself, or of a blank space in a visible text, and uses that quality to defend itself. [*OT*, p. 374]

"It must not be supposed that the Freudian approach is the combination of an interpretation of meaning and a dynamics

---

15. M. Foucault, *The Order of Things: An Archaeology of the Human Sciences* (1966; New York: Pantheon, 1970), p. xi; hereafter abbreviated *OT*.

of resistance and defence," Foucault declares in the next sentence; "by following the same path as the human sciences, but with its gaze turned the other way, psychoanalysis moves towards the moment—by definition inaccessible to any theoretical knowledge of man, *to any continuous apprehension in terms of signification, conflict, or function*—at which the contents of consciousness articulate themselves, or rather stand gaping, upon man's finitude" (p. 374, my emphasis). In this respect Foucault's argument echoes Lacan's point about asymmetry, cited earlier and presented by Lacan in 1957. Indeed, psychoanalysis productively underwrites Foucault's famous antihumanist dictum, the closing words of *this* book, which aspire to decenter humanity so entirely that "man would be erased, like a face drawn in sand at the edge of the sea" (p. 387).[16] In assessing the degree of prescience operating here, we'll see that Freud inaugurated these ideas in the late 1890s, almost seventy years before Foucault published *The Order of Things*.[17]

Since many Foucauldians ignore *Foucault's* perspective on the unconscious, tending to leap in their assessment of psychoanalysis from the conclusion of *Madness and Civilization* to Volume 1 of *The History of Sexuality* (1976), it may not be a bad idea to point to this double erasure of the face drawn in sand, lost to the rising tide of identity politics and new

---

16. For elaboration see M. Cousins and A. Hussain, *Michel Foucault* (New York: St. Martin's, 1984), pp. 70–72.

17. I am referring here to Freud's "Project for a scientific psychology" (*Standard Edition* 1:283–397, 1895) as well as to Freud's letters to Wilhelm Fliess. See also Freud's "Screen memories" 1899; *Standard Edition* 3:300–322, in which Freud questions "whether we have any memories at all *from* our childhood: memories *relating to* our childhood may be all that we possess" (p. 322).

historicism. It should go without saying that such "forgetting" distorts Foucault's understanding of genealogy, which points up doubt about historical meaning far more readily than it advances certainty about political subversion or strategy.[18] Additionally, that proponents of identity politics represent the ego as the "seat" of consciousness skews Lacan's and Foucault's arguments against self-determination in the 1950s and 1960s. Foucault wrote *The Archaeology of Knowledge* (1969) explicitly to oppose arguments about agency and self-determination, and he concluded this book by advising his readers that "archaeology touches on a question that is being posed today by psychoanalysis."[19] That Foucauldians and new historicists attest repeatedly to Foucault's antipathy to Freud nonetheless brings to our attention an ambivalence in Foucault's work concerning links between unreason and the unconscious, and this is what we must assess to engage

18. In "Nietzsche, genealogy, history" (1971), Foucault represents truth and being as "but the exteriority of accidents" (*Language, Counter-Memory, Practice: Selected Essays and Interviews*, ed. D. F. Bouchard, tr. D. F. Bouchard and S. Simon [Ithaca, NY: Cornell University Press, 1977], p. 146); hereafter abbreviated *N*. See also C. Shepherdson, "History and the Real: Foucault with Lacan," *Postmodern Culture* 5(2), 1995; J. Johnston, "Discourse as event: Foucault, writing, and literature," *Modern Language Notes* 105: 800–818, 1990; H. D. Harootunian, "Foucault, genealogy, history: the pursuit of otherness" and J. Sawicki, "Feminism and the power of Foucaldian discourse," both in *After Foucault: Humanistic Knowledge, Postmodern Challenges*, ed. J. Arac (New Brunswick, NJ: Rutgers University Press, 1988), pp. 110–138 and 161–178. See also Judith Butler, *The Psychic Life of Power: Theories in Subjection* (Stanford, CA: Stanford University Press, 1997), especially pp. 86–89; hereafter abbreviated *PL*.

19. M. Foucault, *The Archaeology of Knowledge*, tr. A. M. Sheridan (1969; New York: Harper and Row, 1972), p. 207.

the broader stakes concerning subjective causation and social change.[20]

I turn to Foucault's ambivalence, then, because it serves
a number of diverse aims and underscores his own complex
claims about subjectivity. As Derrida shows in his brilliant
essay on Foucault and madness, Foucault "regularly attempts
to objectify psychoanalysis and to reduce it to that of which
he speaks rather than to that from out of which he speaks"
(*TJ*, p. 62). He does so, Derrida argues, because he "*does and
does not want* to situate Freud in a historical place that is
stabilizable, identifiable, and open to a univocal understanding. . . . Sometimes he wants to credit Freud, sometimes dis-
credit him, unless he is actually doing both indiscernibly and
at the same time. One will always have the choice of attributing this ambivalence to either Foucault or Freud. . . ." (p. 63,
original emphasis). Derrida acknowledges that other commentators have been less reticent in attributing this ambivalence
to Foucault alone (pp. 58, 80). Jacques-Alain Miller, for one,
has argued that the position psychoanalysis occupies in *The
History of Sexuality, Volume I* is "symmetrical and inverse to

---

20. Todd May observes: "psychoanalysis . . . is a practice about which
Foucault was more ambivalent than he was about other psychological prac-
tices." T. May, *Between Genealogy and Epistemology: Psychology, Politics,
and Knowledge in the Thought of Michel Foucault* (University Park: Penn-
sylvania State University Press, 1993), p. 47. Patrick H. Hutton argues that
"Foucault's work is heavy with Freud's unstated presence." P. Hutton,
"Foucault, Freud, and the technologies of the self," in *Technologies of the
Self: A Seminar with Michel Foucault,* ed. L. H. Martin, H. Gutman, and P. H.
Hutton (London: Tavistock, 1988), p. 121. And Johnston reminds us that
"Foucault constantly shifted perspective and reassessed his earlier views"
("Discourse as Event," p. 802).

the position it occupies in [*The Order of Things*]. It is no longer the guiding principle of the enquiry but the object of the enquiry. It does not guide the archaeologist, but is subject to his counterattack. It is not praised. On the contrary, it is crushed with sarcasm."[21]

Later paragraphs in my essay will offer tentative explanations for this shift in Foucault's work, which although palpable between 1966 and 1976, prevails most acutely between *Discipline and Punish* and *The History of Sexuality, Volume I*—books that were published just one year apart.[22] My immediate emphasis concerns the difficulty of isolating this ambivalence in temporal terms: if we limit Foucault's ambivalence about psychoanalysis to 1976, we necessarily eclipse the interesting conceptual tensions of earlier texts such as *Madness and Civilization*. And although Miller is right to underscore the value Foucault placed on psychoanalysis in *The Order of Things*, he is not correct in implying that psychoanalysis, in *The History of Sexuality, Volume I*, is *consistently* "crushed with sarcasm." Foucault understood well that Wilhelm Reich and Herbert Marcuse were the chief proponents of a "repressive hypothesis" he wanted to disband, and he differentiates clearly

---

21. J.-A. Miller, "Michel Foucault and psychoanalysis," in *Michel Foucault: Philosopher*, ed. and tr. T. J. Armstrong (New York: Routledge, 1992), 58; hereafter abbreviated *MFP*. John Forrester similarly remarks: "One has a strange feeling as one reads this book of Foucault's [*The History of Sexuality, Volume I*]. It is like reading Freud, but with all the signs changed." J. Forrester, *The Seductions of Psychoanalysis: Freud, Lacan, and Derrida* (New York: Cambridge University Press, 1990), p. 299; hereafter abbreviated *SP*; see also pp. 301–302.

22. M. Foucault, *Discipline and Punish: The Birth of the Prison,* tr. A. Sheridan (1975) (Harmondsworth: Peregrine, 1979). Gallimard published *Histoire de la sexualité, 1: La Volonté de savoir* in 1976.

in this first volume between both theorists and Freud.[23] Nor can we say unequivocally that Foucault's earlier work is exempt from this ambivalence; I began deliberately with a brief illustration of this tension in *Madness and Civilization*, to underscore the inconsistency between the book's final words and its chapter on "Doctors and Patients."

I suggest that this conceptual tension in *Madness and Civilization* signals the difficulty of attributing to psychoanalysis a clear and static perspective on the gap separating experience from its interpretation—a gap that has dramatic repercussions for arguments about social and political change. One reason for this difficulty is the psychic mutability of unreason itself, which partly demonstrates that the subject is constructed by forces lying beyond conscious apprehension and social meaning. Additionally, the "anti-conceptual . . . indefinite" principle of cause permeating Lacan's work allows us to view psychoanalysis as complicit in policies of self-management only if we confuse psychoanalysis with ego psychology, as Foucault did not.[24] As soon as we recognize with Freud the interminable dimension of psychoanalysis, owing

---

23. See the passage reproduced in note 9 above.

24. J. Lacan, *FFC*, p. 22. As Derrida observes, Foucault argues rather crassly in *Madness and Civilization* that "all nineteenth-century psychiatry really converges on Freud" (*TJ*, p. 74, citing Foucault, *M*, p. 277). Although Foucault's double argument about psychoanalysis "is assured by the workings of a hinge" (*TJ*, p. 64), as Derrida makes clear, Derrida nonetheless is right to indicate that "[f]rom this point on, things are going to deteriorate. 'To do justice to Freud' will more and more come to mean putting on trial a psychoanalysis that will have participated, in its own way, however original that may be, in the order of the immemorial figures of the Father and the Judge, of Family and Law, in the order of Order, of Authority and Punishment. . . ." (*TJ*, 73–74).

largely to what he calls the "violent opposition" between identity and sexuality,[25] we see that psychoanalysis—as distinct from psychiatry—necessarily *departs* from the idea of the confessional and self-policing, as Foucauldians tend to define these terms.[26] Without leaping to the conclusion that Foucault's selective use of Freud underscores his basic aversion to all things psychoanalytic, I therefore propose that Foucault partly shares with psychoanalysis this complex—at times, faltering—relationship to the interpretation of limit experiences.

The difficulty of establishing where psychoanalysis stands relative to experience and its interpretation not only haunted Foucault's career but partly determined it. One strand of Foucault's intellectual project was aimed at complicating historical materialism by building on Nietzsche's work. Another strand—tied conceptually to the first—focused on challenging the intellectual sovereignty in France of Jean-Paul Sartre. But a third and less successful strand devolved on establishing the importance of psychoanalysis for modern thought *without at the same time endorsing Lacan's "return to Freud."*[27]

---

25. S. Freud, "Resistance and repression" *Standard Edition* 16:294, 1916–1917.

26. See for example J. D. Marshall, *Michel Foucault: Personal Autonomy and Education* (Dordrecht: Kluwer Academic, 1996), pp. 116–118.

27. On the question of Foucault's "return" to Freud, see Derrida, *TJ*, p. 65. Lee Grieveson underscores a related point in "'The death of psychoanalysis'? Foucault on Lacan" (*New Formations* 31:189–190, 1997, though he does so to claim that Foucault's theses in Volumes 1 and 2 of *The History of Sexuality* are also partial objections to Lacan's theory of castration. His argument is only partly convincing because it's obliged to downplay Foucault's obvious debt to Lacan at the start of the fourth section of *Volume 1*. Foucault admits here: "In point of fact, the assertion that sex is not "repressed" is not altogether new. Psychoanalysts have been saying the same thing for some time." (*HS*, p. 81, my emphasis). Grieveson

From this perspective, we can view Foucault's early work as not only a profound assault on Sartre's precepts but also an implicit, sometimes ambivalent commentary on Lacan's claims about extimacy and the real, factors far beyond the purview of discourse theory and new historicism.[28]

"Foucault . . . was never fascinated by psychoanalysis," declares Maurice Blanchot in "Michel Foucault as I Imagine Him," but even if we ignore extensive counterevidence in Blanchot's essay we have ample reason to dispute this claim.[29] David Macey, one of Foucault's biographers, writes that before Foucault advanced his early accounts of psychoanalysis in the 1950s and 1960s, he asked the Parisian analyst Daniel Lagache about the prerequisites for a career in psychology.[30] And Didier Eribon, Foucault's first biographer, recalls that

---

also is unable to show convincingly how Foucault managed to get "'beyond' . . . the deployment of sexuality and psychoanalysis" (p. 198). Indeed, as he avows toward the end of his article, restating the "problematic" with which he began, "It is this question of a 'beyond' that seems to haunt Foucault's account of psychoanalysis" (p. 198). My essay aims to show why Foucault couldn't get "beyond" Freud and Lacan, and thus why this "haunt[ing]" was conceptually inevitable.

28. James Miller advances this point in *The Passion of Michel Foucault* (New York: Simon and Schuster, 1993), p. 136. For elaboration on extimacy (*extimité*) and the real, see J.-A. Miller, "Extimité," tr. F. Massardier-Kenney, *Prose Studies* 11.3; pp. 121–131, 1988; and J. Copjec, "The orthopsychic subject," *RMD* pp. 15–38, a superb chapter to which my argument is indebted.

29. M. Blanchot, "Michel Foucault as I imagine him," tr. J. Mehlman, *Foucault, Blanchot* (1986; New York: Zone, 1987), p. 73. Subsequent references to the English translation will be abbreviated *MF*. For indications of this counterevidence, see Blanchot, *MF*, pp. 93–101; J.-A. Miller, *MFP*, p. 58; and Derrida, *TJ*.

30. D. Macey, *The Lives of Michel Foucault* (New York: Pantheon, 1993), p. 37.

Foucault simultaneously considered beginning analysis with Lagache; it was Lagache—not Foucault—who dismissed this possibility.[31] Rejecting Louis Althusser's advice that he receive hospital treatment for depression, Foucault eventually began a brief period of analysis in 1948, and he attended Lacan's seminars in the 1950s while following his work with interest.[32] Macey notes further that Foucault wrote a brief tribute to Lacan, after his death in 1981, calling him "the liberator of psychoanalysis."[33]

Foucault would surely loathe the inclusion of this information, insisting—with sometimes quasimystical resonance —that the personal be erased to avoid reducing the history of twentieth-century French thought to a few internecine rivalries. And though I partly agree with this last caution, I include this material because some Foucauldians—rendering Foucault's perspectives on desire, identity, and even history antipathetic to Freud's—seem almost to believe that these events could not have occurred. That Foucault sought out analysis seems to tarnish this dissociation, as if—in attacking the *dispositif* (apparatus) that allegedly "produced" depression—"Saint Foucault" could never have suffered from the condition himself.

If Foucault's assessment of Lacan as "the liberator of psychoanalysis" apparently was possible only in retrospect, when Lacan had died—and I stress that this is my speculation—how can we assess these thinkers' conceptual rapport when both were alive? Lacan himself recognized in 1966 that

---

31. D. Eribon, *Michel Foucault* (Paris: Flammarion, 1989), pp. 61–62.

32. See D. Macey, *The Lives of Michel Foucault,* pp. 36 and 513 n.26; Forrester, *SP,* p. 293.

33. Foucault, cited in D. Macey, *The Lives of Michel Foucault,* p. 422.

Foucault's relationship to psychoanalysis was uneasy and equivocal. "As for Foucault," Lacan declared, "he follows what I do, and I like his work, but I don't see him as being very interested in Freud's position."[34] "[H]e follows what I do" is perhaps comic—because egregiously narcissistic—but although Lacan attests to Foucault's interest in his work, his statement isn't *entirely* correct. We need only glance at Foucault's oeuvre, pushing on from his essay on dreams to the first volume of his *History of Sexuality*, to see that Foucault framed his ambivalent relationship to Lacan largely by engaging with and disengaging from *Freud*. It was Freud, in other words, who served as a vanishing mediator between Foucault and Lacan—as a figure whose work became a crucial hinge between two bodies of thought that, despite their profound similarities, fail at crucial moments to coalesce. The conceptual implications of this divergence help reveal what is at stake, on Foucault's side, in viewing resistance relative less to failure and impossibility than to relations of power.[35] Since Foucault largely was unwilling to address this divergence, however, there is additional difficulty in assessing this dispute. Admitting that he was eager to engage Foucault on this point, for instance, John Forrester explains in *The Seductions of Psychoanalysis* that interviewing Foucault on this subject proved singularly unenlightening: "My next step in tracking down Foucault's relation to psychoanalysis was to go and ask him about it. Remarkably enough, that was no help at all. . . . He proved genuinely evasive on this topic" (*SP*, p. 289).

---

34. These remarks appeared in *Figaro Littéraire* on December 29, 1966, and are cited in Forrester, *SP*, p. 381 n.27.

35. See Blanchot, *MF*, p. 90.

GENEALOGY AND IMMANENCE

After publishing numerous books detailing abuses of power—
books on incarceration, punishment, psychiatry, and modern
medicine—Foucault published *The History of Sexuality, Volume I* to criticize the way radical sexual movements too readily
had adopted Reich's and Marcuse's hydraulic perspectives on
repression and liberation.[36] As Foucault avowed in April 1983,
however, the first volume of *The History of Sexuality* stymied
as a project because it failed to engage ethics *in the field of
sexuality*.[37] What initially seemed adequate for Foucault, in
theorizing how external forms of power steadily encroach on
individuals, proved deficient when it came to formulating an
ethics of the drive not entirely determined by outside forces.[38]
Foucault's apparent solution to this impasse was to provide
what he called "a historical ontology of ourselves in relation
to truth through which we constitute ourselves as subjects of
knowledge; . . . as subjects acting on others; [and] . . . as moral
agents" (*G*, p. 351). Still, this perspective continued to short-
circuit his engagement with psychic drives and the "defiles"

---

36. See J. Rajchman, *Michel Foucault: The Freedom of Philosophy*, p. 88.

37. See M. Foucault, "On the genealogy of ethics: an overview of
work in progress," an interview with Paul Rabinow and Hubert Drefus,
April 1983, reprinted in *The Foucault Reader*, ed. P. Rabinow (New York:
Pantheon, 1984), pp. 347–349; hereafter abbreviated *G*; J.-A. Miller, *MFP*,
pp. 58–59; and Forrester, *SP*, pp. 311–315. Forrester asks: "So, what is the
failure being addressed in these last two books [*Discipline and Punish* and
The History of Sexuality, Volume I]? I think it is the failure of the intellectual himself—Foucault's own failure" (*SP* p. 115).

38. Another illustration of this conceptual weakness is Foucault's
essay "The subject and power," *Critical Inquiry* 8.4:777–795, 1982, which
elaborates almost entirely on power, but makes only generic statements
about subjectivity.

of the signifier. The solution merely reproduced from another direction the limited advantages of emphasizing self-fashioning. "On the Genealogy of Ethics," for example, shows Foucault invoking an approach to life, common in antiquity, of which "[w]e have hardly any remnant . . . in our society": "In antiquity, this work on the self with its attendant austerity is not imposed on the individual by means of civil law or religious obligation, but is a choice about existence made by the individual. *People decide for themselves whether or not to care for themselves"* (G, p. 361, my emphasis).[39]

Partly because of this emphasis on self-fashioning, *The Use of Pleasure*, Volume 2 of *The History of Sexuality*, became an extensive meditation on Greek and Roman sexual ethics. Foucault shows with remarkable lucidity how these cultures represented passion as a potential threat—even "danger"— to an individual's "self-rule [*pouvoir sur lui-même*]."[40] Nevertheless, as subsequent interviews about this volume underscore, Foucault resisted the suggestion—voiced differently by the cultures of antiquity and the nineteenth century—that sexuality's complex relationship to ontology cannot always be reduced to history and cultural concerns. Foucault's em-

---

39. Foucault advances similar voluntaristic claims about selfhood in *The Care of the Self: Volume 3 of The History of Sexuality,* tr. R. Hurley (1984; New York: Pantheon, 1986), pp. 71 and 85. Elsewhere, as Kate Soper notes dryly, Foucault's "austere and clinical ethics, conducted as far as possible without reference to affectivity . . . cannot bring itself to speak of 'love' but only of the development of a 'stylistics of the individual bond.'" K. Soper, "Forget Foucault?" *New Formations* 25:27, 1995, citing Foucault, *The History of Sexuality, Volume 3,* p. 148.

40. M. Foucault, *The Use of Pleasure: Volume 2 of The History of Sexuality,* tr. R. Hurley (1984; New York: Pantheon, 1985), pp. 79, 81; *Histoire de la sexualité, 2: L'Usage des plaisirs* (Paris: Gallimard, 1984), p. 94; hereafter abbreviated *UP* and *UPS*.

phasis therefore tells us how passion became tied to "1. the expression of a fear, 2. a model of conduct, 3. the image of a stigmatized attitude, and 4. an example of abstinence" (*UP*, p. 15). In refusing the psychoanalytic argument that sexuality isn't determined wholly by discourse and social practices, however, Foucault could understand the ontological *difficulty* of sexuality only the way antiquity represented this phenomenon—that is, as an "effect . . . of errors of regimen [*les erreurs de régime*]" (*UP*, p. 16; *UPS*, p. 23).

Foucault's insistence even here in approaching sexuality from primarily a culturalist perspective exacerbated his self-acknowledged difficulties. Yet his commitment to engaging some of the psychic repercussions of subjectivation— which dovetailed into his study of the modes of subjection (*mode d'assujettisement*, *G*, p. 353)—ironically obliged him to *return* to psychoanalysis for a better understanding of their diverse effects.[41] I am suggesting that throughout Foucault's career this pincer-like approach to psychoanalysis overdetermined his perspective on subjectivity. While his first published essay critiqued works by Ludwig Binswanger and Freud, for example, it didn't dispute the appearance or effect of the unconscious. "Freud . . . restored a psychological dimension to the dream," Foucault argued, "but he did not

---

41. Although Foucault preferred speaking of *subjection* and *subjectivation* rather than *subjectivity*, my purpose is to focus on Foucault's preoccupation with a form of interiority that isn't snared by the *mode d'assujettisement*; to this extent, my reading is consonant with one strand of Foucault's work (see also Butler's questions, cited below). M. Foucault, "Maurice Blanchot: the thought from outside," tr. B. Massumi, *Foucault, Blanchot*, and M. Foucault, *La pensée du dehors* (1966; Paris: Fata Morgana, 1986), p. 34, in both French and English editions. Subsequent references to the English translation will be abbreviated *MB*.

succeed in understanding it as a specific form of experience" (*D*, p. 43). Although this last claim is questionable,[42] Foucault's principal criticism of Freudian technique lay, in John Forrester's words, in "its failure to give sufficient account of the innate expressivity of the image prior to, or beyond, any semantic, representational analysis" (*SP*, p. 289). In "Dream, Imagination, and Existence," Foucault argues that phenomenology offered a more successful—though still inadequate— perspective on dreams: "Phenomenology has succeeded in making dreams speak," he remarks, "but it has given no one the possibility of understanding their language" (*D*, p. 42).[43] A maturer Foucault nonetheless would wonder if he really wanted to understand the language of dreams. The germ of this refusal manifests in "Dream, Imagination, and Existence," in the suggestion that Freud's *Interpretation of Dreams* is so schematic that it almost takes us *away* from the unconscious. This is the flip side of trying to retrieve "the innate expressivity" of the dream without diluting its meaning. Foucault

---

42. Questionable, because "the specific form of experience" Freud details in *The Interpretation of Dreams* necessarily alters—and even destroys—all prior conceptions of the *integrity* of ontology. Hence, in part, his urging us "to conclude . . . that *psychical* reality is a particular form of existence not to be confused with *material* reality" (*Standard Edition* 5:620, 1900, original emphases; see also note 61 below).

43. Foucault's interest in Freud did not wane, however, and he followed up his work on Freud and Binswanger by writing *Maladie mentale et personalité* (1954; 1962), a revised version of which was translated and published in 1987 as *Mental Illness and Psychology*. See also M. Foucault, "La psychologie de 1850 à 1950" and "La recherche scientifique et la psychologie," both in *Michel Foucault: Dits et écrits: 1954–1988, Volume I*, ed. D. Defert and F. Ewald (Paris: Gallimard, 1994), pp. 120–137 and 137–158, respectively.

implies here that aspects of subjectivity (including dreams) be allowed to remain enigmatic.

These arguments reveal the philosophical arc of Foucault's work, which begins in 1954 with Freud and Binswanger, and ends circa 1983 with Foucault's attempt to produce a genealogy of ethics uncoupled from the drives. We might say that these margins of Foucault's work—these bookends to his career—haunt and partly undermine his attempt to define subjectivity as an effect of discursive apparatuses. While subtle differences therefore arise between *The Archaeology of Knowledge* (1969) and *Discipline and Punish* (1975) concerning the role of the *dispositif*—the latter text marking, in Blanchot's words, Foucault's "transition from the study of isolated discursive practices to the study of the social practices that constitute their underpinning" (*MF* p. 83)[44]—the thread linking these books is Foucault's suggestion that "[t]he individual is the product of power."[45] The underside to this conception of subjectivity—and, perhaps, the obvious extension of it—is the near-metaphysical idea that subjectivity, once freed from outside regulation, would lack "inner conviction" (*MF*, pp. 89, 42). This idea surfaces periodically in Foucault's 1954 essay

---

44. We can of course identify other transitions in Foucault's work. Indeed, Jacques-Alain Miller archly points up the one concerning us here when writing: "[P]erhaps this shift in the work of Foucault, between 1966 to 1976 [concerning his perspective on psychoanalysis], will appear to the future archaeologists as the privileged indicator of the moment when the practice of psychoanalysis fell definitively into disuse, deprived of meaning and of hope, becoming as anachronistic for us today as initiation. Maybe" (*MFP*, p. 58).

45. M. Foucault, preface to Deleuze and Guattari, *Anti-Oedipus: Capitalism and Schizophrenia*, p. xiv. On this point see J. S. Ransom, *Foucault's Discipline: The Politics of Subjectivity* (Durham, NC: Duke University Press, 1997), esp. pp. 49 and 56–57.

on dreams, and it culminates logically with the demand that subjectivity be let alone, whether to silence, abstraction, or pleasure.[46] We see this latter perspective in Foucault's statement, "*l'Art de vivre c'est de tuer la psychologie*,"[47] which, following *Madness and Civilization* and *The Order of Things*, can be a judgment on psychology and psychiatry only. The statement would otherwise be misleading and dishonest; as *The Order of Things* made clear, Freud is a crucial ally here, rethinking "subjectivation" seven decades before Foucault published his remarkable attack on ego psychology and the human sciences.

For the sake of brevity, I'll offer one example of Foucault's tautological perspective on subjectivity, which I take from his long and interesting 1971 debate with Noam Chomsky: "[I]f you were to push me to an extreme," Foucault declared, "I would say that our society has been afflicted by a disease, a very curious, a very paradoxical disease, for which we haven't yet found a name; and this mental disease has a very curious symptom, which is that the symptom itself brought the mental disease into being. There you have it."[48] It may be fascinating

---

46. See Foucault, *G*, p. 347, as well as p. 350, where Foucault asks plangently: "[C]ouldn't everyone's life become a work of art? Why should the lamp or the house be an art object, but not our life?"

47. Foucault, cited in L. Bersani, *Homos* (Cambridge, MA: Harvard University Press, 1995), p. 97; hereafter abbreviated *H*. Bersani comments: "Can anyone believe that such peremptory formulas (. . .) make any sense except as an aggressive riposte to an interlocutor Foucault seldom acknowledges or addresses directly? He was so acutely aware of psychoanalysis as yet another episode in a history of disciplinary networks that he never considered that psychoanalysis might provide some answers to questions he himself found urgent" (*H*, pp. 97–98).

48. Foucault (with N. Chomsky), "Human nature: justice versus power," in *Foucault and His Interlocutors*, p. 140.

to view society's afflictions in this way, representing the "symptom" as if it alone can "br[ing] . . . into being . . . the mental
disease" that it comes to represent. Nonetheless, the statement
is perplexing and disingenuous at the level of *cause*. What is
eclipsed here—perhaps necessarily so, for Foucault—are the
precise relations among subject, structure, and drive. In a
tautological way, the subject apparently manifests a symptom that the *dispositif* in question later renders indicative of
its being, suffering, or type.[49] What we lose, therefore, is the
necessity of addressing the symptom's formation relative
to drive or fantasy, and thus the idea that cause is neither
empirical nor discursive.[50] And while Foucauldians might
cheer this result, convinced that it returns causation to the
dispositif, they truncate and impoverish their own perspective on history, society, and desire, as Joan Copjec has shown
us so well, by insisting that power is "*immanent within* society" (*RMD*, p. 5). "Historicism wants to ground being in
appearance and wants to have nothing to do with desire,"

---

49. Foucault makes this clear in *Mental Illness and Psychology*: "[I]t
would be absurd to say that the sick man machinizes his world because he
projects a schizophrenic world in which he is lost; it is even untrue to say
that he is a schizophrenic, because this is the only way open to him of escaping from the constraints of his real world. In fact, when man remains
alienated from what takes place in his language, when he cannot recognize any human, living signification in the productions of his activity, when
economic and social determinations place constraints upon him and he is
unable to feel at home in this world, he lives in a culture that makes a
pathological form like schizophrenia possible" (p. 84).

50. Bersani valuably represents Foucault's claims about subjectivation in the following way: "The mechanisms of power studied by Foucault produce the individuals they are designed to dominate" (*S*, p. 3).

Copjec tells us. "[H]istoricism . . . refuses to believe in re-pression and proudly professes to be *illiterate in desire*. The emergence of a neopopularism cannot be blamed on Fou-cault, but the historicism he cultivated is guilty of effacing the pockets of empty, inarticulable desire that bear the bur-den of proof of society's externality to itself" (p. 14).[51]

SILENCE AND STASIS

Foucault's second and related conception of subjectivity in-terests me more than this perspective on social practices, however, because it deems silence and stasis alternatives to the subject's endless agitation from without. It doesn't sur-prise me that at such moments Foucault would reproduce a scenario comparable to Samuel Beckett's interest in depletion and inertia in *The Unnamable* (1958).[52] Nor does it surprise

---

51. I agree entirely with Copjec's reading of new historicism, but draw attention to Foucault's assertion, in "Nietzsche, Genealogy, History," that the concept of genealogy makes it "wrong" to "reduc[e the] entire history and genesis [of morality] to an exclusive concern for utility" (N, p. 139). The question is therefore whether Foucault "cultivated" histori-cism or whether historicism "produced" the Foucault that it required in order to become "illiterate in desire." Consonant between Foucault and Lacan is the way "genealogy retrieves an indispensable restraint: it must record the singularity of events outside of any monotonous finality" (N, p. 139). Anglo-American Foucauldians might heed that psychoanalysis aids—and even enhances—precisely this *recording* of "the singularity of events." It's really no accident that Foucault concluded *The Order of Things* by making the same point.

52. S. Beckett, *The Unnamable: Three Novels by Samuel Beckett* (1958; New York: Grove, 1991). At the end of Beckett's novella, movement—like life—proves too much of an ordeal; the narrator tries to stop the alienation

me that Foucault would feel drawn to the work of Blanchot, a writer he celebrated in part for depicting "the essence of zeal to be negligent" (p. 30). "Into [a self-effacing] void [language] must go," observes Foucault in his 1966 essay on Blanchot, "consenting to come undone in the rumbling, in the immediate negation of what it says, in a silence that is not the intimacy of a secret but a pure outside where words endlessly unravel" (*MB*, p. 22).

In a section of his essay reproducing the following phrase, however, Foucault seems to grasp that "the *experience* of the outside" is neither silent nor serene; it is *real*, in the Lacanian sense, as Foucault seems to imply in the quotation above. Indeed, the condition of being alive is such that one cannot arrest thought or stimulation. Nor can one identify an outside free of psychic difficulty. One might hope to capture what Foucault calls, apparently without irony, "the sweet interiority of consciousness" (*MB*, p. 33). But "the law," he avows here, "is *not* the principle or inner rule of conduct. It is the outside that envelops conduct, thereby removing it from all interiority; it is the darkness beyond its borders; it is the void that surrounds it, converting, unknown to anyone, its singularity into the gray monotony of the universal and opening around

----

that speech and demand force him to confront. For elaboration on this point, see Bersani and U. Dutoit, *Arts of Impoverishment: Beckett, Rothko, Resnais* (Cambridge, MA: Harvard University Press, 1993), pp. 50–52. Lacan underscores a similar point about speech and alienation in his reading of Edgar Allan Poe's story "The Facts in the Case of M. Valdemar" (1845). See *The Seminar of Jacques Lacan, Book II: The Ego in Freud's Theory and in the Technique of Psychoanalysis, 1954–1955*, tr. S. Tomaselli (New York: Norton, 1988), pp. 231–32; hereafter abbreviated *EF*. In "What Is an Author?" Foucault echoes questions surfacing in Beckett's work. See M. Foucault, *Language, Counter-Memory, Practice*, p. 115.

it a space of uneasiness, of dissatisfaction, of multiplied zeal" (*MB*, p. 34, my emphasis).

Although these words are beautifully measured, what they point up isn't exactly lovely. They ask us to consider what binds subjectivity to "the void that surrounds it," which returns us to the enigma of causation—the paradoxical effects of the death drive—precisely when the subject appears free of "the law." It is here, when Foucault *seems* to refute a Lacanian insistence on nonmaterialist causation, that Blanchot grasps the problem of voluntarism and mysticism. In "Michel Foucault As I Imagine Him," however, he tries to circumvent this problem by chiding Foucault's readers; it is they, apparently, who idealize the subject's vanishing: "[I]t is accepted as a certainty that Foucault . . . got rid of, purely and simply, the notion of the subject: no more oeuvre, no more author, no more creative unity, [and no more drive, we might add]. But things are not that simple. The subject does not disappear; rather its excessively determined unity is put in question" (*MF*, p. 76).[53] It seems only right to direct Blanchot's statement at Foucault himself, however, for if the law "is *not* the principle or inner rule of conduct" (*MB*, p. 34, my emphasis), as Foucault claims quite surprisingly, what is? And if, as Foucault tells us often and in diverse ways, "[t]he individual is the product of power,"[54] what prevents the subject from dis-

---

53. For a more stringent assessment of this fantasy, see Lacan: "Don't . . . get the idea that the ego volatilises after an analysis—be it didactic or therapeutic, one doesn't go to heaven, disembodied and pure symbol" (*EF* p. 325).

54. M. Foucault, preface to Deleuze and Guattari, *Anti-Oedipus: Capitalism and Schizophrenia*, p. xiv.

appearing if the configurations change or even cease? More-over, what form of resistance could emerge at this point that wouldn't collapse the argument back into the materialist regis-ter from which Foucault usefully distances himself in this essay? Blanchot is partly correct in saying that Foucault's readers have extended the argument farther than Foucault took it himself, but I don't think they are entirely misreading him. I suggest they are instead voicing a doubt about the subject's resilience and causation that Foucault raised but seemed unwilling—and perhaps unable—to resolve.

Whenever he touches on this idea of the subject's par-tial release from its *dispositif*, Foucault's language becomes enigmatic; his ideas trail off into silence. Judith Butler identi-fies this problem when asking, in her recent book, "given the radical exteriority of the soul [in *The History of Sexual-ity*], how are we to understand 'interiority' in Foucault? That interiority will not be a soul, and it will not be a psyche, but what will it be?" (*PL*, p. 89). Jacques-Alain Miller also high-lights this tendency to abstraction when stating, in an inter-view with Foucault, published in 1977 as "Le jeu de Michel Foucault" (Michel Foucault's Game—or Trick, or Ploy), "With the introduction of 'apparatuses,' you want to get beyond dis-course. But . . . I can't quite see how you could be getting at a 'non-discursive' domain."[55]

---

55. J.-A. Miller, "The confession of the flesh," an interview with Foucault, recorded on July 10, 1977, with Alain Grosrichard, Gerard Wajeman, Guy Le Gaufey, Dominique Celas, Gerard Miller, Catherine Millot, Jocelyne Livi, and Judith Miller, in M. Foucault, *Power/Knowledge: Selected Interviews and Other Writings 1972–1977*, ed. C. Gordon, tr. C. Gordon, L. Marshall, J. Mepham, and K. Soper (New York: Pantheon, 1980), p. 197; hereafter abbreviated *CF*.

We see glimpses of this "'nondiscursive' domain" in Foucault's work, to be sure, but only in brief intervals between the limit of the apparatus and the subject's abstraction. Moreover, these gaps return us to Foucault's ambivalent relationship to psychoanalysis, for they point up a demand for silence without drive, and pleasure without anxiety. As Blanchot announces in a typical and unsatisfactory move, "Foucault . . . distrusts the marvels of interiority, refuses the traps of subjectivity, asking where and how there emerges a discourse entirely surface and shimmering, but bereft of mirages" (*MF*, p. 68). But one cannot "*refuse* the traps of subjectivity" without producing an abstraction and idealizing the result. Blanchot's point about refusal and distrust seems possible only after he declares—incorrectly so, as three biographies of Foucault attest—that "Foucault . . . was never fascinated by psychoanalysis" (*MF*, p. 73).[56] This scenario need not resurrect a stale binary between the inside and the outside; let me instead address how Foucault's indifference to psychic resistance actually *enabled* his sometimes lyrical assessment of life without identity, death without pain, desire without misery, and attraction without anguish.[57] As Foucault declared in an interview in *Mec*: "There is no anxiety, there is no fantasy behind happi-

---

56. In addition to Eribon's and Macey's biographies, I am also referring to James Miller's here. See J. Miller, *The Passion of Michel Foucault*, pp. 62, 135–136, and 150.

57. For valuable elaboration on these points, see J. Rose, "'Where does the misery come from? Psychoanalysis, feminism, and the event," in *Why War?—Psychoanalysis, Politics, and the Return to Melanie Klein* (Cambridge: Blackwell, 1993), pp. 89–109.

ness."[58] He also told us that "[t]he outside . . . is the void
that surrounds [interiority] . . . opening around it a space
of uneasiness, of dissatisfaction" (MB, p. 34). In light of these
perspectives on anxiety, where do "uneas[e]" and "dissatisfaction" go in Foucault's work?

TWO PERSPECTIVES ON RESISTANCE

Foucault and Lacan would agree that psychic resistance af-
fects our experience of the outside, our relationship to the
"nondiscursive," but they part company over the psychoanalytic argument that resistance is largely an *involuntary* response to external and internal stimuli. The subject's best
solution to this problem, argued Freud and Lacan, is "reality
testing," an idea to which I'll return. The following example
illustrates this conceptual disagreement between Foucault and
psychoanalysis—indeed, the repercussions of this example
take us beyond recent efforts to identify partial resemblances
between Foucault's and Lacan's projects.[59] When Jacques-

58. M. Foucault, cited in "Michel Foucault, le gai savoir," an interview with Jean Le Bitoux, Mec 5 (Juin 1988), p. 35. Foucault is referring
here to the happiness or sexual contentment of gay partners, and I am
adopting Bersani's translation of Foucault's statement, in H, p. 79. Bersani
comments usefully, "It is as if desexualized pleasures were [for Foucault]
pleasures without fantasy, almost pleasure uncomplicated by desire" (H,
p. 80).

59. I am referring to Forrester's Seductions of Psychoanalysis and
Charles Shepherdson's fine essay "History and the Real: Foucault with
Lacan," which Postmodern Culture published in 1995. Despite pointing up
these resemblances, however, both Forrester and Shepherdson are aware
of crucial differences between Foucault and Lacan. See Forrester, SP,
pp. 288, 293, 296; but also 304 and 306–310. And Shepherdson writes: "At

Alain Miller challenged Foucault on the historical apparatus of sexuality, insisting, "There isn't a history of sexuality in the way that there is a history of bread" (*CF*, p. 213), Foucault admitted that "[t]he strength of psychoanalysis consists in its having opened out on to something quite different [from conventional histories of sexuality], namely the logic of the unconscious. And there sexuality is no longer what it was at the outset" (pp. 212–213).[60] More surprising, given his early ambivalence about Freud's account of dreams, is Foucault's claim in this 1977 interview that "the important part of [Freud's work] is not the *Three Essays on the Theory of Sexuality* but

---

the end of [*The History of Sexuality, Volume I*], Foucault [proposes that] sex is . . . what one might call a discursive effect and not a 'natural' basis that is shaped by various restrictions or prohibitions. The question we are asking, with Lacan, however, is whether 'sex' is simply or entirely discursive. To speak of the 'real' is not to speak of a 'pre-discursive reality' such as 'sex,' but it is to ask about what 'remains' outside representation" ("History and the Real," n. 33). Accounts of Foucault's perspective on psychoanalysis that differ slightly from the one I offer here include J. Rajchman, *Michel Foucault: The Freedom of Philosophy*, pp. 88–93; J. Butler, *Subjects of Desire: Hegelian Reflections in Twentieth-Century France* (New York: Columbia University Press, 1987), pp. 217–229 and J. Butler, *PL*, pp. 87–88; and Ann Laura Stoler, who makes clear why "saying 'yes' to Foucault has not always meant saying 'no' to Freud, not even for Foucault himself." A. Stoler, *Race and the Education of Desire: Foucault's History of Sexuality and the Colonial Order of Things* (Durham, NC: Duke University Press, 1995), p. 168. "Despite Foucault's rejection of the repressive hypothesis," she adds, "there are surprising ways in which their projects can and do converge" (pp. 168–169). My interest ultimately lies in where they *cannot* converge.

60. Commenting on this statement, Derrida remarks that Foucault "seemed to be ready for some sort of compromise on this issue, readily and good-spiritedly acknowledging the 'impasses' (that was his word) of his concept of *episteme* and the difficulties into which this new project [*The History of Sexuality*] had led him" (*TJ*, p. 92).

The Interpretation of Dreams. . . . Not the theory of development, nor the sexual secret behind the neuroses or psychoses, but a logic of the unconscious . . ." (*CF*, p. 213). Miller's
reply is worth repeating: "That's very Lacanian, opposing
sexuality and the unconscious. And moreover it's one of the
axioms of that logic that there is no sexual relation." Foucault
responded by saying, "I didn't know there was this axiom"
(p. 213).

This exchange is both amusing and instructive; the status of the sexual relation *as such* clearly determines what kind
of history we can write about sexuality. The exchange also
seems useful in indicating that Foucault and Miller disagree
over the subject's *ability*—and not simply its willingness—to
coalesce with the external world. From Miller's Lacanian perspective, it makes little sense to represent the subject as an
effect of discursive regimes, for the simple reason that the ego's
opposition to reality is constitutive and not contingent. Such
arguments derive from Freud's realization, in the closing paragraphs of *The Interpretation of Dreams*, that "*psychical* reality
is a particular form of existence not to be confused with *material* reality"; and later, in "The Unconscious" (1915), that
unconscious processes "pay . . . little attention to *reality*."[61]
Lacan of course finessed these claims, refusing to separate
either register or endorse the idea that psychic reality is her-
metically sealed against an external world uninfluenced by
psychic principles. As he argued in *The Four Fundamental
Concepts*, "the reality system, however far it is developed,

---

61. See S. Freud, "The interpretation of dreams," *Standard Edition*
5:620, original emphases; this sentence was published in its present form
only in 1919; Freud, "The unconscious" (1915), *Standard Edition* 14:187,
original emphasis.

leaves an essential part of what belongs to the real a prisoner in the toils of the pleasure principle."[62] But important points about causation and freedom obtain from Freud's and Lacan's claims. Whereas Foucault represents the subject's well being as contingent on whether reality is conducive to its happiness, for Lacan (as indeed for Freud) the possibility of well-being derives almost entirely from the ego's limited ability to defend itself *against* reality. Leo Bersani cogently summarizes this perspective when he states: "[T]he ego . . . far from having any original aptitude for dealing with reality, is in a state of radical hostility to the external world."[63]

I dwell on these points about "[in]aptitude" and "radical hostility" to underscore why psychoanalysis departs conclusively from materialist accounts of reality and consciousness, as well as from related critiques of reality's many shortcomings. By insisting on the ego's basic "[in]aptitude for dealing with reality," Bersani—like Freud and Lacan—shows us why the subject's alienation is neither explained nor repaired by altering the diverse forms of political oppression that impede and partly shape us, an argument quite different from the frequent and unjustified claim that psychoanalysis is uninterested in our oppression. Owing to their faith in the underlying influence of these external causes on the subject,

---

62. J. Lacan, *FFC*, p. 55. "The fundamental thesis of Lacanian psychoanalysis," adds Žižek, "is that what we call 'reality' constitutes itself against the background of [symbolic] 'bliss,' i.e., of such an exclusion of some traumatic Real. This is precisely what Lacan has in mind when he says that fantasy is the ultimate support of reality: 'reality' stabilizes itself when some fantasy-frame of a 'symbolic bliss' closes off the view into the abyss of the Real." S. Žižek, *Tarrying with the Negative: Kant, Hegel, and the Critique of Ideology* (Durham, NC: Duke University Press, 1993), p. 118.

63. L. Bersani, *The Freudian Body: Psychoanalysis and Art*, p. 87.

Foucauldian and materialist approaches to subjectivity argue that factors such as gender, ethnicity, and even sexuality are egoic effects of varied, contradictory, and unjust social demands. From this perspective, however, the ego is invested with an ability to modify, subvert, and even repair these demands in order to diminish their effects and sometimes render them meaningless.[64]

Although this faith in the influence of external causes relies erroneously on the ego's capacity for congruency with the outside, I should stress that in opposing this faith I am not refuting the influence of external factors. To do so would undercut my emphasis on the asymmetry of psychical and physical reality; it would reproduce another form of volun-

---

64. I am summarizing the logic of this precept, which scholars in cultural studies now widely invoke. And although a number of theorists have endeavored to complicate these assumptions, the inexorable logic of the assumptions requires that theorists ultimately rephrase them in similar ways. After extensive criticism of her earlier work's psychic voluntarism, for instance, Butler finally concedes in *Bodies That Matter* that "sexuality cannot be summarily made or unmade." J. Butler, *Bodies That Matter: On the Discursive Limits of "Sex,"* (New York: Routledge, 1993), p. 94. The blurb on her most recent book, *The Psychic Life of Power*, nonetheless says that "[t]he author considers the way in which *psychic life is generated by the social operation of power*, and how that social operation of power is concealed and fortified by *the psyche that it produces*" (*PL*, my emphases). While this last book therefore modifies Butler's starker claims about psychic causality in her earlier works, such as *Gender Trouble: Feminism and the Subversion of Identity* (1990), it displays at the outset ambivalence about the psychoanalytic argument that only a *non*social factor—the drive—is capable of *determining* psychic life. More important for us here, *The Psychic Life of Power* restates the logic of external causation, which paradoxically restores *in principle* the forms of social influence that I am challenging here. For invaluable discussion of this point, published just before this essay went to press, see S. Žižek, *The Ticklish Subject: The Absent Centre of Political Ontology* (New York: Verso, 1999), especially pp. 247–312.

tarism, generating precisely the characterizations of psycho-analysis that I am objecting to here. The fantasy that the ego determines consciousness slips easily into solipsism and epistemic relativism, a fantasy that we simply make our own reality. I am objecting instead to the crass suggestion—voiced repeatedly by constructivists and Foucauldians—that subjectivity is merely an "effect" of discourse, a suggestion that renders subjectivity politically transparent, devoid of drives and unconscious causes. This suggestion culminates in a conceptual deadlock, in which social practices and power are caught in a circular relationship that thwarts the possibility of transformation. Let us iterate that Foucault wrote *The Archaeology of Knowledge* precisely in an atttempt to shatter this deadlock.[65]

One way that psychoanalysis departs conclusively from materialism is by insisting that we can't test our reality without confronting our perception of the external world. According to Freud, the structure of loss that frames our perception and desire serves as a guide for all subsequent perspectives on reality. As he argued in "Negation," building on a related and now famous claim in *Three Essays on the Theory of Sexuality*:

> The first and immediate aim . . . of reality-testing is, not to *find* an object in real perception which corresponds to the one presented, but to *re-find* such an object, to convince oneself that it is still there."[66]

---

65. See M. Foucault, *The Archaeology of Knowledge*, p. 13.

66. S. Freud, "Negation," *Standard Edition* 19:233–238, 1925, paraphrasing his earlier claim in *Three Essays and the Theory of Sexuality* (1905), *Standard Edition* 7: "The finding of an object is in fact a refinding of it" (p. 222).

This statement shows us clearly why Freudian psychoanalysis differs from the conservative idea that therapy consists in *adapting* the patient's ego to reality. For Freud and Lacan, the idea of patient adaptation was preposterous, because egregiously coercive. Indeed, the very question of adaptation returns us to *The Order of Things*, where Foucault usefully points up a conclusive split between psychoanalysis and psychiatry. Poised between rationalism and unreason in *Madness and Civilization*, Freudian psychoanalysis surfaces in *The Order of Things* and even Volume 1 of *The History of Sexuality* as one of the primary fields that avoids, and even preempts, the coercive logic of psychiatry. It is psychiatry, Foucault insists, that claims the patient must sacrifice his or her reality for preexisting forms of social reality. Lacan of course agreed, arguing in the 1930s—long before Foucault began publishing—that the very idea of "sacrifice" is both manipulative and delusive, insofar as "adaptation" merely substitutes one fantasy about reality for another.[67]

NEGATION AND CONTINGENCY

Let us return to Freud's argument about reality, however, to put to rest the fallacy that psychoanalysis has nothing to say about social reality. Copjec's account of Freud's essay "Negation" makes clear that Freud's argument has radical consequences for *all* theories of social and political change:

---

67. See J. Lacan, "The direction of the treatment and the principles of its power" (1958), in *Écrits*, pp. 226–231, a passage in which Lacan is quoting G. Devereux, "Some criteria for the timing of confrontations and interpretations," *International Journal of Psycho-Analysis* 32.1:22, 1951.

> Contrary to the common misperception, reality testing is
> not described here as a process by which we match our
> perceptions against an external, independent reality. In
> fact, it is the permanent *loss* of that reality—or real: a re-
> ality that was never present as such—that is the precon-
> dition for determining the objective status of our percep-
> tions. Not only is the real unavailable for comparison with
> our perceptions but, Freud concedes, we can assume that
> the latter are always somewhat distorted, inexact. [*RM*,
> p. 233]

Copjec shows us here why psychoanalysis and historicism
offer quite different perspectives on reality; she illustrates
too that by highlighting the profound repercussions of
Freud's argument about reality, Lacan *completely discredited
the idea that reality can ever be reparative for the subject.* "In
the name of what is social constraint exercised?" he asks
in *Seminar VII.* "[R]eality isn't just there so that we bump
our heads up against the false paths along which the functioning of the pleasure principle leads us."[68] "In truth," Lacan
continues, "we make reality out of pleasure" (*EP*, p. 225),
a statement inverting the standard materialist claim that
we extract whatever pleasure we can from a reality that
pre-exists us. That the ego exists in relation to a structural
méconnaissance overturns all existing claims about false
consciousness: "By definition," Lacan says in *Seminar II*,
"there is something so improbable about all existence that
one is in effect perpetually questioning oneself about its re-

---

68. J. Lacan, *The Seminar of Jacques Lacan, Book VII: The Ethics of
Psychoanalysis, 1959–1960*, ed. J.-A. Miller, tr. D. Porter (New York:
Norton, 1992), p. 225; hereafter abbreviated *EP*.

ality."[69] To take up an earlier thread concerning Foucault's fantasy about Blanchot's work, we can now see why Lacan would remark that "nothing would be more appreciated than locating the ineffable experience beyond what is considered to be the illusion, and not the wall, of language" (EF, p. 245). He nonetheless differs from Foucault in noting that the illusion is possible only because "[i]t is clearly on the imaginary level that one is operating" (EF, p. 245). "We start transparent, and then the cloud thickens," opines the narrator of Virginia Woolf's Jacob's Room, in a statement advancing a similar idea: "All history backs our pane of glass."[70]

In attempting to summarize Foucault's and Lacan's similar but nonidentical perspectives on "the outside," I have chosen to revisit Freud's and Lacan's arguments about the reality principle, Foucault hearing many of the latter directly. One could of course bypass these arguments by proceeding directly to Lacan's conception of the real, which points up a dimension of trauma that can't be assimilated by reality. Or one could ignore the psychoanalytic ramifications of this debate, and revisit its philosophical antecedents, examining texts such as David Hume's Enquiry Concerning Human Understanding.[71] But while each path would eventually return us to

---

69. J. Lacan, EF, p. 229. As he put it later, more concisely, in the same seminar: "the ego is always an alter-ego" (p. 321, original emphases).

70. V. Woolf, Jacob's Room (1922; New York: Harcourt Brace Jovanovich, 1950), p. 49. Woolf is echoing Walter Pater's famous conclusion to The Renaissance (1873; 1893), in which he argues that "[a]t first sight experience seems to bury us under a flood of external objects, pressing upon us with a sharp and importunate reality . . ." The Renaissance: Studies in Art and Poetry, ed. D. L. Hill (Berkeley, CA: University of California Press, 1980), p. 187.

71. See D. Hume, An Enquiry Concerning Human Understanding (1748; Indianapolis: Hackett, 1977), p. 105. For an example of analytical philoso-

a similar problem, it would fail to address Foucault's and Lacan's rather different perspectives on the subject's *structural* relationship to reality and axiomatic dependence on resistance.

To my mind the kernel of this difference arises in Freud's claim, near the end of his study of the Wolfman, that "[a] repression is something very different from a condemning judgement."[72] What Freud brings to our attention here is that repression's importance lies less in what we contain, than in what we can't evade. "I'd say that that is the very essence of the Freudian discovery," remarks Lacan in *Seminar I*.[73] To put this another way, repression, for psychoanalysis, doesn't signify what we can possess of the past; it dramatizes the effort it takes to accomplish forgetting, to remove or dislodge us from a past—and thus a history—that threatens to overwhelm us. This claim points up a form of difficulty that isn't altered or resolved by will, whether individual or collective, and the difficulty helps us refute the simplistic objection that psychoanalysis is ahistorical. Ultimately more political than is Foucault's perspective on force and power, this argument enhances our critique of the *dispositif*, for it shows us that our failure to rid ourselves of the past is one of the factors binding us *involuntarily* to history.

---

phy building on these and related arguments, see D. Davidson, "Mental events" (1970) and "Psychology as philosophy" (1974), both in *Essays on Actions and Events* (Oxford: Clarendon, 1980), pp. 207–227 and 229–244.

72. S. Freud, "From the history of an infantile neurosis," *Standard Edition* 17:79–80, 1918.

73. J. Lacan, *The Seminar of Jacques Lacan, Book I: Freud's Papers on Technique, 1953–1954*, ed. J.-A. Miller, tr. J. Forrester (New York: Norton, 1988), p. 43.

15

The Subject of Homosexuality: Butler's Elision

FRANCES L. RESTUCCIA

> "[P]sychoanalysis proposes castration as an ineluctable law. An identification horsexe entails a refusal of the castration endemic to sexual difference, which alienates one from one's jouissance by requiring that one speak. If castration were not universally operative for those of us who speak, desire simply would not exist."
> —Tim Dean, "Transsexual Identification, Gender Performance Theory, and the Politics of the Real"

In *The Psychic Life of Power*,[1] Judith Butler proposes that subject formation depends on the relinquishing of passionate attachments, to which one is nevertheless forever subjected, and that such psychic subjection renders one vulnerable to a social subjection to power. Foucault has failed to address the question of what psychic form power takes; Butler wishes to answer that question through a reconciliation of psychoanalytic and Foucauldian theories of subject formation. Psychic dependency of the subject on the family renders the subject "exploitable" by society. One's relation of subjection to one's original others appears to result in a susceptibility to Foucault's Power.

---

1. J. Butler, *The Psychic Life of Power: Theories in Subjection.* (Stanford, CA: Stanford University Press, 1997).

Butler doesn't articulate precisely what she means in saying that the subject is primarily dependent, passionately attached. She proposes vaguely that the subject is produced through a "foreclosure" of his or her early objects of love, so that the "I" is "fundamentally threatened by the specter of this (impossible) love's reappearance and remains condemned to reenact that love unconsciously."[2] Nevertheless, the question is whether such a structure institutes desire for subjection, as Butler suggests, or is the very means by which one becomes a desiring subject, having accepted lack or, as Tim Dean phrases it, the "ineluctable law" of castration.[3] Would "desire" for subjection even be desire, or would it rather be a form of masochistic *jouissance*, produced as a result of a blockage of subjectivity?

Yet in a way, Butler's proposition that the subject is constituted through a relinquishment of certain passionate attachments does seem loosely compatible (as she seems to think it is) with Lacan's conception of subject formation that results in an *objet a*, an object cause of desire, that structures the subject by producing and preserving his or her desire. To Lacan, the subject is positioned in relation to a primal experience of trauma, on the border between pleasure and pain. The subject emerges through attraction toward and defense against a primordial, overwhelming experience of *jouissance*. But rather than being subjugated, the subject, in Lacanian theory, is (to quote from *The Four Fundamental Concepts*) "strictly speaking determined by the very separation that de-

---

2. Ibid., pp. 8–9.
3. T. Dean, "Transsexual identification, gender performance theory, and the politics of the real." *Literature and Psychology* 39:20, 1993.

termines the break of the *a*."[4] It is "in this point of lack, that the desire of the subject is constituted."[5] Lack, in Lacanian as well as Kristevan psychoanalytic theory, then, saves the subject from various maladies of the soul (such as depression and perversion, in which myriad forms of "desire" for subjection operate). The oddity is that Butler takes up melancholia, a painful pathology, as if it were the condition of all subjects— the constitutive condition, no less. Butler's sense of subject formation, in my view, confuses melancholic loss with Lacanian lack. It relies upon a distortion of melancholia and points theoretically to an oxymoronic nondesiring "subjectivity" for all.

Still, to make sense of Butler's assumption that desire for subjection is the unappealing outcome of, as well as the apparent "enabler" of, subject formation (an outcome we must avoid, and so we must flee the Law), we need to look at Butler's "loss" in more detail. It eventually comes out in Butler's introduction to *The Psychic Life of Power* that the primary loss she has in mind is that of a homosexual love, a loss experienced by a heterosexual subject. What Butler initially presents as an apparently lacking/desiring generic subject turns out to be a heterosexual melancholic prohibited from loving the homosexual beloved. Butler regards the foreclosure of "someone of similar gender" never loved and so never lost as a function of "the melancholia that grounds the subject." Such a loss, she believes, "inaugurates the subject."[6]

4. J. Lacan, *The Four Fundamental Concepts of Psycho-Analysis*, tr. A. Sheridan. (New York: Norton, 1977), p. 118.

5. Ibid., pp. 218–219.

6. *The Psychic Life of Power*, p. 23.

But, first, how does one make sense of the slide in Butler's work from lost passionate attachments within the family to this lost, yet never lost because never loved, object of the same gender? Is it that this unloved object of the same gender is always linked to a lost familial passionate attachment? Why and how so? Second, if "the homosexual" is the lost object, why isn't the subject in pursuit of it in the form of an *objet a*? In other words, why aren't all heterosexual subjects seeking their lost homosexual loves? Although Foucauldian Power may forbid this pursuit of the homosexual love, what we are forbidden to desire in Lacanian theory forms our *objet a*. "In effect," Lacan writes, "I would not have had the idea to covet it if the Law hadn't said: 'Thou shalt not covet it'"; (again to quote from the *Ethics* seminar) "The dialectical relationship between desire and the Law causes our desire to flare up only in relation to the Law."[7] Third, if "foreclosure" is somehow consistent with uncompleted grief or melancholia, as it appears to be in Butler, it seems that we are to assume, in accord with Freudian and Kristevan theories of melancholia, that the lost homosexual love, in being foreclosed, is also somehow incorporated so as not to be lost after all. Incorporation appears to be what Butler has in mind when she contends that such a loss haunts and thereby threatens the subject. Yet is foreclosure incorporation, or rather *can* a rigorous barring, a preemptive loss possibly produce incorporation? All of which returns us to the central question of whether melancholia can serve as a paradigm for subject formation, since the very lack/loss required for subject formation is incorporated, swallowed, consumed in melancholia and therefore jeopardizes subjectivity.

In Chapter 5 of *The Psychic Life of Power*, "Melancholy Gender/Refused Identification," the focus oddly shifts from the more spacious and complex concept of "the subject" to "gender" in conjunction with the more limited concept of "the ego," as if the subject and the ego were synonymous. Now gender is conceived of as "a kind of melancholy, or as one of melancholy's effects" (p. 132). Butler's task, she asserts, is "to explain the sense in which a melancholic identification is central to the process whereby the ego assumes a gendered character" (pp. 132–133). Propelled by Freud's shift from "Mourning and Melancholia," where he assumes that grief can be resolved, to *The Ego and the Id*,[8] where Freud posits that the lost object is made coextensive with the ego through a melancholic internalization, Butler's Chapter 5 argues that heterosexuality "*preempt*[s] the possibility of homosexual attachment [through] a foreclosure . . . which produces a domain of homosexuality understood as unlivable passion and *ungrievable* loss" (p. 135, my emphasis). Butler assumes that "masculine" and "feminine" are "accomplishments" that "emerge in tandem with the achievement of heterosexuality" (p. 135), which is itself forever internally affixed to its lost, unloved homosexuality.

The question I would raise here is how exactly is a "foreclosure" of homosexual love related to, or indicative of, gender; foreclosure of "the homosexual" would produce male

---

8. S. Freud, "The ego and the id," *Standard Edition* 19:3–66, 1923, and "Mourning and melancholia," *Standard Edition*, 14:243–258, 1917.

heterosexuals as well as female heterosexuals. *Gender*, in this discussion, is really a pleonasm. At no point is Butler interested in gender foreclosure, nor is there room for the possibility of a gendered homosexual. While I grant that it seems to make a certain sense to say that barring homosexuality enables, in some cases, the formation of masculinity—a man must bar a man—as well as, in others, femininity—a woman must bar a woman—in fact, if the idea is to explain gender formation in relation to a foreclosed homosexuality, it seems that Butler must posit prior to her very explanation of gender formation a gender that forecloses the homosexual or "someone of similar gender." That is, to explain the psychic production of masculinity, Butler must initially posit a man (whose very gender is supposedly being explained by her theory) who forecloses a man. One cannot logically claim, then, as Butler writes, that "*any* person of the same gender" is "foreclosed" from the start (p. 139), because if a gender is not yet formed, which is the *same* gender would not yet be apparent.

* * *

At the end of "Melancholy Gender/Refused Identification," Butler presents her under-elaborated hypothesis that "only by risking the *incoherence* of identity is connection [between heterosexuality and homosexuality] possible." (Precisely what is meant by "connection," the crux of Butler's idea, needs to be clarified.) This hypothesis, she points out, correlates with "Leo Bersani's insight that only the decentered subject is available to desire."[9] Here, Butler discloses her own sense that the

---

9. *The Psychic Life of Power*, p. 149.

melancholic structure of "subjectivity" that she has been developing cancels desire, in other words, desire is after all in Butler's view too distinct from "desire" for subjection.

Despite complications that I cannot get entangled in here, at times it does look as if Butler supports the idea of completed mourning (to activate desire)—only curiously for the sake of achieving incoherent identity, rather than subjectivity. Toward the end of *The Psychic Life of Power*, she states that she favors "avowing the trace of loss that inaugurates one's own emergence" (p. 195). Translated specifically into the terms of her thoughts on homosexuality, this would mean avowing the lost homosexual love, and thereby enacting the rebellion of melancholia that has been, Butler says, put down. Butler is not trying to recuperate melancholia, to conceive of it as an ethical form of subjectivity that puts one into intimate contact with one's internalized but cast-out alterior. Instead, it seems that to Butler all, necessarily subjugated, subjects *are* sad, diminished, self-berating, and will be until they assume an incoherent, decentered identity of true desire, which will emerge once homosexual loss is avowed and mourned—that is, no longer lost and consequently no longer incorporated to counter loss.

Forfeiting autonomy, in Butler, enables survival, since then an exclusionary foreclosure no longer operates in order that the ego can emerge "on the condition of the 'trace' of the other." Autonomy, to Butler, forgets this "trace." Not to forget it is, she writes, "to embark upon a process of mourning."

However, here Butler qualifies her comment about the desirability of mourning by adding that it will "never be complete, for no final severance could take place without dissolving the ego" (p. 196). No final severance of what exactly? Must "the homosexual" be somewhat unsevered and incorporated, after all? Why is Butler suddenly anxious about dissolving the ego, after arguing against coherent identity, which entails a necessary exclusion? Moreover, not to sever one's tie to the other but to keep it incorporated, and hence not to complete mourning, would be to wallow in melancholia. Is Butler promoting a melancholic state or not?

While avowing loss in psychoanalytic theory would mean letting go and accepting lack, it does not carry this meaning for Butler, who, in addition, assumes that lack is not required for desire to ensue. Butler believes that there is "no necessary reason for . . . desire to be fueled by repudiation."[10] She instead assumes that submitting to the Law produces a loss/lack that holds one down, that subjugates, and that degrades what becomes externalized. As Butler said in a (Fall 1997) talk on *Antigone* at the Center for Literary and Cultural Studies at Harvard, she opposes the idea that desire is radically determined by a Law. In a theoretical vacuum, Butler defines subjectivity as melancholia and is therefore inspired, for the most part, to promote a notion of incoherent identity that would seem to be (although incoherent) devoid of lack, even as it is capable of desire. Ironically, such a fantasy of plenitude, such a "denial of negation," in Kristeva's terms, would itself also fit Kristeva's description of melancholia, a state of lack of lack that would certainly complicate entry into signification.

Butler advocates an avowal of one's lost, unloved homosexuality, in what would seem to be accurately described as an act of mourning, meant eventually to terminate melancholia. Yet the incoherent identity that she wishes to see emerge as a result also (like the melancholic "subjectivity" with which

---

10. *The Psychic Life of Power*, p. 149.

she begins) differs from the psychoanalytic notion of the subject, founded on lack (versus incorporated loss). That is, were a Freudian or Kristevan melancholic to avow an incorporated loss, she or he would subsequently accept the loss rather than cling to it. But Butler envisions, after avowal of homosexual lost love, incoherent, nonlacking identity, whose advantage, to Butler, would seem to be its extrication from any relation to the Lacanian Law or Foucauldian Power.

But how does one resist such Power, having been made vulnerable to it by early passionate attachments? Is Butler proposing that we no longer, as children, passionately attach, or that we no longer passionately ever detach? Butler needed at least to return to her introductory assertion that subjetivity is dependent upon passionate attachments when she, later in *The Psychic Life of Power*, advocates incoherent identity. How does one overcome the vulnerability that constitutes one, in an effort to *avow* what has been foreclosed? Possibly a traversal of the fundamental fantasy could do the job, but Butler offers no explanation. More crucially, how would such an avowal affect subjectivity? Butler is simultaneously anxious and not anxious about this. What if the "ego" dissolves?

If Butler is right that subjects are formed through the foreclosure of homosexuality, would a subject that avows homosexual loss not face his or her gaze, the Thing whose *lack* constitutes his or her subjectivity, and in doing so, would that subject not be threatened with collapse? The critical difference between avowal of a consumed loss in melancholia and the avowal that Butler describes (in relation to subjectivity) is that in melancholia a loss is usually experienced by a (formed) subject who psychically takes in that loss, or lost object, with whom the subject identifies (and so the loss can be given up without shattering subjectivity), whereas in

Butler's (mis)conception of melancholic subject-formation *loss* is there from the start; it's of course, to her, constitutive. So *how* could a constitutive loss be avowed without producing a severe problem?

The usual psychoanalytic meaning of "foreclosure" turns out to pertain to Butler's work after all. As Žižek conveniently explains, "in psychosis, something is missing, the key signifier (the 'paternal metaphor') is rejected, foreclosed, excluded from the symbolic universe and thence returns in the real in the guise of psychotic apparitions." Such a state is obviously undesirable as well as a way of shutting down desire. For, in order to have a consistent sense of reality, we must maintain an *objet a* that stands in for what is "primordially repressed." "In psychosis, this exclusion is undone: the object . . . is *included* in reality, the outcome of which . . . is the disintegration of our 'sense of reality,' the loss of reality."[11]

As Žižek himself pointed out in a (Spring 1998) lecture at the Center for Literary and Cultural Studies at Harvard, Butler makes a fundamental mistake in conflating two resistances: social and psychoanalytic. While social resistance to Foucauldian Power may very well be a worthy cause (although whether or not Foucault regards it as a possibility is another huge can of theoretical worms), such social resistance is not consonant with psychoanalytic resistance to the Lacanian Law. For, as I have been trying to show by referring to theorists as distinct from one another as Žižek and Tim Dean, foreclosure of the Law—which Butler risks effecting in

---

11. S. Žižek, "'I hear you with my eyes': or the invisible master," in *Gaze and Voice as Love Objects*, ed. R. Salecl and S. Žižek (Durham, NC: Duke University Press, 1996), p. 9.

her effort to escape the subjectivity, gender, and sexual difference that, to her, weigh us down—cancels desire and results in psychosis.

* * *

Let me stress that I am not arguing against avowal of homosexuality; I am not advocating that homosexuality remain "foreclosed" to avoid the abyss of psychosis. I would instead challenge Butler's initial conception of the subject *as* a heterosexual subject founded on a foreclosed homosexuality. Foucauldian Power may require an excluded homosexuality (that nevertheless is a function of the power structure), but it is at least an open question whether or not Lacanian Law makes this demand. I find the possibility of such a demand doubtful, for one thing because in Lacanian theory "the homosexual" remains undertheorized, if not untheorized. There is certainly no Lacanian idea of homosexuality defined by biology or anatomy. A couple comprised of two anatomical men would hardly make a homosexual couple to Lacan, since he is only interested in psychoanalytic conceptions of "sex" or sexuation: "A man is nothing but a signifier. A woman seeks out a man *qua* signifier. . . . A man seeks out a woman *qua* . . . that which can only be situated through discourse, since, if what I claim is true—namely, that woman is not-whole—there is always something in her that escapes discourse."[12]

Two anatomical men, it would seem, could be either "homosexual" or "heterosexual," from a Lacanian point of view, depending upon whether each of them were a "woman"

---

12. J. Lacan, "On feminine sexuality: the limits of love and knowledge 1972–1973," *Encore, The Seminar*, Book xx, tr. B. Fink (New York: Norton, 1998), p. 33.

or a "man." But even the desirability (to Lacan) of their being "heterosexual" in this psychoanalytic sense is presently unclear. In his paper "Lacan Meets Queer Theory," Tim Dean (despite his earlier emphasis on sexual difference) argues that, to Lacan, sexuality is a question of *object a*, of fantasy rather than of "object choice, orientation, or sexual identity."[13] In any case, whether or not Lacan puts a premium on heterosexuality, it should now be apparent, if it was not at the start, that when Butler refers to a certain "foreclosure of homosexuality," it is questionable what "homosexuality" even means. From my point of view, there is no way around the position that a theory of the desiring subject that embraces "the homosexual" (however that concept turns out to be understood) needs to be articulated.

---

13. T. Dean, "Lacan Meets Queer Theory," talk given at Center for Literary and Cultural Theory, Harvard University, 1997.

16

The Philanthropy of Perversion

JUDITH FEHER GUREWICH

One of my very first patients, whose perverse structure became readily apparent in the treatment, soon became suspicious of my status as an analyst. I was at the time trying to find my bearings as a research candidate in an American psychoanalytic institute while getting extra training from a Lacanian school. I had of course no idea of the signals that I was sending off—clearly a mixture of anxiety, arrogance, and hesitation—unaware as I was then of the *jouissance* I was experiencing in getting Lacanian supervision on the side. Shortly after I had started seeing this patient, she sent me a letter describing in detail a murder she was planning to commit that same day. She completed the blow by recommending that I seek supervision for her case. I was trapped and terrified: Which law should I submit to—the police, the psychoanalytic institution, or the law of my desire? What was my responsibility in this acting-out?

Clearly my patient's unconscious intent was to challenge my legitimacy as an analyst, and she had succeeded—she had rightfully sensed that something was fishy. Perhaps she did not expect me to believe her, but she was serious about the supervision. Following her advice, I cleared my ambiguous relation to American pychoanalysis and made official my allegiance to a Lacanian school. As Lacan says, "castration means that jouissance has to be refused in order to be attained on the inverse scale of desire"[1] I therefore went to Paris and submitted my desire to become an analyst to a jury of Lacanian experts.

Their authorization had a paradoxical effect that in retrospect revealed to me the full import of what I would call the philanthropy of my patient's move. Had I had my "pass" at the time of the threatened crime, it would not have reduced my anxiety. In that sense she had exposed how the power of allegiance to a social group provides only a semblance of legitimacy, not a limit to *jouissance*. Yet the recognition of my peers gave me the freedom to detach myself from the imposture of a subject who is presumed to know and doesn't. My patient therefore enabled me to understand how the desire of the analyst struggles with the *jouissance* that necessarily binds the subject to the group—a problem that Lacan himself had difficulty resolving.

This formative distinction did more than put me on track in my analytic work. I came to realize that no one is better than a pervert in exposing in the other, analyst or not, the signifier of desire that waits to be born under the mask of power and knowledge. After all, neither psychotics, nor obsessionals, nor even hysterics, can provide such selfless devotion in revealing to their victims the place where their symbolic castration is obscured by *jouissance*. In that sense, I

---

1. J. Lacan, *Ecrits*, tr. A. Sheridan (Norton, New York, 1977), p. 324.

thought, the diagnostic category based on the logic of perversion should not be ignored simply because of the bad reputation that perverts continue to endure even among—of all people—psychoanalysts and queer theorists. I am not talking here of "perverse" sexual practices, of course; after all, from a Freudian point of view sexuality in general is by definition perverse, since there is nothing natural about it. I am referring here specifically to the logic of perversion as Lacan has defined it, that is, a psychic structure of desire, not a social or sexual behavior.

The fact that psychoanalysts and queer theorists have chosen to ignore what I have called the philanthropy of perversion has certainly not buttressed the dialogue between the two goups—just the opposite. I would even argue that if they stand today in opposing camps it is precisely because they both refuse to acknowledge how the logic of perversion has shaped the thrust of their most radical insights. Or to put my argument yet in another way: queer theory and Lacanian psychoanalysis have elected to disavow the very thing that has caused their estrangement, namely their passionate attachment—to use Butler's term[2]—to the logic of perversion. I must say, however, that this allusion to Butler does not recapitulate her own metapsychological program, that is, the idea that heterosexuality is produced by the subject's disavowal of his or her passionate attachements to a primordial homosexuality—which, of course, has no relation to the structure of perversion. This allusion simply suggests that the falling out between queer theory and psychoanalysis has led to a paradoxical situation: because Butler can no longer rely on psychoanalytic

---

2. J. Butler, *The Psychic Life of Power* (Stanford, CA: Stanford University Press, 1997), pp. 6–10.

insights to devise a new subversive psychic strategy, she re-
verts for better and for worse to a metapsychology of her own
making.

I hope that my attempt to inscribe into discourse such
passionate attachments to the logic of perversion in both
Lacanian psychoanalysis and queer theory will transform
the present status of Lacanian psychoanalysis in academic
discourse. It is certainly a pity that today both queers and
Lacanians have taken a path that no longer does justice to what
brought them together originally. Indeed, it has almost been
forgotten that feminist theory put Lacan on the American map
of gender deconstruction. It is clearly under Lacan's patron-
age that the signifier became "queen," that gender lost its ties
with biological determinism, and that phallic masquerade
became available to all. However, by the time queer theory
—Butler and others—joined forces with the psychoanalytic
branch of feminism, Lacan's hour of glory had already begun
to pass. The breakdown between the normal and the pathological that had been pioneered by psychoanalysis returned
under a new guise: it is the pathological that became compelling. Feminists radically transformed psychic pathologies into
strategies of social resistance, turning Lacan's convincing interpretation of the structure of hysteria against the foundation of his theory. It was claimed that the symbolic order is
itself a masquerade of phallocracy. Hysteria's politics of defiance against "the signification of the phallus" is far preferable
to the degrading submission demanded by the law of the father. Lacan's paternal metaphor is therefore no advance over
Freud's Oedipus complex.[3]

---

3. See, for example, *In Dora's Case*, C. Bernheimer and C. Kahane,
eds. (New York: Columbia University Press, 1985).

Queer theorists such as Michael Warner and others brought the feminist critique of Lacan to yet another level of contempt towards psychoanalysis. The term *heteronormativity* was hurled as a disdainful reproach at Freud and Lacan alike.[4] The talent and humor of Lacan's most famous ambassador, Slavoj Žižek, only led to a new split among cultural theorists: either for Lacan or against. Žižek's uncritical allegiance to the cause prevented him from addressing directly the relation between the symbolic order and the question of sexual difference Moreover, the Lacanian clinicians who have been pressed on this point have reiterated that queer theory is ill-equipped to grasp how, through the transference, imaginary, symbolic, and real become disentangled. Symbolic castration is the trigger of discourse, and the scenarios of defiance adopted by queer theory merely confirm the refusal to recognize the true import of the paternal function. Unfortunately, the fact that these clinical insights are mired in a cultural perspective that is mostly European only deepened the gap between Lacanians and queer theorists. Lacanian psychoanalysis in the United States is above all a theory of subjectivity whose ideological underpinnings must be clearly stated.

Is Lacanian psychoanalysis more normative than it is prepared to acknowledge? After all, the status of homosexuality in relation to symbolic castration continues to be obscure. Now the new party line, at least for Miller is that *"Je suis pour avoir cliniquement constaté l'authenticité de ces liai-*

---

4. M. Warner, "Introduction," *Fear of a Queer Planet: Queer Politcs and Social Theory*, ed. M. Warner (Minneapolis: University of Minnesota Press, 1993), pp. vii–xxxi, cited in T. Dean, *Lacan Meets Queer Theory*, a talk given at the Lacan Seminar at the Center for Literary and Cultural Studies Harvard University, April 1997.

sons homosexuelles."[5] But doesn't the lady protest too much? Did Lacan ever use the word "authenticity" when he spoke of the complicated relation between love and desire?

It is obvious that all clinicians today will agree that perversion as a psychic structure is no more related to homosexuality than to heterosexuality. Yet this is not enough to get Lacanian psychoanalysis out of the woods of heteronormativity. In *The Plague of Fantasy* Žižek found a new strategy to fudge the issue. Perversion in this text is safely aligned with the obscene *jouissance* of a superego that has become, in Žižek's eyes, the new threat of the postmodern, postpatriarchal era.[6] The pressure to enjoy, through cyberspace, virtual warfare or capitalistic globalization "promises the almost perfect materialization of the big Other."[7] Perversion has found a new identity for sure. No longer associated with homosexuality— nor with subversion for that matter—perversion now stands on the side of the establishment. The more things change, the more they stay the same. It would seem that even after Lacan, perversion continues to be the one that is not invited to the party. For who among queer theorists and Lacanian analysts wants to sit with the establishment?

As things stand for Žižek, the perverse *jouissance* of the Law has run amok, since it no longer finds in social institutions a limit to its destructive intention. While this point may be well taken, it nevertheless implicitly reveals a certain nostalgia for a time when the social bond found in the law of

5. J.-A. Miller, "L'inconscient homosexuel," *La cause Freudienne, Revue de psychanalyse,* October 1997, pp. 12–13.

6. S. Žižek, *The Plague of Fantasy* (London, New York: Verso, 1997), p. 86, also pp. 86–124.

7. Ibid., p. 164.

sexual difference the means to divert this perverse *jouissance* into circumscribed areas of social life. Yet this view, which undeniably implies a rather moralizing judgment on the structure of perversion, does not exhaust all aspects of the question.

It is therefore from the perspective of the philanthropic act inflicted upon me by my patient that I shall address what I perceive to be the cause of the estrangement between Lacanian and queer theory. I have to make clear at this point that I don't intend to cover the logic of perversion with the same kind of glory that brought down the anti-Oedipus. Neither madness nor perversion is a mode of functioning that can easily find a place in the social fabric. While psychosis excludes its victims from the realm of social interaction, perversion stands perpetually at the edge of a castration whose liberating power it cannot access. Indeed, perversion remains more often than not incapable of submitting to a process whereby its knowledge of *jouissance* could give way to a desire that does not know. Thus my present analysis primarily concerns the ways in which perversion carries within its logic the potential to bring about social change and paradigm shifts through the process of accentuating in their targets, a psychic division that they would rather ignore. It is in this sense that I understand perversion's relation to philanthropy. Unlike the hysteric, the pervert does not expect to be loved. The pervert works for free. As Lacan says, "The perverse subject offers himself up to the Other's *jouissance*."[8] I shall examine this process in

---

8. J. Lacan, *Seminar X*, December 5, 1962, cited in B. Fink, *A Clinical Introduction to Lacanian Psychoanalysis*, (Cambridge, MA: Harvard University Press, 1997), p. 186.

Lacan's work before discussing the function of the logic of perversion in queer theory.

The ambiguity that hovers over the concept of the name of the father, at least in American academia, stems from the fact that the radical epistemological shift in Lacanian theory—that is, Lacan's move beyond Freud—has remained hidden in the folds of a text whose extraordinary obscurity went beyond the call of duty, even for Lacan. So I am wondering whether the convoluted rhetoric of the famous *Kant avec Sade*[9] does not suggest Lacan's conflict with his own superego, since the superego is—as far as we can tell—the true topic of this paper. For although Kant's sadistic *jouissance* is officially Lacan's target, it is Freud himself, I suggest, whom Lacan implicitly denounces. Therefore, it is not only Horkheimer whose gaze Lacan must confront; it is also Freud's. Could it be possible that this difficult text reveals in its concealment Lacan's own desire and trepidation with regard to being for Freud what Sade is for Kant?

In other words, I would like to propose that *Kant avec Sade* implicitly inaugurates Lacan's progressive unmasking of the lure that led Freud to link the myth of the Oedipus complex to the primordial father of *Totem and Taboo*. As it appears in *Kant avec Sade*, the superego is no longer simply the warrant of the prohibition of incest that condemns *jouissance*; it now also commands the transgression of the very Law that it has enforced. This double-faced superego, which transpires *in Kant avec Sade*, will later be related to Freud's own inability to bring psychoanalysis beyond the bedrock of castration.

What is remarkable in *Kant avec Sade*, in my view, is that, through his identification with Sade, Lacan enacts the logic

---

9. J. Lacan, *Ecrits* (Paris: Seuil, 1966), pp. 765–790.

of perversion that consists in exposing the very place where the other refuses to reckon with castration.[10] In that sense the *jouissance* of Kant that is revealed through Sade may well refer to Freud's inability to recognize his own. Lacan will eventually set forth somewhat more explicitly how Freud was reluctant to abandon the position of the master in the psychoanalytic situation. This idea will reach its climax in Lacan's seminar on Joyce, where he will declare that the Father is a symptom that psychoanalysis must dissolve. Yet we can perhaps argue that the seeds of this radical reversal in Lacan's thinking were planted as early as 1963, just when he was about to be expelled from the Societé Française de Psychanalyse.

All this is to say that, thanks to his identification with Sade, Lacan broke through the bedrock of castration and moved beyond the Oedipus complex and its vicissitudes. This move allowed him to elaborate the structure of fantasy, which in turn led to a radical reconceptualization of the praxis of psychoanalysis: the desire of the analyst is no longer invested in imposing the law of the father but rather in exposing its modus operandi. Under such auspices Freud's concept of castration loses its ties with normative heterosexuality. No longer inscribed in the teleology of a psychic development guided by a dialectic of identification, castration concerns only the structure of a *parlêtre* whose division produces the leitmotif of its existence, namely object little a, the cause of desire.

In that sense we begin to see here how Lacan's enactment of perversion brought about a radical shift in his thinking. Yet

---

10. For a comprehensive description of the structure of perversion in Lacanian theory see B. Fink, *A Clinical Introduction to Lacanian Psychoanalysis*, (Cambridge, MA: Harvard University Press, 1997), pp. 165–202.

we may argue, although not everyone may agree, that Lacan is not a pervert and therefore he did not stop where a pervert would, namely deriving satisfaction and power in having unmasked the underpinnings of Freud's fantasmatic construction of an all-powerful father. Lacan's attitude, rather, reveals that his perverse "acting" is that of an hysteric who wants to protect the master whose weakness he has exposed. Lacan, therefore, continues to declare his allegiance to Freud for fear that psychoanalysis would lose touch with the side of the superego that keeps the social order in place.

This complicated position, whose logic concerns primarily the place of psychoanalysis in the social fabric, caused Lacan never to return to the earlier writings in which his reading of Freud led him to formulate the crucial moments of the becoming of the human subject, namely the mirror stage and the paternal metaphor. By the time he had elaborated the matheme of the fantasy, it had become unclear whether his concept of symbolic castration, which he kept intact, continues to bear any relation to the concept of castration of the previous years, which had divided the sexes between the ones who ought to give the phallus and the ones who ought to receive it. This gap in Lacan's discourse cannot fail to remind us of Lacan's own description of the unconscious as "that chapter of my history that is marked by a blank or occupied by a falsehood."[11] Doesn't this blank stand for the place where his perverse enactment slides under the bar to return in the structure of the fantasy where desire aims at the place where the *jouissance* of an object attempts to plug the lack in the Other, thereby repeating at the level of the repressed the logic of the perverse scenario?

---

11. J. Lacan, *Ecrits*, p. 50.

Of this affinity, Lacan will say only: "I will not deal with
the question of perversion here, except to say that it accen-
tuates to some extent the function of desire in man."[12] "I will
not deal with the question of perversion here"—or anywhere
else, for that matter. Indeed, his elliptic allusions on the topic
of perversion are in sharp contrast with his generous and in-
sightful analysis of the hysterical, obsessional, phobic, and
psychotic structures of psychic functioning. It is as if the
pervert's glaring knowledge of *jouissance* had come to occupy
the place of Lacan's own *objet petit a*. For it is in the pursuit
of this light that Lacan discovered the path that led him to
first identify with Sade before he then took on the task of
debunking Sade himself.

The desire of the analyst and the desire of the pervert are
in fact articulated on the same structural plane. Both propose
themselves to be the instrument—the *objet a*—through which
the other will experience the anxiety that has produced his
or her subjective division. But here it is Lacan who tells the
truth of Sade: it is the ethics of psychoanalysis that reveal the
limit of the logic of perversion. As Serge André has put it,
where the pervert stops there starts the desire of the analyst[13]
because "nobody holds the key to the truth of *jouissance*, nei-

---

12. J. Lacan, *Ecrits*, p. 320, modified. Sheridan's translation does not
quite convey the same meaning and emphasis: "Nous n'aborderons pas ici
la perversion pour autant qu'elle accentue à peine la fonction du désir chez
l'homme, en tant qu'il institue la dominance, à la place privilégiée de la
jouissance, de l'objet a du fantasme qu'il substitue à l'A . . . Seule notre
formule du fantasme permet de faire apparatre que le sujet ici se fait l'instrument
de la jouissance de l'Autre." *Écrits*, p. 823. The passage makes clear how the
structure of fantasy can in turn reveal the structure of perversion.

13. S. André, *L'imposture perverse* (Paris: Editions du Seuil, 1993),
pp. 19–20.

ther the pervert nor God nor Woman nor Lacan himself,"[14] in its stead there is only lack. Unlike the pervert, who believes that castration can be avoided through his or her identification with *objet a*—the analyst recognizes that *objet a* is only a semblance of the *jouissance* of the Other. This is another way to understand what Lacan means when he says at the end of *The Four Fundamental Concepts* that "the desire of the analyst is a desire to obtain absolute difference, a desire which intervenes when, confronted with the primary signifier, the subject is for the first time in a position to subject himself to it."[15] "Absolute difference" here may describe a desire that would no longer be prey to a *jouissance*—the *jouissance* of the Other—that ignores the liberating power of castration. Yet the desire of the analyst for pure difference has a chance to reach its target only in the reduced sphere of the analytic situation. But even here the analyst (alias *objet a*) rarely reaches the point of being reduced to shreds. This explains why Lacan reverted to the hysterical position, so that he could avoid the risk of being cast himself in the position of the new "perverse" father of psychoanalysis.

This hysterical move could therefore be interpreted as an invitation to extract his theory from the constraints of the analytic situation on the one hand, and of the psychoanalytic institution on the other. For in fact Lacan's paradigm shift cannot be accused of bearing any relation to a so-called heteronormative position, since the becoming of the subject in the social fabric is no longer accounted for. The new theory concerns only the tracking down of the speaking subject's

---

14. Ibid., p. 22, my translation.
15. J. Lacan, *The Four Fundamental Concepts of Psychoanalysis*, tr. A. Sheridan, ed. J.-A. Miller (London, New York: Norton, 1978), p. 276.

relation to the cause of its desire, so that the sex or sexual preference of the one who speaks could be perceived as irrelevant. The law that produces desire and that causes the formation of the fantasy is neither the law that enforces sexual difference and its normative effects nor the law of the father as Freud had defined it in *Totem and Taboo*. The Law as Lacan seems to understand it in his later work is what comes to bring a limit to the *jouissance* that the future subject attributes to an all-powerful Other.

It is also true, however, that we cannot have our cake and eat it too without paying the price that the hysteric is only too familiar with: "No one understands me." In this case we might say that Lacan added insult to his own injury. Then again, to revert to hysterical discourse rather than to the discourse of the university was Lacan's best bet for having his strategy exposed, in the sense that hysteria brings out in the other a desire to conquer what has been left out of sight. Nothing should therefore prevent social theorists from picking up the psychoanalytic ball where Lacan left it. In other words, where the desire of the analyst and also the institution cannot venture there could start the desire of those, such as queer theorists, who are eager to explore the place where fantasy can promote social change.

It would appear, then, that the new social and sexual configurations that are presently in the works in queer theory might consider as their compass the limit that human desire necessarily brings to the desubjectifying injunction demanded by *jouissance*. Helped by this psychoanalytic model, they could therefore debunk those social practices that fail to recognize that the law of desire defeats by definition any discourse that gets trapped in the *jouissance* of the subject who is presumed to know.

Yet this is easier said than done. Without the guidance of clinical insights that stem from the transference, social or cultural theory is ill-equipped to elucidate whether *jouissance* has been defeated by the production of a new signifier or whether, on the contrary, it is *jouissance* that is being promoted by a new discourse. Yet this potential new dialogue between queer theory and Lacanian psychoanalysis can be genuine only if both groups retrospectively recognize—as I suggested at the beginning of this paper—how their passionate attachment to perversion had indirectly caused their estrangement. For Lacanian psychoanalysis, as we have seen, has thus far declined to focus its clinical acumen on the ambiguity that has blurred Lacan's legacy. This is where the logic of perversion speaks through those who, like Michael Warner, have opposed "the normalizing methodologies of modern social knowledge."[16] After all, how else to understand the accuracy of the dart that feminist and queer theories have aimed at Lacanian psychoanalysis? Haven't they duplicated to perfection the logic of perversion that led Lacan, alias the Marquis de Sade, to tell the truth of Freud? Hasn't their passionate attachment to perversion became apparent when they accused of deception the *enfant terrible* of psychoanalysis?

It is now the turn of Lacan's followers to show whether they can afford to continue ignoring the passionate attachment to the logic of perversion that has been so instrumental in Lacan's thinking. Can they accept being struck at the place where Freud was unable to surrender and where Lacan disavowed what he had discovered? But how else can psychoanalysts break down the wall between their praxis and the outside world, unless they are prepared to expose not so much

16. M. Warner, *op. cit.*, p. xxvii.

their patients' susceptibility to the call of *jouissance* as their own? It is enough to remember Freud's famous footnote on Dora's passionate attachment to Frau K. to realize that the most important or dialectical reversals in psychoanalytic thought often emerge when the analyst himself realizes in retrospect how his own *jouissance* has produced resistance in his patient. Where would we be today if Freud had not shared with us the turpitude of his prejudices?[17] It is therefore crucial, now more than ever, to bring these types of footnotes into the social realm, so as to permit a better understanding of the stakes involved in the psychoanalytic process: that is, the point when the imaginary phallus of the one who is presumed to know can give way to the signifier of lack, the place where anxiety meets creativity and change. There is no other road towards new conceptualization in psychoanalytic theory.

Indeed, the personal is the political; as I had to deal with my patient's philanthropic denunciation so should psychoanalysis reckon with the finger-pointing of queer theory. Can queer theory, in turn, be willing to acknowledge its passionate attachment to the logic of perversion? Can it recognize the affinity of its calling with a structure destined to repeat over and over the act of unveiling the place where "the normal" usurps the place of *jouissance*? This quest is a lonely one, because they will find few interlocutors who can bear the permanent challenge to values, especially when they are faltering. Can queer theory instead reassess the implications of its strategy through a dialogue with a psychoanalysis that would be prepared—ideology aside—to work through the difficult question of sexual difference in both Lacan and Freud? If the enigma of sexual difference that Freud placed

---

17. S. Freud, *Standard Edition* 7: footnote p. 120.

at the center of his investigation has become, for Lacan, the enigma of the Real filtered through the logic of the fantasy, doesn't this shift require that we examine under a new light the appeasing and liberating function of symbolic castration for the subject of our postmodern era, whether homosexual or heterosexual?

It seems to me imperative that Lacanian psychoanalysis examine seriously its ties with a discourse that wittingly or unwittingly confuses the law of desire with phallocracy, as if the present ethics of psychoanalysis could not tolerate the radical implications of Lacan's theory. If this reflective move is again avoided under the pretext that clinical experience is at odds with the position of queer theory, we will witness, as I suggested at the beginning of my argument, a situation in which queering psychoanalysis will again consist in turning psychoanalysis against itself.

For example, in *The Psychic Life of Power,* Butler equates human alienation and melancholia with the process of submission involved in the formation of heterosexuality and advocates as a form of resistance a sort of partial dissolution of subjectivity. "Risking the incoherence of identity,"[18] as she puts it. Yet if one chooses to see in this model merely a return to the glorification of psychosis, instead of what Butler seems not to realize is a revisitation of Lacan's logic of fantasy, the meeting point between Lacan and Butler will again be missed and with it the possibility of giving Lacan's ethics of desire a new chance. Indeed it is only when Lacanian psychoanalysis acknowledges that the true import of symbolic castration is revealed through the logic of perversion that it can legitimately demonstrate how the ethics of *jouissance*

---

18. J. Butler, *op. cit.,* p. 149.

advocated by Butler seem to run against her subversive intent. After all isn't Butler's project of psychic resistance invested in giving object *a* a political consistency? Instead of falling back on Žižek's critique of the post-patriarchal era—which may possibly include queer theory, although he is careful not to say so—wouldn't it be more productive to demonstrate the subversive value of a desire no longer fooled by the false promises of *jouissance*?

17

On Female Homosexuality: A Lacanian Perspective

MARCIANNE BLÉVIS

Regarding the question of homosexuality, psychoanalysis occupies a paradoxical position. On the one hand, it has played a major role in modifying what is said today about homosexuality by refusing to define the "correct" norm for the love object; on the other hand, psychoanalysis has always refused to give its stamp of approval to any sexual practice. Freud, who always maintained that homosexuality was not a pathological problem, described it solely in terms of identity and object choice and never in terms of homosexual identity, since he did not believe in the existence of a homosexual or heterosexual nature. As for Jacques Lacan, who cared little for anything that credited itself with being "normal," or what he liked to call the "normal male," he was radically opposed to the phrase that Freud had borrowed from Napoleon: "Anatomy is destiny." Instead, Lacan spoke of a choice of positions whereby men and women are identified by their modes of *jouissance*. According to Lacan, subjects have the choice between two ways of inscribing themselves in the phallic function.

Thus, the bell has tolled for any idea of a natural norm. People today identify so little with their anatomy that they are often very worried about their gender. "Am I a man, a real man?" they ask, or "Am I a real woman?" Meanwhile, analytical theory is still faced with the problem of defining sexual membership, since, although anatomy may determine one's civil status, it in no way determines the destiny of one's desires. One's sexual identity is the result of the psychic elaboration of the sexual real—and such an elaboration is no easy task.

My own interest in female homosexuality is linked to the fact that analytical theory does not seem to know how to address it and neglects it in very much the same way history has always done. Even though female homosexuality was an area whose importance Freud confessed to having underestimated in the course of several treatments and about which he found himself at times "in complete perplexity" (his own terms)[1] when he was confronted with something akin to it in the transference, female homosexuality has nevertheless suffered the same ambiguous fate as female sexuality: everyone knows it exists, but no one can say much about it. Either its specificity is mimimized, or it is inscribed in exclusively phallic terms not incompatible with an undisguised fascination for female *jouissance.*

First of all, in some brilliant pages from his Seminar on the Object Relation, Lacan provides a brilliant critique of Freud's article "On the Psychogenesis of a Case of Female Homosexuality"[2] published in 1920, and gives us the major

---

1. S. Freud, *Dora: An Analysis of a Case of Hysteria* (New York: Touchstone, 1997), p. 110.
2. S. Freud, *Standard Edition* 18:147–172.

part of his own thinking on the subject.[3] Lacan returned to this topic in 1973,[4] perhaps feeling the pressure of the powerful and nascent feminist movements of the seventies. At that time he stated that male and female homosexuality were so asymmetrical that it would be more appropriate to use the term "heterosexual" for anyone who loved women whatever his, or her, own sex might be! Seen from this angle, female homosexuality quite simply does not exist. Indeed, to be able to speak of it, one would have to assume that it is not really a woman that the female homosexual desires in her partner, a view that S. André supports in his book *L'Imposture Perverse*.[5]

Similarly, although the changes in women's status in the twentieth century owe so much to the struggles in which the female homosexual movement took an active part, or even initiated, the social role of female homosexuality has been downplayed, or sometimes flatly denied. For society as a whole, male homosexuality seems to be much more intimidating, since in the exercise of its sexual function male homosexuality calls into question the division of male and female roles between two men, something that never fails to bring about an "alteration" of virility, as Jean Genet wrote to Sartre.[6] In other words, male homosexuality seems to be much more condemned and condemnable than female homosexuality, because the former imperils the reign of the phallus, whereas female homosexuality, at the very worst, leaves the phallus alone, and, in the best case scenario, puts it on a pedestal.

---

3. J. Lacan, *Le séminaire, Livre IV, La relation d'objet* (Paris: Seuil, 1994) pp. 95–131.

4. J. Lacan, *Le séminaire, Livre XX, Encore* (Paris: Seuil, 1975).

5. S. André, *L'imposture perverse* (Paris: Seuil, 1993).

6. E. White, *Jean Genet—Biographies* (Paris: Gallimard, 1993), p. 384.

Curiously enough, as we shall see, when female homosexuality does actually privilege the phallus, it is often no less provocative. Thus, however one considers it, female homosexuality is either reduced to nothing, or recuperated by the phallus. Need it be said that the two positions contradict both the history and the clinical reality of female homosexuality? In addition, both positions seek to erase the unique way in which female homosexuality calls into question phallocentrism, so unique that neither Freud nor Lacan escape unscathed.

An examination of Lacan's incisive analysis will, I believe, afford us a better understanding of the meaning of the deceit that Freud felt the young homosexual woman practiced on him. We shall thus be able to give this deceit another dimension than that of mere phallic rivalry. However, we will still have to determine how female homosexuality can be inscribed in the destiny of female sexuality since, as Lacan notes, female homosexuality is encountered "each time that the discussion touches upon the stages that a woman must go through to achieve her own symbolic realization."[7] And there is still another question that remains: When we leave the area of negotiations necessary for each stage (which lead us to assume that we are dealing with unconscious homosexuality) and go to that of active and conscious homosexuality, are we then in the presence of a radical change between two positions, or do both positions continue without any notable interruption?

Although Freud reestablished the rights of female pleasure and desire in respect to the monosexism that history had forced upon women, including even the way women regarded

7. J. Lacan, *Le séminaire, Livre IV*, p. 96.

their own body as Laqueur has shown,[8] it is still true that Freud pays tribute to a position that gives female homosexuality a dimension that he believed was perverse—a dimension based on the inversion of the love choice and on the inversion of identifications. None of these criteria, however, can justify Freud's position. In Freud's account of the young female homosexual, three terms are used to describe her relationship with her father and with her analyst: challenge, disappointment, and deceitfulness. In masterful fashion, Lacan rereads the interlinkage of these three terms.

Thus, when the young female homosexual offers Freud an accommodating transferential dream in which she sees herself surrounded by husband and children, Freud denounces in his patient a desire to deceive him, the analyst. For Lacan, however, the desire that the young woman reveals is not so much aimed at deceiving Freud as at addressing the desire to deceive in itself. On a symbolic level, the desire to deceive has as much to do with the desire to see the deceit that one has undergone recognized, as with the desire to deceive the other person.

For both Lacan and Freud, however, the story of the young female homosexual is an unshakeable paradigm of all forms of female homosexuality. The young woman, as the story goes, is said to be awaiting, in the course of normal development, a symbolic phallic gift from her father. After her expectations are disappointed (by her mother's pregnancy), she regresses to "a stage of frustration." "Frustrated of the symbolic phallus," Lacan adds, "she finds a way of maintaining her desire in her imaginary relationship with

---

8. T. W. Laqueur, *Making Sex: Body and Gender from the Greeks to Freud* (Cambridge, MA: Harvard University Press, 1990).

the Lady."[9] The symbolic phallus longed for from the father is reduced, through regression, to an imaginary phallus. The child who imaginarizes the phallus instead of symbolizing it becomes henceforth an attribute of the mother, something that in all logic hints at the possibility of fetishism.

Like all women, the young female homosexual knows where the phallus is. In her eyes her father has not proven that he has it. She thinks that since he has, in reality, given her mother a child equivalent to the phallus, he has lost the power to give it symbolically. In her disappointment, the young woman wishes to show her father what the real love is that one should give a woman. This is a double challenge. First, it challenges her father, and men in general. Since she (or any woman for that matter) does not have it, the young female homosexual claims to be better able to love a woman than a man is, because she knows that to love means to love, beyond the other, the phallus that the other does not have. But it is also a challenge addressed to the mother, and to women in general; she wants to show both her mother and all women that she can love them better since she is not a man. "Since I am not provided with a penis," she seems to be saying, "I am all the more likely to give you the phallus that you await."

In all love there is a dimension of promise, just as a distinction should be made in any elaboration of the phallic attribution between possessing a penis and possessing a phallus, and in this respect the female homosexual is no different from any other. However, since she seems to be more altruistic than other women, and more of a woman than any woman, the female homosexual, in Lacan's eyes, affirms radically the disjunction of the penis and the phallus and shows to women and men alike

---

9. J. Lacan, *Le séminaire, Livre IV*, p. 96.

what real love is—"in that such a love prides itself more than any other on being the love which gives what it does not have, so it is precisely in this that the homosexual woman excels in relation to what is lacking to her," as Lacan writes in his article on female sexuality.[10] Nevertheless, like Freud, although he deploys all the imaginary and symbolic registers of this promise of love wherein more than any other woman the female homosexual knows that "such love prides itself in giving what it does not have," Lacan still reads only a challenge addressed to men.

Of course, if the imaginary quest of female homosexuality is read solely in terms of a challenge, all psychoanalytical interpretations will, by necessity, be exclusively defensive. However, a young woman who presented herself to me as a perfect transsexual reassured me of the contrary, adding that what she enjoyed doing most was to talk to men about women. "I know women," she said, "much better than men do." Here one cannot help thinking that there is an opening in her discourse. The fact that she challenged men meant that she had continued to address them symbolically, albeit minimally. But better that than shutting oneself off completely in transsexual autism. If the female homosexual often seems to seek the other's pleasure more than her own (which is often feared), is it to be seen as a challenge (to do better erotically than men), or is it because it is impossible for her to take pleasure in her own female sex? If she appears to refer to the presence of a third male term, is it because the latter is, as J. Dor writes, "the inevitable witness of the challenge that the female homosexual addresses to any man inasmuch as he is castrated,"[11]

---

10. J. Lacan, "Guiding remarks for a congress on feminine sexuality," in *Feminine Sexuality*, ed. J. Mitchell and J. Rose, tr. J. Rose (New York: Norton, 1982), p. 96.

11. J. Dor, *Structure et perversion* (Paris: Denoël, 1987), p. 231.

or is it rather because she is trying to formulate a question concerning femininity—a question that, for a woman, involves the other?

Lacan, once again, did not dissociate himself from Freud on this point. The question of female homosexuality remains, for him also, reduced to the sole register of the phallic challenge. And although he deploys brilliantly all the imaginary and symbolic registers, this challenge is not so much questioned as it is described.

The importance of the symbolic child that the young female homosexual awaited quite belatedly from her father can be properly understood only when placed against the backdrop of a fierce rivalry with the mother. Indeed, it is the presence of the child identified with the imaginary phallus possessed by the mother that catalyzed her homosexual choice. The young woman's hope was perhaps to be separated from the imaginary phallus that both mother and daughter were vying for. Placed in this quandary, the young woman seems to have tried to free herself from the hope of receiving an answer from a man. Her homosexuality is perhaps the sign that she is attempting to free herself from any expectation—which she knows now to be vain—in respect to her father, and now prefers to negotiate her sexuality, and her coming of age as a woman, with another woman. Why does this choice have to be regarded in terms of phallic provocation, rather than considered as something closer to her own truth? In other words, by placing the phallus issue at the core of the female homosexual choice, Freud and Lacan address neither the question of whether the female homosexual really positions herself within the sphere of phallic attribution in respect to other women, nor the question of what she expects from other women.

In actual fact, the father is brought on to the scene in hopes of being given a symbolic phallus only through the metonomy of a mother for a daughter. Thus, in the story of the young female homosexual, there may well be two mutually disappointed people—the daughter and the father.

In any case, Lacan's contribution to the question of female homosexuality, if it were to be summed up in these few pages, is not to be found within a phallocentrism that, as we have seen, seems to take no account of the particularities of the destiny of female sexuality. No, as I suggested earlier, the real contribution we can gain from Lacan is in the use of some of his concepts, which, at first sight, may seem very removed from the issue at hand.

At this point, I suppose that some of you may want to treat such a difficult question by contrasting the various types of female homosexuality, just as there exist several types of male homosexuality. It is true that the ways of being in homosexuality are quite varied. One could say that there are as many types of homosexuality as there are women. Nothing in female hysteria, even the most banal type, distinguishes its constant ill treatment and mending of the phallus from what animates in identical fashion the female homosexual. And I don't think that it advances the argument to speak of psychotic, neurotic, or perverse homosexuality, since the homosexuality represented in each case is no more psychotic, in terms of homosexuality, than it is perverse or neurotic. However, it is true that female homosexuality leads us to reconsider the benevolent eviction of women from the sphere of perversions and, in particular, fetishism. Does this eviction hint at how hard it is to accept that the real of the maternal sex might be a source of anxiety for women themselves, or is it because only the missing penis is deemed worthy of giving rise to denial? Is it merely a sign of the times that cases of female exhibitionism have been reported, along with an increase in female sexual deviations? And is it merely another accident that the term *perverse maternity* has been used on occasion—for cases (denied less and less) of child abuse by mothers? These phenomena show, in any case, that the question of the imaginary phallus and fetishism in women still holds a number of secrets. Furthermore, several authors have reported among female transsexuals a more or less forthright belief in an internal and immortal phallic organ, although this leaves unanswered the question of whether, for them, the penis can function as a fetish that masks the symbolic hole.

At the very most there has been some talk, for quite a while now, of a "primary homosexuality" in women (Stoller),[12] or of a "homosexuality by birth" (Perrier)[13]—a homosexuality that women never abandon. However, it cannot be inferred from this that there is a natural continuity between this primary homosexuality and active adult homosexuality. Here, I tend to adapt Lacan's caution concerning terms like "primary homosexuality" or "homosexuality by birth." It is difficult for me to use a term like *homosexuality*, which means "same sex," for a period when the child does not yet perceive the mother as being different from itself, much less "gendered."

The various theoretical positions must nevertheless be taken into account inasmuch as they seek recourse in a form of female essentialism to counter a theory like Freud's, which formulates female homosexuality in exclusively phallic terms. The approach taken, for example, by Helene Deutsch, should

---

12. R. J. Stoller, *Sex and Gender* (New York: Jason Aronson, 1974).
13. F. Perrier, "L'amatride," in *La Chaussée d'Antin* (Paris: Albin Michel, 1994) p. 439.

be mentioned; she saw in the female homosexual position a reconciliaton with a pre-conflictual good mother. This is a theoretical position that sidelines the phallus and gives maternity—seen as the fulfillment of femininity—pride of place. Concerning Lacan's own position, one must say that it is, at the very least, wavering and unclear. For Lacan, as it is for Freud, female homosexuality is in the realm of perversion, but Lacan seems to sense, a few lines after asserting this view, that there is perhaps another way that leads, as he says, "from female sexuality to desire itself,"[14] and that might be seen as the effort "of a *jouissance* enveloped in its own contiguity . . . to fulfill itself out of the envy of the desire that castration frees in the male by granting it its signifier in the phallus." But the question remains: To counter female essentialism are there only two solutions, nostalgia and phallus envy?

"Unnameable and irrepresentable"—such was for François Perrier any homosexuality between mother and daughter, and he made no distinction between the unconscious homosexuality formed at the time of the acquisition of sexual difference and those first moments when the child is the object of his mother's *jouissance*. Is it true that it is more difficult for a girl than for a boy to separate herself from the real of maternal *jouissance*? Does she have less access to the elaboration of fantasms needed for such a separation? And if so, why? Furthermore, it should be pointed out that a source of much anguish for some women is an incapacity—often observed—for a certain type of homosexual investment. This is another way of saying that unconscious homosexuality is a major factor in human sexuality (for both sexes), something, of course, of great benefit to heterosexuality. Many issues that are con-

---

14. J. Lacan, *Ecrits*, p. 735.

sidered solely in terms of the phallic challenge may be reread in this light. The loathing that many female homosexuals have of being touched by another woman, a fear hidden behind a craving to give more pleasure to their partner than any man could possibly give, is much more the result of an insurmountable anguish concerning their own sex, or as Joyce McDougall[15] notes, the expression of a fear of having the interior of their bodies damaged.

From the very beginning, the female child is in contact with the gendered being who takes care of her, and with the unconscious representations of this being, her points of *jouissance*. Just as for the male child, the female child's link with the mother is sexual by definition and, thus, traumatic. The imaginary that is exchanged in the first contacts between mother and daughter covers the real of the gendered body and makes it a symbolic reality in which a woman can live and take delight in her sex. It appears difficult, therefore, to continue to speak of female homosexuality, be it primary or other, without addressing the role of the mother in the elaboration of the child's imaginary and symbolic world.

Although the mirror image is the first object of which a child is enamored, this image is invested by the child inasmuch as the representative of the *objet a* (or the small a object), but especially of the phallus. When the child, first looking into the mirror, turns and looks at the mother, it shows that it is seeking what has founded it. Indeed, what the child is seeking when it turns around is the mother's face, and beyond the mother's eye her gaze, and beyond her gaze what has founded her gaze. For the child, the mother's gaze con-

---

15. J. McDougall, *Eros aux Mille et un Visages* (Paris: Gallimard, 1996).

tains the real, and her gaze provides a support for the child's first attempts to construct an imaginary that surrounds the sexual real with a web of signifiers well before the mirror stage begins. Winnicott suggests as much in some of his writings. However, Lacan's ideas on the specular realm, which he never ceased to explore, as Guy Le Gaufey has shown,[16] enable us to understand better the woof and warp of the imaginary in its narcissistic relationship with a symbolic third term. If the child does not encounter in the mother's gaze any sign of what founds it symbolically, it will be forced to maintain the axis of its phallic identification exclusively in the imaginary register, and will need to be constantly acknowledged by some gaze that must be present in actual reality. There is nothing specifically homosexual (be it female or male), in the need for a person to maintain him- or herself, in the imaginary axis in respect to the mother's gaze, and to seek reassurances insatiably, if only that it points to the extreme narcissistic fragility of all types of homosexuality.

The female child, too, loves herself first of all in the mother's gaze. In that gaze, she loves herself both as a child and as a gendered child. Later, she will love herself with the gaze with which she surrounds her mother and in accordance with what her mother gives her in return. Thus, from the very outset the daughter is confronted with the way in which her mother invests her as a gendered being, which in turn depends on the mother's own setbacks in dealing with her imaginary castration. In her mother's gaze, the daughter may be seen more or less exclusively as an imaginary phallus, or as a prolongation of the mother who thus refuses any separation, or as an object of *jouissance*. However, although the specular

---

16. G. Le Gaufey, *Le Lasso Spéculaire* (Paris: EPEL, 1997).

realm provides an allegory for the way in which the child has been separated, or not, by the symbolic agency from its position as the mother's phallus, the child still has, in all cases, to give up being the *objet a* (or small object a) of the mother.

The absence of the mother's symbolizing gaze will make it impossible for the daughter to find the signifiers that serve to separate her from the arena of maternal ravages. Secondarily, the formation of an unconscious homosexuality needed to gain access to the other sex also becomes impossible. The maternal sex thus will remain more or less completely unwritten, a nonword, a nonlanguage. Only unconscious homosexuality enables the daughter to love her mother as a sexual object and to love the man who loves her mother. On the other hand, when the mother's gaze disavows the daughter's sex and the mother thus expresses her submission to imaginary castration alone, the daughter is left only with the rage and hatred that tear to shreds her own narcissistic image. In her sexuality, the Other will exist only in a traumatic realm. Here we can see that it is mainly the dysfunctions of unconscious homosexuality that account for all sorts of pathologies and problems in women. It is, however, extremely difficult to distinguish between the apparently "normal" solutions of female sexuality—which may be yet another submission to the imaginary phallus—and the solution that consists in active homosexuality.

Perhaps there is, indeed, an insurmountable difficulty involved in giving up one's position as the object of the mother's *jouissance* and at the same time giving up loving women in order to become another woman, when the *jouissance* that wreaks havoc in the mother is turned against the gendered female body. Many homosexual patients complain bitterly about their mother's criticism of their body: they were always too fat, or too tall; they were never quite right in their mother's eyes. "A real hook," one mother used to call her daughter, because she couldn't stand the fact that her daughter took shorter steps than her and would hang on to her arm. The woman who told this story watched herself very carefully in later life, so as never to be treated as a "hanger-on" or a hindrance, and thus in her masochistic relationships lets her female companions "hang around" her place and live off her income.

Joyce McDougall writes that the female homosexual seems "to be still waiting to possess the mother in order to have the right to possess female prerogatives, and these expectations surface again and again in her homosexual scenarios."[17] In her scenarios, the female homosexual seeks, through another woman, to regain access to signifiers of the desire that separates her from a maternal gaze filled more or less overtly with scorn and hatred of female sexuality. The daughters of passive mothers, seemingly crushed by violent fathers who are jealous of everything that escapes their control, seek in their homosexuality to escape their fathers and their phallic order, but also to reconstruct a narcissizing myth for themselves and their own mothers. Others seek through a woman and through the body contact of sexual relationships to escape their mother's enclosure in the phallic and narcissistic One. A female child can lay hold of the signifiers of desire in a mother's gaze, which will allow her to elaborate them as a symbolic phallus and thus confront the mother's lack. However, for want of such signifiers the same child may be thrown into the position of the *objet a* of the Other's *jouissance*.

---

17. J. McDougall, *op. cit.*, p. 56.

The sublimation or transformation of the economy of feminine archaic *jouissance* that Montrelay[18] seems to devoutly wish for all women still does not solve the enigma of what exactly the daughter must abandon in order to find a point of reference for herself, her mother, and her femininity. Although Lacan makes a clear distinction between imaginary and symbolic castration (the former is transmitted to the female with particulary ruinous effects), it is nevertheless true that there is, in Lacan's theory, a major difficulty in the way he approaches female homosexuality, since for Lacan all discourse goes back to the phallic system. How can the law of female desire be thought out in a system that is not founded on the Name of the Father?

Perhaps Lacan himself has obscured the issue somewhat, first by refusing to really dissociate himself from Freud regarding the quest of the young homosexual woman, which remains an exclusively phallic quest, and, next, by failing to make "the female something other than the internal limit of the male" as David-Ménard[19] noted. Female sexuality remains, for Lacan, inscribed in the enigma that he gives to women's position in respect to the symbolic. Perhaps it is, indeed, very difficult to acknowledge that the phallus is not the emblem of all access to the symbolization of desire, and that there exists a more intrinsically female mode of symbolization that cannot make of the penis either the emblem of symbolization or the imaginary support "of displacements and substitutions of erotic objects." In this respect, the *jouissance* that a woman has to lose is not, as Lacan would have it, a phallic *jouissance*,

---

18. M. Montrelay, *L'Ombre et le Nom* (Paris: Minuit, 1976).

19. M. David-Ménard, *Les Constructions de l'Universel* (Paris: PUF, 1997), p. 113.

but rather the maternal *jouissance* that separates irrevocably the phallus and the penis as an object of erotic value. It is precisely here that female homosexuality asserts something crucial for all women: it affirms a radical disjunction between the penis and the phallus, which is a disjunction necessary for everybody (and not just for women!), and, finally, a disjunction that will always be perceived as scandalous in respect to the phallic discourse. Female homosexuality emancipates itself from the penis as an emblem of symbolization, but at the same time this total separation, in my opinion, underscores the fact that the penis cannot be invested with the ludic symbolic character needed to grant it erotic valence. The reduction of the penis to an exclusive partial object that reunites for the female homosexual both her own sex and that of a man as a piece of waste, leads her to save, through the sex of another woman, a little of her own sex.

Thus—and I do not claim to have given an exhaustive view of female homosexuality, or an explanation of all the various types of homosexuality—one cannot fail to see that the other of the same sex, for a female homosexual, plays a major role in the equilibrium of a system that involves a complex ordering of several interdictions of which she sees herself the object. However, for the female homosexual there is a dramatic wavering between what is possible or impossible and what is forbidden, a wavering that points to the difficulty of finding signifiers that skirt and contain the maternal *jouissance* subjected to the effects of imaginary castration. She struggles hard between her wish to take pleasure in her sex and the necessity for her to submit to her hopes of receiving from the mother signifiers that do not exist. Finally, it seems impossible for her to rearticulate the male penis (and thus take pleasure in it) with the symbolic phallus, which does not belong to any sex. The transgression of these interdictions is awaited from another woman.

On the journey from the same to the Other, a journey that everyone travels in the course of a lifetime, there are ports of call and way stations more or less close to the Same, or to the Other. This is a completely different option from the one Lacan calls "the bachelor's ethic," an ethic "outside of sex" that also short-circuits the Other in favor of the Same. Soler[20] points out that in the bachelor's ethic "the subject shuts himself off from otherness and seeks refuge in the phallic One." The ethic of female homosexuality makes room for the Other, and thus Lacan could say that everything that loves women is heterosexual. In order to explain what seems to be a paradox, let us remember all the efforts that a female homosexual makes to regain access to signifying configurations that go beyond the phallic limits to which she feels condemned. Sometimes she does, indeed, submit herself completely, and deliriously, to the phallic order—we have seen this in female transsexuals. However, in most cases, she seeks through another woman to make the Other take on existence. The ethic of female homosexuality seems to me to always have a nostalgic vocation not for the phallus, but for otherness.

If the unconscious knows nothing of the Other, if it knows only the One, then it is homosexual and "bachelor" by definition, and the conquest of the Other will always remain uncertain, even in our theories. Nevertheless, female homosexuality positions itself, often in hushed undertones, in the disturbing axis of otherness, even when it seems to submit itself to male truths given as universals. Where the male gaze

---

20. C. Soler, "La malédiction sur le sexe," in *L'Inconscient Homosexuel*, Revue de la Cause Freudienne, 37:60–67.

reads only phallic provocation, perhaps it would be more fitting to read the suffering of phallic condemnation. No one, however, is sheltered from the bachelor's ethic, no more the homosexual than anyone else. No one is safe from seeking refuge in the many hiding places of the Phallic One and its mirages.[21]

21. Translated from the French by John Monahan.

Contributors

Marcianne Blévis is a psychiatrist and a psychoanalyst active in Paris. She is director of the Psychoanalytic Psychotherapeutic Services of the Hospital Sainte-Anne. Co-founder of the journal *Patio*, she has published numerous articles on various topics in psychoanalysis and art.

Néstor A. Braunstein, a supervisory analyst and Professor at the Universidad Nacional de Mexico, where he teaches the epistemology of psychoanalysis, is also Director of the *Centro de Investigaciones Psicoanaliticas*. He is the author of numerous articles and books on psychoanalysis published internationally. His most recent books include *Psiquiatria, teoria sujeto y psicoanalisis: el lenguaje y el inconsciente freudiano*; *Goce*, also published in French as *La Jouissance: un concept lacanien*, is forthcoming in English by Verso.

Joan Copjec is Professor in Comparative Literature and the Humanities at the University of New York at Buffalo. She has published *Read My Desire: Lacan against the Historicists* (1994) and edited Lacan's *Television* (1990), as well as *Shades of Noir* (1993), *Supposing the Subject* (1994), and *Radical Evil* (1996). She is currently the editor of the "S" series at Verso, and has recently co-edited with M. Sorkin, *Giving Ground: The Politics of Propinquity* (1999).

Erich D. Freiberger is Professor of Philosophy at Jacksonville University, and is a member of the Association for the Philosophy of the Unconscious in the American Philosophical Association. He has published various articles on Lacan.

Patricia Gherovici, formerly director of a clinic in North Philadelphia, is a practicing psychoanalyst who has published internationally and has most recently contributed to *The Subject of Lacan* (SUNY Press, 2000). She is now completing a book entitled *The Puerto Rican Syndrome* (Other Press, 2001).

Judith Feher Gurewich, psychoanalyst, is a member of the Boston Psychoanalytic Institute and of the Association de Formation Psychanalytique et de Recherches Freudiennes. After having edited "The Lacanian Clinical Field" series at Jason Aronson, she is now editing this series with Other Press. She has co-edited the volume *Lacan avec la Psychanalyse Américaine* (Denoël, 1996) with Michel Tort as well as *Lacan and the New Wave in American Psychoanalysis* (Other Press, 1999), also with Michel Tort.

Christopher Lane is Associate Professor of English and Director of Psychoanalytic Studies at Emory University. He is the author of *The Burdens of Intimacy: Psychoanalysis and Victorian Masculinity* (Chicago, 1999) and *The Ruling Passion: British Colonial Allegory and the Paradox of Homosexual Desire* (Duke, 1995), as well as editor of *The Psychoanalysis of Race* (Columbia, 1998) and co-editor of *Homosexuality and*

Psychoanalysis (2001). He is currently completing a book on nineteenth-century misanthropy, entitled *Civilized Hatred: The Antisocial Life in Victorian Fiction.*

Steven Z. Levine is Professor in the Humanities and Professor of History of Art at Bryn Mawr College, Pennsylvania. He is the author of *Monet, Narcissus, and Self-Reflection: The Modernist Myth of the Self* (1994), and various essays on psychoanalysis and art; they include "Virtual Narcissus" in *American Imago* (Spring 1996), and "Between Art History and Psychoanalysis" in *The Subjects and Objects of Art History* (1997).

Catherine Liu, a professor in Comparative Literature at the University of Minnesota, has published articles on psycho-analytic theory, French literature, Walter Benjamin, and con-temporary art. She has curated shows in New York City and Los Angeles, and has published a novel, *Oriental Girls Desire Romance* (Kaya Press, 1997). Forthcoming are a second novel, *Suicide of an Assistant Professor*, a book, *Copying Machines: Taking Notes for the Automaton*, and a translation of Gérard Pommier's *Du bon usage de la colère érotique.*

Kareen Ror Malone is Professor in Psychology and on the Women's Studies faculty at State University of West Georgia. She is co-editor, with Stephen Friedlander, of *The Subject of Lacan: A Lacanian Reader for Psychologists* (Albany, NY: SUNY, 2000) and has published articles on psychoanalysis and Lacan in various journals.

Arkady Plotnitsky is Professor of English at Purdue Univer-sity. He has published several books and numerous articles on Continental philosophy, literary and critical theory, Ro-manticism, and the relationships among literature, philoso-phy, and science. His most recent books are *Reconfigurations*

(1993), *Complementarity: Anti-epistemology after Bohr and Derrida* (1994), and co-edited a volume of essays, *Mathematics, Science, and Postclassical Theory* (1995).

Gérard Pommier is a psychiatrist and a psychoanalyst active in Paris, where he founded the *Fondation Européenne de la Psychanalyse*; he has published more than ten books, which include *D'une logique de la psychose*; *L'exception féminine*; *L'ordre sexuel*; *Naissance et renaissance de l'écriture*; *La néurose infantile de la psychanalyse*; *Ceci n'est pas un Pape*; and *Du bon usage érotique de la colère*, forthcoming in English from the University of Minnesota Press.

Jean-Michel Rabaté, Professor of English and Comparative Literature at the University of Pennsylvania, has published books on esthetics, literary theory, Samuel Beckett, Thomas Bernhard, Ezra Pound, and James Joyce. His most recent books are *The Ghosts of Modernity* (1996), *Writing the Image after Roland Barthes*, (1997), and *Jacques Lacan: The Last Word* (2000).

Frances L. Restuccia is professor of English at Boston College. She is the author of *James Joyce and the Law of the Father* (1989) and of *Melancholics in Love: Representing Women's Depression and Domestic Abuse* (2000). She has written articles in several journals such as *Raritan, Genre, Contemporary Literature, Genders, American Imago*, and *Gender and Psychoanalysis*. She is currently working on the ethics of psychoanalysis and on the concept of Lacanian love.

Paul Roazen's numerous books, *Freud: Political and Social Thought; Brother Animal: The Story of Freud and Tausk; Freud and his Followers; Encountering Freud: The Politics and Histo-*

ries of Psychoanalysis, and *Oedipus in Britain* distinguish him as a leading historian of psychoanalysis.

C. Edward Robins is a psychoanalyst and psychologist active in New York, where he also teaches Clinical Psychology at Fordham University. He is a co-founder of the *Nomos* Association and a member of the Lacan Clinical Forum (Austin Riggs Center). He has published widely and internationally on Lacan and psychoanalysis.

Joseph H. Smith is a psychoanalyst and the founding editor of the "Psychiatry and the Humanities" series: among its volumes, *Psychoanalysis and Language* (1978), *Literary Freud* (1980), *Interpreting Lacan* (1981), *Taking Chances: Derrida, Psychoanalysis and Literature* (1984), and *Psychoanalysis, Feminism, and the Future of Gender* (1994). He has been president of the Washington Psychoanalytic Society, is a Professor of Clinical Psychiatry, and is the author of several books, including *Arguing with Lacan: Ego Psychology and Language* (1991).

Michel Tort is a psychoanalyst and a Professor at the University of Paris VII (Denis-Diderot), currently serving as Chair of the Department of Clinical Human Sciences. He is also Program Director at the Collège International de Philosophie (Paris). He has published several books, which include *Le Désir Froid* (1992) and *Le Nom du Père Incertain* (1997). He has edited with Judith Feher Gurewich *Lacan and the New Wave in American Psychoanalysis: The Subject and the Self* (Other Press, 1999).

Index